India's Approach towards Sustainable Development Goals

India's Approach towards Sustainable Development Goals

Dr. Bedprakas Syam Roy
Dr. Maniparna Syam Roy

KALPAZ

First Published, 2019

Published by

Kalpaz Publications
C-30, Satyawati Nagar,
Delhi – 110052
Ph.: 011-47034999, 9811692060
www.kalpazpublications.com
E-mail: kalpaz@hotmail.com

Printed at: G. Print Process, Delhi

Cataloging in Publication Data—DK
Courtesy: D.K. Agencies (P) Ltd. <docinfo@dkagencies.com>

Shyamroy, Bedprakash, author.
India's approach towards sustainable development goals / Dr. Bedprakas Syam Roy, Dr. Maniparna Syam Roy.
pages cm
Includes bibliographical references.
ISBN 9789353240219

1. Sustainable development—India. 2. Economic development—India. 3. India—Economic policy. 4. India—Social policy. I. Syam Roy, Maniparna, author. II. Title.

LCC HC440.E5S59 2019 | DDC 338.9270954 23

Contents

PART - V

GOAL-WISE SUSTAINABLE DEVELOPMENT INITIATIVES IN INDIA

To our affectionate Manichandrima

Preface

Human civilization is a continuous process punctuated by visible and invisible events and future shaping monumental inventions, discoveries and improvements by sons and daughters of its human beings- visionaries, scientists, academicians, statesmen, leaders, social workers and also of the numerous faceless human beings residing at different period of their earthly existence over the centuries in plural and diversified parts of this universe. Incremental contributions of individuals over time are as important and as meaningful as the big ticket inventions of its worthy children. The synthesis of such contributions has coalesced to give a distinct character to different phases of civilization. The civilization of today is an overtime product of that synthetic outcome.

The plurality and diversity of human resources in different geographical locations also spawned, different and distinct version of its own regional civilization with a unique identity, as reflected in its human development index. It is an irony of human civilization that all human beings do not enjoy similar quality of life and, for the same diversity, there have taken place asymmetric human development index, broadly classified as the developed and the under-developed. As a result, there exists perceptible quality difference in the pattern of life and standard of civilization in between the developed and the less developed countries. The conscience of humanity is, however, extremely unhappy and concerned about the unacceptable gaps in the inter-country variation of human development index and ponder how best it could be bridged through appropriate interventions. The conscience of humanity is also equally concerned about the diminishing stock of natural resources around the global and regional eco-system accompanied with the onset of alarming climate change scenario and its fall-out. The collective wisdom of world leaders also agreed in international conferences that it owes to the human system's responsibility to protect and safeguard the human civilization by making a considered choice and balance in between developmental efforts and its stock of natural resources and that it must preserve the reservoir of its current stock of resources to enable to bequeath and meet the needs of future generations.

Historically, the UN Millennium Summit, 2000 was the most eventful beginning to scale –up human development issues by global initiative through an outcome document called the Millennium Declaration- a Declaration that contained a statement of values, principles and objectives for the international agenda for the 21st century which ultimately got shaped as the Millennium Development Goals(MDGs) with a deadline for accomplishing the goals set for 2015. The international community meanwhile felt that since the MDGs targeted developing countries, particularly the poorest, the need for Sustainable Development Goals for the entire world, developed and developing countries, was to be explored worldwide for the post -2015 scenario. The UN Conference on Sustainable Development (UNCSD, or Rio+20), in June 2012, was instrumental to launch the process of sustainability and develop a set of Sustainable Development Goals(SDGs). After a series of follow-up efforts towards achieving the MDGs and intergovernmental negotiations on the post-2015 agenda, a Global Summit namely, Sustainable Development Summit took place in September 2015 to adopt "Transforming Our World: The 2030 Agenda for Sustainable Development," with 17 SDGs and 169 targets by addressing the root causes of poverty and the universal need for development that works for all people covering in the process the three dimensions of sustainable development: economic growth, social inclusion and environmental protection. The then UN Secretary-General envisioned it as a universal, transformative and integrated agenda that heralds an historic turning point for our world" and observed :"This is the People's Agenda, a plan of action for ending poverty in all its dimensions, irreversibly, everywhere, and leaving no one behind".

The SDGs recognize that tackling climate change is essential for sustainable development and poverty eradication. The SDG 13 specifically aims to promote urgent action to combat climate change and its impacts. Indeed, Climate change has been impacting public health, food and water security, migration, peace and security in all over the world. Investments in sustainable development will help address climate change by reducing emissions and building climate resilience. Action on climate change will drive sustainable development and vice versa. Thus, while concluding the 2030 Agenda and its SDGs, it has been widely noted that the true legacy of 2015 will only be known once the Paris Climate Change Conference concludes, as the 2030 Agenda and the Paris agreement are mutually supportive, and jointly it will establish the framework of the global development agenda for the next 15 years.

India is an important signatory to the Declaration of Sustainable Development Goals (SDGs) at the Sustainable Development Summit, 2015 and also at the Paris Agreement on Climatic Change Conference, COP 21. The visionary and game-changing SDGs are now to be reached by the world in general and India in particular with reference to the country's obligation under COP 21. The country-specific Road-map for SDGs is now the order of the day.

This book intends to probe the Road-map of the Sustainable Development Goals in India by way of examining the approach, programmes and the state of preparedness to reach sustainable development. This exercise is a joint study of Dr. Maniparna SyamRoy and myself. As a matter of record, apart from designing the study format and writing the very important chapters on 'The theoretical framework of Sustainable Development' and 'The linkage between Climatic Change and Sustainable Development Goals, the Paris Agreement and its way forward', she revised the draft and constantly guided me in the writing of other chapters. Besides, she has been my constant source of inspiration and assistance to complete the manuscripts in time.

In undertaking this Study, I have made use of related publications of the Government of India. For the record, among others, I owe a great debt to the websites of the UN system, Sustainable Development Summit Conference, Sustainable Development Knowledge platform, The Paris Agreement on Climatic Change Conference, COP 21 etc and also to websites of different Ministries, Government of India, and NITI Aayog, and also of numerous others for making liberal use of relevant materials to prepare the book. Moreover, I put on record the constant encouragement and support that I received from co-author to complete the study.

Finally, I deeply acknowledge the exemplary guidance and assistance that I received from Shri Amit Garg, publishing Director, Kalpaz to agree to publish the book at the quickest possible time.

Saltlake,
20, August, 2018

Dr. Bedprakas Syam Roy
bpsyamroy@yahoo.co.in

PART - I
SUSTAINABLE DEVELOPMENT ISSUES

Chapter - 1

The Theoretical Framework of Sustainable Development

The UN Sustainable Development Goals (SDGs) adopted on 25th September, 2015 aimed to end hunger, assure gender equity, and build a life of dignity for all over the world. It gave a clarion call of a new framework of "Transforming Our World: the 2030 Agenda for Sustainable Development". The SDGs composed of 17 goals and 169 targets to wipe out poverty, fight inequality and tackle climate change over the next 15 years. Among the 17 goals to this agenda, focus was on complete poverty eradication, zero hunger, quality education, gender equality, sustainable cities and communities and clean water and sanitation. The 193-member General Assembly of the United Nations described the agenda as 'clarion call' to share prosperity, empower people's livelihood, ensure peace and heal our planet for the benefit of this and future generations. The new agenda is a universal, integrated and transformative vision for a better world. It is an agenda for the people, to end poverty in all its forms and dimensions. The 17 SDGs are our guide and to-do list for people and planet, and a blue print to look beyond national boundaries and short term interests and act in solidarity for the long term.

The Sustainable Development Goals is a blend of several superfine ideas and concepts tailored to improve the quality and destiny of the homo sapiens in the changing and challenging landscape of terrestrial life. It is intended to meet Humanity's quest for a fairly equitable quality life ' For All' even in the midst of all great diversities around the world. It is also endeared that such improvement of quality of life would not be one-off affair or transient in nature; it needs to have a reasonable foundation of strength of continuity in a sustainable manner. The concept of sustainability is the central pillar to the new approach to development. The concept of Sustainable development thus requires to be understood at the first instance both in terms of sequence of development stages and more particularly in terms of its generic meaning and dimensions. It would be prudent to begin with stages of concepts of development as perceived by economic theoreticians along with several inter-linked concepts, some of which are described below:

Stages of concept of economic development: from GDP to Sustainable Development

Improvement in the standard of living of the countrymen is the avowed goal of all governments in any part of the world. Mere well-wishing does not have meaning and value in this area; the incremental improvement has to be visibly reflected and buttressed by hard facts of reality. For a reality check of the status of the evolving standard of living, an acceptable tool is essential. However, at the nascent stage of economic and social development, no reliable measurement index came up and it was hardly possible to have a fair assessment of ongoing changes in the standard of living based on objective reality until the Gross Domestic Product(GDP) concept was born.This was the first acceptable indicator of improment in the standard of living.

Gross Domestic Product(GDP):

The GDP as a concept of tool of measurement of a country's overall economic wellbeing came into being in 1937 when Simon Kuznets,the Russian economist mentioned it as the system of measurement in a report to the U.S. Congress in response to the Great Depression. The GDP was widely adopted as the standard means for measuring national economies after the Bretton Woods conference in 1944.

There are three methods by which GDP can be worked out namely, the expenditure approach, the output (or production) approach and the income approach. The expenditure approach or spending approach is the most common method which essentially measures the total sum of everything used in developing a finished product for sale. The production approach on the other hand is the reverse of the expenditure approach in that instead of exclusively measuring input costs that feed economic activity, it estimates the total value of economic output and deducts costs of intermediate goods that are consumed in the process, like those of materials and services. The third approach is called the Income approach under which income earned by all the factors of production in an economy are included, namely, the wages paid to labor, the rent earned by land, the return on capital in the form of interest, as well as an entrepreneur's profits.

Beginning from 1950 onwords, the idea that the GDP is an absolute indicator of a nation's economic progress began to be questioned on its failure to account for the health status, distribution of wealth of the nation, the extent of discrimination and on several aspects of public welfare. In other words, the GDP, the critics pointed out, is unable to reflect the distinction between economic progress and social progress. The criticisms against GDP as an indicator of a country's economic wellbeing may be summarized as below:

- GDP usually relies on official data and therefore cannot take into account the vast network of the informal sector which significantly contributes to the volume of economic wellbeing in a country. Similarly, GDP also fails to quantify the value of volunteer work. .
- GDP does not take into account profits earned in a country by overseas companies which are remitted back to foreign investors. This can overstate a country's actual economic output.
- GDP growth per se does not reflect a country's real development or its citizens' real well-being. For example, rapid GDP growth may be accompanied by adverse environmental cost and or an increase in income disparity. In practical term, GDP serves more as a measure of productivity or material wellbeing rather as overall human wellbeing of its citizens.
- Finally, the GDP does not reflect environmental cost and reveal human development status

Standard of living concept

Standard of living as a concept of wellbeing came into being in June 1949 when President Trumen mentioned the necessity of assisting people of economically underdeveloped countries to raise standard of living. Incidentally, the Charter of United Nations had also affirmed in 1945 in Article 55 'to promote higher standard of living'. In economic sense, Standard of living refers to material wellbeing, and is also susceptible to measurement, similar to per capita Gross National Product. According to Jean Fourastie, Standard of living is measured by the average national income and also by the quality of goods and services which may be produced and consumed. Any increase in the level of this indicator is considered the logical consequences of economic development.

The concept of Standard of living as an indicator of economic development has, however, been questioned. It is being held that Standard of living is not a measurable index; quantitative and normative measures are largely absent. Further, this concept has not matured as a technical tool for obtaining a precise and statistically determined economic aggregate. In fact it remains as a general notion that is largely imprecise and subjective. For the same reason, the Standard of living concept is not considered as a better indicator of economic development than the GDP.

Human Development and HDI

GDP as indicator of economic development is criticized because it does not take into consideration other aspects that define human well-being like life expectancy and educational attainment. It is for these reasons that alternative ways of measuring human well- being have emerged. One of these is the Human Development Index or HDI. The UNDP introduced the concept in 1990 which takes into account GDP and adds other aspects to measure human development: knowledge, longevity and decent standard of living. The HDI showed that countries with same level of income does not necessarily have the same level of human development. The HDI included indicators of health and education, and income level to represent means for achieving capabilities in a country. The areas covered are life expectancy, adult literacy rate and gross enrolment ratio and per capita GDP. HDI index values range from 0 to 1. Those countries with an HDI of over 0.800 are part of the High Human Development group. Those between 0.500 and 0.800, are considered as Medium Human Development group.

Gender Development and GDI

The HDI reveals maro scenario of well-being of all human beings in aggregate-male or female in a given country. It has been felt in a short span of time that real life status of male and female does not necessarily fall in the same grade ;in fact in a large number countries the relative position is rather asymmetric. Women enjoy a considerably deprived position and status on components of HDI. Accordingly, the UNDP introduced GDI and GEM in the HDR in 1995 'to provide some degree of quantification on gender inequality that would enable comparisons between different points in time or across countries or regions.' It is also likely to set in motion policy correction of the gender imbalance.

The composite indexes, however, represent only a crude and limited way to gender inequality and women's empowerment. Moreover, neither GDI nor GEM can be used as a measure of gender equality. The composite index is also a summary measure and do not reveal differences across various indicators. The UNDP, thereafter, introduced a new measure of gender inequity by overhauling the methodology of HDI and put in place the Gender Inequality Index(GII) in replacement of GDI and GEM. The GII is an inequality index. It measures gender inequalities in three important aspects of human development—reproductive health, measured by maternal mortality ratio and adolescent birth rates; empowerment, measured by proportion of parliamentary seats occupied by females and proportion of adult females and males aged 25 years and older with at least some secondary education; and economic status, expressed as labour market participation and measured by labour force participation rate of female and male populations aged 15 years and older.

Sustainable Development and SDI

The measuring rods of economic well-being – the GDP and HDI including GDI and GII have one common feature in that these concepts are static in character and are related with a definite point of time and never take into account depleting stock of resources. Since the economic growth is closely linked with the state of stock of capital and its use, the over exploitation of them in any given period results a higher GDP but only at the cost of growth of future generation. For realistic and economic reasons, therefore, the real growth of that period has to be discounted. The concept of sustainable development owes its origin to balanced use of its stock of resources.

Brundtland, the pioneer of the Sustainable Development, defined it in 'Our Common Future' as that *development that meets the needs of the present without compromising the ability of future generations to meet their own needs. The concept has been addressed subsequently by scholars from various angles, examples of which are given hereunder:*

Sustainable development (SD) is a process for meeting human development goals while maintaining the ability of natural systems to continue to provide the natural resources and ecosystem services upon which the economy and society depend. Sustainable development has in that sense three dimensions, domains or pillars, namely "economic, environmental and social" or "ecology, economy and equity" while some scholars include a fourth pillar, namely, culture, institutions or governance. The ecological sustainability of human settlements is part of the relationship between humans and their natural, social and built environments. Ecological economists look upon it from the premise of natural capital of intergenerational equity and irreversibility of environmental change in that sustainability requires that human activity has to use up such amount of nature's resources that can be replenished naturally.

The meaning of Sustainable Development is also linked with several inter-linked analogous concepts, some of which are described below:

Carrying capacity

Carrying capacity in simple language means the maximum number of individuals that an area of land can support with their food requirements, and without any detrimental effects. Ecologists define carrying capacity as the maximal population size of a given species that an area can support without reducing its ability to support the same species in the future. Because of variation of types and quantities of consumption, carrying capacity, for human habitations, varies markedly with culture and level of economic development. With a particular culture, the types of resource used and with a particular level of economic development, the quantities of resources consumed vary signalling different carrying capacity of the locations. Carrying capacity may thus be defined as biophysical carrying capacity (the maximal population size that could be sustained biophysically under given technological capabilities) and social carrying capacities (the maxima that could be sustained under various social systems especially, the associated patterns of resource consumption).

Population Matters in its website has dealt on Carrying capacity in a very lucid way: "the maximum number of individuals that can be supported sustainably by a given environment is known as its 'carrying capacity'. For most non-human species, the concept is quite simple. If carrying capacity is exceeded, the population declines because its environment can no longer support the excess numbers. In many situations this can happen very rapidly because excessive demand degrades or even devastates the environment and there is a sudden and catastrophic feedback effect. Such a feedback effect can not only eradicate those numbers of population in excess of the carrying capacity of an environment but under certain circumstances it can cause the near extinction of an entire species. A population can exceed the carrying capacity of its environment for a short while by using up the stored resources (ie natural capital) of its environment, but sooner or later the 'overshoot' will catch up. Once the capital is exhausted, population numbers inevitably fall because there are no longer enough resources available to support the number of individuals.

In the case of human populations, there is a large variation in per capita consumption levels between poor and affluent communities, so the basic definition of carrying capacity needs to be qualified and the given level of per capita consumption and waste generation needs to be taken into consideration. The carrying capacity of a given environment is much greater for people living at a subsistence level than it is for people with a typical Western European or North American lifestyle. It is also important to note that different geographic regions have a greater or smaller carrying capacity. Climate and local geography both play a crucial part."

Sustainability

Sustainability has been defined by Geir B. Ascheim in 1994 in the World Bank document as a requirement of our generation to manage the resource base such that the average quality of life that we ensure ourselves can be potentially shared by future generations. Development is sustainable if it is involved a non-decreasing average quality of life. A sustainable process is thus one that can be maintained without interruption. Sustainability is a necessary and sufficient condition for a population to be at or below any carrying capacity. Incidentally, Brundtland, the author of Sustainable development concept way back in 1983 defined it as "development that meets the needs and aspirations of the present without compromising the ability of future generations to meet their own needs". Implicit in the desire for sustainability is the moral conviction that the current generation should pass on its inheritance of natural wealth, not unchanged, but undiminished in potential to support future generations. In other words, Living sustainably means balancing our consumption, our technology choices and our population numbers in order to live within the resources of the planet. It means maintaining a stable and healthy environment for both humanity and biodiversity.

The sustainability equation

Another way of looking upon up on sustainable development is from a mathematical equation. Paul R. Ehrlich, the eminent American biologist and educator, in his book, *The Population Bomb* summarised what is known as the Ehrlich or IPAT equation, I=PAT. I = impact on the environment or demand for resources, P = population size, A = affluence and T = technology.

The two most important conclusions deriving from this relationship are that Earth can support only a limited number of people in a sustainable manner and humanity has a clear choice between more people who have poorer lifestyles and fewer people who have a better quality of life.

Biocapacity and ecological footprint

Population Matters in its website has brought out two concepts relating to sustainable development -Biocapacity and ecological footprint developed by the Global Footprint Network and are quantified as global hectares (gha) which provide a common basis on which to compare the biological capability of the environment to provide food and other essential needs versus the demands placed by human communities on these ecological services. If the ecological footprint of a human population exceeds the biocapacity of its environment, the situation is unsustainable. Disturbingly, worldwide the total human ecological foot -print is 2.6 global hectares per capita (gha/cap) compared with a total worldwide bio-capacity of only 1.8 gha/cap (GFN Ecological Footprint Atlas 2009). This overshoot means that humanity is already using 1.4 times as many resources as are sustainably available. It means that we are in effect already 'living on the capital of the planet rather than its income'. The overshoot for high income countries is much more extreme than the overall average. Whereas low income countries have a typical footprint of 1.0 gha/cap, the average for high income countries is 6.1, of which the UK is typical at 6.12. Thus for the current population, we would need 3.4 Planet Earths (ie 6.12/1.8) to support the total world population of 6.8 billion if everyone was to have typical UK living standards. Though the foot printing approach explicitly accounts for different levels of per capita consumption, it doesn't factor in the biocapacity needed for the preservation of other species – a clear moral problem that would concern many people and one with significant economic consequences for humanity. If capacity for other species is allowed for, we are in a situation of greater overshoot than the figures suggest.

Sustainable Development Goals: An outcome of systemic thinking

All definitions of sustainable development look upon the world as a system—a system that connects space; and a system that connects time. When the world is looked as a system over space, air quality from one place to another or the harmful effect of pesticides from one country on to another can be felt. And when the world is thought of as a system over time, the decisions of older generations over any subject areas continue to affect today; and the economic policies of today will have an impact on outcome of those policies tomorrow. Finally, when quality of life in the world is considered as a system, it boils down to outreach and access of ingredients of human development to all places in the nation and beyond. Thus the concept of sustainable development is rooted in this sort of systems thinking and the SDGs are the outcome of such systemic thinking. SGDs are a shining example of sustainable development.

Chapter - 2

The Background, Process and the Overview of the Sustainable Development Summit, 2015

The Sustainable Development Summit, 2015 took place at UN head quarter in New York from 25-27 September, bringing together Heads of State / Government from all UN Member States to formally adopt the outcome document on the post-2015 agenda. International summit usually takes place through a process of serious consultations with all possible stakeholders-the member states, specialised regional agencies of the UN system, other international bodies, academic institutions of repute, international experts and personalities and the like. It proceeds step by step through a designed format of interactions in working out a draft Agenda and thereafter refining the same with the core principles of UN value system and fine-tuning them where ever necessary. The validation process of possible goal-posts and outcome ensurance is also worked with extreme care and caution with the best professional experts of the world to make such goals measurable in nature, which could as well be monitored in a designed time frame through defined indicators. However, it is also a fact that not all international summits follow any unique model or a fixed format of consultations; every summit has its own way of addressing them. Thus the format of consultation of international conference on ICPD is different from the MDG Summit or that the building-up process of SDG Summit, 2015 is also unique of its own. However, it goes without saying that there is some commonality in form and content of all such intensive consultations in that all core partners and stakeholders must be active partners to own the decision and then implement it through its own Programme of Action. Since the Sustainable Development Summit, 2015 is the outcome of the UN Conference on Sustainable Development (UNCSD, or Rio+20) and in a way the next forward step for post MDGs scenario also, all international events connected therewith played crucial role leading to the Sustainable Summit, 2015.

Process of arriving the post 2015 development agenda for sustainable Development

Based on broad participation from Major Groups, civil society, scientific and knowledge institutions, parliaments, local authorities and the private sector and their views, the process of arriving at the post 2015 development agenda was led by Member States reflecting therein the expressed views of the Open Working Group on Sustainable Development Goals in accordance with resolution 69/244. The "Major Groups" formalized by the Earth Summit for broad participation included nine sectors: namely, Women, Children and Youth, Indigenous Peoples, Non-Governmental Organizations, Local Authorities, Workers and Trade Unions, Business and Industry and Scientific and Technological Community. Numerous inputs to the agenda, including a set of Sustainable Development Goals (SDGs) were proposed by an open working group of the General Assembly, an intergovernmental committee of experts on sustainable development on financing, GA dialogues on technology facilitation and many others. The UN General Assembly called upon the Secretary-General to synthesize the full range of inputs and to present a synthesis report before the end of 2014 as a contribution to the intergovernmental negotiations in the lead up to the Summit. The United Nations High-level Political Forum on Sustainable Development (HLPF) had a central role in the follow-up and review of the 2030 Agenda for Sustainable Development and Sustainable Development Goals (SDGs) at the global level. The Forum adopted inter-governmentally negotiated political declarations. The United Nations played the facilitating role in the global conversation on the post 2015 development agenda and supported broad consultations. It also has the responsibility of supporting Member States by providing evidence-based inputs, analytical thinking and field experience.

It would be worthwhile to record several milestones of the Process which ultimately led to the culmination of the post 2015 development agenda for sustainable development. Those are captured as follows:

(a) UNCSD: The international community gathered at the UN Conference on Sustainable Development (UNCSD, or Rio+20), in Rio de Janeiro, Brazil in 20-22 June 2012, agreed to launch a process to develop a set of SDGs. The Rio+20 outcome called for establishing an Open Working Group (OWG) that would submit a proposal for SDGs. The Rio+20 outcome document outlines, *inter alia*:

- the importance of remaining firmly committed to the full and timely achievement of the MDGs and of respecting all Rio principles, taking into account different national circumstances, capacities and priorities;

- the need to ensure coordination and coherence with the processes considering the post-2015 development agenda, and to receive initial input to the OWG's work from the UN Secretary-General in consultation with national governments; and
- the need to assess progress towards the achievement of the goals, accompanied by targets and indicators, while taking into account different national circumstances, capacities and levels of development.

The UNGA endorsed the outcome document, titled "The Future We Want," in resolution 66/288 on 27 July 2012.

(b) **UNGA Special Event to Follow-up Efforts Towards Achieving the MDGS:** This Special Event took place on 25 September 2013, at UN Headquarters in New York. The Outcome Document called for, *inter alia*: a single framework and set of goals that are universal in nature and applicable to all countries, and that promote peace and security, democratic governance, the rule of law, gender equality and human rights for all; intergovernmental negotiations on the post-2015 agenda; the Secretary-General to release, by the end of 2014, a synthesis report on all post-2015 development agenda inputs; and adopting the new agenda at a summit in September 2015.

(c) **OWG:** The OWG on SDGs held its first eight meetings, also referred to as the "input" or "stocktaking" phase, between March 2013 and February 2014 at UN Headquarters in New York. In February 2014, the Co-Chairs, Macharia Kamau (Kenya) and Csaba Kõrösi (Hungary), released a "stocktaking" document, reviewing the discussions to date, and outlining 19 focus areas as the basis for further discussion. A "zero draft" of the goals and targets was issued on 2 June 2014. After two sessions held primarily in informal consultations, at the conclusion of the 13th session of the OWG, on 19 July 2014, the Group adopted by acclamation a report containing 17 proposed SDGs and 169 targets, and agreed to submit the proposal to the UNGA for consideration and action at its 68th session.

(d) **Synthesis Report of the UN Secretary – General:** The UNGA called on the UN Secretary-General, in resolution 68/6 of September 2013, to synthesize inputs on the post-2015 development agenda in a report before the end of 2014, so as to feed into the intergovernmental negotiations on the post-2015 development agenda. Secretary-General Ban Ki-moon released an advance version of "The Road to Dignity by 2030: Ending Poverty, Transforming All Lives and Protecting the Planet" on 6 December 2014 and formally presented it to UN

Member States on 8 January 2015. The report proposes an integrated set of six essential elements: dignity, people, prosperity, planet, justice, and partnership.

(e) **UN General Assembly :** A number of UNGA resolutions have established and set parameters for the post-2015 development agenda negotiations and related processes.

- On 30 June 2014, the UNGA adopted resolution 68/279, titled "Modalities for the third International Conference on Financing for Development (FfD3)." The resolution included the decision to hold FfD3 and emphasizes the need for effective coordination with the preparations for the summit to adopt the post-2015 development agenda.
- On 10 September 2014, the UNGA adopted resolution 68/309, by which it acknowledged the conclusion of the work of the OWG; welcomed its report; and decided that the proposal of the OWG contained in its report shall be the main basis for integrating the SDGs into the post-2015 development agenda, while recognizing that other inputs will also be considered in the intergovernmental negotiating process in 2015.
- On 29 December 2014, the UNGA adopted resolution 69/244 on the organization of the UN summit for the adoption of the post-2015 development agenda, noting it will take place on 25-27 September 2015, in New York with the 70th session of the UN General Debate beginning on 28 September.
- On 16 January 2015, the UNGA adopted a decision on modalities for the intergovernmental negotiations on the post-2015 development agenda (A/69/L.46). The decision states, *inter alia:*
- the proposal of the OWG on SDGs will be the main basis for integrating the SDGs into the post-2015 development agenda, while other inputs will also be taken into consideration;
- "every effort shall be made" to ensure effective coordination between the intergovernmental negotiations on the post-2015 development agenda and the preparatory process for FfD3, and other relevant UN intergovernmental processes;
- the outcome document for adoption at the summit "may include" as main components: a declaration; the SDGs and targets; means of implementation and global partnership for sustainable development; and follow-up and review; and
- the initial draft of the outcome document shall be prepared by the Co-Facilitators "on the basis of views provided by Member States," as well as "taking into account substantive discussions

in the process of intergovernmental negotiations," and issued by May 2015.

(f) **Intergovernmental Negotiations on the Post -2015 Development Agenda:** A series of eight week-long sessions to prepare the outcome of the UN Summit to adopt the post-2015 development agenda at UN Headquarters in New York began in January 2015, and included interactive dialogues with Major Groups and other stakeholders.

- The first session, from 19-21 January, conducted a stocktaking of governments' views on the agenda. On the basis of this session, the Co-Facilitators prepared an Elements Paper for discussion at the second session.
- The second session convened from 17-20 February 2015. This session focused on the declaration component of the Summit outcome document. The session also included a briefing with the Director of the UN Statistics Division regarding the development of SDG indicators.
- The third session convened from 23-27 March 2015. This meeting focused on: the SDGs and targets; a proposed timeline and roadmap for the UN Statistical Commission (UNSC) to create an indicator framework for the SDGs; country experiences in implementing sustainable development; and arrangements for a joint meeting with the FfD3 preparatory process during its April session.
- The fourth session convened as a joint meeting with the FfD3 process from 21-24 April 2015. Delegates focused on: the deliberations during the second FfD3 preparatory meeting, which had convened the previous week; a discussion with representatives from the World Bank and the International Monetary Fund; proposals for the creation of a technology facilitation mechanism and other science, technology and innovation issues; the relationship between FfD3 and post-2015 processes; follow-up and review of FfD3 and means of implementation; and coherence between the outcome documents from the two processes, outstanding issues and the way forward.
- The fifth session took place from 18-22 May 2015. During the course of the week, delegates discussed: follow-up and review of the post-2015 development agenda; goals, targets and indicators; themes for the interactive dialogues during the post-2015 summit in September, and the way forward. Delegates also adopted the six themes for the interactive dialogues.
- The sixth session took place from 22-25 June 2015. Delegations and Major Groups provided their reactions and amendments to the zero draft, which included a preamble, a political declaration,

the 17 SDGs and supporting targets, a section on means of implementation and the Global Partnership, and a section on a framework for follow-up and review.

- The final two-week negotiating session began on 20 July 2015, with discussion of a draft outcome document dated 8 July. The session was scheduled to finish on 31 July. The Co-Facilitators produced new drafts on 26, 30 and 31 July. Delegates reviewed a revised text dated 1 August, and adopted this with oral amendments during the closing plenary on Sunday 2 August. The final package, titled "Transforming Our World: The 2030 Agenda for Sustainable Development," contains the preamble, declaration, 17 SDGs and 169 targets, means of implementation and the Global Partnership, and a framework for follow-up and review of implementation.

Overview of the UN Sustainable Development Summit 2015

The UN Summit took place in New York from 25-27 September,2015 to adopt the outcome document on the post-2015 agenda, entitled Transforming our world: the 2030 Agenda for Sustainable Development containing 17 Sustainable Development Goals (SDGs) for all countries to reach by 2030, by way of addressing the interconnected economic, social and environmental challenges that the world faces now. The global discourse underwent a paradigm shift of focus from policy to action on specific commitments towards national and regional strategies and accountability mechanisms for the achievement of the SDGs. Before going to the outcome of the Sustainable Development Summit 2015 in chapter-3, it would be useful to know the framework of the approaches on the many pressing areas that the international summit recognized for appropriate intervention. Accordingly, the Informal summary of the 70th Session of the General Assembly United Nations Summit on Sustainable Development 2015, as noted in the UN website, is produced below:

"Informal summary 25-27 September 2015 United Nations Headquarters, New York

Contents

I. Overview

The United Nations Summit on Sustainable Development 2015 garnered visibility, political support and impetus for a truly transformative 2030 Agenda and its implementation. The very large number of Heads of State or Government as well as high-level leaders from business and civil society who participated is evidence of the enthusiasm generated by this new Agenda. The sense of achievement was reinforced by the address by His Holiness Pope Francis prior to the opening plenary.

Over 200 speakers addressed the high -level plenary session of the Summit, including the Co-Chairs of the Summit,Heads of State and Government, other high-level representatives of Member States, the United Nations Secretary General, and representatives from international organizations, business sector and civil society. Large numbers also contributed actively to the in -depth discussions on the issues addressed in the interactive dialogues.

Throughout the Summit, Heads of State and Government welcomed the 2030 Agenda and emphasized its transformative, universal and inclusive nature, its applicability to all countries and stakeholders and its motto of leaving no one behind. Its linkages with peace, security, human rights and good governance were also lauded.

Many said that the success of the 2030 Agenda would not be measured by what was promised, but what would be delivered. The debates focused on many themes of global concern addressed in the Agenda. Regional and national development challenges were stressed by many, with emphasis on the needs of countries in special situations. The central roles of global partnership, means of implementation and partnerships in the Agenda's implementation were prominent.

The engagement of stakeholders, including through partnership, was highly emphasised and over fifty partnership events were held during the Summit. The participation of development partners, including civil society organisations and the private sector, in the preparation of the SDGs and the 2030 Agenda has been unprecedented. In order to fully achieve the Agenda, it will be necessary to continue to be inclusive, bringing together stakeholders everywhere to be engaged in the Agenda's implementation.

The Summit's six Interactive Dialogues covered a broad range of issues. Participants underscored that national ownership of the 2030 Agenda is key for implementation, together with citizen engagement and breaking down silos. Much emphasis was also placed on the need to forge innovative partnerships between governments, businesses and civil society.

II. Main messages

Speakers at the Summit welcomed the adoption of the 2030 Agenda for Sustainable Development and its 17 Sustainable Development Goals (SDGs). They reflected on the Millennium Development Goals (MDGs) and outlined the impressive international and national achievements in implementing them, yet noted that progress has been uneven and there remains unfinished business. The SDGs were recognised as more comprehensive and complex and a springboard for continued progress.

Implementing the 2030 Agenda for Sustainable Development

There was an important focus on implementing the Agenda. Many countries expressed a strong resolve to follow through on their commitments. Participants emphasized that national ownership of the 2030 Agenda is key for implementation, together with citizen engagement and breaking down silos between institutions as well as the various strands of policy making.

A fervent call was made for strengthening international institutions, with multilateral regional and international organisations contributing more towards sustainable development. Coherence between national, regional and international policies and priorities will also need to increase significantly over the next fifteen years. Several countries reported on initiatives they have already taken to implement the Agenda by reviewing their strategies, adopting new ones, or adjusting institutions.

A major challenge will now be to ensure that countries build on the momentum created by the Summit and truly undertake to adapt the 2030 Agenda to their national situations by reviewing policies, plans and institutions. Developed countries acknowledged that the Agenda extends beyond development cooperation, and are considering relevant reforms in their domestic policies to address its provisions.

Much emphasis was placed on the need to forge innovative partnerships between governments, businesses and civil society. Regional and national development challenges were stressed by many, with emphasis on countries in special situations.

Speakers underscored the integrated nature of the Agenda. Many stated that ending poverty and hunger and achieving sustainable development can only be attained by addressing many interconnected factors. To achieve the 2030 Agenda, reducing inequalities was considered essential, including the empowerment of women and the most marginalized. Balanced and sustainable economic growth with employment creation is fundamental for addressing the multidimensional nature of poverty and must be decoupled from environmental degradation.

There was consensus that special attention should be paid to the Least Developed Countries, Landlocked Developing Countries and Small-Island Developing States. The needs of countries emerging from conflict and of Africa were highlighted, and the special challenges of middle-income countries were also emphasized.

It was underscored throughout the Summit that people must be at the centre of the Agenda and that no one must be left behind. A globalised world will not work if many are excluded. In recognition of a major humanitarian crisis not only in Europe but worldwide, many speakers noted the importance of addressing the essential needs of refugees while also tackling the root causes of migration and displacement.

Addressing climate change

Climate change was repeatedly stressed as an existential threat that jeopardizes hard-won development gains and undermines efforts for future sustainable development. Without addressing climate change, achieving the 2030 Agenda and the other SDGs will not be possible. Its negative impacts are putting at risk the potential for progress in the economic, social and environmental areas.

The transition to renewable energy sources was underscored as particularly important, while improving the efficiency of energy and natural resources. National policies can help attract investment in renewable energy. There were also calls for ending subsidies to fossil fuel sources.

The significance of the upcoming Conference of the Parties in Paris (COP21) was seen as crucial to the implementation and success of the 2030 Agenda. Many called for continued momentum and a revitalised political will to ensure a comprehensive and ambitious global agreement at COP21, one that is legally binding and reflects the ambition necessary for averting irreversible environmental damage.

There was a strong call for the agreement to include mechanisms for both adaptation and mitigation. In addition, many countries called for the inclusion in the agreement of a stand-alone mechanism for loss and damage. Many stated that the new agreement needed to have a strong, transparent and flexible monitoring and evaluation mechanism.

Strengthening the means of implementation and a revitalized global partnership for sustainable development

There was wide-ranging consensus that a revitalized, strong and inclusive global partnership for sustainable development is crucial for the implementation of the SDGs. Some also mentioned that the spirit of the global partnership needs to shift from a North-South approach to reflect the universality of the new agenda, while taking into account differences in national circumstances and capacities and giving national policy space to countries.

The private sector and civil society were recognised as critical partners in building a strong global partnership. Public and private initiatives, involving both local and international actors, will be needed. Cooperation in all forms, with multiple stakeholders, will help to facilitate knowledge-sharing, harness technical expertise and mobilize financial resources.

Many called for renewed attention to strengthening the means of implementation. While significant progress has been made, inadequate financial resources were seen as the main impediment for achieving greater progress towards international development goals. In this context, the interlinkages between the SDGs means that investments seeking to benefit the achievement of one goal will also benefit the achievement of others.

Clear linkages were made between the means of implementation for the 2030 Agenda and the outcome of the Addis Ababa Action Agenda. Many speakers emphasised that the Addis Agenda provides a strong framework for financing sustainable development and that its full implementation is essential to the achievement of the SDGs. The importance of adequate, consistent and predictable resources was underscored. The role of official development assistance (ODA) was emphasised. Many called for prompt action towards the ODA target of 0.7 percent of Gross National Income.

The means of implementation must draw on all sources of finance, including other transfers,such as remittances, curbing illicit financial flows, preventing tax evasion, addressing debt sustainability and systemic issues. Some also stressed the need to place an emphasis on delivering an efficient funding mechanism, especially in the context of the broader application of innovative finance mechanisms and forms of aid, in conjunction with private sector engagement.

Several speakers highlighted the importance of trade as an enabler for the realization of the new agenda. Putting in place the right policies at the national and international levels was also mentioned as paramount. Trade facilitation and enhanced market access were deemed important. Many underscored that national science, technology and innovation systems should be strengthened with support from the international community. Several speakers mentioned the importance of capacity building and technical assistance, through both bilateral and multilateral channels, in order to harness technology and innovation.

Common but differentiated responsibilities were emphasized by many, as well as that implementation should take into account different national realities, capacities and levels of development.

Many developing countries referred to their own primary responsibility for mobilizing resources to implement the 2030 Agenda and to integrate it into their national development plans, strategies and priorities. The importance of international cooperation was highlighted, including South-South and triangular cooperation, complementing North-South cooperation. It was affirmed that the financing mechanism for the SDGs must be coupled with a strong technology facilitation mechanism; speakers welcomed the Summit's launch of the global Technology Facilitation Mechanism.

Engaging all stakeholders

Speakers stressed the importance of engaging all stakeholders to actively take ownership of, and participate in, the implementation of the 2030 Agenda. The many development stakeholders, including civil society and the private sector, were recognised as critical for implementation; the 2030 Agenda will not be achievable without their engagement and partnership.

Most of the SDGs will be implemented at the national and local levels. Empowering parliaments, national and local stakeholders and involving citizens will be crucial for achieving the SDGS. It will also be important to develop indicators that capture the goals' impact on ordinary citizens.

Putting in place a robust follow-up and review mechanism

Speakers highlighted that the successful implementation of the 2030 Agenda will be reliant on putting in place a robust follow-up and review mechanism to ensure that commitments are translated into time -bound results. Many underscored the important role of the United Nations to assess progress and identify shortcomings in achieving the SDGs. In this regard, the central role of the high-level political forum on sustainable development (HLPF) at the global level was emphasized.

The Economic and Social Council's annual forum on financing for development to review the development financing outcome and the means of implementation was also welcomed. The need for increased capacity development and improved, credible and realistic statistical data for follow up and review was stressed by many speakers. Robust data and global evidence, supported by harnessing the data revolution, were seen as critical.

Making the United Nations 'fit for purpose'

The 2030 Agenda must be supported by targeted institutional reforms to make the UN system'fit-for-purpose ' and reflect today's realities. Further, the UN system needs to realign itself to effectively support the implementation of the SDGs. There was also a call for reforms to address regional dimensions.

III. Interactive Dialogues

Interactive Dialogue 1: Ending poverty and hunger

Interactive Dialogue 1 on ending poverty and hunger was Co-chaired by H.E. Dr. Miro Cerar, Prime Minister of Slovenia, and H.E. Mr. Ralph Gonzalves, Prime Minister of Saint Vincent and the Grenadines.

- Participants noted that ending poverty is a matter of human dignity. The Millennium Development Goals were an important catalyst in the significant progress in reducing poverty and hunger globally However, this progress has been deeply uneven. Too many are still poor and undernourished, and poverty continues to exist in all countries.
- Eradicating poverty and hunger, and leaving no one behind will require a multi-dimensional perspective that addresses their social, economic and environmental drivers. It must also tackle inequality and systemic and structural issues.
- Ending poverty and hunger can only be achieved by addressing interconnected factors, such as: inclusive growth; livelihoods and

employment; access to basic infrastructure and services; food security; nutrition; health; education; greater equality; improved agricultural productivity and the sustainable use of natural resources. We also highlighted the important role of social protection schemes.

- Economic growth is necessary, but not sufficient, to accelerate the reduction of poverty and hunger. Future prosperity will also require that economic growth no longer degrades the environment. Climate change must be halted.
- Participants emphasized the importance of national ownership and political commitment, citizen engagement, effective fiscal policies, an integrated and coherent approach to policy making, adequate resources, monitoring of progress, and accountability and transparency. Increased participation of developing countries in global decision-making is also needed.
- There is a need for financing and investments from a range of actors, including national and regional development banks, the private sector and other institutional investors, such as pension funds and insurance companies. It is also important to raise additional resources, for example, through improved national tax systems and innovative sources of financing.
- Investing in the health and education of women and girls is crucial. Youth employment and inclusion should receive priority attention. Marginalized groups should be included in decision-making processes.
- Peaceful and just societies are a necessary precondition for sustainable development; many conflicts are driven by poverty, hunger and hopelessness.
- We noted that reversals in development gains could be avoided by building resilience to shocks and disasters, and will require appropriate risk management plans and strategies, together with strong social protection frameworks.
- Participants stressed the need to strengthen the global partnership for development at both the international and national levels.

Interactive Dialogue 2: Tackling inequalities, empowering women and girls and leaving no one behind

Interactive Dialogue 2 on Tackling inequalities, empowering women and girls and leaving no one behind was Co-chaired by H.E. Ms. Kolinda Grabar-Kitarovic, President of the Republic of Croatia, and H.E. Mr. Uhuru Kenyatta, President of the Republic of Kenya.

- Participants noted that the 2030 Agenda for Sustainable Development calls unprecedented attention to the need to reduce inequalities both within and among nations. Only by doing so can we build a world that is more just, stable and peaceful.

- It was agreed that translating the goals and targets in national policies and programmes is a commitment which will mobilize us all for the next fifteen years. The 2030 Agenda is ambitious: it encompasses all human rights and aims at eliminating all forms of discrimination.
- It was recognized that the goals cannot be achieved unless progress includes all, especially women as half of the world's population. Addressing gender equality is key and will have a multiplier effect on achieving all goals.
- While acknowledging the significant progress made in advancing gender equality, discussions highlighted some of the areas for further action:
  - First, universal access to quality education for girls must be reached by all means in the given timeframe.
  - Second, women must be given equal opportunities in the economic sphere, including at the workplace.
  - Third, more representation of women in political positions and leadership needs to be ensured.
  - And fourth, violence against women must be eliminated and investments made in sexual and reproductive health.
- Participants agreed that tackling inequalities requires not only change in policies or laws but also strengthened capacities and empowerment at the community level. The most marginalized, including rural, indigenous, disabled or older persons, must have equal opportunities and access to resources. They must also be given a voice.
- A sustainable world should give every person a fair chance. The humanitarian crises that the word faces now, particularly the situation of migrants and refugees, remind us to prioritize the needs of the most vulnerable.
- Participants highlighted that all are accountable for taking the 2030 Agenda forward. The right data, new technologies and broad partnerships are needed. Above all, there is a need for sustained political will to reach our common objective of ensuring dignity and equal opportunities for all.

Interactive Dialogue 3: Fostering sustainable economic growth, transformation and promoting sustainable consumption and production

Interactive Dialogue 3 on Tackling inequalities, empowering women and girls and leaving no one behind was Co-chaired by H.E. Mr. Charles Michel,

Prime Minister of Belgium, and H.E. Ms.Sheikh Hasina, Prime Minister of the People's Republic of Bangladesh.

- The discussions confirmed that prosperity has risen and many people have been lifted out of poverty. But, much more needs to be done, especially for the most vulnerable. Further reducing poverty levels, addressing the structural causes of inequality, ensuring access to justice and respecting human rights remain critical priorities.
- Participants noted that balanced and sustainable economic growth is fundamental to poverty reduction and sustainable development. It is our obligation to pursue this in response to the many current and emerging global challenges.
- It was acknowledged that jobless growth, rising income inequalities, and youth unemployment are some of the key widespread global concerns. Promoting decent jobs, labour rights and the expansion of social protection, including social protection floors, are crucial for maintaining equitable and inclusive societies.
- To ensure inclusiveness of our economies, we need to pursue full and productive employment and decent work for all women and men, reduce income disparities and promote gender equality. Investing in women's health and education, eliminating gender violence and promoting women's entrepreneurship are essential to achieving the sustainable development goals.
- Our economies will need to undertake structural and technological transformation in order to attain higher technological intensity, greater value added and productivity and full integration in international trade. Wider Connectivity, including access to the Internet, is a key enabler for accelerating such a transformation, as are building strong institutions and empowering communities.
- Enhancing regional and international trade is essential for sustainable development. Access to markets and technology are needed for integration into global value chains. More investment is needed, particularly in Africa, in sectors such as renewable energy, infrastructure, transport and agriculture.
- Public finance can be used as a catalyst to mobilize both foreign and domestic investments. In this regard, new partnerships are needed between the public and private sectors.
- Economic growth must be decoupled from environmental degradation and combat climate change to protect future generations. Accelerating a real shift towards more sustainable lifestyles will require changing how we consume and use valuable resources.

Interactive Dialogue 4: Protecting our planet and combatting climate change

Interactive Dialogue 4 on Protecting our planet and combatting climate change was Co-chaired by H.E. Mr. François Hollande, President of France, and H.E.Mr.Ollanta Humala, President of the Republic of Peru.

- Climate change is one of our biggest challenges. The negative impacts of climate change are putting into question the potential for progress in all economic and social areas. In order to achieve the objectives of sustainable development, it is essential to ensure a high level of consistency between the actions to address climate change and poverty eradication.
- Integrated actions are needed in order to achieve a sustainable biodiversity management and use of natural resources, forests, land, mountains, oceans, and seas. This is the only way to meet the growing demand for food, water and energy. It is essential to ensure that women, indigenous peoples and other vulnerable groups have equitable access to land, forests and fisheries.
- It is also essential to make sure that we limit the global temperature rise to 1.5 or 2 degrees. The only way to limit the rise of temperature is through the de-carbonization of the economy, especially priority in countries with higher emissions of greenhouse gases. The transition to renewable energy sources is particularly important, while improving the efficiency of the use of energy and natural resources.
- Developing countries, especially small-island developing States and the least developed countries, are highly vulnerable to climate change. Losses incurred by the increased frequency of natural disasters have high costs on people and the economies of these countries.
- Adaptation to climate change requires a greater international effort in the form of financial resources, technology transfer, and capacity building. Enhanced international cooperation is especially important in the context of small-island developing States and the least developed countries.
- It is imperative to strengthen the contributions of all stakeholders (particularly from the private sector) to all level --global, regional and national–and establish, where possible, a carbon price to guide investment decisions to a low carbon economy.
- Several countries reported the existence of ambitious national plans to reduce greenhouse gas emissions and mitigate the impacts of climate change. These plans constitute a good sign for the negotiations that will start at the 21st session of the Conference of the Parties (COP) of the UN Convention on Climate Change (UNFCCC) in Paris next December.

- All countries signalled high expectations for the outcome of the Conference of the Parties of the UN Convention on Climate Change in December. It appears that the general will is to achieve an ambitious and legally binding global agreement with the aim of keeping the temperature rise below 1.5 or 2 degrees. This agreement will be the test of our collective commitment to the Sustainable Development Goals.

Interactive Dialogue 5: Building effective, accountable and inclusive institutions

Interactive Dialogue 5 on Building effective, accountable and inclusive institutions was Co-chaired by H.E. Ms. Park Guen-hye, President of the Republic of Korea, and H.E. Ms.Micelle Bachelet, President of Chile.

- There was a strong sentiment during the dialogue that effective, accountable and inclusive institutions that are transparent and free of corruption are essential prerequisites for our common vision for sustainable development. While Goal 16 is an important goal in its own right, it facilitates and accelerates the success of all other goals.
- Participants agreed that increased involvement of citizens is needed in order to create full ownership of the 2030 Agenda. This can be achieved only through high quality education, non-discrimination, gender equality, access to justice and information, as well as reliable and timely data. This must include the most vulnerable and marginalized groups. It should uphold the highest standards of human rights and freedoms.
- The full engagement of citizens will also help to build a bridge between rich and poor, men and women, urban and rural constituencies, and provide an enabling environment for all people. This will be essential in promoting integrity and building trust between governments and citizens.
- It was acknowledged that strong institutions, based on the rule of law, and not on rule by law, are essential for building peaceful societies where people live free from fear and want. A culture of justice needs to be created, and upheld, to empower all people, including the most marginalised.
- Breaking down silos through building partnerships across sectors and among all stakeholders is a precondition for implementation of Goal 16 and all other Sustainable Development Goals.
- Participants concurred that the SDGs must be integrated into national plans and strategies, supported by sound monitor ing and review frameworks. The important roles of parliaments and local authorities need to be recognized and enhanced.

- Partnerships and a stable environment provided through strong institutions are necessary for vibrant private sector engagement and domestic and international resource mobilization.
- Full gender equality needs to be achieved and women's potential must be unlocked. Young people are the prime beneficiaries of peaceful states and societies. Children and youth living in conflict are often the most immediate victims of violence and displacement. We owe it to them to create a peaceful, just and prosperous world.

Interactive Dialogue 6: A strengthened global partnership for realizing the post-2015 development agenda

Interactive Dialogue 6 on A strengthened global partnership for realizing the post-2015 development agenda was Co-chaired by H.E. Mr. Macky Sall, President of Senegal, and Mr. Ahmet Davutoglu, Prime Minister of Turkey.

- Noting that reaching the SDGs will hinge on a revitalized global partnership, participants agreed that it should be universal and relevant to all, while addressing the needs of the most vulnerable and leaving no one behind. All stakeholders must be engaged and the needs of current and future generations taken into account.
- It was underscored the need to mobilize public and private, domestic and international finance, as well as technologies and capacity building for sustainable development. ODA will remain critical, in particular for the poorest and most vulnerable countries. Domestic resource mobilization, enhanced international tax cooperation and combating illicit flows, plus sound policies, private investments and effective partnerships will also play important roles.
- Participants urged that commitments on ODA and in other areas must be met without delay. We also underscored the importance of effective, predictable, country-driven and results-focused development cooperation.
- Participants agreed on the need for coherent financial, trade, debt and technology policies in support of sustainable development. We also stressed good governance and the rule of law, an enabling environment and combating corruption, and the empowerment of women and girls and inclusion of youth.
- Recognizing that global goals have to be localized, we highlighted the need to reflect them in effective national development plans, developed in open consultations with civil society, to guide national policy and international development cooperation. Capacities of local actors need to be strengthened and access to financial services expanded. We also emphasized the contributions of regional institutions, which provide platforms for sharing of experiences and know-how.

- Participants agreed on the need to forge innovative partnerships between governments, businesses and civil society, to ensure the tapping of all available resources and expertise. The potential of public policies and public funding to leverage private investments in support of the SDGs was recognized.
- Participants stressed the importance of open and transparent data to monitor progress, inform policy and ensure accountability of all stakeholders. The need for innovative, effective and inclusive approaches to monitoring and review was emphasized. Participants agreed on the need to engage all stakeholders and create space for civil society to participate, while supporting mutual learning as we work together towards the SDGs."

Chapter - 3

Meeting the Unfinished Tasks of MDGs

The humanity's journey for ending poverty by the UN system began with the landmark commitment in the year 2000 to "spare no effort to free our fellow men, women and children from the abject and dehumanizing conditions of extreme poverty" which shaped into an inspiring framework of eight goals, known as Millennium Development Goals(MDGs). The MDGs was an agreed set of goals that international community set for itself for the first time around at the UN Millennium Summit in September 2000, a common 15-year agenda to tackle the indignity of poverty. It encompassed universally accepted human values and rights such as freedom from hunger, the right to basic education, the right to health and responsibility to future generations. The MDGs, as set for implementation and monitoring, were as follows:

Goal 1: Eradicate extreme poverty and hunger

Goal 2: Achieve universal primary education

Goal 3: Promote gender equality and empower women

Goal 4: Reduce child mortality

Goal 5: Improve maternal health

Goal 6: Combat HIV/AIDS, malaria and other diseases

Goal 7: Ensure Environmental Sustainability

Goal 8: Develop a global partnership for development

Along with these eight goals, the MDGs had set itself targets for each of the goals totalling 21 targets, and also monitoring indicators within each of such targets aggregating 60 in all. The 15-year MDGs effort has produced the most successful anti-poverty movement in history as brought out by 'The Millennium Development Goals Report 2015'. A summary of such achievements, Goal wise, from the said Report is shown hereunder:

Goal 1: Eradicate extreme poverty and hunger

- Extreme poverty has declined significantly over the last two decades. In 1990, nearly half of the population in the developing world lived on less than $1.25 a day; that proportion dropped to 14% in 2015.
- Globally, the number of people living in extreme poverty has declined by more than half, falling from 1.9 billion in 1990 to 836 million in 2015. Most progress has occurred since 2000.
- The number of people in the working middle class—living on more than $4 a day—has almost tripled between 1991 and 2015. This group now makes up half the workforce in the developing regions, up from just 18% in 1991.
- The proportion of undernourished people in the developing regions has fallen by almost half since 1990, from 23.3% in 1990–1992 to 12.9% in 2014–2016.

Goal 2: Achieve universal primary education

- The primary school net enrolment rate in the developing regions has reached 91% in 2015, up from 83% in 2000.
- The number of out-of-school children of primary school age worldwide has fallen by almost half, to an estimated 57 million in 2015, down from 100 million in 2000.
- Sub-Saharan Africa has had the best record of improvement in primary education of any region since the MDGs were established. The region achieved a 20% point increase in the net enrolment rate from 2000 to 2015, compared to a gain of 8% points between 1990 and 2000.
- The literacy rate among youth aged 15–24 has increased globally from 83 to 91% between 1990 and 2015. The gap between women and men has narrowed

Goal 3: Promote gender equality and empower women

- Many more girls are now in school compared to 15 years ago. The developing regions as a whole have achieved the target to eliminate gender disparity in primary, secondary and tertiary education.
- In Southern Asia, only 74 girls were enrolled in primary school for every 100 boys in 1990. Today, 103 girls are enrolled for every 100 boys.
- Women now make up 41% of paid workers outside the agricultural sector, an increase from 35% in 1990.
- Between 1991 and 2015, thse proportion of women in vulnerable employment as a share of total female employment has declined

13% points. In contrast, vulnerable employment among men fell by 9% points.

- Women have gained ground in parliamentary representation in nearly 90% of the 174 countries with data over the past 20 years. The average proportion of women in parliament has nearly doubled during the same period. Yet still only one in five members are women.

Goal 4: Reduce child mortality

- The global under-five mortality rate has declined by more than half, dropping from 90 to 43 deaths per 1000 live births between 1990 and 2015.
- Despite population growth in the developing regions, the number of deaths of children under five has declined from 12.7 million in 1990 to almost 6 million in 2015 globally.
- Since the early 1990s, the rate of reduction of under-five mortality has more than tripled globally.
- In sub-Saharan Africa, the annual rate of reduction of under-five mortality was over five times faster during 2005–2013 than it was during 1990–1995.
- Measles vaccination helped prevent nearly 15.6 million deaths between 2000 and 2013. The number of globally reported measles cases declined by 67% for the same period.
- About 84% of children worldwide received at least one dose of measles-containing vaccine in 2013, up from 73% in 2000.

Goal 5: Improve maternal health

- Since 1990, the maternal mortality ratio has declined by 45% worldwide, and most of the reduction has occurred since 2000.
- In Southern Asia, the maternal mortality ratio declined by 64% between 1990 and 2013, and in sub-Saharan Africa it fell by 49%.
- More than 71% of births were assisted by skilled health personnel globally in 2014, an increase from 59% in 1990.
- In Northern Africa, the proportion of pregnant women who received four or more antenatal visits increased from 50 to 89% between 1990 and 2014.
- Contraceptive prevalence among women aged 15 to 49, married or in a union, increased from 55% in 1990 worldwide to 64% in 2015.

Goal 6: Combat HIV/AIDS, malaria and other diseases

- New HIV infections fell by approximately 40% between 2000 and 2013, from an estimated 3.5 million cases to 2.1 million.

- By June 2014, 13.6 million people living with HIV were receiving antiretroviral therapy (ART) globally, an immense increase from just 800,000 in 2003. ART averted 7.6 million deaths from AIDS between 1995 and 2013.
- Over 6.2 million malaria deaths have been averted between 2000 and 2015, primarily of children under five years of age in sub-Saharan Africa. The global malaria incidence rate has fallen by an estimated 37% and the mortality rate by 58 %.
- More than 900 million insecticide-treated mosquito nets were delivered to malaria-endemic countries in sub-Saharan Africa between 2004 and 2014.
- Between 2000 and 2013, tuberculosis prevention, diagnosis and treatment interventions saved an estimated 37 million lives. The tuberculosis mortality rate fell by 45% and the prevalence rate by 41% between 1990 and 2013.

Goal 7: Goal 7 : Ensure Environmental Sustainability

- Ozone-depleting substances have been virtually eliminated since 1990, and the ozone layer is expected to recover by the middle of this century.
- Terrestrial and marine protected areas in many regions have increased substantially since 1990. In Latin America and the Caribbean, coverage of terrestrial protected areas rose from 8.8 to 23.4% between 1990 and 2014.
- In 2015, 91% of the global population is using an improved drinking water source, compared to 76% in 1990.
- Of the 2.6 billion people who have gained access to improved drinking water since 1990, 1.9 billion gained access to piped drinking water on premises. Over half of the global population (58 %) now enjoys this higher level of service.
- Globally, 147 countries have met the drinking water target, 95 countries have met the sanitation target and 77 countries have met both.
- Worldwide, 2.1 billion people have gained access to improved sanitation. The proportion of people practicing open defecation has fallen almost by half since 1990.
- The proportion of urban population living in slums in the developing regions fell from approximately 39.4% in 2000 to 29.7% in 2014.

Goal 8: Develop a global partnership for development

- Official development assistance from developed countries increased by 66% in real terms between 2000 and 2014, reaching $135.2 billion.

- In 2014, Denmark, Luxembourg, Norway, Sweden and the United Kingdom continued to exceed the United Nations official development assistance target of 0.7% of gross national income.
- In 2014, 79% of imports from developing to developed countries were admitted duty free, up from 65% in 2000.
- The proportion of external debt service to export revenue in developing countries fell from 12% in 2000 to 3% in 2013.
- As of 2015, 95% of the world's population is covered by a mobile-cellular signal.
- The number of mobile-cellular subscriptions has grown almost tenfold in the last 15 years, from 738 million in 2000 to over 7 billion in 2015.
- Internet penetration has grown from just over 6% of the world's population in 2000 to 43% in 2015. As a result, 3.2 billion people are linked to a global network of content and applications.

The MDG Report, 2015 captures the significant achievements of the targets worldwide, as mentioned above, but the progress has been uneven across regions and countries. This is more so to the poorer and to the disadvantages on ground of sex, age, disabilities, ethnicity and geographic considerations. The big gap still exists between the poorest and richer households, and between rural and urban areas. Further, climate change and environmental degradation still remains a critical challenge for the global community. Another gap that surfaced related to conflicts in the global scenario which account for a serious threat to human development. Millions of poor people still live in poverty and hunger without access to basic services. In fine, the MDG Report 2015 which documents the aspirational goals set out to achieve Millennium Declaration and highlights many success areas also mentions gaps that still remain. This has posed a new challenge at the end of MDGs' tenure.

The UN Secretary General observed at the summary of 'The Millennium Development Goals Report 2015' that 'the global mobilization behind the Millennium Development Goals has produced the most successful anti-poverty movement in history. The global initiative helped to lift more than one billion people out of extreme poverty, to make inroads against hunger and galvanized international and national public opinion to put people and their immediate needs at the forefront. The Report also noted that despite enormous progress, 800 millions of poor people still live in poverty and hunger at the end of the life span of the MDGs. Over 160 million children under age five have inadequate height for their age due to insufficient food. Almost half of global workers are still working in vulnerable conditions, rarely enjoying the benefits associated with decent work. With global action, these numbers can only be turned around".

Historically, the MDGs initiative is a path breaking event of monumental importance in that it set on motion a set on common social priorities worldwide.. Further, it brought a paradigm shift on the role of global partner and global awareness, political accountability and public pressure to the Report Card of development, as Bill Gate liked to look at the MDGs Report.

The Sustainable Development Summit Declaration, briefly summarised the background, the achievements and the limitations of MDGs initiatives at paragraphs 16-17 in the following manner:

> "16. Almost 15 years ago, the Millennium Development Goals were agreed. These provided an important framework for development and significant progress has been made in a number of areas. But the progress has been uneven, particularly in Africa, least developed countries, landlocked developing countries and small island developing States, and some of the Millennium Development Goals remain off track, in particular those related to maternal, newborn and child health and to reproductive health. We recommit ourselves to the full realization of all the Millennium Development Goals, including the off-track Millennium Development Goals, in particular by providing focused and scaled-up assistance to least developed countries and other countries in special situations, in line with relevant support programmes. The new Agenda builds on the Millennium Development Goals and seeks to complete what they did not achieve, particularly in reaching the most vulnerable.
>
> 17. In its scope, however, the framework we are announcing today goes far beyond the Millennium Development Goals. Alongside continuing development priorities such as poverty eradication, health, education and food security and nutrition, it sets out a wide range of economic, social and environmental objectives. It also promises more peaceful and inclusive societies. It also, crucially, defines means of implementation. Reflecting the integrated approach that we have decided on, there are deep interconnections and many cross-cutting elements across the new Goals and targets".

The paradigm shift of approach of the MDGs to SDGs can be explained by means of an illustration. MDGs incorporated targets on drinking water and sanitation but did not address other aspects crucial to sustainable development, such as water resources management, waste-water management, water quality and enhancing resilience to water-related disasters. The SDG-6 addresses issues relating to drinking water, sanitation and hygiene along with the quality and sustainability of water resources worldwide.In fact, the SDG- 6 expands the MDG focus on drinking water and sanitation to cover the entire water cycle, including the management of water, wastewater and ecosystem resources. Further, with water at the very core of sustainable development, the SDG- 6 does not only have strong linkages to all of the other SDGs, it also underpins them; meeting SDG 6 would go a long way towards achieving much of the 2030 Agenda.

Sustainable Development Goals also go beyond MDGs in focusing on global system reforms to remove the barriers to sustainable development. While the first set of SDGs (No 1-7) appears to be just an extension of MDGs, the later set of goals are indeed an extension of the agenda itself. The later parts have in turn two distinct characteristics: SDGs falling under numbers 8,9 and 10 are reforms centred enablers of development covering areas like inclusion and jobs, infrastructure and industrialisation, and distribution. The final set of goals under SDGs No 11-17 lays down the framework of governance covering areas like urbanization, consumption and production, climate change, resources and environment, peace and justice, and means of implementation and global partnership. Considerable shift in approaches has also been visible from MDGs to SDGs in that SDGs have now 5 Ps-people, planet, prosperity, peace and partnership.

Chapter - 4

Declaration of the Sustainable Devclopment Summit, 2015

A preamble is a kind of introductory statement or a preface setting forth the general principles. The Constitution of a country usually begins with a Preamble setting out its vision embodying therein in a summary form core spirit, philosophy, values and principles enshrined in different provisions under various Articles. The Constitution of India, for example, begins with a Preamble as vision statement before its chapter-1. Similarly, Seventy years ago, when an earlier generation of world leaders came together to create the United Nations from the ashes of war and fashioned the Charter of the United Nations it began with a Preamble which incorporated the values of peace, dialogue and international cooperation which under pin it. The supreme embodiment of those values is the Charter of the United Nations. Likewise, the Sustainable Development Summit,2015 brought out a 'Declaration', which espouses the values and principle of Sustainable Development initiative, and is indeed a model kind of preamble to set its great perspective 'to build a better future for all people, including the millions who have been denied the chance to lead decent, dignified and rewarding lives and to achieve their full human potential.' As a matter of fact, the Sustainable Goals and Targets form a very part of the 'Declaration' It would, therefore, be appropriate to keep in upfront the salient points of Declaration before proceeding towards the Sustainable Development Goals and targets of the Summit in detalis.

The core focus of the SDG Summit, as highlighted in the historic Declaration, was the setting out of a comprehensive, far-reaching and people-centred set of universal and transformative new global Sustainable Development Goals and targets. Recognizing that eradicating poverty in all its forms and dimensions is the greatest global challenge and an indispensable requirement for sustainable development, it took a pledge to achieving sustainable development in its three dimensions-economic, social and environmental in a balanced and integrated manner. Built upon the achievements of the Millennium Development Goals, SDG summit sought to address their unfinished Agenda for global action for the next 15 years -a charter for people and planet on making world a better place in 2030., This journey will involve Governments as well as parliaments, the United Nations system and other international institutions, local authorities, indigenous peoples, civil society, business and the private sector, the scientific and the academic community. The abiding concern for this great collective endeavour and journey was to ensure that no one will be left behind.

Following an inclusive process of negotiations, the Sustainable Development Goals and targets have been worked out as integrated and indivisible manner. Global in nature and universally applicable, the targets took into account different national realities, capacities and levels of development, and also factored in national policies and priorities. The Targets are aspirational in character with each Government requiring to set its own national targets guided by the global level of ambition but taking into account national circumstances.

The SDG Summit declaration is a call for action to change our world with an Agenda for global action for the next 15 years. Children and young women and men are critical agents of change and will find in the new Goals a platform to channel their infinite capacities for activism into the creation of a better world. Since the SDG Summit declaration, as adopted on September 2015, on new global Sustainable Development Goals incorporating all finer points leading to the setting of the 17 SDGs and 169 Targets, it would therefore, be appropriate to put in place the entire declaration, in original, to appreciate the perspective in formulation of SDGs and targets as below:

Declaration

Introduction

"1. We, the Heads of State and Government and High Representatives, meeting at United Nations Headquarters in New York from 25 to 27 September 2015 as the Organization celebrates its seventieth anniversary, have decided today on new global Sustainable Development Goals.

2. On behalf of the peoples we serve, we have adopted a historic decision on a comprehensive, far-reaching and people-centred set of universal and transformative Goals and targets. We commit ourselves to working tirelessly for the full implementation of this Agenda by 2030. We recognize that eradicating poverty in all its forms and dimensions, including extreme poverty, is the greatest global challenge and an indispensable requirement for sustainable development. We are committed to achieving sustainable development in its three dimensions – economic, social and environmental – in a balanced and

integrated manner. We will also build upon the achievements of the Millennium Development Goals and seek to address their unfinished business.

3. We resolve, between now and 2030, to end poverty and hunger everywhere; to combat inequalities within and among countries; to build peaceful, just and inclusive societies; to protect human rights and promote gender equality and the empowerment of women and girls; and to ensure the lasting protection of the planet and its natural resources. We resolve also to create conditions for sustainable, inclusive and sustained economic growth, shared prosperity and decent work for all, taking into account different levels of national development and capacities.

4. As we embark on this great collective journey, we pledge that no one will be left behind. Recognizing that the dignity of the human person is fundamental, we wish to see the Goals and targets met for all nations and peoples and for all segments of society. And we will endeavour to reach the furthest behind first.

5. This is an Agenda of unprecedented scope and significance. It is accepted by all countries and is applicable to all, taking into account different national realities, capacities and levels of development and respecting national policies and priorities. These are universal goals and targets which involve the entire world, developed and developing countries alike. They are integrated and indivisible and balance the three dimensions of sustainable development.

6. The Goals and targets are the result of over two years of intensive public consultation and engagement with civil society and other stakeholders around the world, which paid particular attention to the voices of the poorest and most vulnerable. This consultation included valuable work done by the Open Working Group of the General Assembly on Sustainable Development Goals and by the United Nations, whose Secretary-General provided a synthesis report in December 2014.

Our vision

7. In these Goals and targets, we are setting out a supremely ambitious and transformational vision. We envisage a world free of poverty, hunger, disease and want, where all life can thrive. We envisage a world free of fear and violence.A world with universal literacy. A world with equitable and universal access to quality education at all levels, to health care and social protection, where physical,mental and social well-being are assured. A world where we reaffirm our commitments regarding the human right to safe drinking water and sanitation and where there is improved hygiene; and where food is sufficient, safe, affordable and nutritious. A world where human habitats are safe, resilient and sustainable and where there is universal access to affordable, reliable and sustainable energy.

8. We envisage a world of universal respect for human rights and human dignity, the rule of law, justice, equality and non-discrimination; of respect for

race, ethnicity and cultural diversity; and of equal opportunity permitting the full realization of human potential and contributing to shared prosperity. A world which invests in its children and in which every child grows up free from violence and exploitation. A world in which every woman and girl enjoys full gender equality and all legal, social and economic barriers to their empowerment have been removed. A just, equitable, tolerant, open and socially inclusive world in which the needs of the most vulnerable are met.

9. We envisage a world in which every country enjoys sustained, inclusive and sustainable economic growth and decent work for all. A world in which consumption and production patterns and use of all natural resources – from air to land, from rivers, lakes and aquifers to oceans and seas – are sustainable. One in which democracy, good governance and the rule of law, as well as an enabling environment at the national and international levels, are essential for sustainable development, including sustained and inclusive economic growth, social development, environmental protection and the eradication of poverty and hunger. One in which development and the application of technology are climate-sensitive, respect biodiversity and are resilient. One in which humanity lives in harmony with nature and in which wildlife and other living species are protected.

Our shared principles and commitments

10. The new Agenda is guided by the purposes and principles of the Charter of the United Nations, including full respect for international law. It is grounded in the Universal Declaration of Human Rights, 1 international human rights treaties, the Millennium Declaration2 and the 2005 World Summit Outcome.3 It is informed by other instruments such as the Declaration on the Right to Development.4

11. We reaffirm the outcomes of all major United Nations conferences and summits which have laid a solid foundation for sustainable development and have helped to shape the new Agenda. These include the Rio Declaration on Environment and Development, 5 the World Summit on Sustainable Development, the World Summit for Social Development, the Programme of Action of the International Conference on Population and Development, 6 the Beijing Platform for Action 7 and the United Nations Conference on Sustainable Development. We also reaffirm the follow-up to these conferences, including the outcomes of the Fourth United Nations Conference on the Least Developed Countries, the third International Conference on Small Island Developing States, the second United Nations Conference on Landlocked Developing Countries and the Third United Nations World Conference on Disaster Risk Reduction.

12. We reaffirm all the principles of the Rio Declaration on Environment and Development, including, inter alia, the principle of common but differentiated responsibilities, as set out in principle 7 thereof.

13. The challenges and commitments identified at these major conferences and summits are interrelated and call for integrated solutions. To address them effectively, a new approach is needed. Sustainable development recognizes that eradicating poverty in all its forms and dimensions, combating inequality within and among countries, preserving the planet, creating sustained, inclusive and sustainable economic growth and fostering social inclusion are linked to each other and are interdependent.

Our world today

14. We are meeting at a time of immense challenges to sustainable development. Billions of our citizens continue to live in poverty and are denied a life of dignity. There are rising inequalities within and among countries. There are enormous disparities of opportunity, wealth and power. Gender inequality remains a key challenge. Unemployment, particularly youth unemployment, is a major concern. Global health threats, more frequent and intense natural disasters, spiralling conflict, violent extremism, terrorism and related humanitarian crises and forced displacement of people threaten to reverse much of the development progress made in recent decades. Natural resource depletion and adverse impacts of environmental degradation, including desertification, drought, land degradation, freshwater scarcity and loss of biodiversity, add to and exacerbate the list of challenges which humanity faces. Climate change is one of the greatest challenges of our time and its adverse impacts undermine the ability of all countries to achieve sustainable development. Increases in global temperature, sea level rise, ocean acidification and other climate change impacts are seriously affecting coastal areas and low-lying coastal countries, including many least developed countries and small island developing States. The survival of many societies, and of the biological support systems of the planet, is at risk.

15. It is also, however, a time of immense opportunity. Significant progress has been made in meeting many development challenges. Within the past generation, hundreds of millions of people have emerged from extreme poverty. Access to education has greatly increased for both boys and girls. The spread of information and communications technology and global interconnectedness has great potential to accelerate human progress, to bridge the digital divide and to develop knowledge societies, as does scientific and technological innovation across areas as diverse as medicine and energy.

16. Almost 15 years ago, the Millennium Development Goals were agreed. These provided an important framework for development and significant progress has been made in a number of areas. But the progress has been uneven, particularly in Africa, least developed countries, landlocked developing countries and small island developing States, and some of the Millennium Development Goals remain off track, in particular those related to maternal, newborn and child health and to reproductive health. We recommit ourselves

to the full realization of all the Millennium Development Goals, including the off-track Millennium Development Goals, in particular by providing focused and scaled-up assistance to least developed countries and other countries in special situations, in line with relevant support programmes. The new Agenda builds on the Millennium Development Goals and seeks to complete what they did not achieve, particularly in reaching the most vulnerable.

17. In its scope, however, the framework we are announcing today goes far beyond the Millennium Development Goals. Alongside continuing development priorities such as poverty eradication, health, education and food security and nutrition, it sets out a wide range of economic, social and environmental objectives. It also promises more peaceful and inclusive societies. It also, crucially, defines means of implementation. Reflecting the integrated approach that we have decided on, there are deep interconnections and many cross-cutting elements across the new Goals and targets.

The new Agenda

18. We are announcing today 17 Sustainable Development Goals with 169 associated targets which are integrated and indivisible. Never before have world leaders pledged common action and endeavour across such a broad and universal policy agenda. We are setting out together on the path towards sustainable development, devoting ourselves collectively to the pursuit of global development and of "win-win" cooperation which can bring huge gains to all countries and all parts of the world. We reaffirm that every State has, and shall freely exercise, full permanent sovereignty over all its wealth, natural resources and economic activity. We will implement the Agenda for the full benefit of all, for today's generation and for future generations. In doing so, we reaffirm our commitment to international law and emphasize that the Agenda is to be implemented in a manner that is consistent with the rights and obligations of States under international law.

19. We reaffirm the importance of the Universal Declaration of Human Rights, as well as other international instruments relating to human rights and international law. We emphasize the responsibilities of all States, in conformity with the Charter of the United Nations, to respect, protect and promote human rights and fundamental freedoms for all, without distinction of any kind as to race, colour, sex, language, religion, political or other opinion, national or social origin, property,birth, disability or other status.

20. Realizing gender equality and the empowerment of women and girls will make a crucial contribution to progress across all the Goals and targets. The achievement of full human potential and of sustainable development is not possible if one half of humanity continues to be denied its full human rights and opportunities. Women and girls must enjoy equal access to quality education, economic resources and political participation as well as equal opportunities with men and boys for employment,leadership and decision-

making at all levels. We will work for a significant increase in investments to close the gender gap and strengthen support for institutions in relation to gender equality and the empowerment of women at the global, regional and national levels. All forms of discrimination and violence against women and girls will be eliminated, including through the engagement of men and boys. The systematic mainstreaming of a gender perspective in the implementation of the Agenda is crucial.

21. The new Goals and targets will come into effect on 1 January 2016 and will guide the decisions we take over the next 15 years. All of us will work to implement the Agenda within our own countries and at the regional and global levels, taking into account different national realities, capacities and levels of development and respecting national policies and priorities. We will respect national policy space for sustained, inclusive and sustainable economic growth, in particular for developing States, while remaining consistent with relevant international rules and commitments. We acknowledge also the importance of the regional and sub-regional dimensions, regional economic integration and interconnectivity in sustainable development. Regional and sub-regional frameworks can facilitate the effective translation of sustainable development policies into concrete action at the national level.

22. Each country faces specific challenges in its pursuit of sustainable development. The most vulnerable countries and, in particular, African countries, least developed countries, landlocked developing countries and small island developing States, deserve special attention, as do countries in situations of conflict and post-conflict countries. There are also serious challenges within many middle income countries.

23. People who are vulnerable must be empowered. Those whose needs are reflected in the Agenda include all children, youth, persons with disabilities (of whom more than 80 per cent live in poverty), people living with HIV/AIDS, older persons, indigenous peoples, refugees and internally displaced persons and migrants. We resolve to take further effective measures and actions, in conformity with international law, to remove obstacles and constraints, strengthen support and meet the special needs of people living in areas affected by complex humanitarian emergencies and in areas affected by terrorism.

24. We are committed to ending poverty in all its forms and dimensions, including by eradicating extreme poverty by 2030. All people must enjoy a basic standard of living, including through social protection systems. We are also determined to end hunger and to achieve food security as a matter of priority and to end all forms of malnutrition. In this regard, we reaffirm the important role and inclusive nature of the Committee on World Food Security and welcome the Rome Declaration on Nutrition and the Framework for Action.8 We will devote resources to developing rural areas and sustainable agriculture and fisheries, supporting smallholder farmers, especially women

farmers, herders and fishers in developing countries, particularly least developed countries.

25. We commit to providing inclusive and equitable quality education at all levels – early childhood, primary, secondary, tertiary, technical and vocational training. All people, irrespective of sex, age, race or ethnicity, and persons with disabilities, migrants, indigenous peoples, children and youth, especially those in vulnerable situations, should have access to life-long learning opportunities that help them to acquire the knowledge and skills needed to exploit opportunities and to participate fully in society. We will strive to provide children and youth with a nurturing environment for the full realization of their rights and capabilities, helping our countries to reap the demographic dividend, including through safe schools and cohesive communities and families.

26. To promote physical and mental health and well-being, and to extend life expectancy for all, we must achieve universal health coverage and access to quality health care. No one must be left behind. We commit to accelerating the progress made to date in reducing newborn, child and maternal mortality by ending all such preventable deaths before 2030. We are committed to ensuring universal access to sexual and reproductive health-care services, including for family planning, information and education. We will equally accelerate the pace of progress made in fighting malaria, HIV/AIDS, tuberculosis, hepatitis, Ebola and other communicable diseases and epidemics, including by addressing growing anti-microbial resistance and the problem of unattended diseases affecting developing countries. We are committed to the prevention and treatment of non-communicable diseases, including behavioural, developmental and neurological disorders, which constitute a major challenge for sustainable development.

27. We will seek to build strong economic foundations for all our countries. Sustained, inclusive and sustainable economic growth is essential for prosperity. This will only be possible if wealth is shared and income inequality is addressed. We will work to build dynamic, sustainable, innovative and people-centred economies, promoting youth employment and women's economic empowerment, in particular, and decent work for all. We will eradicate forced labour and human trafficking and end child labour in all its forms. All countries stand to benefit from having a healthy and well-educated workforce with the knowledge and skills needed for productive and fulfilling work and full participation in society. We will strengthen the productive capacities of least developed countries in all sectors, including through structural transformation. We will adopt policies which increase productive capacities, productivity and productive employment; financial inclusion; sustainable agriculture, pastoralist and fisheries development; sustainable industrial development; universal access to affordable, reliable, sustainable and modern energy services; sustainable transport systems; and quality and resilient infrastructure.

28. We commit to making fundamental changes in the way that our societies produce and consume goods and services. Governments, international organizations, the business sector and other non-State actors and individuals must contribute to changing unsustainable consumption and production patterns, including through the mobilization, from all sources, of financial and technical assistance to strengthen developing countries' scientific, technological and innovative capacities to move towards more sustainable patterns of consumption and production. We encourage the implementation of the 10-Year Framework of Programmes on Sustainable Consumption and Production Patterns. All countries take action, with developed countries taking the lead, taking into account the development and capabilities of developing countries.

29. We recognize the positive contribution of migrants for inclusive growth and sustainable development. We also recognize that international migration is a multidimensional reality of major relevance for the development of countries of origin, transit and destination, which requires coherent and comprehensive responses. We will cooperate internationally to ensure safe, orderly and regular migration involving full respect for human rights and the humane treatment of migrants regardless of migration status, of refugees and of displaced persons. Such cooperation should also strengthen the resilience of communities hosting refugees, particularly in developing countries. We underline the right of migrants to return to their country of citizenship, and recall that States must ensure that their returning nationals are duly received.

30. States are strongly urged to refrain from promulgating and applying any unilateral economic, financial or trade measures not in accordance with international law and the Charter of the United Nations that impede the full achievement of economic and social development, particularly in developing countries.

31. We acknowledge that the United Nations Framework Convention on Climate Change9 is the primary international, intergovernmental forum for negotiating the global response to climate change. We are determined to address decisively the threat posed by climate change and environmental degradation. The global nature of climate change calls for the widest possible international cooperation aimed at accelerating the reduction of global greenhouse gas emissions and addressing adaptation to the adverse impacts of climate change. We note with grave concern the significant gap between the aggregate effect of parties' mitigation pledges in terms of global annual emissions of greenhouse gases by 2020 and aggregate emission pathways consistent with having a likely chance of holding the increase in global average temperature below 2 degrees Celsius, or 1.5 degrees Celsius above pre-industrial levels.

32. Looking ahead to the twenty-first session of the Conference of the Parties in Paris, we underscore the commitment of all States to work for an ambitious and universal climate agreement. We reaffirm that the protocol,

another legal instrument or agreed outcome with legal force under the Convention applicable to all parties shall address in a balanced manner, inter alia, mitigation, adaptation, finance, technology development and transfer and capacity-building; and transparency of action and support.

33. We recognize that social and economic development depends on the sustainable management of our planet's natural resources. We are therefore determined to conserve and sustainably use oceans and seas, freshwater resources,as well as forests, mountains and drylands and to protect biodiversity, ecosystems and wildlife. We are also determined to promote sustainable tourism, to tackle water scarcity and water pollution, to strengthen cooperation on desertification, dust storms, land degradation and drought and to promote resilience and disaster risk reduction. In this regard, we look forward to the thirteenth meeting of the Conference of the Parties to the Convention on Biological Diversity to be held in Mexico.

34. We recognize that sustainable urban development and management are crucial to the quality of life of our people. We will work with local authorities and communities to renew and plan our cities and human settlements so as to foster community cohesion and personal security and to stimulate innovation and employment. We will reduce the negative impacts of urban activities and of chemicals which are hazardous for human health and the environment, including through the environmentally sound management and safe use of chemicals, the reduction and recycling of waste and the more efficient use of water and energy. And we will work to minimize the impact of cities on the global climate system. We will also take account of population trends and projections in our national rural and urban development strategies and policies. We look forward to the upcoming United Nations

Conference on Housing and Sustainable Urban Development to be held in Quito.35. Sustainable development cannot be realized without peace and security; and peace and security will be at risk without sustainable development. The new Agenda recognizes the need to build peaceful, just and inclusive societies that provide equal access to justice and that are based on respect for human rights (including the right to development), on effective rule of law and good governance at all levels and on transparent, effective and accountable institutions. Factors which give rise to violence, insecurity and injustice, such as inequality, corruption, poor governance and illicit financial and arms flows, are addressed in the Agenda. We must redouble our efforts to resolve or prevent conflict and to support post-conflict countries, including through ensuring that women have a role in peace-building and State-building.We call for further effective measures and actions to be taken, in conformity with international law, to remove the obstacles to the full realization of the right of self-determination of peoples living under colonial and foreign occupation, which continue to adversely affect their economic and social development as well as their environment.

36. We pledge to foster intercultural understanding, tolerance, mutual respect and an ethic of global citizenship and shared responsibility. We acknowledge the natural and cultural diversity of the world and recognize that all cultures and civilizations can contribute to, and are crucial enablers of, sustainable development.

37. Sport is also an important enabler of sustainable development. We recognize the growing contribution of sport to the realization of development and peace in its promotion of tolerance and respect and the contributions it makes to the empowerment of women and of young people, individuals and communities as well as to health, education and social inclusion objectives.

38. We reaffirm, in accordance with the Charter of the United Nations, the need to respect the territorial integrity and political independence of States.

Means of implementation

39. The scale and ambition of the new Agenda requires a revitalized Global Partnership to ensure its implementation. We fully commit to this. This Partnership will work in a spirit of global solidarity, in particular solidarity with the poorest and with people in vulnerable situations. It will facilitate an intensive global engagement in support of implementation of all the Goals and targets, bringing together Governments, the private sector, civil society, the United Nations system and other actors and mobilizing all available resources.

40. The means of implementation targets under Goal 17 and under each Sustainable Development Goal are key to realizing our Agenda and are of equal importance with the other Goals and targets. The Agenda, including the Sustainable Development Goals, can be met within the framework of a revitalized Global Partnership for Sustainable Development, supported by the concrete policies and actions as outlined in the outcome document of the third International Conference on Financing for Development, held in Addis Ababa from 13 to 16 July 2015. We welcome the endorsement by the General Assembly of the Addis Ababa Action Agenda, 10 which is an integral part of the 2030 Agenda for Sustainable Development. We recognize that the full implementation of the Addis Ababa Action Agenda is critical for the realization of the Sustainable Development Goals and targets

41. We recognize that each country has primary responsibility for its own economic and social development. The new Agenda deals with the means required for implementation of the Goals and targets. We recognize that these will include the mobilization of financial resources as well as capacity-building and the transfer of environmentally sound technologies to developing countries on favourable terms, including on concessional and preferential terms, as mutually agreed. Public finance, both domestic and international, will play a vital role in providing essential services and public goods and in catalysing

other sources of finance. We acknowledge the role of the diverse private sector, ranging from micro-enterprises to cooperatives to multinationals, and that of civil society organizations and philanthropic organizations in the implementation of the new Agenda.

42. We support the implementation of relevant strategies and programmes of action, including the Istanbul Declaration and Programme of Action, the SIDS Accelerated Modalities of Action (SAMOA) Pathway and the Vienna Programme of Action for Landlocked Developing Countries for the Decade 2014–2024, and reaffirm the importance of supporting the African Union's Agenda 2063 and the programme of the New Partnership for Africa's Development, all of which are integral to the new Agenda. We recognize the major challenge to the achievement of durable peace and sustainable development in countries in conflict and post-conflict situations.

43. We emphasize that international public finance plays an important role in complementing the efforts of countries to mobilize public resources domestically, especially in the poorest and most vulnerable countries with limited domestic resources. An important use of international public finance, including official development assistance (ODA), is to catalyse additional resource mobilization from other sources, public and private. ODA providers reaffirm their respective commitments, including the commitment by many developed countries to achieve the target of 0.7 per cent of gross national income for official development assistance (ODA/GNI) to developing countries and 0.15 per cent to 0.2 per cent of ODA/GNI to least developed countries.

44. We acknowledge the importance for international financial institutions to support, in line with their mandates, the policy space of each country, in particular developing countries. We recommit to broadening and strengthening the voice and participation of developing countries – including African countries, least developed countries, landlocked developing countries, small island developing States and middle-income countries – in international economic decision-making, norm-setting and global economic governance.

45. We acknowledge also the essential role of national parliaments through their enactment of legislation and adoption of budgets and their role in ensuring accountability for the effective implementation of our commitments. Governments and public institutions will also work closely on implementation with regional and local authorities, sub-regional institutions, international institutions, academia, philanthropic organizations, volunteer groups and others.

46. We underline the important role and comparative advantage of an adequately resourced, relevant, coherent, efficient and effective United Nations system in supporting the achievement of the Sustainable Development Goals and sustainable development. While stressing the importance of strengthened national ownership and leadership at the country level, we express our support

for the ongoing dialogue in the Economic and Social Council on the longer-term positioning of the United Nations development system in the context of this Agenda.

Follow-up and review

47. Our Governments have the primary responsibility for follow-up and review, at the national, regional and global levels, in relation to the progress made in implementing the Goals and targets over the coming 15 years. To support accountability to our citizens, we will provide for systematic follow-up and review at the various levels, as set out in this Agenda and the Addis Ababa Action Agenda. The high-level political forum under the auspices of the General Assembly and the Economic and Social Council will have the central role in overseeing follow-up and review at the global level.

48. Indicators are being developed to assist this work. Quality, accessible, timely and reliable disaggregated data will be needed to help with the measurement of progress and to ensure that no one is left behind. Such data is key to decision making. Data and information from existing reporting mechanisms should be used where possible. We agree to intensify our efforts to strengthen statistical capacities in developing countries, particularly African countries, least developed countries, landlocked developing countries, small island developing States and middle-income countries. We are committed to developing broader measures of progress to complement gross domestic product.

A call for action to change our world

49. Seventy years ago, an earlier generation of world leaders came together to create the United Nations. From the ashes of war and division they fashioned this Organization and the values of peace, dialogue and international cooperation which underpin it. The supreme embodiment of those values is the Charter of the United Nations.50. Today we are also taking a decision of great historic significance. We resolve to build a better future for all people, including the millions who have been denied the chance to lead decent, dignified and rewarding lives and to achieve their full human potential. We can be the first generation to succeed in ending poverty; just as we may be the last to have a chance of saving the planet. The world will be a better place in 2030 if we succeed in our objectives.

51. What we are announcing today – an Agenda for global action for the next 15 years – is a charter for people and planet in the twenty-first century. Children and young women and men are critical agents of change and will find in the new Goals a platform to channel their infinite capacities for activism into the creation of a better world.

52. "We the peoples" are the celebrated opening words of the Charter of the United Nations. It is "we the peoples" who are embarking today on the

road to 2030. Our journey will involve Governments as well as parliaments, the United Nations system and other international institutions, local authorities, indigenous peoples, civil society, business and the private sector, the scientific and academic community – and all people. Millions have already engaged with, and will own, this Agenda. It is an Agenda of the people, by the people and for the people – and this, we believe, will ensure its success.

53. The future of humanity and of our planet lies in our hands. It lies also in the hands of today's younger generation who will pass the torch to future generations. We have mapped the road to sustainable development; it will be for all of us to ensure that the journey is successful and its gains irreversible.

Sustainable Development Goals and targets

54. Following an inclusive process of intergovernmental negotiations, and based on the proposal of the Open Working Group on Sustainable Development Goals,which includes a chapeau contextualizing the latter, set out below are the Goals and targets which we have agreed.

55. The Sustainable Development Goals and targets are integrated and indivisible,global in nature and universally applicable, taking into account different national realities, capacities and levels of development and respecting national policies and priorities. Targets are defined as aspirational and global, with each Government setting its own national targets guided by the global level of ambition but taking into account national circumstances. Each Government will also decide how these aspirational and global targets should be incorporated into national planning processes, policies and strategies. It is important to recognize the link between sustainable development and other relevant ongoing processes in the economic, social and environmental fields.

56. In deciding upon these Goals and targets, we recognize that each country faces specific challenges to achieve sustainable development, and we underscore the special challenges facing the most vulnerable countries and, in particular, African countries, least developed countries, landlocked developing countries and small island developing States, as well as the specific challenges facing the middle income countries. Countries in situations of conflict also need special attention.

57. We recognize that baseline data for several of the targets remains unavailable, and we call for increased support for strengthening data collection and capacity building in Member States, to develop national and global baselines where they do not yet exist. We commit to addressing this gap in data collection so as to better inform the measurement of progress, in particular for those targets below which do not have clear numerical targets.

58. We encourage ongoing efforts by States in other forums to address key issues which pose potential challenges to the implementation of our Agenda, and we respect the independent mandates of those processes. We intend that

the Agenda and its implementation would support, and be without prejudice to, those other processes and the decisions taken therein.

59. We recognize that there are different approaches, visions, models and tools available to each country, in accordance with its national circumstances and priorities, to achieve sustainable development; and we reaffirm that planet Earth and its ecosystems are our common home and that "Mother Earth" is a common expression in a number of countries and regions.

59. We recognize that there are different approaches, visions, models and tools available to each country, in accordance with its national circumstances and priorities, to achieve sustainable development; and we reaffirm that planet Earth and its ecosystems are our common home and that "Mother Earth" is a common expression in a number of countries and regions.

Sustainable Development Goals

Goal 1. End poverty in all its forms everywhere

Goal 2. End hunger, achieve food security and improved nutrition and promote sustainable agriculture

Goal 3. Ensure healthy lives and promote well-being for all at all ages

Goal 4. Ensure inclusive and equitable quality education and promote lifelong learning opportunities for all

Goal 5. Achieve gender equality and empower all women and girls

Goal 6. Ensure availability and sustainable management of water and sanitation for all

Goal 7 Ensure access to affordable, reliable, sustainable and modern energy for all

Goal 8. Promote sustained, inclusive and sustainable economic growth, full and productive employment and decent work for all

Goal 9. Build resilient infrastructure, promote inclusive and sustainable industrialization and foster innovation

Goal 10. Reduce inequality within and among countries

Goal 11. Make cities and human settlements inclusive, safe, resilient and sustainable

Goal 12. Ensure sustainable consumption and production patterns

Goal 13. Take urgent action to combat climate change and its impacts*

Goal 14. Conserve and sustainably use the oceans, seas and marine resources for sustainable development

Goal 15. Protect, restore and promote sustainable use of terrestrial ecosystems, sustainably manage forests, combat desertification, and halt and reverse land degradation and halt biodiversity loss

Goal 16. Promote peaceful and inclusive societies for sustainable development, provide access to justice for all and build effective, accountable and inclusive institutions at all levels

Goal 17. Strengthen the means of implementation and revitalize the Global Partnership for Sustainable Development

* Acknowledging that the United Nations Framework Convention on Climate Change is the primary international, intergovernmental forum for negotiating the global response to climate change.

Transforming our world: the 2030 Agenda for Sustainable Development A/RES/70/1 15/35

Goal 1. End poverty in all its forms everywhere

1.1 By 2030, eradicate extreme poverty for all people everywhere, currently measured as people living on less than $1.25 a day

1.2 By 2030, reduce at least by half the proportion of men, women and children of all ages living in poverty in all its dimensions according to national definitions

1.3 Implement nationally appropriate social protection systems and measures for all, including floors, and by 2030 achieve substantial coverage of the poor and the vulnerable

1.4 By 2030, ensure that all men and women, in particular the poor and the vulnerable, have equal rights to economic resources, as well as access to basic services, ownership and control over land and other forms of property, inheritance, natural resources, appropriate new technology and financial services, including microfinance

1.5 By 2030, build the resilience of the poor and those in vulnerable situations and reduce their exposure and vulnerability to climate-related extreme events and other economic, social and environmental shocks and disasters

1.a Ensure significant mobilization of resources from a variety of sources, including through enhanced development cooperation, in order to provide adequate and predictable means for developing countries, in particular least developed countries, to implement programmes and policies to end poverty in all its dimensions

1.b Create sound policy frameworks at the national, regional and international levels, based on pro-poor and gender-sensitive development strategies, to support accelerated investment in poverty eradication actions

Goal 2. End hunger, achieve food security and improved nutrition and promote sustainable agriculture

2.1 By 2030, end hunger and ensure access by all people, in particular the poor and people in vulnerable situations, including infants, to safe, nutritious and sufficient food all year round

2.2 By 2030, end all forms of malnutrition, including achieving, by 2025, the internationally agreed targets on stunting and wasting in children under 5 years of age, and address the nutritional needs of adolescent girls, pregnant and lactating women and older persons

2.3 By 2030, double the agricultural productivity and incomes of small-scale food producers, in particular women, indigenous peoples, family farmers, pastoralists and fishers, including through secure and equal access to land, other productive resources and inputs, knowledge, financial services, markets and opportunities for value addition and non-farm employment

2.4 By 2030, ensure sustainable food production systems and implement resilient agricultural practices that increase productivity and production, that help maintain ecosystems, that strengthen capacity for adaptation to climate change, extreme weather, drought, flooding and other disasters and that progressively improve land and soil quality

2.5 By 2020, maintain the genetic diversity of seeds, cultivated plants and farmed and domesticated animals and their related wild species, including through soundly managed and diversified seed and plant banks at the national, regional and international levels, and promote access to and fair and equitable sharing of benefits arising from the utilization of genetic resources and associated traditional knowledge, as internationally agreed

2.a Increase investment, including through enhanced international cooperation, in rural infrastructure, agricultural research and extension services, technology development and plant and livestock gene banks in order to enhance agricultural productive capacity in developing countries, in particular least developed countries

2.b Correct and prevent trade restrictions and distortions in world agricultural markets, including through the parallel elimination of all forms of agricultural export subsidies and all export measures with equivalent effect, in accordance with the mandate of the Doha Development Round

2.c Adopt measures to ensure the proper functioning of food commodity markets and their derivatives and facilitate timely access to market information, including on food reserves, in order to help limit extreme food price volatility

Goal 3. Ensure healthy lives and promote well-being for all at all ages

3.1 By 2030, reduce the global maternal mortality ratio to less than 70 per 100,000 live births

3.2 By 2030, end preventable deaths of newborns and children under 5 years of age, with all countries aiming to reduce neonatal mortality to at least as low as 12 per 1,000 live births and under-5 mortality to at least as low as 25 per 1,000 live births

3.3 By 2030, end the epidemics of AIDS, tuberculosis, malaria and neglected tropical diseases and combat hepatitis, water-borne diseases and other communicable diseases

3.4 By 2030, reduce by one third premature mortality from non-communicable diseases through prevention and treatment and promote mental health and wellbeing

3.5 Strengthen the prevention and treatment of substance abuse, including narcotic drug abuse and harmful use of alcohol

3.6 By 2020, halve the number of global deaths and injuries from road traffic accidents

3.7 By 2030, ensure universal access to sexual and reproductive health-care services, including for family planning, information and education, and the integration of reproductive health into national strategies and programmes

3.8 Achieve universal health coverage, including financial risk protection, access to quality essential health-care services and access to safe, effective, quality and affordable essential medicines and vaccines for all

3.9 By 2030, substantially reduce the number of deaths and illnesses from hazardous chemicals and air, water and soil pollution and contamination

3.a Strengthen the implementation of the World Health Organization Framework Convention on Tobacco Control in all countries, as appropriate

3.b Support the research and development of vaccines and medicines for the communicable and non-communicable diseases that primarily affect developing countries, provide access to affordable essential medicines and vaccines, in accordance with the Doha Declaration on the TRIPS Agreement and Public Health,which affirms the right of developing countries to use to the full the provisions in the Agreement on Trade-Related Aspects of Intellectual Property Rights regarding flexibilities to protect public health, and, in particular, provide access to medicines for all

3.c Substantially increase health financing and the recruitment, development,training and retention of the health workforce in developing countries, especially in least developed countries and small island developing States

3.d Strengthen the capacity of all countries, in particular developing countries, for early warning, risk reduction and management of national and global health risks

Goal 4. Ensure inclusive and equitable quality education and promote lifelong learning opportunities for all

4.1 By 2030, ensure that all girls and boys complete free, equitable and quality primary and secondary education leading to relevant and effective learning outcomes

4.2 By 2030, ensure that all girls and boys have access to quality early childhood development, care and pre-primary education so that they are ready for primary education

4.3 By 2030, ensure equal access for all women and men to affordable and quality technical, vocational and tertiary education, including university

4.4 By 2030, substantially increase the number of youth and adults who have relevant skills, including technical and vocational skills, for employment, decent jobs and entrepreneurship

4.5 By 2030, eliminate gender disparities in education and ensure equal access to all levels of education and vocational training for the vulnerable, including persons with disabilities, indigenous peoples and children in vulnerable situations

4.6 By 2030, ensure that all youth and a substantial proportion of adults, both men and women, achieve literacy and numeracy

4.7 By 2030, ensure that all learners acquire the knowledge and skills needed to promote sustainable development, including, among others, through education for sustainable development and sustainable lifestyles, human rights, gender equality, promotion of a culture of peace and non-violence, global citizenship and appreciation of cultural diversity and of culture's contribution to sustainable development

4.a Build and upgrade education facilities that are child, disability and gender sensitive and provide safe, non-violent, inclusive and effective learning environments for all

4.b By 2020, substantially expand globally the number of scholarships available to developing countries, in particular least developed countries, small island developing States and African countries, for enrolment in higher education, including vocational training and information and communications technology,technical, engineering and scientific programmes, in developed countries and other developing countries

4.c By 2030, substantially increase the supply of qualified teachers, including through international cooperation for teacher training in developing countries, especially least developed countries and small island developing States

Goal 5. Achieve gender equality and empower all women and girls

5.1 End all forms of discrimination against all women and girls everywhere

5.2 Eliminate all forms of violence against all women and girls in the public and private spheres, including trafficking and sexual and other types of exploitation

5.3 Eliminate all harmful practices, such as child, early and forced marriage and female genital mutilation

5.4 Recognize and value unpaid care and domestic work through the provision of public services, infrastructure and social protection policies and the promotion of shared responsibility within the household and the family as nationally appropriate

5.5 Ensure women's full and effective participation and equal opportunities for leadership at all levels of decision-making in political, economic and public life

5.6 Ensure universal access to sexual and reproductive health and reproductive rights as agreed in accordance with the Programme of Action of the International Conference on Population and Development and the Beijing Platform for Action and the outcome documents of their review conferences

5.a Undertake reforms to give women equal rights to economic resources, as well as access to ownership and control over land and other forms of property, financial services, inheritance and natural resources, in accordance with national laws

5.b Enhance the use of enabling technology, in particular information and communications technology, to promote the empowerment of women

5.c Adopt and strengthen sound policies and enforceable legislation for the promotion of gender equality and the empowerment of all women and girls at all levels

Goal 6. Ensure availability and sustainable management of water and sanitation for all

6.1 By 2030, achieve universal and equitable access to safe and affordable drinking water for all

6.2 By 2030, achieve access to adequate and equitable sanitation and hygiene for all and end open defecation, paying special attention to the needs of women and girls and those in vulnerable situations

6.3 By 2030, improve water quality by reducing pollution, eliminating dumping and minimizing release of hazardous chemicals and materials, halving the proportion of untreated wastewater and substantially increasing recycling and safe reuse globally

6.4 By 2030, substantially increase water-use efficiency across all sectors and ensure sustainable withdrawals and supply of freshwater to address water scarcity and substantially reduce the number of people suffering from water scarcity

6.5 By 2030, implement integrated water resources management at all levels, including through transboundary cooperation as appropriate

6.6 By 2020, protect and restore water-related ecosystems, including mountains, forests, wetlands, rivers, aquifers and lakes

6.a By 2030, expand international cooperation and capacity-building support to developing countries in water- and sanitation-related activities and programmes, including water harvesting, desalination, water efficiency, wastewater treatment, recycling and reuse technologies

6.b Support and strengthen the participation of local communities in improving water and sanitation management

Goal 7. Ensure access to affordable, reliable, sustainable and modern energy for all

7.1 By 2030, ensure universal access to affordable, reliable and modern energy services

7.2 By 2030, increase substantially the share of renewable energy in the global energy mix

7.3 By 2030, double the global rate of improvement in energy efficiency

7.a By 2030, enhance international cooperation to facilitate access to clean energy research and technology, including renewable energy, energy efficiency and advanced and cleaner fossil-fuel technology, and promote investment in energy infrastructure and clean energy technology

7.b By 2030, expand infrastructure and upgrade technology for supplying modern and sustainable energy services for all in developing countries, in particular least developed countries, small island developing States and landlocked developing countries, in accordance with their respective programmes of support

Goal 8. Promote sustained, inclusive and sustainable economic growth, full and productive employment and decent work for all

8.1 Sustain per capita economic growth in accordance with national circumstances and, in particular, at least 7 per cent gross domestic product growth per annum in the least developed countries

8.2 Achieve higher levels of economic productivity through diversification, technological upgrading and innovation, including through a focus on high-value added and labour-intensive sectors

8.3 Promote development-oriented policies that support productive activities, decent job creation, entrepreneurship, creativity and innovation, and encourage the formalization and growth of micro-, small- and medium-sized enterprises, including through access to financial services

8.4 Improve progressively, through 2030, global resource efficiency in consumption and production and endeavour to decouple economic growth from environmental degradation, in accordance with the 10-Year Framework of Programmes on Sustainable Consumption and Production, with developed countries taking the lead

8.5 By 2030, achieve full and productive employment and decent work for all women and men, including for young people and persons with disabilities, and equal pay for work of equal value

8.6 By 2020, substantially reduce the proportion of youth not in employment, education or training

8.7 Take immediate and effective measures to eradicate forced labour, end modern slavery and human trafficking and secure the prohibition and elimination of the worst forms of child labour, including recruitment and use of child soldiers, and by 2025 end child labour in all its forms

8.8 Protect labour rights and promote safe and secure working environments for all workers, including migrant workers, in particular women migrants, and those in precarious employment

8.9 By 2030, devise and implement policies to promote sustainable tourism that creates jobs and promotes local culture and products

8.10 Strengthen the capacity of domestic financial institutions to encourage and expand access to banking, insurance and financial services for all

8.a Increase Aid for Trade support for developing countries, in particular least developed countries, including through the Enhanced Integrated Framework for Trade-related Technical Assistance to Least Developed Countries

8.b By 2020, develop and operationalize a global strategy for youth employment and implement the Global Jobs Pact of the International Labour Organization

Goal 9. Build resilient infrastructure, promote inclusive and sustainable industrialization and foster innovation

9.1 Develop quality, reliable, sustainable and resilient infrastructure, including regional and transborder infrastructure, to support economic development and human well-being, with a focus on affordable and equitable access for all

9.2 Promote inclusive and sustainable industrialization and, by 2030, significantly raise industry's share of employment and gross domestic product, in line with national circumstances, and double its share in least developed countries

9.3 Increase the access of small-scale industrial and other enterprises, in particular in developing countries, to financial services, including affordable credit, and their integration into value chains and markets

9.4 By 2030, upgrade infrastructure and retrofit industries to make them sustainable, with increased resource-use efficiency and greater adoption of clean and environmentally sound technologies and industrial processes, with all countries taking action in accordance with their respective capabilities

9.5 Enhance scientific research, upgrade the technological capabilities of industrial sectors in all countries, in particular developing countries, including, by 2030, encouraging innovation and substantially increasing the number of research and development workers per 1 million people and public and private research and development spending

9.a Facilitate sustainable and resilient infrastructure development in developing countries through enhanced financial, technological and technical support to African countries, least developed countries, landlocked developing countries and small island developing States

9.b Support domestic technology development, research and innovation in developing countries, including by ensuring a conducive policy environment for,inter alia, industrial diversification and value addition to commodities

9.c Significantly increase access to information and communications technology and strive to provide universal and affordable access to the Internet in least developed countries by 2020

Goal 10. Reduce inequality within and among countries

10.1 By 2030, progressively achieve and sustain income growth of the bottom 40 per cent of the population at a rate higher than the national average

10.2 By 2030, empower and promote the social, economic and political inclusion of all, irrespective of age, sex, disability, race, ethnicity, origin, religion or economic or other status

10.3 Ensure equal opportunity and reduce inequalities of outcome, including by eliminating discriminatory laws, policies and practices and promoting appropriate legislation, policies and action in this regard

10.4 Adopt policies, especially fiscal, wage and social protection policies, and progressively achieve greater equality

10.5 Improve the regulation and monitoring of global financial markets and institutions and strengthen the implementation of such regulations

10.6 Ensure enhanced representation and voice for developing countries in decision-making in global international economic and financial institutions in order to deliver more effective, credible, accountable and legitimate institutions

10.7 Facilitate orderly, safe, regular and responsible migration and mobility of people, including through the implementation of planned and well-managed migration policies

10.a Implement the principle of special and differential treatment for developing countries, in particular least developed countries, in accordance with World Trade Organization agreements

10.b Encourage official development assistance and financial flows, including foreign direct investment, to States where the need is greatest, in particular least developed countries, African countries, small island developing States and landlocked developing countries, in accordance with their national plans and programmes

10.c By 2030, reduce to less than 3 per cent the transaction costs of migrant remittances and eliminate remittance corridors with costs higher than 5 per cent

Goal 11. Make cities and human settlements inclusive, safe, resilient and sustainable

11.1 By 2030, ensure access for all to adequate, safe and affordable housing and basic services and upgrade slums

11.2 By 2030, provide access to safe, affordable, accessible and sustainable transport systems for all, improving road safety, notably by expanding public transport, with special attention to the needs of those in vulnerable situations, women, children, persons with disabilities and older persons

11.3 By 2030, enhance inclusive and sustainable urbanization and capacity for participatory, integrated and sustainable human settlement planning and management in all countries

11.4 Strengthen efforts to protect and safeguard the world's cultural and natural heritage

11.5 By 2030, significantly reduce the number of deaths and the number of people affected and substantially decrease the direct economic losses relative to global gross domestic product caused by disasters, including water-related disasters, with a focus on protecting the poor and people in vulnerable situations

11.6 By 2030, reduce the adverse per capita environmental impact of cities, including by paying special attention to air quality and municipal and other waste management

11.7 By 2030, provide universal access to safe, inclusive and accessible, green and public spaces, in particular for women and children, older persons and persons with disabilities

11.a Support positive economic, social and environmental links between urban, peri-urban and rural areas by strengthening national and regional development planning

11.b By 2020, substantially increase the number of cities and human settlements adopting and implementing integrated policies and plans towards inclusion, resource efficiency, mitigation and adaptation to climate change, resilience to disasters, and develop and implement, in line with the Sendai Framework for Disaster Risk Reduction 2015–2030, holistic disaster risk management at all levels

11.c Support least developed countries, including through financial and technical assistance, in building sustainable and resilient buildings utilizing local materials

Goal 12. Ensure sustainable consumption and production patterns

12.1 Implement the 10-Year Framework of Programmes on Sustainable Consumption and Production Patterns, all countries taking action, with developed countries taking the lead, taking into account the development and capabilities of developing countries

12.2 By 2030, achieve the sustainable management and efficient use of natural resources

12.3 By 2030, halve per capita global food waste at the retail and consumer levels and reduce food losses along production and supply chains, including post harvest losses

12.4 By 2020, achieve the environmentally sound management of chemicals and all wastes throughout their life cycle, in accordance with agreed international frameworks, and significantly reduce their release to air, water and soil in order to minimize their adverse impacts on human health and the environment

12.5 By 2030, substantially reduce waste generation through prevention, reduction, recycling and reuse

12.6 Encourage companies, especially large and transnational companies, to adopt sustainable practices and to integrate sustainability information into their reporting cycle

12.7 Promote public procurement practices that are sustainable, in accordance with national policies and priorities

12.8 By 2030, ensure that people everywhere have the relevant information and awareness for sustainable development and lifestyles in harmony with nature

12.a Support developing countries to strengthen their scientific and technological capacity to move towards more sustainable patterns of consumption and production

12.b Develop and implement tools to monitor sustainable development impacts for sustainable tourism that creates jobs and promotes local culture and products

12.c Rationalize inefficient fossil-fuel subsidies that encourage wasteful consumption by removing market distortions, in accordance with national circumstances, including by restructuring taxation and phasing out those harmful subsidies, where they exist, to reflect their environmental impacts, taking fully into account the specific needs and conditions of developing countries and minimizing the possible adverse impacts on their development in a manner that protects the poor and the affected communities

Goal 13. Take urgent action to combat climate change and its impacts*

13.1 Strengthen resilience and adaptive capacity to climate-related hazards and natural disasters in all countries

13.2 Integrate climate change measures into national policies, strategies and planning

13.3 Improve education, awareness-raising and human and institutional capacity on climate change mitigation, adaptation, impact reduction and early warning

13.a Implement the commitment undertaken by developed-country parties to the United Nations Framework Convention on Climate Change to a goal of mobilizing jointly $100 billion annually by 2020 from all sources to address the needs of developing countries in the context of meaningful mitigation actions and transparency on implementation and fully operationalize the Green Climate Fund through its capitalization as soon as possible

13.b Promote mechanisms for raising capacity for effective climate change-related planning and management in least developed countries and small island developing States, including focusing on women, youth and local and marginalized communities

Goal 14. Conserve and sustainably use the oceans, seas and marine resources for sustainable development

14.1 By 2025, prevent and significantly reduce marine pollution of all kinds, in particular from land-based activities, including marine debris and nutrient pollution

14.2 By 2020, sustainably manage and protect marine and coastal ecosystems to avoid significant adverse impacts, including by strengthening their resilience, and take action for their restoration in order to achieve healthy and productive oceans

14.3 Minimize and address the impacts of ocean acidification, including through enhanced scientific cooperation at all levels

* Acknowledging that the United Nations Framework Convention on Climate Change is the primary international, intergovernmental forum for negotiating the global response to climate change.

A/RES/70/1 Transforming our world: the 2030 Agenda for Sustainable Development 24/35

14.4 By 2020, effectively regulate harvesting and end overfishing, illegal,unreported and unregulated fishing and destructive fishing practices and implement science-based management plans, in order to restore fish stocks in the shortest time feasible, at least to levels that can produce maximum sustainable yield as determined by their biological characteristics

14.5 By 2020, conserve at least 10 per cent of coastal and marine areas, consistent with national and international law and based on the best available scientific information

14.6 By 2020, prohibit certain forms of fisheries subsidies which contribute to overcapacity and overfishing, eliminate subsidies that contribute to illegal,unreported and unregulated fishing and refrain from introducing new such subsidies,recognizing that appropriate and effective special and differential treatment for developing and least developed countries should be an integral part of the World Trade Organization fisheries subsidies negotiation

14.7 By 2030, increase the economic benefits to small island developing States and least developed countries from the sustainable use of marine resources, including through sustainable management of fisheries, aquaculture and tourism

14.a Increase scientific knowledge, develop research capacity and transfer marine technology, taking into account the Intergovernmental Oceanographic Commission Criteria and Guidelines on the Transfer of Marine Technology, in order to improve ocean health and to enhance the contribution of marine biodiversity to the development of developing countries, in particular small island developing States and least developed countries

14.b Provide access for small-scale artisanal fishers to marine resources and markets

14.c Enhance the conservation and sustainable use of oceans and their resources by implementing international law as reflected in the United Nations Convention on the Law of the Sea, which provides the legal framework for the conservation and sustainable use of oceans and their resources, as recalled in paragraph 158 of "The future we want"

Goal 15. Protect, restore and promote sustainable use of terrestrial ecosystems, sustainably manage forests, combat desertification, and halt and reverse land degradation and halt biodiversity loss

15.1 By 2020, ensure the conservation, restoration and sustainable use of terrestrial and inland freshwater ecosystems and their services, in particular forests, wetlands,mountains and drylands, in line with obligations under international agreements

15.2 By 2020, promote the implementation of sustainable management of all types of forests, halt deforestation, restore degraded forests and substantially increase afforestation and reforestation globally

15.3 By 2030, combat desertification, restore degraded land and soil, including land affected by desertification, drought and floods, and strive to achieve a land degradation-neutral world

15.4 By 2030, ensure the conservation of mountain ecosystems, including their biodiversity, in order to enhance their capacity to provide benefits that are essential for sustainable development

15.5 Take urgent and significant action to reduce the degradation of natural habitats, halt the loss of biodiversity and, by 2020, protect and prevent the extinction of threatened species

15.6 Promote fair and equitable sharing of the benefits arising from the utilization of genetic resources and promote appropriate access to such resources, as internationally agreed

15.7 Take urgent action to end poaching and trafficking of protected species of flora and fauna and address both demand and supply of illegal wildlife products

15.8 By 2020, introduce measures to prevent the introduction and significantly reduce the impact of invasive alien species on land and water ecosystems and control or eradicate the priority species

15.9 By 2020, integrate ecosystem and biodiversity values into national and local planning, development processes, poverty reduction strategies and accounts

15.a Mobilize and significantly increase financial resources from all sources to conserve and sustainably use biodiversity and ecosystems

15.b Mobilize significant resources from all sources and at all levels to finance sustainable forest management and provide adequate incentives to developing countries to advance such management, including for conservation and reforestation

15.c Enhance global support for efforts to combat poaching and trafficking of protected species, including by increasing the capacity of local communities to pursue sustainable livelihood opportunities

Goal 16. Promote peaceful and inclusive societies for sustainable development, provide access to justice for all and build effective, accountable and inclusive institutions at all levels

16.1 Significantly reduce all forms of violence and related death rates everywhere

16.2 End abuse, exploitation, trafficking and all forms of violence against and torture of children

16.3 Promote the rule of law at the national and international levels and ensure equal access to justice for all

16.4 By 2030, significantly reduce illicit financial and arms flows, strengthen the recovery and return of stolen assets and combat all forms of organized crime

16.5 Substantially reduce corruption and bribery in all their forms

16.6 Develop effective, accountable and transparent institutions at all levels

16.7 Ensure responsive, inclusive, participatory and representative decision making at all levels

16.8 Broaden and strengthen the participation of developing countries in the institutions of global governance

16.9 By 2030, provide legal identity for all, including birth registration

16.10 Ensure public access to information and protect fundamental freedoms, in accordance with national legislation and international agreements

16.a Strengthen relevant national institutions, including through international cooperation, for building capacity at all levels, in particular in developing countries, to prevent violence and combat terrorism and crime

16.b Promote and enforce non-discriminatory laws and policies for sustainable development

Goal 17. Strengthen the means of implementation and revitalize the Global Partnership for Sustainable Development

Finance

17.1 Strengthen domestic resource mobilization, including through international support to developing countries, to improve domestic capacity for tax and other revenue collection

17.2 Developed countries to implement fully their official development assistance commitments, including the commitment by many developed countries to achieve the target of 0.7 per cent of gross national income for official development assistance (ODA/GNI) to developing countries and 0.15 to 0.20 per cent of ODA/GNI to least developed countries; ODA providers are encouraged to consider setting a target to provide at least 0.20 per cent of ODA/GNI to least developed countries

17.3 Mobilize additional financial resources for developing countries from multiple sources

17.4 Assist developing countries in attaining long-term debt sustainability through coordinated policies aimed at fostering debt financing, debt relief and debt restructuring, as appropriate, and address the external debt of highly indebted poor countries to reduce debt distress

17.5 Adopt and implement investment promotion regimes for least developed Countries

Technology

17.6 Enhance North-South, South-South and triangular regional and international cooperation on and access to science, technology and innovation and enhance knowledge sharing on mutually agreed terms, including through improved coordination among existing mechanisms, in particular at the United Nations level, and through a global technology facilitation mechanism

17.7 Promote the development, transfer, dissemination and diffusion of environmentally sound technologies to developing countries on favourable terms, including on concessional and preferential terms, as mutually agreed

17.8 Fully operationalize the technology bank and science, technology and innovation capacity-building mechanism for least developed countries by 2017 and enhance the use of enabling technology, in particular information and communications technology Capacity-building

17.9 Enhance international support for implementing effective and targeted capacity-building in developing countries to support national plans to implement all the Sustainable Development Goals, including through North-South, South-South and triangular cooperation

Trade

17.10 Promote a universal, rules-based, open, non-discriminatory and equitable multilateral trading system under the World Trade Organization, including through the conclusion of negotiations under its Doha Development Agenda

17.11 Significantly increase the exports of developing countries, in particular with a view to doubling the least developed countries' share of global exports by 2020

17.12 Realize timely implementation of duty-free and quota-free market access on a lasting basis for all least developed countries, consistent with World Trade Organization decisions, including by ensuring that preferential rules of origin applicable to imports from least developed countries are transparent and simple, and contribute to facilitating market access

Systemic issues

Policy and institutional coherence

17.13 Enhance global macroeconomic stability, including through policy coordination and policy coherence

17.14 Enhance policy coherence for sustainable development

17.15 Respect each country's policy space and leadership to establish and implement policies for poverty eradication and sustainable development

Multi-stakeholder partnerships

17.16 Enhance the Global Partnership for Sustainable Development, complemented by multi-stakeholder partnerships that mobilize and share knowledge, expertise, technology and financial resources, to support the achievement of the Sustainable Development Goals in all countries, in particular developing countries

17.17 Encourage and promote effective public, public-private and civil society partnerships, building on the experience and resourcing strategies of partnerships

Data, monitoring and accountability

17.18 By 2020, enhance capacity-building support to developing countries, including for least developed countries and small island developing States, to increase significantly the availability of high-quality, timely and reliable data disaggregated by income, gender, age, race, ethnicity, migratory status, disability, geographic location and other characteristics relevant in national contexts

17.19 By 2030, build on existing initiatives to develop measurements of progress on sustainable development that complement gross domestic product, and support statistical capacity-building in developing countries

Means of implementation and the Global Partnership

60. We reaffirm our strong commitment to the full implementation of this new Agenda. We recognize that we will not be able to achieve our ambitious Goals and targets without a revitalized and enhanced Global Partnership and comparably ambitious means of implementation. The revitalized Global Partnership will facilitate an intensive global engagement in support of implementation of all the Goals and targets, bringing together Governments, civil society, the private sector, the United Nations system and other actors and mobilizing all available resources.
61. The Agenda's Goals and targets deal with the means required to realize our collective ambitions. The means of implementation targets under each Sustainable Development Goal and Goal 17, which are referred to above, are key to realizing our Agenda and are of equal importance with the other Goals and targets. We shall accord them equal priority in our implementation efforts and in the global indicator framework for monitoring our progress.
62. This Agenda, including the Sustainable Development Goals, can be met within the framework of a revitalized Global Partnership for Sustainable Development, supported by the concrete policies and actions outlined in the Addis Ababa Action Agenda, which is an integral part of the 2030 Agenda for Sustainable Development.The Addis Ababa Action Agenda supports, complements and helps to contextualize the 2030 Agenda's means of implementation targets. It relates to domestic public resources, domestic and international private business and finance, international development cooperation, international trade as an engine for development, debt and debt sustainability, addressing systemic issues and science, technology, innovation and capacity-building, and data, monitoring and follow-up.
63. Cohesive nationally owned sustainable development strategies, supported by integrated national financing frameworks, will be at the heart of our efforts. We reiterate that each country has primary responsibility for its own economic and social development and that the role of national policies and development strategies cannot be overemphasized. We will respect each country's policy space and

leadership to implement policies for poverty eradication and sustainable development, while remaining consistent with relevant international rules and commitments. At the same time, national development efforts need to be supported by an enabling international economic environment, including coherent and mutually supporting world trade, monetary and financial systems, and strengthened and enhanced global economic governance. Processes to develop and facilitate the availability of appropriate knowledge and technologies globally, as well as capacity building,are also critical. We commit to pursuing policy coherence and an enabling environment for sustainable development at all levels and by all actors, and to reinvigorating the Global Partnership for Sustainable Development.

64. We support the implementation of relevant strategies and programmes of action, including the Istanbul Declaration and Programme of Action, the SIDS Accelerated Modalities of Action (SAMOA) Pathway and the Vienna Programme of Action for Landlocked Developing Countries for the Decade 2014–2024, and reaffirm the importance of supporting the African Union's Agenda 2063 and the programme of the New Partnership for Africa's Development, all of which are integral to the new Agenda. We recognize the major challenge to the achievement of durable peace and sustainable development in countries in conflict and post-conflict situations.

65. We recognize that middle-income countries still face significant challenges to achieve sustainable development. In order to ensure that achievements made to date are sustained, efforts to address ongoing challenges should be strengthened through the exchange of experiences, improved coordination, and better and focused support of the United Nations development system, the international financial institutions, regional organizations and other stakeholders.

66. We underscore that, for all countries, public policies and the mobilization and effective use of domestic resources, underscored by the principle of national ownership, are central to our common pursuit of sustainable development, including achieving the Sustainable Development Goals. We recognize that domestic resources are first and foremost generated by economic growth, supported by an enabling environment at all levels.

67. Private business activity, investment and innovation are major drivers of productivity, inclusive economic growth and job creation. We acknowledge the diversity of the private sector, ranging from micro-enterprises to cooperatives to multinationals. We call upon all businesses to apply their creativity and innovation to solving sustainable development challenges. We will foster a dynamic and well functioning business sector, while protecting labour rights and

environmental and health standards in accordance with relevant international standards and agreements and other ongoing initiatives in this regard, such as the Guiding Principles on Business and Human Rights and the labour standards of the International Labour Organization, the Convention on the Rights of the Child and key multilateral environmental agreements, for parties to those agreements.

68. International trade is an engine for inclusive economic growth and poverty reduction, and contributes to the promotion of sustainable development. We will continue to promote a universal, rules-based, open, transparent, predictable, inclusive, non-discriminatory and equitable multilateral trading system under the World Trade Organization, as well as meaningful trade liberalization. We call upon all members of the World Trade Organization to redouble their efforts to promptly conclude the negotiations on the Doha Development Agenda. We attach great importance to providing trade-related capacity-building for developing countries, including African countries, least developed countries, landlocked developing countries, small island developing States and middle-income countries, including for the promotion of regional economic integration and interconnectivity.

69. We recognize the need to assist developing countries in attaining long-term debt sustainability through coordinated policies aimed at fostering debt financing, debt relief, debt restructuring and sound debt management, as appropriate. Many countries remain vulnerable to debt crises and some are in the midst of crises, including a number of least developed countries, small island developing States and some developed countries. We reiterate that debtors and creditors must work together to prevent and resolve unsustainable debt situations. Maintaining sustainable debt levels is the responsibility of the borrowing countries; however we acknowledge that lenders also have a responsibility to lend in a way that does not undermine a country's debt sustainability. We will support the maintenance of debt sustainability of those countries that have received debt relief and achieved sustainable debt levels.

70. We hereby launch a Technology Facilitation Mechanism which was established by the Addis Ababa Action Agenda in order to support the Sustainable Development Goals. The Technology Facilitation Mechanism will be based on a multi-stakeholder collaboration between Member States, civil society, the private sector, the scientific community, United Nations entities and other stakeholders and will be composed of a United Nations inter-agency task team on science, technology and innovation for the Sustainable Development Goals,

a collaborative multi-stakeholder forum on science, technology and innovation for the Sustainable Development Goals and an online platform.

- The United Nations inter-agency task team on science, technology and innovation for the Sustainable Development Goals will promote coordination, coherence and cooperation within the United Nations system on science, technology and innovation-related matters, enhancing synergy and efficiency, in particular to enhance capacity-building initiatives. The task team will draw on existing resources and will work with 10 representatives from civil society, the private sector and the scientific community to prepare the meetings of the multi-stakeholder forum on science, technology and innovation for the Sustainable Development Goals, as well as in the development and operationalization of the online platform, including preparing proposals for the modalities for the forum and the online platform. The 10 representatives will be appointed by the Secretary-General, for periods of two years. The task team will be open to the participation of all United Nations agencies, funds and programmes and the functional commissions of the Economic and Social Council and it will initially be composed of the entities that currently integrate the informal working group on technology facilitation, namely, the Department of Economic and Social Affairs of the Secretariat, the United Nations Environment Programme, the United Nations Industrial Development Organization, the United Nations Educational, Scientific and Cultural Organization, the United Nations Conference on Trade and Development, the International Telecommunication Union, the World Intellectual Property Organization and the World Bank.
- The online platform will be used to establish a comprehensive mapping of, and serve as a gateway for, information on existing science, technology and innovation initiatives, mechanisms and programmes, within and beyond the United Nations. The online platform will facilitate access to information, knowledge and experience, as well as best practices and lessons learned, on science, technology and innovation facilitation initiatives and policies. The online platform will also facilitate the dissemination of relevant open access scientific publications generated worldwide. The online platform will be developed on the basis of an independent technical assessment which will take into account best practices and lessons learned from other initiatives, within and beyond the United Nations, in order to ensure that it

will complement, facilitate access to and provide adequate information on existing science, technology and innovation platforms, avoiding duplications and enhancing synergies.

- The multi-stakeholder forum on science, technology and innovation for the Sustainable Development Goals will be convened once a year, for a period of two days, to discuss science, technology and innovation cooperation around thematic areas for the implementation of the Sustainable Development Goals, congregating all relevant stakeholders to actively contribute in their area of expertise. The forum will provide a venue for facilitating interaction, matchmaking and the establishment of networks between relevant stakeholders and multi-stakeholder partnerships in order to identify and examine technology needs and gaps, including on scientific cooperation, innovation and capacity-building, and also in order to help to facilitate development, transfer and dissemination of relevant technologies for the Sustainable Development Goals. The meetings of the forum will be convened by the President of the Economic and Social Council before the meeting of the high-level political forum under the auspices of the Council or, alternatively, in conjunction with other forums or conferences, as appropriate, taking into account the theme to be considered and on the basis of a collaboration with the organizers of the other forums or conferences. The meetings of the forum will be co-chaired by two Member States and will result in a summary of discussions elaborated by the two co-Chairs, as an input to the meetings of the high-level political forum, in the context of the follow-up and review of the implementation of the post-2015 development agenda.
- The meetings of the high-level political forum will be informed by the summary of the multi-stakeholder forum. The themes for the subsequent multi-stakeholder forum on science, technology and innovation for the Sustainable Development Goals will be considered by the high-level political forum on sustainable development, taking into account expert inputs from the task team.

71. We reiterate that this Agenda and the Sustainable Development Goals and targets, including the means of implementation, are universal, indivisible and interlinked.

Follow-up and review

72. We commit to engaging in systematic follow-up and review of the implementation of this Agenda over the next 15 years. A robust,

voluntary, effective, participatory, transparent and integrated follow-up and review framework will make a vital contribution to implementation and will help countries to maximize and track progress in implementing this Agenda in order to ensure that no one is left behind.

73. Operating at the national, regional and global levels, it will promote accountability to our citizens, support effective international cooperation in achieving this Agenda and foster exchanges of best practices and mutual learning. It will mobilize support to overcome shared challenges and identify new and emerging issues. As this is a universal Agenda, mutual trust and understanding among all nations will be important.

74. Follow-up and review processes at all levels will be guided by the following principles:

    (a) They will be voluntary and country-led, will take into account different national realities, capacities and levels of development and will respect policy space and priorities. As national ownership is key to achieving sustainable development, the outcome from national-level processes will be the foundation for reviews at the regional and global levels, given that the global review will be primarily based on national official data sources.

    (b) They will track progress in implementing the universal Goals and targets, including the means of implementation, in all countries in a manner which respects their universal, integrated and interrelated nature and the three dimensions of sustainable development.

    (c) They will maintain a longer-term orientation, identify achievements, challenges, gaps and critical success factors and support countries in making informed policy choices. They will help to mobilize the necessary means of implementation and partnerships, support the identification of solutions and best practices and promote the coordination and effectiveness of the international development system.

    (d) They will be open, inclusive, participatory and transparent for all people and will support reporting by all relevant stakeholders.

    (e) They will be people-centred, gender-sensitive, respect human rights and have a particular focus on the poorest, most vulnerable and those furthest behind.

    (f) They will build on existing platforms and processes, where these exist, avoid duplication and respond to national circumstances, capacities, needs and priorities. They will evolve over time, taking into account emerging issues and the development of new methodologies, and will minimize the reporting burden on national administrations.

(g) They will be rigorous and based on evidence, informed by country-led evaluations and data which is high-quality, accessible, timely, reliable and disaggregated by income, sex, age, race, ethnicity, migration status, disability and geographic location and other characteristics relevant in national contexts.

(h) They will require enhanced capacity-building support for developing countries, including the strengthening of national data systems and evaluation programmes, particularly in African countries, least developed countries, small island developing States, landlocked developing countries and middle-income countries.

(i) They will benefit from the active support of the United Nations system and other multilateral institutions.

75. The Goals and targets will be followed up and reviewed using a set of global indicators. These will be complemented by indicators at the regional and national levels which will be developed by Member States, in addition to the outcomes of work undertaken for the development of the baselines for those targets where national and global baseline data does not yet exist. The global indicator frame work, to be developed by the Inter-Agency and Expert Group on Sustainable Development Goal Indicators, will be agreed by the Statistical Commission by March 2016 and adopted thereafter by the Economic and Social Council and the General Assembly, in line with existing mandates. This framework will be simple yet robust, address all Sustainable Development Goals and targets, including for means of implementation, and preserve the political balance, integration and ambition contained therein.

76. We will support developing countries, particularly African countries, least developed countries, small island developing States and landlocked developing countries, in strengthening the capacity of national statistical offices and data systems to ensure access to high-quality, timely, reliable and disaggregated data. We will promote transparent and accountable scaling-up of appropriate public-private cooperation to exploit the contribution to be made by a wide range of data, including earth observation and geospatial information, while ensuring national ownership in supporting and tracking progress.

77. We commit to fully engage in conducting regular and inclusive reviews of progress at the subnational, national, regional and global levels. We will draw as far as possible on the existing network of follow-up and review institutions and mechanisms. National reports

will allow assessments of progress and identify challenges at the regional and global level. Along with regional dialogues and global reviews, they will inform recommendations for follow-up at various levels.

National level

78. We encourage all Member States to develop as soon as practicable ambitious national responses to the overall implementation of this Agenda. These can support the transition to the Sustainable Development Goals and build on existing planning instruments, such as national development and sustainable development strategies, as appropriate.
79. We also encourage Member States to conduct regular and inclusive reviews of progress at the national and sub-national levels which are country-led and country-driven. Such reviews should draw on contributions from indigenous peoples, civil society, the private sector and other stakeholders, in line with national circumstances, policies and priorities. National parliaments as well as other institutions can also support these processes.

Regional level

80. Follow-up and review at the regional and sub-regional levels can, as appropriate, provide useful opportunities for peer learning, including through voluntary reviews, sharing of best practices and discussion on shared targets. We welcome in this respect the cooperation of regional and sub-regional commissions and organizations. Inclusive regional processes will draw on national-level reviews and contribute to follow-up and review at the global level, including at the high level political forum on sustainable development.
81. Recognizing the importance of building on existing follow-up and review mechanisms at the regional level and allowing adequate policy space, we encourage all Member States to identify the most suitable regional forum in which to engage. United Nations regional commissions are encouraged to continue supporting Member States in this regard.

Global level

82. The high-level political forum will have a central role in overseeing a network of follow-up and review processes at the global level, working coherently with the General Assembly, the Economic and Social Council and other relevant organs and forums, in accordance with existing mandates. It will facilitate sharing of experiences, including successes, challenges and lessons learned, and provide

political leadership, guidance and recommendations for follow-up. It will promote system-wide coherence and coordination of sustainable development policies. It should ensure that the Agenda remains relevant and ambitious and should focus on the assessment of progress, achievements and challenges faced by developed and developing countries as well as new and emerging issues. Effective linkages will be made with the follow-up and review arrangements of all relevant United Nations conferences and processes, including on least developed countries, small island developing States and landlocked developing countries.

83. Follow-up and review at the high-level political forum will be informed by an annual progress report on the Sustainable Development Goals to be prepared by the Secretary-General in cooperation with the United Nations system, based on the global indicator framework and data produced by national statistical systems and information collected at the regional level. The high-level political forum will also be informed by the *Global Sustainable Development Report*, which shall strengthen the science-policy interface and could provide a strong evidence-based instrument to support policymakers in promoting poverty eradication and sustainable development. We invite the President of the Economic and Social Council to conduct a process of consultations on the scope, methodology and frequency of the global report as well as its relation to the progress report, the outcome of which should be reflected in the ministerial declaration of the session of the high-level political forum in 2016.

84. The high-level political forum, under the auspices of the Economic and Social Council, shall carry out regular reviews, in line with General Assembly resolution 67/290 of 9 July 2013. Reviews will be voluntary, while encouraging reporting, and include developed and developing countries as well as relevant United Nations entities and other stakeholders, including civil society and the private sector. They shall be State-led, involving ministerial and other relevant high-level participants.They shall provide a platform for partnerships, including through the participation of major groups and other relevant stakeholders.

85. Thematic reviews of progress on the Sustainable Development Goals, including cross-cutting issues, will also take place at the high-level political forum. These will be supported by reviews by the functional commissions of the Economic and Social Council and other intergovernmental bodies and forums which should reflect the integrated nature of the Goals as well as the inter-linkages between them. They will engage all relevant stakeholders and, where possible,

feed into, and be aligned with, the cycle of the high-level political forum.

86. We welcome, as outlined in the Addis Ababa Action Agenda, the dedicated follow-up and review for the financing for development outcomes as well as all the means of implementation of the Sustainable Development Goals which is integrated with the follow-up and review framework of this Agenda. The inter-governmentally agreed conclusions and recommendations of the annual Economic and Social Council forum on financing for development will be fed into the overall follow-up and review of the implementation of this Agenda in the high-level political forum.

87. Meeting every four years under the auspices of the General Assembly, the high-level political forum will provide high-level political guidance on the Agenda and its implementation, identify progress and emerging challenges and mobilize further actions to accelerate implementation. The next high-level political forum under the auspices of the General Assembly will be held in 2019, with the cycle of meetings thus reset, in order to maximize coherence with the quadrennial comprehensive policy review process.

88. We also stress the importance of system-wide strategic planning, implementation and reporting in order to ensure coherent and integrated support to the implementation of the new Agenda by the United Nations development system. The relevant governing bodies should take action to review such support to implementation and to report on progress and obstacles. We welcome the ongoing dialogue in the Economic and Social Council on the longer-term positioning of the United Nations development system and look forward to taking action on these issues, as appropriate.

89. The high-level political forum will support participation in follow-up and review processes by the major groups and other relevant stakeholders in line with resolution 67/290. We call upon those actors to report on their contribution to the implementation of the Agenda.

90. We request the Secretary-General, in consultation with Member States, to prepare a report, for consideration at the seventieth session of the General Assembly in preparation for the 2016 meeting of the high-level political forum, which outlines critical milestones towards coherent, efficient and inclusive follow-up and review at the global level. The report should include a proposal on the organizational arrangements for State-led reviews at the high-level political forum under the auspices of the Economic and Social Council, including recommendations on voluntary common reporting guidelines. It should clarify institutional responsibilities and provide guidance on

annual themes, on a sequence of thematic reviews, and on options for periodic reviews for the high-level political forum.

91. We reaffirm our unwavering commitment to achieving this Agenda and utilizing it to the full to transform our world for the better by 2030."

Chapter - 5

The Sustainable Development Goals

The declaration of Sustainable Development Summit, 2015, as pointed out at chapter-4, contained a historic decision on a comprehensive, far-reaching and people-centred set of universal and transformative Goals and targets for the full implementation of the Sustainable Development Goals Agenda by 2030 for eradicating poverty in all its forms and dimensions, and achieving sustainable development in its three dimensions – economic, social and environmental – in a balanced and integrated manner. Built upon the achievements of the MDGs, the new SDGs are set to address its unfinished agenda and go beyond. The SDGs were arrived at after a process of serious consultations with all possible stakeholders-the member states, specialised regional agencies of the UN system, other international bodies, academic institutions of repute, international experts and personalities and the like. The 17-SDGs that were adopted are the following:

Sustainable Development Goals (SDGs):

- Goal 1. End poverty in all its forms everywhere
- Goal 2. End hunger, achieve food security and improved nutrition and promote sustainable agriculture
- Goal 3. Ensure healthy lives and promote well-being for all at all ages
- Goal 4. Ensure inclusive and equitable quality education and promote lifelong learning opportunities for all
- Goal 5. Achieve gender equality and empower all women and girls
- Goal 6. Ensure availability and sustainable management of water and sanitation for all
- Goal 7. Ensure access to affordable, reliable, sustainable and modern energy for all

- Goal 8. Promote sustained, inclusive and sustainable economic growth, full and productive employment and decent work for all
- Goal 9. Build resilient infrastructure, promote inclusive and sustainable industrialization and foster innovation
- Goal 10. Reduce inequality within and among countries
- Goal 11. Make cities and human settlements inclusive, safe, resilient and sustainable
- Goal 12. Ensure sustainable consumption and production patterns
- Goal 13. Take urgent action to combat climate change and its impacts*
- Goal 14. Conserve and sustainably use the oceans, seas and marine resources for sustainable development
- Goal 15. Protect, restore and promote sustainable use of terrestrial ecosystems, sustainably manage forests, combat desertification, and halt and reverse land degradation and halt biodiversity loss
- Goal 16. Promote peaceful and inclusive societies for sustainable development, provide access to justice for all and build effective, accountable and inclusive institutions at all levels
- Goal 17. Strengthen the means of implementation and revitalize the global partnership for sustainable development

Before proceeding to Goal specific SDG targets, it would be worthwhile to reiterate the Journey from MDGs to SDGs. Historically, the MDGs initiative is a path breaking event of monumental importance in that it set on motion a set on common social priorities worldwide.. Further, it brought a paradigm shift on the role of global partner and global awareness, political accountability and public pressure to the Report Card of development, as Bill Gate liked to look at the MDGs Report.

The SDGs go beyond the MDGs in focusing on global system reforms to remove the barriers to sustainable development. While the first set of SDGs (No 1-7) appears to be just an extension of MDGs, the later set of goals are indeed an extension of the agenda itself. The later parts have in turn two distinct characteristics: SDGs falling under numbers 8,9 and 10 are reforms centred enablers of development covering areas like inclusion and jobs, infrastructure and industrialisation, and distribution. The final set of goals under SDGs No 11-17 lays down the framework of governance covering areas like urbanization, consumption and production, climate change, resources and environment, peace and justice, and means of implementation and global partnership.

Considerable shift in approaches has also been visible from MDGs to SDGs in that SDGs have now 5 Ps-people, planet, prosperity, peace and partnership.

Given the above perspective, the details of goals and targets of Sustainable Development Goals that were settled in the historic UN Summit on Sustainable Development are noted below:

Goal 1. End poverty in all its forms everywhere

1.1 By 2030, eradicate extreme poverty for all people everywhere, currently measured as people living on less than $1.25 a day

1.2 By 2030, reduce at least by half the proportion of men, women and children of all ages living in poverty in all its dimensions according to national definitions

1.3 Implement nationally appropriate social protection systems and measures for all, including floors, and by 2030 achieve substantial coverage of the poor and the vulnerable

1.4 By 2030, ensure that all men and women, in particular the poor and the vulnerable, have equal rights to economic resources, as well as access to basic services, ownership and control over land and other forms of property, inheritance, natural resources, appropriate new technology and financial services, including microfinance

1.5 By 2030, build the resilience of the poor and those in vulnerable situations and reduce their exposure and vulnerability to climate-related extreme events and other economic, social and environmental shocks and disasters

1.a Ensure significant mobilization of resources from a variety of sources, including through enhanced development cooperation, in order to provide adequate and predictable means for developing countries, in particular least developed countries, to implement programmes and policies to end poverty in all its dimensions

1.b Create sound policy frameworks at the national, regional and international levels, based on pro-poor and gender-sensitive development strategies, to support accelerated investment in poverty eradication actions

Goal 2. End hunger, achieve food security and improved nutrition and promote sustainable agriculture

2.1 By 2030, end hunger and ensure access by all people, in particular the poor and people in vulnerable situations, including infants, to safe, nutritious and sufficient food all year round

2.2 By 2030, end all forms of malnutrition, including achieving, by 2025, the internationally agreed targets on stunting and wasting in children under 5 years of age, and address the nutritional needs of adolescent girls, pregnant and lactating women and older persons

2.3 By 2030, double the agricultural productivity and incomes of small-scale food producers, in particular women, indigenous peoples, family farmers, pastoralists and fishers, including through secure and equal access to land, other productive resources and inputs, knowledge, financial services, markets and opportunities for value addition and non-farm employment

2.4 By 2030, ensure sustainable food production systems and implement resilient agricultural practices that increase productivity and production, that help maintain ecosystems, that strengthen capacity for adaptation to climate change, extreme weather, drought, flooding and other disasters and that progressively improve land and soil quality

2.5 By 2020, maintain the genetic diversity of seeds, cultivated plants and farmed and domesticated animals and their related wild species, including through soundly managed and diversified seed and plant banks at the national, regional and international levels, and promote access to and fair and equitable sharing of benefits arising from the utilization of genetic resources and associated traditional knowledge, as internationally agreed

2.a Increase investment, including through enhanced international cooperation, in rural infrastructure, agricultural research and extension services, technology development and plant and livestock gene banks in order to enhance agricultural productive capacity in developing countries, in particular least developed countries

2.b Correct and prevent trade restrictions and distortions in world agricultural markets, including through the parallel elimination of all forms of agricultural export subsidies and all export measures with equivalent effect, in accordance with the mandate of the Doha Development Round

2.c Adopt measures to ensure the proper functioning of food commodity markets and their derivatives and facilitate timely access to market information, including on food reserves, in order to help limit extreme food price volatility

Goal 3. Ensure healthy lives and promote well-being for all at all ages

3.1 By 2030, reduce the global maternal mortality ratio to less than 70 per 100,000 live births

3.2 By 2030, end preventable deaths of newborns and children under 5 years of age, with all countries aiming to reduce neonatal mortality to at least as low as 12 per 1,000 live births and under-5 mortality to at least as low as 25 per 1,000 live births

3.3 By 2030, end the epidemics of AIDS, tuberculosis, malaria and neglected tropical diseases and combat hepatitis, water-borne diseases and other communicable diseases

3.4 By 2030, reduce by one third premature mortality from non-communicable diseases through prevention and treatment and promote mental health and well-being

3.5 Strengthen the prevention and treatment of substance abuse, including narcotic drug abuse and harmful use of alcohol

3.6 By 2020, halve the number of global deaths and injuries from road traffic accidents

3.7 By 2030, ensure universal access to sexual and reproductive health-care services, including for family planning, information and education, and the integration of reproductive health into national strategies and programmes

3.8 Achieve universal health coverage, including financial risk protection, access to quality essential health-care services and access to safe, effective, quality and affordable essential medicines and vaccines for all

3.9 By 2030, substantially reduce the number of deaths and illnesses from hazardous chemicals and air, water and soil pollution and contamination

3.a Strengthen the implementation of the World Health Organization Framework Convention on Tobacco Control in all countries, as appropriate

3.b Support the research and development of vaccines and medicines for the communicable and non-communicable diseases that primarily affect developing countries, provide access to affordable essential medicines and vaccines, in accordance with the Doha Declaration on the TRIPS Agreement and Public Health, which affirms the right of developing countries to use to the full the provisions in the Agreement on Trade-Related Aspects of Intellectual Property Rights regarding flexibilities to protect public health, and, in particular, provide access to medicines for all

3.c Substantially increase health financing and the recruitment, development, training and retention of the health workforce in developing countries, especially in least developed countries and small island developing States

3.d Strengthen the capacity of all countries, in particular developing countries, for early warning, risk reduction and management of national and global health risks

Goal 4. Ensure inclusive and equitable quality education and promote lifelong learning opportunities for all

4.1 By 2030, ensure that all girls and boys complete free, equitable and quality primary and secondary education leading to relevant and effective learning outcomes

4.2 By 2030, ensure that all girls and boys have access to quality early childhood development, care and pre-primary education so that they are ready for primary education

4.3 By 2030, ensure equal access for all women and men to affordable and quality technical, vocational and tertiary education, including university

4.4 By 2030, substantially increase the number of youth and adults who have relevant skills, including technical and vocational skills, for employment, decent jobs and entrepreneurship

4.5 By 2030, eliminate gender disparities in education and ensure equal access to all levels of education and vocational training for the vulnerable, including persons with disabilities, indigenous peoples and children in vulnerable situations

4.6 By 2030, ensure that all youth and a substantial proportion of adults, both men and women, achieve literacy and numeracy

4.7 By 2030, ensure that all learners acquire the knowledge and skills needed to promote sustainable development, including, among others, through education for sustainable development and sustainable lifestyles, human rights, gender equality, promotion of a culture of peace and non-violence, global citizenship and appreciation of cultural diversity and of culture's contribution to sustainable development

4.a Build and upgrade education facilities that are child, disability and gender sensitive and provide safe, non-violent, inclusive and effective learning environments for all

4.b By 2020, substantially expand globally the number of scholarships available to developing countries, in particular least developed countries, small island developing States and African countries, for enrolment in higher education, including vocational training and information and communications technology, technical, engineering and scientific programmes, in developed countries and other developing countries

4.c By 2030, substantially increase the supply of qualified teachers, including through international cooperation for teacher training in developing countries, especially least developed countries and small island developing States

Goal 5. Achieve gender equality and empower all women and girls

5.1 End all forms of discrimination against all women and girls everywhere

5.2 Eliminate all forms of violence against all women and girls in the public and private spheres, including trafficking and sexual and other types of exploitation

5.3 Eliminate all harmful practices, such as child, early and forced marriage and female genital mutilation

5.4 Recognize and value unpaid care and domestic work through the provision of public services, infrastructure and social protection policies and the promotion of shared responsibility within the household and the family as nationally appropriate

5.5 Ensure women's full and effective participation and equal opportunities for leadership at all levels of decision-making in political, economic and public life

5.6 Ensure universal access to sexual and reproductive health and reproductive rights as agreed in accordance with the Programme of Action of the International Conference on Population and Development and the Beijing Platform for Action and the outcome documents of their review conferences

5.a Undertake reforms to give women equal rights to economic resources, as well as access to ownership and control over land and other forms of property, financial services, inheritance and natural resources, in accordance with national laws

5.b Enhance the use of enabling technology, in particular information and communications technology, to promote the empowerment of women

5.c Adopt and strengthen sound policies and enforceable legislation for the promotion of gender equality and the empowerment of all women and girls at all levels

Goal 6. Ensure availability and sustainable management of water and sanitation for all

6.1 By 2030, achieve universal and equitable access to safe and affordable drinking water for all

6.2 By 2030, achieve access to adequate and equitable sanitation and hygiene for all and end open defecation, paying special attention to the needs of women and girls and those in vulnerable situations

6.3 By 2030, improve water quality by reducing pollution, eliminating dumping and minimizing release of hazardous chemicals and materials, halving the proportion of untreated wastewater and substantially increasing recycling and safe reuse globally

6.4 By 2030, substantially increase water-use efficiency across all sectors and ensure sustainable withdrawals and supply of freshwater to address water scarcity and substantially reduce the number of people suffering from water scarcity

6.5 By 2030, implement integrated water resources management at all levels, including through transboundary cooperation as appropriate

6.6 By 2020, protect and restore water-related ecosystems, including mountains, forests, wetlands, rivers, aquifers and lakes

6.a By 2030, expand international cooperation and capacity-building support to developing countries in water- and sanitation-related activities and programmes, including water harvesting, desalination, water efficiency, wastewater treatment, recycling and reuse technologies

6.b Support and strengthen the participation of local communities in improving water and sanitation management

Goal 7. Ensure access to affordable, reliable, sustainable and modern energy for all

7.1 By 2030, ensure universal access to affordable, reliable and modern energy services

7.2 By 2030, increase substantially the share of renewable energy in the global energy mix

7.3 By 2030, double the global rate of improvement in energy efficiency

7.a By 2030, enhance international cooperation to facilitate access to clean energy research and technology, including renewable energy, energy efficiency and advanced and cleaner fossil-fuel technology, and promote investment in energy infrastructure and clean energy technology

7.b By 2030, expand infrastructure and upgrade technology for supplying modern and sustainable energy services for all in developing countries, in particular least developed countries, small island developing States, and land-locked developing countries, in accordance with their respective programmes of support

Goal 8. Promote sustained, inclusive and sustainable economic growth, full and productive employment and decent work for all

8.1 Sustain per capita economic growth in accordance with national circumstances and, in particular, at least 7 per cent gross domestic product growth per annum in the least developed countries

8.2 Achieve higher levels of economic productivity through diversification, technological upgrading and innovation, including through a focus on high-value added and labour-intensive sectors

8.3 Promote development-oriented policies that support productive activities, decent job creation, entrepreneurship, creativity and innovation, and encourage the formalization and growth of micro-, small- and medium-sized enterprises, including through access to financial services

8.4 Improve progressively, through 2030, global resource efficiency in consumption and production and endeavour to decouple economic growth from environmental degradation, in accordance with the 10-year framework of programmes on sustainable consumption and production, with developed countries taking the lead

8.5 By 2030, achieve full and productive employment and decent work for all women and men, including for young people and persons with disabilities, and equal pay for work of equal value

8.6 By 2020, substantially reduce the proportion of youth not in employment, education or training

8.7 Take immediate and effective measures to eradicate forced labour, end modern slavery and human trafficking and secure the prohibition and elimination of the worst forms of child labour, including recruitment and use of child soldiers, and by 2025 end child labour in all its forms

8.8 Protect labour rights and promote safe and secure working environments for all workers, including migrant workers, in particular women migrants, and those in precarious employment

8.9 By 2030, devise and implement policies to promote sustainable tourism that creates jobs and promotes local culture and products

8.10 Strengthen the capacity of domestic financial institutions to encourage and expand access to banking, insurance and financial services for all

8.a Increase Aid for Trade support for developing countries, in particular least developed countries, including through the Enhanced Integrated Framework for Trade-Related Technical Assistance to Least Developed Countries

8.b By 2020, develop and operationalize a global strategy for youth employment and implement the Global Jobs Pact of the International Labour Organization

Goal 9. Build resilient infrastructure, promote inclusive and sustainable industrialization and foster innovation

9.1 Develop quality, reliable, sustainable and resilient infrastructure, including regional and transborder infrastructure, to support economic development and human well-being, with a focus on affordable and equitable access for all

9.2 Promote inclusive and sustainable industrialization and, by 2030, significantly raise industry's share of employment and gross domestic product, in line with national circumstances, and double its share in least developed countries

9.3 Increase the access of small-scale industrial and other enterprises, in particular in developing countries, to financial services, including affordable credit, and their integration into value chains and markets

9.4 By 2030, upgrade infrastructure and retrofit industries to make them sustainable, with increased resource-use efficiency and greater adoption of clean and environmentally sound technologies and industrial processes, with all countries taking action in accordance with their respective capabilities

9.5 Enhance scientific research, upgrade the technological capabilities of industrial sectors in all countries, in particular developing countries, including, by 2030, encouraging innovation and substantially increasing the number of research and development workers per 1 million people and public and private research and development spending

9.a Facilitate sustainable and resilient infrastructure development in developing countries through enhanced financial, technological and technical support to African countries, least developed countries, landlocked developing countries and small island developing States

9.b Support domestic technology development, research and innovation in developing countries, including by ensuring a conducive policy environment for, inter alia, industrial diversification and value addition to commodities

9.c Significantly increase access to information and communications technology and strive to provide universal and affordable access to the Internet in least developed countries by 2020

Goal 10. Reduce inequality within and among countries

10.1 By 2030, progressively achieve and sustain income growth of the bottom 40 per cent of the population at a rate higher than the national average

10.2 By 2030, empower and promote the social, economic and political inclusion of all, irrespective of age, sex, disability, race, ethnicity, origin, religion or economic or other status

10.3 Ensure equal opportunity and reduce inequalities of outcome, including by eliminating discriminatory laws, policies and practices and promoting appropriate legislation, policies and action in this regard

10.4 Adopt policies, especially fiscal, wage and social protection policies, and progressively achieve greater equality

10.5 Improve the regulation and monitoring of global financial markets and institutions and strengthen the implementation of such regulations

10.6 Ensure enhanced representation and voice for developing countries in decision-making in global international economic and financial institutions in order to deliver more effective, credible, accountable and legitimate institutions

10.7 Facilitate orderly, safe, regular and responsible migration and mobility of people, including through the implementation of planned and well-managed migration policies

10.a Implement the principle of special and differential treatment for developing countries, in particular least developed countries, in accordance with World Trade Organization agreements

10.b Encourage official development assistance and financial flows, including foreign direct investment, to States where the need is greatest, in particular least developed countries, African countries, small island developing States and landlocked developing countries, in accordance with their national plans and programmes

10.c By 2030, reduce to less than 3 per cent the transaction costs of migrant remittances and eliminate remittance corridors with costs higher than 5 per cent

Goal 11. Make cities and human settlements inclusive, safe, resilient and sustainable

11.1 By 2030, ensure access for all to adequate, safe and affordable housing and basic services and upgrade slums

11.2 By 2030, provide access to safe, affordable, accessible and sustainable transport systems for all, improving road safety, notably by expanding public transport, with special attention to the needs of those in vulnerable situations, women, children, persons with disabilities and older persons

11.3 By 2030, enhance inclusive and sustainable urbanization and capacity for participatory, integrated and sustainable human settlement planning and management in all countries

11.4 Strengthen efforts to protect and safeguard the world's cultural and natural heritage

11.5 By 2030, significantly reduce the number of deaths and the number of people affected and substantially decrease the direct economic losses relative to global gross domestic product caused by disasters, including water-related disasters, with a focus on protecting the poor and people in vulnerable situations

11.6 By 2030, reduce the adverse per capita environmental impact of cities, including by paying special attention to air quality and municipal and other waste management

11.7 By 2030, provide universal access to safe, inclusive and accessible, green and public spaces, in particular for women and children, older persons and persons with disabilities

11.a Support positive economic, social and environmental links between urban, peri-urban and rural areas by strengthening national and regional development planning

11.b By 2020, substantially increase the number of cities and human settlements adopting and implementing integrated policies and plans towards inclusion, resource efficiency, mitigation and adaptation to climate change, resilience to disasters, and develop and implement, in line with the Sendai Framework for Disaster Risk Reduction 2015-2030, holistic disaster risk management at all levels

11.c Support least developed countries, including through financial and technical assistance, in building sustainable and resilient buildings utilizing local materials

Goal 12. Ensure sustainable consumption and production patterns

12.1 Implement the 10-year framework of programmes on sustainable consumption and production, all countries taking action, with developed countries taking the lead, taking into account the development and capabilities of developing countries

12.2 By 2030, achieve the sustainable management and efficient use of natural resources

12.3 By 2030, halve per capita global food waste at the retail and consumer levels and reduce food losses along production and supply chains, including post-harvest losses

12.4 By 2020, achieve the environmentally sound management of chemicals and all wastes throughout their life cycle, in accordance with agreed international frameworks, and significantly reduce their release to air, water and soil in order to minimize their adverse impacts on human health and the environment

12.5 By 2030, substantially reduce waste generation through prevention, reduction, recycling and reuse

12.6 Encourage companies, especially large and transnational companies, to adopt sustainable practices and to integrate sustainability information into their reporting cycle

12.7 Promote public procurement practices that are sustainable, in accordance with national policies and priorities

12.8 By 2030, ensure that people everywhere have the relevant information and awareness for sustainable development and lifestyles in harmony with nature

12.a Support developing countries to strengthen their scientific and technological capacity to move towards more sustainable patterns of consumption and production

12.b Develop and implement tools to monitor sustainable development impacts for sustainable tourism that creates jobs and promotes local culture and products

12.c Rationalize inefficient fossil-fuel subsidies that encourage wasteful consumption by removing market distortions, in accordance with national circumstances, including by restructuring taxation and phasing out those harmful subsidies, where they exist, to reflect their environmental impacts, taking fully into account the specific needs and conditions of developing countries and minimizing the possible adverse impacts on their development in a manner that protects the poor and the affected communities

Goal 13. Take urgent action to combat climate change and its impacts*

13.1 Strengthen resilience and adaptive capacity to climate-related hazards and natural disasters in all countries

13.2 Integrate climate change measures into national policies, strategies and planning

13.3 Improve education, awareness-raising and human and institutional capacity on climate change mitigation, adaptation, impact reduction and early warning

13.a Implement the commitment undertaken by developed-country parties to the United Nations Framework Convention on Climate Change to a goal of mobilizing jointly $100 billion annually by 2020 from all sources to address the needs of developing countries in the context of meaningful mitigation actions and transparency on implementation and fully operationalize the Green Climate Fund through its capitalization as soon as possible

13.b Promote mechanisms for raising capacity for effective climate change-related planning and management in least developed countries and small island developing States, including focusing on women, youth and local and marginalized communities

* Acknowledging that the United Nations Framework Convention on Climate Change is the primary international, intergovernmental forum for negotiating the global response to climate change.

Goal 14. Conserve and sustainably use the oceans, seas and marine resources for sustainable development

14.1 By 2025, prevent and significantly reduce marine pollution of all kinds, in particular from land-based activities, including marine debris and nutrient pollution

14.2 By 2020, sustainably manage and protect marine and coastal ecosystems to avoid significant adverse impacts, including by strengthening their resilience, and take action for their restoration in order to achieve healthy and productive oceans

14.3 Minimize and address the impacts of ocean acidification, including through enhanced scientific cooperation at all levels

14.4 By 2020, effectively regulate harvesting and end overfishing, illegal, unreported and unregulated fishing and destructive fishing practices and implement science-based management plans, in order to restore fish stocks in the shortest time feasible, at least to levels that can produce maximum sustainable yield as determined by their biological characteristics

14.5 By 2020, conserve at least 10 per cent of coastal and marine areas, consistent with national and international law and based on the best available scientific information

14.6 By 2020, prohibit certain forms of fisheries subsidies which contribute to overcapacity and overfishing, eliminate subsidies that contribute to illegal, unreported and unregulated fishing and refrain from introducing new such subsidies, recognizing that appropriate and effective special and differential treatment for developing and least developed countries should be an integral part of the World Trade Organization fisheries subsidies negotiation

14.7 By 2030, increase the economic benefits to Small Island developing States and least developed countries from the sustainable use of marine resources, including through sustainable management of fisheries, aquaculture and tourism

14.a Increase scientific knowledge, develop research capacity and transfer marine technology, taking into account the Intergovernmental Oceanographic Commission Criteria and Guidelines on the Transfer of Marine Technology, in order to improve ocean health and to enhance the contribution of marine biodiversity to the development of developing countries, in particular small island developing States and least developed countries

14.b Provide access for small-scale artisanal fishers to marine resources and markets

14.c Enhance the conservation and sustainable use of oceans and their resources by implementing international law as reflected in UNCLOS, which provides the legal framework for the conservation and sustainable use of oceans and their resources, as recalled in paragraph 158 of The Future We Want

Goal 15. Protect, restore and promote sustainable use of terrestrial ecosystems, sustainably manage forests, combat desertification, and halt and reverse land degradation and halt biodiversity loss

15.1 By 2020, ensure the conservation, restoration and sustainable use of terrestrial and inland freshwater ecosystems and their services, in particular forests, wetlands, mountains and drylands, in line with obligations under international agreements

15.2 By 2020, promote the implementation of sustainable management of all types of forests, halt deforestation, restore degraded forests and substantially increase afforestation and reforestation globally

15.3 By 2030, combat desertification, restore degraded land and soil, including land affected by desertification, drought and floods, and strive to achieve a land degradation-neutral world

15.4 By 2030, ensure the conservation of mountain ecosystems, including their biodiversity, in order to enhance their capacity to provide benefits that are essential for sustainable development

15.5 Take urgent and significant action to reduce the degradation of natural habitats, halt the loss of biodiversity and, by 2020, protect and prevent the extinction of threatened species

15.6 Promote fair and equitable sharing of the benefits arising from the utilization of genetic resources and promote appropriate access to such resources, as internationally agreed

15.7 Take urgent action to end poaching and trafficking of protected species of flora and fauna and address both demand and supply of illegal wildlife products

15.8 By 2020, introduce measures to prevent the introduction and significantly reduce the impact of invasive alien species on land and water ecosystems and control or eradicate the priority species

15.9 By 2020, integrate ecosystem and biodiversity values into national and local planning, development processes, poverty reduction strategies and accounts

15.a Mobilize and significantly increase financial resources from all sources to conserve and sustainably use biodiversity and ecosystems

15.b Mobilize significant resources from all sources and at all levels to finance sustainable forest management and provide adequate incentives to developing countries to advance such management, including for conservation and reforestation

15.c Enhance global support for efforts to combat poaching and trafficking of protected species, including by increasing the capacity of local communities to pursue sustainable livelihood opportunities

Goal 16. Promote peaceful and inclusive societies for sustainable development, provide access to justice for all and build effective, accountable and inclusive institutions at all levels

16.1 Significantly reduce all forms of violence and related death rates everywhere

16.2 End abuse, exploitation, trafficking and all forms of violence against and torture of children

16.3 Promote the rule of law at the national and international levels and ensure equal access to justice for all

16.4 By 2030, significantly reduce illicit financial and arms flows, strengthen the recovery and return of stolen assets and combat all forms of organized crime

16.5 Substantially reduce corruption and bribery in all their forms

16.6 Develop effective, accountable and transparent institutions at all levels

16.7 Ensure responsive, inclusive, participatory and representative decision-making at all levels

16.8 Broaden and strengthen the participation of developing countries in the institutions of global governance

16.9 By 2030, provide legal identity for all, including birth registration

16.10 Ensure public access to information and protect fundamental freedoms, in accordance with national legislation and international agreements

16.a Strengthen relevant national institutions, including through international cooperation, for building capacity at all levels, in particular in developing countries, to prevent violence and combat terrorism and crime

16.b Promote and enforce non-discriminatory laws and policies for sustainable development

Goal 17. Strengthen the means of implementation and revitalize the global partnership for sustainable development

Finance

17.1 Strengthen domestic resource mobilization, including through international support to developing countries, to improve domestic capacity for tax and other revenue collection

17.2 Developed countries to implement fully their official development assistance commitments, including the commitment by many developed countries to achieve the target of 0.7 per cent of ODA/GNI to developing countries and 0.15 to 0.20 per cent of ODA/GNI to least developed countries; ODA providers are encouraged to consider setting a target to provide at least 0.20 per cent of ODA/GNI to least developed countries

17.3 Mobilize additional financial resources for developing countries from multiple sources

17.4 Assist developing countries in attaining long-term debt sustainability through coordinated policies aimed at fostering debt financing, debt relief and debt restructuring, as appropriate, and address the external debt of highly indebted poor countries to reduce debt distress

17.5 Adopt and implement investment promotion regimes for least developed countries

Technology

17.6 Enhance North-South, South-South and triangular regional and international cooperation on and access to science, technology and innovation and enhance knowledge sharing on mutually agreed terms, including through improved coordination among existing mechanisms, in particular at the United Nations level, and through a global technology facilitation mechanism

17.7 Promote the development, transfer, dissemination and diffusion of environmentally sound technologies to developing countries on favourable terms, including on concessional and preferential terms, as mutually agreed

17.8 Fully operationalize the technology bank and science, technology and innovation capacity-building mechanism for least developed countries by 2017 and enhance the use of enabling technology, in particular information and communications technology

Capacity-building

17.9 Enhance international support for implementing effective and targeted capacity-building in developing countries to support national plans to implement all the sustainable development goals, including through North-South, South-South and triangular cooperation

Trade

17.10 Promote a universal, rules-based, open, non-discriminatory and equitable multilateral trading system under the World Trade Organization, including through the conclusion of negotiations under its Doha Development Agenda

17.11 Significantly increase the exports of developing countries, in particular with a view to doubling the least developed countries' share of global exports by 2020

17.12 Realize timely implementation of duty-free and quota-free market access on a lasting basis for all least developed countries, consistent with World Trade Organization decisions, including by ensuring that preferential rules of origin applicable to imports from least developed countries are transparent and simple, and contribute to facilitating market access

Systemic issues

Policy and institutional coherence

17.13 Enhance global macroeconomic stability, including through policy coordination and policy coherence

17.14 Enhance policy coherence for sustainable development

17.15 Respect each country's policy space and leadership to establish and implement policies for poverty eradication and sustainable development

Multi-stakeholder partnerships

17.16 Enhance the global partnership for sustainable development, complemented by multi-stakeholder partnerships that mobilize and share knowledge, expertise, technology and financial resources, to support the achievement of the sustainable development goals in all countries, in particular developing countries

17.17 Encourage and promote effective public, public-private and civil society partnerships, building on the experience and resourcing strategies of partnerships

Data, monitoring and accountability

17.18 By 2020, enhance capacity-building support to developing countries, including for least developed countries and small island developing States, to increase significantly the availability of high-quality, timely and reliable data disaggregated by income, gender, age, race, ethnicity, migratory status, disability, geographic location and other characteristics relevant in national contexts

17.19 By 2030, build on existing initiatives to develop measurements of progress on sustainable development that complement gross domestic product, and support statistical capacity-building in developing countries.

Part - II

Requisites for the Sustainable Development Goals

Chapter - 6

Important Requisites for Ensuring Sustainable Development Goals including the need of a Nodal Agency at the Appropriate Levels

International goals are always philosophical; those are invariably looked upon from a very high stand-post of human values, human dignity and also from the perspective of human-civilization.. Such international conferences are guided and inspired by greater good of humanity irrespective of current status of human development in various parts of the world. At such Conferences, universality of outcome is the sole and only concern. Indeed there cannot exist any variation or alternative narratives for such a gathering of best human minds. Because of such high moral and ethical stand on vision on good of humanity, mundane issues like geographical, cultural and differentiated Homo sapiens seldom surface. The Goals of such international conferences turn out to be a kind of new Magna Carta for human welfare. The Sustainable Development Summit at United Nations in September,2015 adopted 17 such visionary roadmap for sustainable development goals to be achieved by 2030 by the humanity at large across this world.

The Sustainable Development Summit was aware of challenging issues of implementation and endeavoured to bring in "helping each other" spirit for smoothening out the gulf of variations in material and human development success, keeping in mind looming danger of climatic change.The Summit also adopted a separate Goal -17 (namely, Strengthen the means of implementation and revitalize the global partnership for sustainable development in line with the spirit of the Declaration) to address a host of issues to ensure that the world agenda of sustainable developments goals are put in shape. The Summit declaration also set up a mechanism for periodical Voluntary National Review

Report on Implementation of Sustainable Development Goals to see whether implementation of goals are on track.

Admittedly, the implementation process is not easy; it is more challenging than the MDGs. Every goal has its own domain specific functional responsibilities as there are certain common requisites which factor as conditionalities to reach the targets and maximise outcome. Incidentally, requisites denote necessary requirements that have to be put in place in general for all SDGs but also separate requisites for each of SDGs independently..

One of the essential requisites in a democratic set- up is to undertake serious deliberation on the Sustainable Development Summit and the broader features of each of the SDGs at the national parliament and take a national commitment on its implementation. The Parliament needs to take a view with reference to existing policy relevant to each of the SDGs and revisit them wherever it is required. The Parliament may require the government to design appropriate strategy thereafter for way forward either through existing programmes or by way of launching new initiatives for the kind of intervention needed to reach out the SDGs in the given pathway. The Parliament should also also empower a particular Sub-committee to review the progress of implementation of SDGs in the country. Similar exercise is also needed for our federal states in a parliamentary form of democracy.

For implementation of a particular SDG, dedicated programmes/schemes are needed for targeted outcome. Having regard to the nature of a particular SDG target and the gaps in reaching the targets, a country may require a number of schemes/programmes, but it has to be guarded against preponderances of schemes which may not be implementation-friendly. It is possible that any country may opt to continue existing schemes drawn even on pre-Sustainable Development Summit era; it may require to revisit them having regard to the SDG and associated targets and whether such schemes are qualified to continue based on its inherent strength to produce the desired outcome. Additionally, since some of the SDGs are interlinked, the schemes/programmes chosen might need to have features of interconnectedness and should also be convergence-friendly.

The Sustainable Development Summit empowers country governments to design SDGs –specific monitoring indicators if they have reservation on monitoring indicators as designed by the UN Statistical Commission. Monitoring is usually defined as a process of measuring, recording, collecting, processing and communicating information to assist policy makers and project management to take right decision in a given situation. Monitoring is essentially a functioning tool to understand the flow character of a programme or a scheme right from the time of its commencement. It helps to locate the gaps or deficiencies and be in a position to suggest right prescription for course correction. National government shall either accept the UN Statistical Commission- designed SDGs indicators or of her own national indicators.

There cannot exist any vacuum in this regard; public at large should have access to the ' Monitoring Report Card ' to verify whether the government of the day is doing enough to outreach SDGs to all.

Accountability is an important area to ensure outcome of intended goals. Both the Union Government and the State Governments are jointly and severally responsible for ensuring appropriate and adequate interventions to reach the targets and the outcomes in time. In other words, the implementation of SDGs is the central government's responsibility as much as it is the responsibility of the concerned state for the given jurisdiction. As a matter of fact, the responsibility of state governments is decisively more in that they happen to be addressing most of the SDGs by their line departments and also through linked-up support of rural and urban local bodies. The actions on SDGs implementation on the part of state government need to be adequate and visible; Goal-wise responsibility need to be confusion-free and formally fixed. It is true that the Cabinet is ultimately responsible for all programmes in a state; however, the Cabinet also allocates ministers' responsibility following Rules of Business under Article 166(3) of the Constitution. It is time that Goal-wise subject responsibility is also included under Rules of Business under Article 166(3) so as to enable the ministers and the related departments to pay required attention on SDGs under its constitutional obligation.

The various goals and targets under SDGs are interlinked and even inter-dependent. There exists a strong case for consultation, coordination and convergence among the programme partners both at the policy and implementation level. The scope for a Nodal Ministry looking after coordination of SDGs related programmes/schemes etc has assumed critical importance. Similarly, a Nodal Authority down below to oversee the implementation behaviour of SDGs related interventions, both by the Union Government and also by the federal states has become sin- qua –non for ensuring that the SDGs implementation processes are on right track.

The SDGs are now the new development agenda of the humanity and the Sustainable Development Summit,2015, at para 82 of the Declaration requires the member states to submit annual progress report on the Sustainable Development Goals for review by the High-Level Political Forum (HLPF) under the auspices of the UN Economic and Social Council (ECOSOC). In the given situation, it is imperative that that the Union Government and the respective state government publish evidence-based annual report on SDGs before the Annual Budget and submit the same before the Parliament. and respective Legislative Assembly.

Chapter - 7

Requisites of Sustainable Population for Ensuring Sustainable Development Goals for India's Perceived Challenges

The core philosophy and guiding spirit of Sustainable Development Summit is that nobody should be left behind. The implication is very important in Indian context where the size of population is abnormally large and keeps on increasing at a runaway rate. India, as a signatory to the Declaration of the Sustainable Development Summit (SDS),has to reach out the intended benefits to all of her population, today and day after tomorrow. The SDS, however, did not bother itself with the population size of any country consciously; otherwise it would have come into conflict with the clarion call of reaching out to all Homo sapiens of the world. Be that as it may, the huge population size and its annual increment is an important factor for any country's tryst with development journey. The effective demand originating from population size stimulates its development process up to some point of time; it, however, acts as a spanner on economic growth at a later stage. To be more specific, rapidly growing population enlarges effective demand, releases economic forces, motivation and incentives to speed up initiatives and efforts to take up in a big way the challenges for economic development for the potential big market for goods and services and to make full use of the available resources by all possible ways. On the other hand, hugely growing population stands as great obstacle to economic growth in a number of ways. A high percentage of unproductive population and a higher size of BPL among the huge size of population, forces the government to make provision for huge subsidy and other attendant social sector expenditures thereby compromising its own economic priority programme. It also aggravates the unemployment problems of all kinds - disguised, under-employed or unemployed, both in rural and urban areas. Finally, it acts as a deterrent to improve quality of life of all its citizens and affects the country's capacity to save and invest- a crucial factor for economic growth.

Economists are now in agreement that a country has to aim at sustainable population growth, one that can be maintained without adversely impacting the environment or the quality of life of the members of that population. Sustainable population growth means the rate at which the number of inhabitants of a given area can increase without overburdening the area's economic, social and natural resources. Many demographers use the term "carrying capacity" to refer to the number of inhabitants who can be supported in a particular area without degrading the physical and social environment at present or for future generations. When population growth exceeds an area's carrying capacity, growth is considered unsustainable because the existing resources, such as water and food, are not sufficient to sustain the growing population.

Climate change has added a new dimension to any estimate of sustainable population and the planet's ability to support all 7+ billion of population. Climate scientists foresee lower crop yields of major grains such as wheat, rice, and maize. Rising sea levels may create hundreds of millions of climate refugees in years to come in addition to climate disruption followed by likely increasing levels of resource conflict and civil unrest. Adaptation to climate disruption will only be easier with a much smaller global population. Thus, the world in general and the individual countries in particular need to be circumspect of the hard reality of changing resource base to uphold the existing size of population and factor in certain and irreversible climatic change of foreseeable nature and degrees. In addressing sustainable population, appropriate consideration need to be placed on demand pull forces that hit upon resource scenario in the post-climate changing scenario that the local area of the Earth can support. Naturally, as a signatory to the SDS, each of Individual countries has to draw up a road-map for sustainable population by arresting and reversing the birth rate, immigration and infiltration, and the resource use. Sustainable population is the only requisite for sustainable development and the SDGs. The SDGs will remain illusory if sustainable population is not in place.

The destination point of UN Sustainable Development Goals (SDGs) is to put in place a new world free from hunger, gender inequity, and human indignity. Thus, one of the collateral objectives of sustainable development is to put in place the state of sustainable population in a given country. Unless sustainable population is secured, it is well-nigh impossible to have sustainable development. With 121,05,69,573 number of population as per census, 2011, India happens to be second most populous country in the world, sustaining 17.5 per cent of the world population on 2.4 per cent of the world's surface area as per India's Census, 2011. It is now on way to overtake China on carrying maximum load of population in the world. In the circumstances, it is very important to have an objective assessment as to whether India will be able to secure sustainable population and meet the essential requirement for sustainable development.

The carrying capacity of sustainable population depends, among other requirements, the geographical size of a country. In fact, availability of geographical space may be considered as the primary requirement for maintaining a particular size of population. It would thus be relevant to see the relative geographical area of India vis-à-vis size of the earth and of other major countries of the world. In Table 7.1, the relative geographical position of India has been shown

Table 7.1: The First 10 largest countries of the World

Country/Territory	*Rank*	*Area(KM2)*	*% of Total*	*Continent/Region*
Earth	-	148940000	-	Solar System
Russia	1	17,098,242	11.3	Asia/Europe
Canada	2	9,984,670	6.7	America/North
United States	3	9,629,091	6.5	America/North
P.R. China	4	9,598,094	6.4	Asia/Easter
Brazil	5	8,514,877	5.7	America/South
Australia	6	7,692,024	5.2	Australia
India	7	3,287,263	2.3	Asia/South-Central
Argentina	8	2,780,400	2	America/South
Kazakhstan	9	2,780,400	1.8	Asia/South Central
Algeria	10	2,381,741	1.6	Africa/Northern

Source: Source:www.nationsonline.org/one world/country_ by_area.htm

The dynamics of population load changes fast and the respective Population clock of the country aims to capture such dynamic growth of population. At Table 7.2 the relative position of India and other major populous countries of the world, as revealed in the Population clock, has been captured as on 12th March, 2018. It is a fact that the figures on population clock may not be as exact as the census figures; nonetheless it is a dependable indicator of the emerging scenario. Thus the population load of India, which

Table 7.2: Dependence of population

Rank	*Country*	*Estimated Population, in 2018*	*Yearly Change-%*	*Net Change*	*Density*	*Fertility*	*% of World Population*
1.	China	1415045928	0.39	5528531	151	1.6	18.54
2.	India	1354051854	1.11	14871727	455	2.4	17.74
3.	United States	326766748	0.71	2307285	36	1.9	4.28
4.	Indonesia	266794890	1.06	2803601	147	2.5	3.50
5.	Brazil	210867954	0.75	1579676	25	1.8	2.76
6.	Pakistan	200813818	1.93	3797863	260	3.7	2.63
7.	Nigeria	195875237	2.6	4988926	215	5.7	2,57
8	Bangladesh	166368149	1.03	1698598	1278	2.2	2.18
9.	Russia	143964709	-0.02	-25045	9	1.7	1.89
10.	Mexico	130759074	1.24	1595798	67	2.3	1.71

Source: **World Population** Database - Platinum Edition,,www.geodatasource.com/, Human **Population** in Top Cities. Get **World Population** Database Now! (as on 12.03.2018)

represented 17.5 per cent of the world population in 2011, moved up- words at 17.74 per cent as per Population clock on 12th March, 2018 as would be evident from the following Population and Development in volume 41 Number 3,September 2015, in section Documents, at page 557 mentioned the UN Population Division's series of population projections for twenty-first century, termed the 2015 Revision which was released in July 2015. The 2015 Revision's medium-variant projections for the ten largest countries, as of 2015 (together making up 58 per cent of the world's population), are shown at Table 3.

Table 7.3: Projected population in 2015 and projected population (medium-variant) in 2030,2050, and 2100 of the ten largest countries in 2018 (millions)

Country	*2015*	*2030*	*2050*	*2100*
China	1376	1416	1348	1004
India	1311	1526	1705	1660
United States	322	356	389	450
Indonesia	258	295	322	314
Brazil	208	229	238	200
Pakisthan	189	245	310	364
Nigeria	182	263	399	752
Bangladesh	161	186	202	170
Russian Federation	143	139	129	117
Mexico	127	148	164	148

Source: United Nations Department of Economic and Social Affairs/Population Division, World Population Prospects: The 2015 Revision. Key Findings and Advance Tables 52.

Based on the related data in Table 7.1 and Table 7.2, a Table has been prepared to indicate the relative population size of India in the year 2030, the terminal year of SDGs.

Table 7.4: Size of geographical area vis-à-vis the size of population and its projection on 2030

Country/ Territory	*% of geographical area of the earth*	*Projected population in 2015*	*Population estimation in 2018*	*% of World Population in 2018*	*Projected population in 2030*
China	6.4	1376	1415	18.54	1416
India	2.3	1311	1354	17.74	1526
United States	6.5	322	326	4.28	356
Indonesia	1,3	258	266	3.50	295
Brazil	5.7	208	210	2.76	229
Pakistan	0.53	189	200	2.63	245
Nigeria	0.62	182	195	2.57	263
Bangladesh	0.10	161	166	2.18	186
Russian Federation	11.3	143	143	1.89	139
Mexico	1.3	127	130	1.71	148

The data speak volumes of the population load of India and its alarming scenario. Geographically speaking, India is projected to carry the highest number of population in 2030 with a mere 2.3 (or 2.4 as per Census India's estimate) per cent of space of the earth. This itself raise a question as to whether India will be able to absorb this size of population without any damage to the fundamentals of the Indian economy and be in a position to meet the 17 sustainable development goals and 169 targets in 2030. Normal economic sense does suggest that such a scenario will bring about untold stress on all aspects of economic and social life. Further, the incremental per year addition of around 14.8 million population per year is fearsome, to say the least. The UN projection of 1705 million in 2050 and 1660 million in 2100 are figures that signal the onset of a period of population disaster.

The National Population Policy (NPP), 2000 in India has lost its relevance after the census, 2011.The country has urgency to firm-up its actionable role on Sustainable population in the context of SDGs. India is in need of framing a robust Sustainable Population Policy and also its Strategy. The uppermost consideration should always be the realisation that there are physical limits to the earth-space of India and its life support systems. Technology may give temporary respite in some areas with perceptible fortune for short duration, the limits to population growth are permanent. India is a case of limitless population growth. It is a classic case of over population. India has now no choice but to pursue a regime of hard options for a period of time as there is no quick fix for sustainable population.

In fine, the world in general and the individual countries in particular, such as India, need to stabilise population size at a level consistent with sustainable population level in that demand pull forces do not hit upon resources at a rate the Earth of the local area can support. As a signatory to the World summit of sustainable development goals, each of such individual countries has to draw up a road-map for arresting and reversing the birth rate, immigration and infiltration. Sustainable population is a major requisite for sustainable development and SDGs.

PART- III

THE UN SUSTAINABLE DEVELOPMENT GOALS REPORT 2016

Chapter - 8

An Overview from the UN Sustainable Development Goals Report 2016

The Sustainable Development Goals Report 2016 provides the first account on the status of 17 SDGs for the world as a whole which may stand as benchmark for monitoring our journey towards a sustainable future for people and the planet. Using the data currently available and based on proposed global indicator framework, the inaugural progress report presents an overview of the 17 Sustainable Development Goals.The data and its analysis in the report will serve to locate gaps and challenges so as to address them. It will also enable us also to revisit programme and performance correction. Required new initiatives and supplementation may also be added to bridge the identified gaps and deficits. Performance monitoring is a continuous process and that the clarion call that nobody should be left behind can only be realised when periodical reports are regularly published and analysed. With this brief introduction, the Sustainable Development Goals Report 2016,the first edition of the series, as prepared by the Statistics Division of the Department of Economic and Social Affairs, based on the data and information provided by UN and other international agencies, is presented.

In the Overview of the Sustainable Development Goals Report 2016, it has been mentioned that " this inaugural report on the global Sustainable Development Goals (SDGs) is a first accounting of where the world stands at the start of our collective journey to 2030. The report analyses selected indicators from the global indicator framework for which data are available as examples to highlight some critical gaps and challenges. The list of SDG indicators agreed upon by the UN Statistical Commission in March 2016 will be subject to refinements and improvements as methods and data availability improve. Every journey has a beginning and an end. Plotting that journey and establishing key milestones along the way requires accessible, timely and reliable disaggregated data. The data requirements for the global indicators are almost as unprecedented as the SDGs themselves and constitute a tremendous challenge to all countries. Nevertheless, fulfilling these requirements through building national statistical capacity is an essential step in establishing where we are now, charting away forward and bringing our collective vision closer to reality".

The Sustainable Development Goals Report 2016 presents the status position of 17 SDGs, goal wise, in sequential number. Those are reproduced hereunder:

The Sustainable Development Goals Report 2016 on Goal-1.

End poverty in all its forms everywhere

Goal 1 calls for an end to poverty in all its manifestations, including extreme poverty, over the next 15 years. All people everywhere, including the poorest and most vulnerable, should enjoy a basic standard of living and social protection benefits.

- The proportion of the global population living below the extreme poverty line dropped by half between 2002 and 2012, from 26 to 13 per cent. This translated to one in eight people worldwide living in extreme poverty in 2012.Poverty remains widespread in sub-Saharan Africa, where more than 40 per cent of people lived on less than 1.90 US dollars a day in 2012.In 2015, 10 per cent of the world's workers and their families were living on less than 1.90 US dollars per person per day, down from 28 per cent in 2000.
- Young people aged 15 to 24 are most likely to be among the working poor: 16 per cent of all employed youth were living below the poverty line in 2015,compared to 9 per cent of working adults.
- About one in five people received any type of social assistance or social protection benefits in low-income countries compared with two in three people in upper-middle-income countries.

The Sustainable Development Goals Report 2016 on Goal-2

End hunger, achieve food security and improved nutrition and promote sustainable agriculture

Goal 2 seeks to end hunger and all forms of malnutrition and to achieve sustainable food production by 2030. It is premised on the idea that everyone should have access to sufficient nutritious food, which will require widespread promotion of sustainable agriculture, a doubling of agricultural productivity, increased investments and properly functioning food markets.

- The proportion of the population suffering from hunger declined globally from 15 per cent in 2000-2002 to 11 per cent in 2014-2016. However, nearly 800 million people worldwide still lack access to adequate food.

- More than half of the adult population in sub-Saharan Africa faced moderate or severe food insecurity in 2015; the level was severe for one-quarter of adults in the region.
- One in four children under age 5 had stunted growth in 2014—an estimated 158.6 million children.
- The share of overweight children under age 5 increased by nearly 20 per cent between 2000 and 2014. Approximately 41 million children in this age group worldwide were overweight in 2014; almost half of them lived in Asia.

The Sustainable Development Goals Report 2016 on Goal-3

Ensure healthy lives and promote well-being for all at all ages

Goal 3 aims to ensure health and well-being for all at all ages by improving reproductive, maternal and child health; ending the epidemics of major communicable diseases; reducing non-communicable and environmental diseases; achieving universal health coverage; and ensuring access to safe, affordable and effective medicines and vaccines for all.

- Between 1990 and 2015, the global maternal mortality ratio declined by 44 per cent, and the mortality rate of children under age 5 fell by more than half. Still, an estimated 5.9 million children under 5 died in 2015, mostly from preventable causes.
- The incidence of HIV, malaria and tuberculosis declined globally between 2000 and 2015. However, in 2015, 2.1 million people became newly infected with HIV, and an estimated 214 million people contracted malaria. Almost half the world's population is at risk of malaria, but sub-Saharan Africa accounted for 89 per cent of all cases in 2015.
- Worldwide in 2015, approximately three in four women of reproductive age (15 to 49 years) who were married or in a union satisfied their need for family planning by using modern contraceptive methods.
- In 2012, almost two-thirds of deaths from non-communicable diseases in people under age 70 were attributed to cardiovascular diseases and cancer.

The Sustainable Development Goals Report 2016 on Goal-4

Ensure inclusive and equitable quality education and promote lifelong learning opportunities for all

Goal 4 focuses on the acquisition of foundational and higher-order skills; greater and more equitable access to technical and vocational education and training and higher education; training throughout life; and the knowledge, skills and values needed to function well and contribute to society.

- In 2013, 59 million children of primary school age were out of school. ffSurveys from 63 low- and middle-income countries between 2008 and 2012 show that children from the poorest 20 per cent of households are more than four times as likely to be out of school as their richest peers.
- Data from 38 countries in developed regions show that, in the majority of these countries, 75 per cent or more of young people had at least minimum proficiency in reading and/or mathematics; the same was true for only 5 of the 22 developing countries with data.
- In 2013, there were still 757 million adults (aged 15 and over) unable to read and write, of whom two-thirds were women.

The Sustainable Development Goals Report 2016 on Goal-5

Achieve gender equality and empower all women and girls

Goal 5 aims to empower women and girls to reach their full potential, which requires eliminating all forms of discrimination and violence against them, including harmful practices. It seeks to ensure that they have every opportunity for sexual and reproductive health and reproductive rights; receive due recognition for their unpaid work; have full access to productive resources; and enjoy equal participation with men in political, economic and public life.

- Globally, the proportion of women aged 20 to 24 who reported that they were married before their eighteenth birthdays dropped from 32 per cent around 1990 to 26 per cent around 2015.
- In 30 countries where the practice of female genital mutilation is concentrated,more than a third of girls aged 15 to 19 have undergone the procedure.
- Based on time-use surveys conducted between 2000 and 2014 in 59 countries,women said they spend 19 per cent of their time each day on unpaid labour versus 8 per cent for men.
- The proportion of seats held by women in single or lower houses of parliament rose to 23 per cent in 2016—a rise of 6 percentage points over the last decade.

The Sustainable Development Goals Report 2016 on Goal-6

Ensure availability and sustainable management
of water and sanitation for all

Goal 6 goes beyond drinking water, sanitation and hygiene to also address the quality and sustainability of water resources. Achieving this Goal, which is critical to the survival of people and the planet, means expanding international cooperation and garnering the support of local communities in improving water and sanitation management.

- In 2015, 6.6 billion people, or 91 per cent of the global population, used an improved drinking water source, compared with 82 per cent in 2000. However, in 2015 an estimated 663 million people were still using unimproved sources or surface water.
- Between 2000 and 2015, the proportion of the global population using improved sanitation increased from 59 per cent to 68 per cent. However,2.4 billion were left behind. Among them were 946 million people without any facilities at all who continue to practise open defecation.
- Water stress affects more than 2 billion people around the globe, a figure that is projected to rise.
- Integrated Water Resources Management plans are under way in every region of the world.

The Sustainable Development Goals Report 2016 on Goal-7

Ensure access to affordable, reliable, sustainable and modern energy for all

Goal 7 seeks to promote broader energy access and increased use of renewable energy, including through enhanced international cooperation and expanded infrastructure and technology for clean energy.

- The proportion of the global population with access to electricity increased steadily, from 79 per cent in 2000 to 85 per cent in 2012. Despite these improvements, 1.1 billion people were still without this essential service in 2012.
- In 2014, some 3 billion people, over 40 per cent of the world's population, relied on polluting and unhealthy fuels for cooking.
- Modern renewables grew rapidly, at a rate of 4 per cent a year between 2010 and 2012.
- Global energy intensity improved by 1.3 per cent a year from 2000 to 2012. About 68 per cent of the energy savings between 2010 and 2012 came from developing regions, with Eastern Asia as the largest contributor.

The Sustainable Development Goals Report 2016 on Goal-8

Promote sustained, inclusive and sustainable economic growth, full and productive employment and decent work for all

Continued, inclusive and sustainable economic growth is a prerequisite for global prosperity. Goal 8 aims to provide opportunities for full and productive employment and decent work for all while eradicating forced labour, human trafficking and child labour.

- The average annual growth rate of real gross domestic product (GDP) per capita in the least developed countries (LDCs) declined from 4.7 per cent over the period 2005-2009 to 2.6 per cent in 2010-2014. This was less than half the target rate of 7 per cent per year.

- While labour productivity increased in the developing regions from 2005 to 2015, the value for developed regions was still more than twice that of any developing region, and around 20 times greater than the values for sub-Saharan Africa and Southern Asia.
- In 2015, the unemployment rate for women was 6.7 per cent versus 5.8 per cent for men. Gender disparities were most striking in Western Asia and Northern Africa, where the unemployment rate of women was more than twice that of men.
- While the share of adults with bank accounts rose by 20 per cent in four years,some 2 billion people still lack this important financial service.

The Sustainable Development Goals Report 2016 on Goal-9

Goal 9. Build resilient infrastructure, promote inclusive and sustainable industrialization and foster innovation

Goal 9 focuses on the promotion of infrastructure development, industrialization and innovation. This can be accomplished through enhanced international and domestic financial, technological and technical support, research and innovation, and increased access to information and communication technology.

- In 2015, manufacturing value added per capita was less than 100 US dollars a year in the LDCs versus nearly 5,000 US dollars in developed regions.
- Globally, energy efficiency and cleaner fuels and technologies reduced carbon dioxide (CO2) emissions per unit of value added by 13 per cent from 2000 to 2013.
- In 2013, global investment in research and development (R&D) stood at 1.7 trillion US dollars (purchasing power parity, PPP), up from 732 billion US dollars in 2000. Developed regions dedicated almost 2.4 per cent of their GDP to R&D in 2013, while the average for LDCs and landlocked developing countries was less than 0.3 per cent.
- Third-generation (3G) mobile-broadband covered 89 per cent of the urban population but only 29 per cent of the rural population in 2015.

The Sustainable Development Goals Report 2016 on Goal-10

Reduce inequality within and among countries

Goal 10 calls for reducing inequalities in income, as well as those based on sex,age, disability, race, class, ethnicity, religion and opportunity—both within and among countries. It also aims to ensure safe, orderly and regular migration and addresses issues related to representation of developing countries in global decision-making and development assistance.

- In 56 out of 94 countries with data for the period 2007-2012, the per capita income of the poorest 40 per cent of households grew more rapidly than the national average.
- The share of imports from the least developed and developing countries entering developed countries duty-free increased between 2000 to 2014,from 70 to 84 per cent and from 65 to 79 per cent, respectively.
- The cost of sending money across international borders averaged 7.5 per cent of the amount remitted in 2015, more than double the target rate of 3 per cent.

The Sustainable Development Goals Report 2016 on Goal-11

Make cities and human settlements inclusive,
safe, resilient and sustainable

Goal 11 aims to renew and plan cities and other human settlements in a way that fosters community cohesion and personal security while stimulating innovation and employment.

- In 2014, 880 million people lived in urban slums, or 30 per cent of the global urban population, compared to 39 per cent in 2000.
- In many burgeoning cities around the world, populations are moving outwards,far beyond administrative boundaries.
- In 2014, about half the urban population globally was exposed to air pollution levels at least 2.5 times above the standard of safety set by the World Health Organization.
- As of 2015, 142 countries were developing national-level urban policies;of these, 82 countries were already in the process of implementation and 23 had reached the monitoring and evaluation stage.

The Sustainable Development Goals Report 2016 on Goal-12

Ensure sustainable consumption and production patterns

Goal 12 aims to promote sustainable consumption and production patterns through measures such as specific policies and international agreements on the management of materials that are toxic to the environment.

- In 2010, the material footprint per unit of GDP (amount of primary materials used) of developed regions stood at 23.6 kilograms per unit of GDP, compared with 14.5 kilograms per unit of GDP in developing regions.

- That same year, domestic material consumption per capita in developed regions was 72 per cent higher than in developing regions.
- With six exceptions, all Member States of the United Nations are party to at least one of the conventions (Basel, Rotterdam or Stockholm) dedicated to the management of hazardous wastes and other chemicals.

The Sustainable Development Goals Report 2016 on Goal-13

Take urgent action to combat climate change and its impacts*

Climate change presents the single biggest threat to development, and its widespread, nprecedented effects disproportionately burden the poorest and the most vulnerable. Urgent action is needed not only to combat climate change and its impacts, but also to build resilience in responding to climate-related hazards and natural disasters.

- In April 2016, 175 Member States signed the historic Paris Agreement, which sets the stage for ambitious climate action by all to ensure that global temperatures rise no more than 2 degrees Celsius.
- An average of 83,000 people died and 211 million were affected each year as a result of natural disasters occurring from 2000 to 2013.
- In 2015, only 83 countries reportedly had legislative and/or regulatory provisions in place for managing disaster risk.

The Sustainable Development Goals Report 2016 on Goal-14

Conserve and sustainably use the oceans, seas and marine resources for sustainable development

This Goal seeks to promote the conservation and sustainable use of marine and coastal ecosystems, prevent marine pollution and increase the economic benefits to small island developing States and LDCs from the sustainable use of marine resources.

- Marine resources are particularly important for people living in coastal communities, who represented 37 per cent of the world's population in 2010.
- The proportion of global marine fish stocks within biologically sustainable levels declined from 90 per cent in 1974 to 69 per cent in 2013.
- In 2014, 8.4 per cent of the marine environment under national jurisdiction (up to 200 nautical miles from shore) was under protection. From 2000 to 2016, the share of marine key biodiversity areas that were completely covered by protected areas increased from 15 per cent to 19 per cent.

- The five large marine ecosystems most at risk from coastal eutrophication are the Bay of Bengal, East China Sea, Gulf of Mexico, North Brazil Shelf and South China Sea—areas that provided ecosystem services for coastal populations totalling 781 million in 2010.

The Sustainable Development Goals Report 2016 on Goal-15

Protect, restore and promote sustainable use of terrestrial ecosystems, sustainably manage forests, combat desertification, and halt and reverse land degradation and halt biodiversity loss

Goal 15 focuses on managing forests sustainably, restoring degraded lands and successfully combating desertification, reducing degraded natural habitats and ending biodiversity loss. All of these efforts in combination will help ensure that livelihoods are preserved for those that depend directly on forests and other ecosystems, that biodiversity will thrive, and that the benefits of these natural resources will be enjoyed for generations to come.

- Global net loss in forest area declined from 7.3 million hectares per year in the 1990s to 3.3 million hectares per year during the period 2010-2015.
- The percentage of global terrestrial, inland freshwater and mountain key biodiversity areas covered by protected areas increased from 16.5 per cent to 19.3 per cent, 13.8 per cent to 16.6 per cent and 18.1 per cent to 20.1 per cent, respectively, from 2000 to 2016.
- As of 2015, over 23,000 species of plants, fungi and animals were known to face a high probability of extinction. Human activities are causing species extinctions at rates three orders of magnitude higher than those normal throughout the Earth's history.
- Since 1999, at least 7,000 species of animals and plants have been detected in illegal trade affecting 120 countries.

The Sustainable Development Goals Report 2016 on Goal-16

Promote peaceful and inclusive societies for sustainable development, provide access to justice for all and build effective, accountable and inclusive institutions at all levels

Goal 16 envisages peaceful and inclusive societies based on respect for human rights, the rule of law, good governance at all levels, and transparent, effective and accountable institutions. Many countries still face protracted violence and armed conflict, and far too many people are poorly supported by weak institutions and lack access to justice, information and other fundamental freedoms.

- Between 2008 and 2014, the homicide rate in developing countries was twice that of developed countries.

- At the peak in 2011, 34 per cent of the victims of human trafficking at the global level were children, up from 13 per cent in 2004.
- Globally, 30 per cent of people held in detention over the period 2012-2014 had not been sentenced.
- The births of more than one in four children under age 5 worldwide go unrecorded.In the LDCs, one in two children have not been registered by their fifth birthdays.

The Sustainable Development Goals Report 2016 on Goal-17

Strengthen the means of implementation and revitalize the global partnership for sustainable development

The 2030 Agenda requires a revitalized and enhanced global partnership that mobilizes all available resources from Governments, civil society, the private sector,the United Nations system and other actors. Increasing support to developing countries, in particular LDCs, landlocked developing countries and small island developing States is fundamental to equitable progress for all.

- Official development assistance totalled 131.6 billion US dollars in 2015, which was 6.9 per cent higher in real terms than in 2014 and represents the highest level ever reached.
- The debt service to export ratio fell significantly over the period 2000-2012,dropping from 11.7 in 2000 to under 2.7 in 2012.
- In 2015, fixed-broadband Internet penetration reached 29 per cent in developed regions, but only 7.1 per cent in developing regions and 0.5 per cent in LDCs.
- Although the share of LDC merchandise exports in total exports nearly doubled from 2000 to 2014, it still represented only a small fraction of global exports in 2014, at 1.1 per cent.
- Ninety per cent of all countries and 88 per cent of developing countries conducted population and housing censuses over the period 2006-2015, a key source of essential data.

The Sustainable Development Goals Report 2016 also embodied the comments of the Under-Secretary-General for Economic and Social Affairs on the overwhelming principal objective of Sustainable Development Goals in 'Ensuring that no one is left behind'. The comments are produced below:

"In launching the 2030 Agenda for Sustainable Development,Member States recognized that the dignity of the individual is fundamental and that the Agenda's Goals and targets should be met for all nations and people and for all segments of society. Furthermore, they will endeavour to reach first those who are furthest behind. Going beyond rhetoric in this regard will be no simple matter because disaggregated data tell us that the benefits of development are far from equally shared.

- In 2015, the youth unemployment rate (among people aged 15 to 24) globally was 15 per cent—more than three times the rate for adults (4.6 per cent).
- Globally in 2015, births in the richest 20 per cent of households were more than twice as likely to be attended by skilled health personnel as those in the poorest 20 per cent of households (89 per cent versus 43 per cent).
- Children from the poorest households are more than twice as likely to be stunted as their richest peers.
- Almost 80 per cent of urban inhabitants have access to piped water versus one-third of the rural population.
- The LDCs, landlocked developing countries and small island developing States all reported a prevalence of undernourishment that was substantially higher than that of developing regions as a whole (13.6, 9.8 and 5.1 percentage points higher, respectively) in 2014-2016.

Leaving no one behind is the overarching principle of the 2030 Agenda. However, without data and indicators that address specific groups within a population, including the most vulnerable, full implementation of the commitments made in the SDGs will not be possible. A global effort to improve data availability and use, including through improvements in the integration of data sources, has already begun. But much work lies ahead. The global statistical community stands ready to transform and modernize the way this work is undertaken in order to fully meet current needs and to fulfil our promise to present and future generations".

PART - IV
SUSTAINABLE DEVELOPMENT GOALS INITIATIVES IN INDIA

Chapter - 9

An Overview of the Sustainable Development Goals approaches and initiatives in India

India's approach to Sustainable Development is summed up in the visionary statement of the Prime Minister at the Sustainable Development Summit when he spoke of the birth of a new hope for our age, to collectively rise to its obligation to the world and responsibility to the future, and to chart a course for our humanity and our planet. He went on to state that:

"Mahatma Gandhi had once said, "One must care about the world one will not see". Indeed, humanity has progressed when it has collectively risen to its obligation to the world and responsibility to the future.

Seventy years after the end of a tragic war and birth of a new hope for our age, we are meeting to chart a course for our humanity and our planet. I consider this a very important summit and thank UN Secretary General for organizing it."

The seriousness of the pledge got reflected when the Prime Minister of India took it up in the BRICS Leaders' Meeting that G20 must place priority on effective implementation of Sustainable Development Agenda 2030 and ensure adequate funding for it. At the national level, this urgency of approach got in motion when the NITI Aayog, the erstwhile Planning Commission of India, was entrusted with the role to co-ordinate 'Transforming our world: the 2030 Agenda for Sustainable Development Goals'. In a way, the NITI Aayog has been entrusted to perform a kind of nodal role in the implementation of SDGs in India.

The NITI Aayog, in this new role, has been tasked to periodically collect SDGs related data, facilitate the process to fructify SDGs and targets, and monitoring quantitative and quality performance. Further, just as the Inter-

Agency and Expert Group on Sustainable Development of the UN has been designing and finalising the performance indicators of SDGs targets, the NITI Aayog in collusion with the Ministry of Statistics and Programme Implementation (MoSPI) of India, has also set in motion a parallel exercise to identify gaps in baseline data for several SDGs targets for the country and also for the states of India, and also help in evolving indicators for the SDG goals and targets as the country does not have clear numerical targets for many of SDGs targets in India and the states.

The Philosophy of 'One World' is embedded in the core values of India's civilization which echoes and resonates with the SD Summit Declaration and is very compatible with SDGs's spirit. The said spirit is the hall-mark of all SDG-related initiatives in India.A brief description of the overall approach and initiatives are covered hereunder.

Sabka Saath Sabka Vikas

The country's national development goals are interwoven with the very spirit of SDGs even before it got fully crystallized. Sabka Saath Sabka Vikas, forms the cornerstone of India's national development agenda and reflected towards "Collective Effort, Inclusive Development". This has also been fast-tracked in the recently released Three-Year Action Agenda covering years 2017-18 to 2019-20 in the post Summit days.

Role of Parliament

Another notable feature in the way-forwarding of the SDG initiatives is through the Parliament of the country. Lok Sabha, the Lower House of the Parliament, has organized several discussions on the SDGs with parliamentarians from both Houses as part of the Speaker's Research Initiative. It has also organized several forums to develop policy and action perspectives on elimination of poverty, promoting gender equality and addressing climate change. These include the National Women's Legislators' Conference as well as the second BRICS Women Parliamentarians Forum. The Forum observed that women parliamentarians can make a significant contribution towards shaping public opinion in favour of the new global development goals. The Forum brought out the 'Jaipur Declaration' expressing its commitment to the SDGs.

The South Asian Speakers' Summit on SDGs was another regional initiative organized in 2017. The Summit deliberated on the theme 'Strengthening Regional Cooperation and Resources for SDGs'. It urged parliamentarians to collectively advance action among all stakeholders for mobilizing additional resources in order to achieve the SDG targets in a timely manner.

Key role of sub-national set-ups

An important aspect of SDG initiatives in India is its close linkage with sub-national set-ups. Given India's federal structure of governance, the focus has been on laying down the groundwork for common understanding on concept building, values clarifications, coordination and monitoring and reporting mechanisms in the midst of great diversity of the country. Responsibilities have been divided among various bodies that will lead the efforts of implementing ministries, departments and agencies at central and state levels. The appropriate role of rural and urban local bodies have been worked for them.

Revisiting India's statistical system

India's statistical system and institutions are being reoriented in the context of huge need for data collection, analysis and monitoring and reporting for 17 SDGs for national and sub-national levels. The Ministry of Statistics & Programme Implementation (MoSPI) is about to evolve national indicators in light of the global SDG indicators. After extensive discussions and a national workshop, the Ministry is about to finalise a monitoring framework for SDG indicators after wider consultation in the public domain. Along with the development of the national SDG indicators, the statistical system is also geared to measure achievements at sub-national levels.

Partnership with Civil Society Groups and Corporate sector organisations

Civil Society Organizations have been working on SDG-related issues from the grassroots to the national level. Working individually and in coalitions, they have also partnered with the government to provide inputs, create awareness and offer feedback. Their initiatives include the following:

(a) Preparing information education and communication materials on SDGs, conducting capacity building workshops and awareness campaigns;

(b) Supporting states with integrating SDGs into the planning and implementation process;

(c) Highlighting issues of sustainable energy management and climate justice for necessary policy action at the state and national levels; and

(d) Conducting research and documentation on SDGs as well as their relevance to the rights and entitlements of various vulnerable sections of society.

Similarly, Corporate sector organisations have been playing import role in holding extensive consultations and initiated actions in various areas including environmental sustainability, innovative climate action and inclusive development strategies on various themes. Apart from working with organisations within the industry and related sectors, they have also worked jointly with the government and civil society to develop innovative solutions and courses of action.

Eradication of poverty

The national approach towards economic growth, infrastructure development and industrialisation have been kept in the forefront in country's commitment towards eradication of poverty and social inclusion and empowerment of the poor Under Nationally Determined Contributions, India remains committed to protecting the environment even while combating poverty and made efforts to minimising the emissions intensity of GDP as well as creating an additional carbon sink.

A noteworthy initiative for eradication of poverty is the Mahatma Gandhi National Rural Employment Guarantee Act (MGNREGA) which provides a legal guarantee of a minimum of 100 days of wage employment per household every year for unskilled workers in rural areas. The programme generated over 2 billion person-days of employment during 2016-17. Women and disadvantaged groups have been the largest beneficiaries of the programme accounting for 56% and 39% of person-days of work generated during the said period. Another initiative relevant to this Goal is the Pradhan Mantri Jan Dhan Yojana (PMJDY), launched in 2014 for ensuring access to the entire gamut of financial services, including banking, credit, insurance and pension. Under this programme, 280 million new accounts have been opened thus far with deposits amounting to INR 639 billion (USD 9.9 billion).

Importance assigned to the Centrally Sponsored Schemes

Centrally Sponsored Schemes(CSS) play critical role in providing flexible fund to address any given objective through dedicated scheme (s) to the states of India. These on-going CSS have big role to provide funding support to the implementation of SDGs sustainably. Accordingly, the NITI Aayog carried out a detailed mapping of Centrally Sponsored Schemes and major government initiatives of Nodal Central Ministries as relevant to 17 Goals and 169 targets. Most sub-national governments have also carried out a similar mapping of the SDGs and targets to the departments and programmes in their respective states. This strategy has been of immense help in addressing the SDGs.

Diversity of State Level Initiatives

Based on geo-physical, socio-cultural and economic diversity of the states of India, most of the states, have designed their own model of SDGS initiatives based on ground realities and meet deficits of the intended SDG outcome. The state level initiatives that deserve special mention include Assam's Centre for SDGs under the Planning and Development, Andhra Pradesh's Vision 2029, Bihar's roadmap for SDG implementation, Haryana's Vision 2030 document, Maharashtra's focus on balanced regional development, Kerala's elaborate indicators and standards for achieving the SDGs, Karnataka's focus on technology,Madhya Pradesh's SDG cell at State Planning Commission, Tamil Nadu's focus on infrastructure development in six major sectors and Punjab's SDGs support process under the Planning Department.

Chapter - 10

India's Voluntary National Review Report on Implementation of Sustainable Development Goals on July 2017

At para 82 of the Declaration of the Sustainable Development Summit, 2015 it has been enjoined that a high-level political forum will be set up to work coherently with the General Assembly, the Economic and Social Council and others to review annual progress report on the Sustainable Development Goals. The central platform for international follow-up and review of the 2030 Agenda is the High-Level Political Forum (HLPF), which has started meeting annually since 2016 under the auspices of the UN Economic and Social Council (ECOSOC).The high-level political forum(HLPF) would provide a strong evidence-based instrument to support policymakers in promoting poverty eradication and sustainable development. Reviews will be based on reports submitted voluntarily by stake holders including the developed and developing countries as well as relevant United Nations entities. India submitted the Voluntary National Review Report(VNR) on Implementation of Sustainable Development Goals to the High-Level Political Forum on Sustainable Development on July 2017. The VNR captures, in a way, the status report in the post SDG Summit on SDGs which could be the basis for future monitoring. A summary statement, as collected from the website of the NITI Aayog, as presented to the High-Level Political Forum on Sustainable Development, on July 2017 is captured hereunder:

India's efforts to operationalize SDGs have been conceptualised to run through intensification of national development goals already in place. The core philosophy for the big historical journey towards realisation of SDGs is based on "Sabka Saath Sabka Vikas" meaning "Collective Efforts for Inclusive Development" as coined by the Prime Minister of India and has become the very cornerstone of India's national development agenda.The NITI Aayog, the coordinator on SDGs in India, has recently released ' Three-Year Action Agenda' covering years 2017-18 to 2019-20,prepared with active participation of the sub-national governments. While targeting economic growth, infrastructure development and industrialisation, the country's war against poverty focussed social inclusion and empowerment of the poor. India remains committed to protecting the environment. Under its Nationally Determined Contributions, India has committed to minimising the emissions intensity of GDP as well as creating an additional carbon sink. Reinforcing India's commitment to the national development agenda and SDGs, the country's Parliament has organized several forums to develop policy and action perspectives on elimination of poverty, promoting gender equality and addressing climate change. The NITI Aayog, with the Prime Minister as its chairperson, provides overall coordination and leadership. The institution has carried out a detailed mapping of the 17 Goals and 169 targets to Nodal Central Ministries, Centrally Sponsored Schemes and major government initiatives. Most sub-national governments have carried out a similar mapping of the SDGs and targets to the departments and programmes in their respective states. The Ministry of Statistics & Programme Implementation has developed a list of draft national indicators in light of the global SDG indicators. This draft has been placed in the public domain for wider consultation. Several of the Government's programmes are set to directly contribute to advancement of the SDG agenda. A noteworthy example is the Pradhan Mantri Jan Dhan Yojana (PMJDY) which is the world's largest financial inclusion programme. By leveraging PMJDY, Aadhaar (biometric identity system) and mobile telephony, the Government has disbursed a cumulative amount of INR 1.6 trillion (USD 25 billion) to 329 million beneficiaries through Direct Benefit Transfers.This has helped to significantly enhance the efficiency of Government programmes. While the central government has sponsored schemes to provide employment, connect villages to cities through roads, build houses for the poor and offer education in the states, various sub-groups of Chief Ministers have come forward to give valuable advice to the central government on such important matters as digital payments, skill development and the Swachh Bharat Abhiyaan (Clean India Campaign).

The process of VNR preparation,as stated earlier, was led by the NITI Aayog, the principal coordinator for SDGs in India. Based on reports from sub-national level, state and union territory governments on various facets of the SDGs, this VNR restricts on the progress made towards achieving Goals 1, 2, 3, 5, 9, 14 and 17, as agreed upon in the HLPF as focus areas for the year 2017. Needless to mention, however, is that the nature of SDGs is such that the advancement of one global goal may lead to progress in other goals as well.

Goal 1: End Poverty in All its Forms Everywhere

The report says that the rapid growth in India has achieved following the economic reforms initiated in 1991 and led to significant reduction in poverty. Poverty has fallen across all economic, social and religious groups nationally and in all states in the post-reform era. Sustained growth (6.2% from 1993-94 to 2003-04 and 8.3% from 2004-05 to 2011-12) has created gainful employment and helped raise wages thereby directly empowering the poor. It has also brought the government an increased volume of revenues enabling it to sustain a high level of social spending and, thus, doubling the direct effect of growth on poverty.

Several large-scale anti-poverty programmes have been implemented. The Mahatma Gandhi National Rural Employment Guarantee Act, for instance, has generated over 2 billion person-days of employment during 2016-17 alone, largely for the disadvantaged sections of society. Additionally, initiatives have been launched for providing pension and insurance to workers in the unorganised sector, widows and the differently abled. Over 130 million people have accessed life and accident insurance under these programmes.

Further, efforts are underway to universalise access to basic services. In order to achieve the goal of housing for all by 2022, direct financial assistance is being extended to poor households. Nearly 3.21 million houses were constructed last year as part of this initiative in rural areas. Programmes are also being implemented for ensuring access to education, health and nutrition security, with a special focus on vulnerable groups such as women and children. Other priority areas are drinking water and sanitation. Currently, nearly 77.5% of rural habitations are being provided with 40 litres of drinking water per capita on a daily basis. Another 18.9% habitations have been covered partially thus far. Over 63.7% of households in rural areas had access to an improved sanitation facility in 2016-17 as compared to 29.1% in 2005-06. With respect to clean sources of cooking fuel, over 22 million families have been provided with Liquefied Petroleum Gas connections under the Pradhan Mantri Ujjwala Yojana. Between 2005-06 and 2015-16, households having access to clean fuel have increased from 25.5% to 43.8%.

Goal 2: End hunger, achieve food security and improved nutrition and promote sustainable

Agriculture

The report says that significant progress has been made in improving food and nutrition security. For instance, stunting among children less than 5 years has declined from 48% to 38.4% between 2005-06 and 2015-16. During the same period, the percentage of underweight children has declined from 42.5% to 35.7%.The absolute levels of stunted and underweight children, however, remain high. To address this, a number of schemes are being implemented. For instance, more than 800 million people are covered in India by providing the food grains at affordable prices through the Public Distribution System. The Mid-Day-Meal Programme is providing nutritious cooked meals to 100 million children in primary schools. Additionally,food distribution governance is being strengthened through the digitization of ration cards and an online grievance redressal mechanism. Further, sustainable and climate-adaptive agriculture has been boosted by, inter alia, promoting organic farming and issuing of 62 million Soil Health Cards to farmers. A comprehensive plan is also being implemented for doubling farmers' income by 2022

Goal 3: Ensure healthy lives and promote wellbeing for all at all ages

The report says that India has made significant strides in improving various health indicators. The Infant Mortality Rate has declined from 57 in 2005-06 to 41 in 2015-16. Similarly, Under-5 Mortality Rate has fallen from 74 to 50 over the same period. This has been enabled, at least partially, by a significant improvement in vaccination coverage for children between 12-23 months of age. Moreover, institutional deliveries have increased from 38.7% in 2005-06 to 78.9% in 2015-16. The country's strategy in health is focused on providing essential services to the entire population, with a special emphasis on the poor and vulnerable groups.

The National Health Policy, 2017 has specified targets for universalising primary health care, achieving further reductions in infant and under-5 mortality, preventing premature deaths due to non-communicable diseases as well as increasing government expenditure on health. A composite index is being used to monitor and incentivise improvements in health services delivery across states in the country. The government is aiming to immunize all unimmunized and partially immunized children against vaccine preventable diseases by 2020. Towards achieving universal health coverage, a health insurance cover of INR 100,000 (USD 1,563) is being extended to all poor families.

Goal 5: Achieve gender equality and empower all women and girls

The report says that while much progress remains to be made, a number of indicators pertaining to the status of women in India have moved in the right direction over the years. For instance, 68.4% of women were literate in 2015-16, as compared to 55.1% in 2005-06. Additionally, 53% of women were independently using a bank or savings account in 2015-16, which is a significant improvement from 15.1% in 2005-06.

Numerous measures have been put in place for promoting gender equality. For example, the Beti Bachao Beti Padao (Save the Girl Child, Educate the Girl Child) initiative focuses on a comprehensive package of interventions for the girl child including those pertaining to education and protection.

The Maternity Benefit Programme protects women from wage loss during the first six months after childbirth. Further, several programmes are being implemented for enabling greater participation of women in the work force.

Goal 9: Build resilient infrastructure, promote inclusive and sustainable industrialization and foster innovation

The report says that all forms of transportation - roads, railways, civil aviation and waterways - are being rapidly expanded. Road connectivity and electricity are being brought to all villages. The Bharat Broadband Network Ltd. initiative is aiming to provide high-speed broadband connectivity to all village councils in the country. Over the last five years, there has been a consistent growth in installed electricity generation capacity. The installed capacity in non-fossil-fuel sectors has grown by 51.3% and more than doubled in the renewable energy sector (solar, wind, bio- and small hydro power).Further, India is making efforts to become an Information Technology and manufacturing hub through its 'Make in India' campaign. These efforts have greatly accelerated Foreign Direct Investment (FDI) inflows and helped the country sustain an average growth of 7.5% during the last three financial years (2014-15 to 2016-17). Employment-intensive manufacturing segments are being boosted by providing easy credit to small-scale business entrepreneurs. Additionally, the 'Start-up India' programme promotes entrepreneurship and labour-intensive economic growth.

Goal 14: Conserve and sustainably use the oceans, seas and marine resources

The report says that a clear agenda has been formulated for promoting the 'Blue Revolution'. For tracking the levels of marine pollution along the coastline, the country has developed the Coastal Ocean Monitoring and Prediction. System. Additionally, an oil spill management system has been put in place for responding to emergencies arising out of oil spills. Further, the Integrated National Fisheries Action Plan, 2016 is being implemented to promote the livelihoods of fishing communities as well as the ecological integrity of the marine environment. Giving new impetus to port-led development, the Sagarmala programme is improving port connectivity, port-linked industrialization and coastal community development.

Goal 17: Revitalize the global partnership for sustainable development

The report says that while working towards revitalising the global partnership for the achievement of the SDGs, India reaffirms the principle of common but differentiated responsibilities. Despite significant efforts for domestic resource mobilisation, India is unlikely to gather sufficient revenues for achieving the SDGs. Therefore, India reiterates that the developed countries have an essential obligation to provide financial assistance to the developing countries, especially for global public goods such as climate change mitigation and control of pandemics, so that they can fully achieve the SDGs. India also highlights the need for international cooperation for curbing illicit financial flows, defining aid unambiguously and establishing robust systems for monitoring commitments made by donor countries.

A path-breaking tax reform agenda is being readied in the country to optimise domestic resource mobilization. This includes direct tax reforms as well as the Goods and Services Tax (GST), a uniform and simplified form of indirect taxation. An innovative tax like the Swachh Bharat Cess (Clean India Cess) has also been levied for mobilizing resources for the Clean India Mission. Additionally, implementation of the budget responsibility legislation is ensuring predictable and sustainable budgeting as well as long-term debt sustainability. Proactive policy reforms have boosted the FDI flows during the last three fiscal years to USD 156 billion including a record-breaking USD 56 billion in the latest fiscal year.

To enable the implementation of development interventions by sub-national governments, the fiscal devolution to states has been increased substantially (from 32 to 42% of the central pool of tax proceeds).Initiatives are also being undertaken to enhance development cooperation with neighbouring and other countries of the global South. For instance, the South Asia Satellite was launched in May 2017 for sharing data with neighbours.

Lastly, efforts are underway at the national-level for finalizing the indicators that will enable monitoring of the progress made on the SDGs. The government is also considering setting up a high-level Committee headed by the Chief Statistician of India to oversee the monitoring framework for SDGs at the nationallevel.While national efforts are paramount, global technical support is important in various areas including developing methodologies for data collection as well as monitoring and evaluation.

Part - V

Goal-wise Sustainable Development Initiatives in India

Chapter - 11

Sustainable Development Goal 1
End poverty in all its forms everywhere

The humanity's journey for ending poverty by the UN system began with the landmark commitment in the year 2000 to "spare no effort to free our fellow men, women and children from the abject and dehumanizing conditions of extreme poverty" which shaped into an inspiring framework of eight goals, known as Millennium Development Goals(MDGs). The UN Secretary General observed at the summary of 'The Millennium Development Goals Report 2015' that 'the global mobilization behind the Millennium Development Goals has produced the most successful anti-poverty movement in history. The global initiative helped to lift more than one billion people out of extreme poverty, to make inroads against hunger and galvanized international and national public opinion to put people and their immediate needs at the forefront. The Report also noted that despite enormous progress, 800 millions of poor people still live in poverty and hunger at the end of the life span of the MDGs. Over 160 million children under age five have inadequate height for their age due to insufficient food. Almost half of global workers are still working in vulnerable conditions, rarely enjoying the benefits associated with decent work. With global action, these numbers can only be turned around.

The Interactive Dialogue initiated for ending poverty and hunger before the Sustainable Development Summit,2015 noted that 'Ending poverty is a matter of human dignity, and leaving no one behind' will require a multi-dimensional perspective that addresses their social, economic and environmental drivers. It must also tackle inequality and systemic and structural issues and interconnected factors. It was also noted that Economic growth is necessary, but not sufficient condition, to accelerate the reduction of poverty and hunger. Future prosperity also demands that economic growth no longer degrades the environment. Climate change must be halted. It also emphasised the need on building resilience to shocks and disasters and appropriate risk management plans and strategies, together with strong social protection frameworks.

The Fact-sheet on Goal 1 that was placed at the time of Sustainable Development Summit, 2015 says that globally, the number of people living in extreme poverty has declined by more than half from 1.9 billion in 1990. However, 836 million people still live in extreme poverty. About one in five persons in developing regions lives on less than $1.25 per day. High poverty rates are often found in small, fragile and conflict-affected countries and one in four children under age five in the world has inadequate height for his or her age.

The UN Secretary General's observation on "Progress towards the Sustainable Development Goals" vide E/2016/75 stated that for removing poverty in all its manifestations, the access to basic services has to be increased along with those harmed by climate-related extreme events as well. He noted that the international poverty line has since been revised at $1.90 or below per person per day. For eliminating extreme poverty will require a significant change from historical growth rates as distinct from those witnessed from 2002 to 2015 level. In the decade beginning in 2002, with international poverty rate on less than $1.25 per day, the proportion of the world's population living below the poverty line dropped by half, from 26 per cent to 13 per cent. If growth rates during those 10 years prevail for the next 15 years, the global extreme poverty rate will likely to fall to 4 per cent by 2030, assuming that growth benefits all income groups of the population equally. However, if the growth rates over the longer period of 20 years prevail, the global poverty rate will likely to be around 6 per cent. In 2015, 10.2 per cent of the world's workers were living with their families on less than $1.90 per person per day. Young people happened to be in the category of the working poor: 16 per cent of all employed youth aged 15 to 24 were considered working poor, compared to 9 per cent of adults. In other words, eliminating extreme poverty will require a significant change from historical growth rates.

Referring further for an end to poverty in all its manifestations by 2030, the UN Secretary General also pointed out the need to ensure social protection for the poor and vulnerable and support to people harmed by climate-related extreme events and other economic, social and environmental shocks and disasters. He also cautioned that despite progress over the past decade, increasing social protection for those most in need remains a priority. Globally, 18,000 children still die each day from poverty-related causes, and only 28 per cent of employed women are effectively protected through contributory and non-contributory maternity cash benefits. Most poor people remain outside social protection systems, especially in low-income countries. Of the entire population, only 1 out of 5 receive any type of social protection in low-income countries, compared with 2 out of 3 in upper-middle-income countries. He also observed that Disaster risk reduction is essential to ending poverty and fostering sustainable development and that Disaster risk is disproportionally higher in poorer countries with weaker institutions.

Based on the above observations, it would be appropriate to reiterate the Goal 1 of the SDGs, its targets and related indicators to keep it in the up-fronts, in sequential order, before addressing India's initiatives on ending poverty in all its forms everywhere. It would be worth mentioning the indicators captured here under contained the revised list of global Sustainable Development Goal Indicators as agreed by the Statistical Commission at its forty seventh session, in March 2016

Goal 1. End poverty in all its forms everywhere

1.1 By 2030, eradicate extreme poverty for all people everywhere, currently measured as people living on less than $1.25 a day

1.1.1 Proportion of population below the international poverty line, by sex, age, employment status and geographical location (urban/rural)

1.2 By 2030, reduce at least by half the proportion of men, women and children of all ages living in poverty in all its dimensions according to national definitions

1.2.1 Proportion of population living below the national poverty line, by sex and age

1.2.2 Proportion of men, women and children of all ages living in poverty in all its dimensions according to national definitions

1.3 Implement nationally appropriate social protection systems and measures for all, including floors, and by 2030 achieve substantial coverage of the poor and the vulnerable

1.3.1 Proportion of population covered by social protection floors/ systems, by sex, distinguishing children, unemployed persons, older persons, persons with disabilities, pregnant women, newborns, working jury victims and the poor and the vulnerable

1.4 By 2030, ensure that all men and women, in particular the poor and the vulnerable, have equal rights to economic resources, as well as access to basic services, ownership and control over land and other forms of property, inheritance, natural resources, appropriate new technology and financial services, including microfinance

1.4.1 Proportion of population living in households with access to basic services

1.4.2 Proportion of total adult population with secure tenure rights to land, with legally recognized documentation and who perceive their rights to land as secure, by sex and by type of tenure

1.5 By 2030, build the resilience of the poor and those in vulnerable situations and reduce their exposure and vulnerability to climate-related extreme events and other economic, social and environmental shocks and disasters

1.5.1 Number of deaths, missing persons and directly affected persons attributed to disasters per 100,000 populations

1.5.2 Direct economic loss attributed to disasters in relation to global gross domestic product (GDP)

1.5.3 Number of countries that adopt and implement national disaster risk reduction strategies in line with the Sendai Framework for Disaster Risk Reduction 2015-2030

1.5.4 Proportion of local governments that adopt and implement local disaster risk reduction strategies in line with national disaster risk reduction strategies

1.a Ensure significant mobilization of resources from a variety of sources, including through enhanced development cooperation, in order to provide adequate and predictable means for developing countries, in particular least developed countries, to implement programmes and policies to end poverty in all its dimensions

1.a.1 Proportion of domestically generated resources allocated by the government directly to poverty reduction programmes

1.a.2 Proportion of total government spending on essential services (education, health and social protection)

1.a.3 Sum of total grants and non-debt-creating inflows directly allocated to poverty reduction programmes as a proportion of GDP

1.b Create sound policy frameworks at the national,regional and international levels, based on pro-poor and gender-sensitive development strategies, to support accelerated investment in poverty eradication actions

1.b.1 Proportion of government recurrent and capital spending to sectors that disproportionately benefit women, the poor and vulnerable groups

The goals and targets per se are important from the angle of programme vision and intended outcome; however from the perspective of monitoring the performance, indicators do play critical role. Since indicator-design is essentially an expert professional skill- job requiring to keep harmony with overall goals and targets of the Sustainable Development Summit as embodied in paragraph 75 of Transforming our World: The 2030 Agenda for Sustainable Development mentioned: "the Goals and targets will be followed-up and reviewed using a set of global indicators. These will be complemented by indicators at the regional and national levels which will be developed by member states, in addition to the outcomes of work undertaken for the development of the baselines for those targets where national and global baseline data does not yet exist".

Needless to mention that purpose of SDG indicators is twofold; first it acts as a management tool to help countries develop implementation and monitoring strategies for achieving the SDGs and to monitor progress and secondly, it works as a report card, to measure progress towards achieving a target and ensure the accountability of governments to their citizens. As a matter of fact Agenda 21 of the SD Summit also called on countries and the international community to develop indicators of sustainable development. Such indicators were needed to increase focus on sustainable development and assist decision-makers at all levels to adopt sound national sustainable development policies.

Be that as it may, the Global Indicator Framework as designed by the UN Statistical Commission at its 47th Session in March 2016 and adopted thereafter by the Economic and Social Council and the General Assembly, are as follows:

Indicators of Goal-1

1.1.1 Proportion of population below the international poverty line, by sex, age, employment status and geographical location (urban/rural)

1.2.1 Proportion of population living below the national poverty line, by sex and age

1.2.2 Proportion of men, women and children of all ages living in poverty in all its dimensions according to national definitions

1.3.1 Proportion of population covered by social protection floors/systems, by sex, distinguishing children, unemployed persons, older persons, persons with disabilities, pregnant women, newborns, working jury victims and the poor and the vulnerable

1.4.1 Proportion of population living in households with access to basic services

1.4.2 Proportion of total adult population with secure tenure rights to land, with legally recognized documentation and who perceive their rights to land as secure, by sex and by type of tenure

1.5.1 Number of deaths, missing persons and directly affected persons attributed to disasters per 100,000 population

1.5.2 Direct economic loss attributed to disasters in relation to global gross domestic product (GDP)

1.5.3 Number of countries that adopt and implement national disaster risk reduction strategies in line with the Sendai Framework for Disaster Risk Reduction 2015-2030

1.5.4 Proportion of local governments that adopt and implement local disaster risk reduction strategies in line with national disaster risk reduction strategies

1.a.1 Proportion of domestically generated resources allocated by the government directly to poverty reduction programmes

1.a.2 Proportion of total government spending on essential services (education, health and social protection)

1.a.3 Sum of total grants and non-debt-creating inflows directly allocated to poverty reduction programmes as a proportion of GDP

1.b.1 Proportion of government recurrent and capital spending to sectors that disproportionately benefit women, the poor and vulnerable groups

Given the task of eradicating poverty and hunger and leaving no one behind, it would require every country to adopt and adapt the 2030 Agenda to their national situations by reviewing policies, plans and institutions to ensure that the efforts to eradicate poverty is addressed in all interconnected issues, such as: inclusive growth, livelihoods and employment, access to basic infrastructure and services, food security; nutrition, health; education, greater equality, improved agricultural productivity and the sustainable use of natural resources. In this gigantic task of removing poverty of all persons in India, it would be appropriate to understand, at the beginning, the extent of poverty size at national and regional level in our country context. The statistical data base, even if it is not updated, provides the needed background of poverty-profile of the country as it very often captures disaggregated regional and rural and urban data as well. It would be worthwhile to cover the said historical poverty journey.

Historically, the poverty estimate of India has been the onerous duty of the erstwhile Planning Commission and the first poverty line study in India was undertaken in 1962 by a Working Group set up by the Government of India. The Planning Commission defined the poverty level as below the average per capita daily intake of 2400 calories in rural areas and 2100 calories for urban areas. Based on this accepted norms, poverty estimates were made from time to time with adjustment in the cost of living index. The simplest measure of poverty was given by head count ratio, which essentially measured the percentage of people below the poverty line. All estimates of poverty usually follow the head count ratio in India for simplicity as against world bank norm of S1 earlier or S I.9 now. The floor level of poverty monitoring for SDG-1 remains, however, at S 1.25.

Be that as it may, let us follow the norms of poverty estimate of India, as captured in the MDG 2014 India Country Report. It has shown the Poverty Head Count Ratio (Tendulkar Methodology), as published by the erstwhile Planning Commission.

Table 11.1: Poverty Head Count Ratio (Tendulkar Methodology)

Sl. No.	*States/U.T.'s*	*1990 est*	*1993-94*	*2004-05*	*2011-12*	*Likely achievement 2015*	*2015*
1.	Andhra Pradesh	49.74	44.6	29.9	9.2	8.27	24.87
2.	Arunachal Pradesh	63.51	54.5	31.1	34.67	27.72	31.76
3.	Assam	57.92	51.8	34.4	31.98	27.34	28.96
4.	Bihar	62.28	60.5	54.4	33.74	33.03	31.14
5.	Chhattisgarh	51.32	50.9	49.4	39.93	39.82	25.66
6.	Delhi	16.49	15.7	13.1	9.91	9.34	8.25
7.	Goa	19.78	20.8	25	5.09	5.09	9.89
8.	Gujarat	39.62	37.8	31.8	16.63	15.98	19.81
9.	Haryana	40.02	35.9	24.1	11.16	9.87	20.01
10.	Himachal Pradesh	38.72	34.6	22.9	8.06	7.17	19.36
11.	Jammu& Kashmir	31.74	26.3	13.2	10.35	7.99	15.87
12.	Jharkhand	65.74	60.7	45.3	36.96	33.25	32.87
13.	Karnataka	55.11	49.5	33.4	20.91	18.29	27.55
14.	Kerala	35.51	31.3	19.7	7.05	6.15	17.76
15.	Madhya Pradesh	43.57	44.6	48.6	31.65	31.65	21.78
16.	Maharashtra	50.85	47.8	38.1	17.35	16.42	25.43
17.	Manipur	75.40	65.1	38	36.89	29.93	37.70
18.	Meghalaya	43.57	35.2	16.1	11.87	8.86	21.79
19.	Mizoram	10.99	11.8	15.3	20.4	20.40	5.50
20.	Nagaland	25.50	20.4	9	18.88	13.29	12.75
21.	Odisha	59.63	59.1	57.2	32.59	32.96	29.81
22.	Puducherry	38.27	30.9	14.1	9.69	7.25	19.14
23.	Punjab	22.83	22.4	20.9	8.26	8.36	11.41
24.	Rajasthan	39.44	38.3	34.4	14.71	14.62	19.72
25.	Sikkim	31.99	31.8	31.1	8.19	8.59	16.00
26.	Tamil Nadu	50.20	44.6	28.9	11.28	9.91	25.10
27.	Tripura	31.07	32.9	40.6	14.05	15.96	15.53
28.	Uttarakhand	31.81	32	32.7	29.43	29.81	15.91
29.	Uttar Pradesh	50.67	48.4	40.9	11.26	11.14	25.34
30.	West Bengal	40.92	39.4	34.3	19.98	19.37	20.46
	All India	47.80	45.3	37.2	21.9	20.74	23.90

Source: MDG 2014 India Country Report.

It appears from Table-11.1 that the all-India Poverty Head Count Ratio (PHCR - percentage below the national poverty line) has declined by 15 percentage points from 37.2% in 2004-05 to 21.9% in 2011-12. The percentage of people below the national poverty line has narrowed down to a level less than half of its position in 1990,and met the MDG target year of 2015.However, this percentage is really high for eradication of poverty when viewed from the SDG target of Eradicating poverty and hunger, and leaving no one behind.

It is worthwhile to mention that Tendulkar methodology, adopted for the poverty estimate, came in for sharp criticism subsequent to publication of 2011-12 poverty estimate and the erstwhile Planning Commission had to set up an Expert Group to 'Review the Methodology for Measurement of Poverty 'under a Technical Group of eminent economists under the Chairmanship of Dr. C. Rangarajan. The Report, since published, mentions that three out of ten Indians are poor. The report also mentioned that poverty was at 38.2 per cent in 2009-10 and then came down to 29.5 per cent in 2011-12.The Rangarajan panel also recommended to raise the daily per capita expenditure to Rs 32 from Rs 27 for the rural poor.

Based on State-wise Poverty Line in Rural and Urban areas for 2011-12, Poverty Ratio and Number of Poor in 2011-12 for the States of India, as per the methodology of the Rangarajan Committee, is as follows:

Table 11.2: Poverty Ratio and Number of Poor in 2011-12

Sl. No.	*States*	*Rural*		*Urban*		*Total*	
		% of persons	*No. of persons (in lakhs)*	*% of persons*	*No. of persons (in lakhs)*	*% of persons*	*No. of persons (in lakhs)*
1.	Andhra Pradesh	12.7	71.5	15.6	45.7	13.7	117.3
2.	Arunachal Pradesh	39.3	4.3	30.9	1.0	37.4	5.3
3.	Assam	42.0	114.1	34.2	15.4	40.9	129.5
4.	Bihar	40.1	376.8	50.8	61.4	14.3	438.1
5.	Chhattisgarh	49.2	97.9	43.7	26.9	47.9	124.8
6.	Delhi	11.9	0.5	15.7	26.3	15.6	26.7
7.	Goa	1.4	0.1	9.1	0.8	6.3	0.9
8.	Gujarat	31.4	109.8	22.2	58.9	27.4	168.8
9.	Haryana	11.0	18.4	15.3	14.0	12.5	32.4
10.	Himachal Pradesh	11.1	6.9	8.8	0.6	10.9	7.5
11.	Jammu & Kashmir	12.6	11.7	21.6	7.6	15.1	19.3
12.	Jharkhand	45.9	117.0	31.3	25.5	42.4	142.5
13.	Karnataka	19.8	74.8	25.1	60.9	21.9	136.7
14.	Kerala	7.3	12.3	15.3	26.0	11.3	38.3
15.	Madhya Pradesh	45.2	241.4	42.1	86.3	44.3	327.8
16.	Maharashtra	22.5	139.9	17.0	88.4	20.0	228.3
17.	Manipur	34.9	6.7	73.4	6.3	46.7	18.9
18.	Meghalaya	26.3	6.4	16.7	1.0	24.4	7.4
19.	Mizoram	33.7	1.8	21.5	1.2	27.4	3.1
20.	Nagaland	6.1	0.8	32.1	1.9	14.0	2.8

(Contd...)

21.	Odisha	47.8	169.0	36.3	26.0	45.9	195.0
22.	Punjab	7.4	12.9	17.6	18.7	11.3	31.6
23.	Rajasthan	21.4	112.0	22.5	39.5	21.7	151.5
24.	Sikkim	20.0	0.9	11.7	0.2	17.8	1.1
25.	Tamil Nadu	24.3	91.1	20.3	72.8	22.4	163.9
26.	Tripura	22.5	6.1	31.3	3.2	24.9	9.3
27.	Uttar Pradesh	38.1	600.9	45.7	208.2	39.8	809.1
28.	Uttarakhand	12.6	8.9	29.5	9.4	17.8	18.4
29.	West Bengal	30.1	188.6	29.0	86.8	29.7	275.4
30.	Puducherry	5.9	0.2	8.6	0.7	7.7	1.0
31.	Andaman & Nicobar Islands#	6.6	0.2	4.9	0.1	6.0	0.2
32.	Chandigarh#	12.0	0.0	21.5	2.3	21.3	2.3
33.	Dadra & Nagar Haveli#	55.2	1.0	15.3	0.3	35.6	1.3
34.	Daman & Diu#	0.0	0.0	17.6	0.4	13.7	0.4
35	Lakshadweep#	0.6	0.0	7.9	0.0	6.5	0.0
	All India	30.9	2605.2	26.4	1024.7	29.5	3629.9

UT Source: Rangarajan Committee Report.

The significance of the Rangarajan Committee Report, from the perspective of SDG, is that it has quantified the size of BPL population in India. It is a fact that this quantum of BPL population has undergone changes overtime. Nonetheless, it gives an indication of magnitude of BPL population that has to be taken care of for SDG-1.

Other benchmark data relating to poverty situation in India, as available in the MDG Report, 2015 published by the United Nations on 6th July, 2015 are also very relevant to understand the kind of SDG initiatives needed in India. The related indicators and its performance status over time are indicated below:

- Series Name: Children under five moderately or severely underweight percentage

  Goal 1. Eradicate extreme poverty and hunger

  Target 1.C Halve, between 1990 and 2015, the proportion of people who suffer from hunger

  Indicator 1.8 Prevalence of underweight children under five years of age

Last updated 6 July 2015

Country	1992	1993	1997	1999	2006
India	52.8	51.2	38.4	46.3	43.5

Source: unstat/Millennium Indicators.

- Series Name: Children under five severely under-weight, percentage

  Goal 1. Eradicate extreme poverty and hunger

Target 1.C Halve, between 1990 and 2015, the proportion of people who suffer from hunger

Indicator 1.8 Prevalence of underweight children under five years of age

Last updated 6 July 2015

Country	1992	1993	1997	1999	2006
India	-	24.3	-	20.6	17.4

Source: unstat/Millennium Indicators.

- Series Name: Population under nourishment, percentage

  Goal 1. Eradicate extreme poverty and hunger

  Target 1.C Halve, between 1990 and 2015, the proportion of people who suffer from hunger

  Indicator 1.9 Proportion of population below minimum level of dietary energy consumption

Last updated 6 July 2015

Country	1991	1992	1993	1994	1995	1996	1997	1998	1999	2000	2001
India	23.7	22.2	22.4	22.1	21.6	20.5	19.2	18.0	17.3	17.0	17.5

contd...

2002	2003	2004	2005	2006	2007	2008	2009	2010	2011	2012	2013
18.6	19.9	20.9	21.2	20.5	18.9	17.2	16.2	17.2	15.7	15.6	15.4

Source: unstat/Millennium Indicators.

At the international level, the World Bank is recognised as the nodal agency for the estimation of poverty. The World Bank has of late revised the global poverty line from $1.25 a day to $1.90 a day (approximately Rs. 130). Based on the new cut-off ceiling of poverty rate, the World Bank has however, not worked out any revised poverty estimate for India. Under 'Global Monitoring Report 2015/2016, with caption 'Why Poverty in India could even be less', it has stated as follows:

> *"Poverty measures for India are based on the household expenditure surveys done as part of the National Sample Survey (NSS).Since the survey in the 50s,it has used 30 day recall for consumption of both food and non-food items to measure expenditures. The so called uniform reference period(URP) consumption aggregates collected in every consumption survey (except 1999/2000) provide the longest consistent series for measuring poverty in India. Historically, they have been the basis of the World Bank's poverty estimates in India at the international poverty line.*
>
> *Since 2015 is the target year for the Millennium Development Goals, the assessment of changes in poverty overtime is best based on the URP method which was used to set the baseline poverty rates for India in*

1990. As reported at this Global Monitoring Report, for 2011/12, India's poverty rate using URP based consumption was 21.2 percent.

The National Sample Survey organisation introduced a new consumption series based on modified mixed reference period(MMRP) in the 2009/11 survey. The MMRP series (which modified the 30 day recall period to a 7 day recall for some food items, and to a larger recall for low-recovery non-food consumption items was recommended as a more accurate reflexion of consumption expenditures, following experimental rounds to examine non-sampling errors. As a result of the short term recall period for food items, MMRP-based consumption expenditures in both rural and urban areas are 10-12 larger than URP-based aggregates. The higher expenditures, combined with a high population density around the poverty line, translate to a significantly lower poverty rate of 12.4 percent from 2011/12.

The MMRP, which is available from 2009/10 onword, is expected to be the consumption aggregate of choice for monitoring poverty in the future. This year MMRP-based estimate of 12.4 percent will set the baseline for future India at Global poverty estimate, one consequence of which will be a break- in the Global service."

The significance of poverty estimates, of whatever be the method and origin, is to understand the kind of journey needed to reach a poverty-free milestone by 2030. The national data on poverty estimates on the basis of given parameter is as important as the international poverty estimates on the basis of different parameters/criteria as both of them are mutually inclusive in that one may be considered as a necessary condition for addressing national programme efforts while the later may be termed as the sufficient condition to qualify as poverty-free country in the comity of nations. Furthermore, even the poverty estimates may undergo transformational change in between 2016-30,and every country might require to keep pace with the same in its poverty eradication drive.

SDG-1 and the initiatives in India :

(a) The NITI Aayog and Mapping of Initiatives under SDG-1:

The roadmap for Sustainable development Goal -1 need to be examined with reference to the basic approach and goal-specific initiatives undertaken in India. The NITI Aayog has been tasked to oversee the implementation of SDGs by the ministries of the Central Government and coordinate with States for the achievement of developmental targets as enshrined in the SDGs. The NITI Aayog tasked itself to prepare a initial draft based on mapping of the goals and targets proposed by Nodal and other Ministries in consultation with MoSPI. The schemes so mapped for Goal-1 include Urban Livelihood Mission (Core){2013}, National Rural Employment Guarantee Scheme,(Core of the

Core){2005},National Rural Livelihood Mission,(Core){2011}, National Social Assistance Programme (Core of the Core){1995} and National Land Record Management Programme {2008}.Additionally, it has done a mapping of the other relevant Centrally Sponsored Schemes (CSSs), and 'optional' Schemes being implemented by the States on goal-specific area. Most of the state governments have also carried out a similar mapping of the SDGs and targets to the departments and programmes in their respective states. A good number of ongoing Government's programmes like Pradhan Mantri Jan Dhan Yojana {2014}, Pradhan Mantri Jeevan Jyoti Bima and Yojana {2015} and Atal Pension Yojana (APY) {2015} would also directly serve the advancement of the SDG agenda Incidentally, Pradhan Mantri Jan Dhan Yojana (PMJDY) is the world's largest financial inclusion programme covering million beneficiaries through Direct Benefit Transfers. However, the most important flagship programme for poverty eradication in the country is the Mahatma Gandhi National Rural Employment Guarantee Act, largely for the disadvantaged sections of society. Additionally, for providing pension and insurance to workers in the unorganised sector, widows and the differently-abled persons schemes have benefitted over 130 million people. The universal access to basic services has been strengthened. For achieving the goal of housing for all by 2022, direct financial assistance is being extended to poor households. Similarly, schemes have been put in place including drinking water and sanitation for ensuring access to health and nutrition security to the poor with a special focus on women and children.

(b) The Voluntary National Review Report,2017

The outcomes of initiatives under SDG-1 cannot bear result overnight since outcome is a process that takes time to mature and reflect its final outcome. Be that as it may, the Voluntary National Review Report on Implementation of Sustainable Development Goals presented for United Nations High Level Political Forum 2017 is a good reference point for understanding the latest position on SDG-1 status in India. The report says that with the sustained growth (6.2% from 1993-94 to 2003-04 and 8.3% from 2004-05 to 2011-12) in India in the post-reform era of 1991, significant reduction in poverty across all economic, social and religious groups nationally and in all states has taken place by way of creating gainful employment and raised wages. The resultant increased volume of revenues also enabled it to sustain a high level of social spending which also made direct effect of growth on poverty. The flagship programme on poverty. namely, the Mahatma Gandhi National Rural Employment Guarantee Act has generated over 2 billion person-days of employment during 2016-17 alone, largely for the disadvantaged sections of society. Additionally, under pension and insurance programmes in the unorganised sector, widows and the differently –abled persons were also provided life and accident insurance for over 130 million people..

Under the goal of housing for all by 2022, direct financial assistance is being extended to poor households. Nearly 3.21 million houses were constructed in the 2016-17 as part of this initiative in rural areas. Access to education, health and nutrition security are also being provided with a special focus on vulnerable groups, women and children. Of the other basic services like drinking water and sanitation, 77.5% of rural habitations are being provided with 40 litres of drinking water per capita on a daily basis so far. Another 18.9% habitations have been covered partially thus far. Over 63.7% of households in rural areas had access to an improved sanitation facility in 2016-17 as compared to 29.1% in 2005-06. With respect to clean sources of cooking fuel, over 22 million families have been provided with Liquefied Petroleum Gas connections under the Pradhan Mantri Ujjwala Yojana. Between 2005-06 and 2015-16, households having access to clean fuel have increased from 25.5% to 43.8%.

(c) The NITI Aayog on Three Year Action Agenda

To fast-track this agenda, NITI Aayog, has recently released a Three-Year Action Agenda covering years 2017-18 to 2019-20 which begins with the objective of eliminating poverty in all its dimensions such that every citizen has access to a minimum standard of food, education, health, clothing, shelter, transportation and energy. Earlier, the Parliament of India organized several forums to develop policy and action perspectives on elimination of poverty, promoting gender equality and addressing climate change. Incidentally, the Ministry of Statistics & Programme Implementation has developed a list of draft national indicators in light of the global SDG indicators which has been placed in the public domain for wider consultation.

Addressing the poverty related issues, the NITI Aayog, in its Overview on Three Year Action Agenda stated the following:

> "The objective of eliminating poverty in all its dimensions such that every citizen has access to a minimum standard of food, education, health, clothing, shelter, transportation and energy has been at the heart of India's development efforts since Independence. The extremely low level of per-capita income and widespread poverty made it impossible for us to achieve this objective without growing the economy. Tax revenues were so meagre and the economy's needs so vast that no serious dent into poverty could be made through redistribution alone. While we substantially improved economic performance during the first four decades of independence over that during the preceding fifty years, growth remained below 4%, which was woefully inadequate for a meaningful decline in poverty.
>
> 1.2. But the signs of change began to emerge during the second half of the 1980s, with 1991 proving to be a turning point. The reforms that followed first under Prime Minister Narasimha Rao and then under Prime Minister Atal Bihari Vajpayee placed India first on a 6% growth trajectory

and then, beginning in 2003-04, on an 8% plus trajectory. Rising wages accompanied faster growth and pulled many out of abject poverty. Growth also yielded handsome gains in tax revenues, which helped expand social spending manifold, reinforcing the direct effect of growth on poverty reduction.

1.3. Although a combination of global economic developments and domestic policy choices led to a dip in the growth rate to 5.6% in 2012-13, quick corrective action in 2014, followed by sustained policy reforms, has helped the economy sustain 7% plus growth during the three years ending on 31 March 2017. Indeed, there are good prospects that we will return to the 8% plus growth trajectory in another two to three years if not sooner. Therefore, the chances of a massive cut in the poverty rate in the upcoming decade are excellent'.

(d) *Economic Survey of India, 2017-18*

The Government of India tabled the Economic Survey of India, 2017-18 in the Parliament in the Budget Session on 29th January,2018 to set the stage for the Government for the Annual Budget. The Survey contains an indepth analysis, serious research as well new policy ideas. The said Survey however, has not captured any updated status of poverty nor has specifically commented anything on outcome of any policy related interventions on poverty. It has indicated instead growth of per capita real income which has distant relationship with poverty status. Be that as it may, the real per capita income (measured in terms of per capita net national income at constant (2011-12) prices is one of the important indicators representing the welfare of people of a country. It is expected to increase from Rs. 77,803 in 2015-16 to Rs. 86,660 in 2017-18, growing at an annual average rate of 5.5 per cent. In nominal terms it increased by an average of 9.0 per cent per annum from Rs. 94,130 in 2015-16 to Rs. 111,782 in 2017-18..

(e) *Budget Initiatives of 2018-19*

The Budget document embodies not only a financial statement on resources availability and its projected expenditure, it also expresses alongside overtly and covertly the policy statement of the Government of the day. The Budget Speech of the Finance Minister of India delivered on First February,2018 is taken up to relate its relevance on SDGs. In so far as SDG-1 is concerned, the Budget Speech focuses extensively on Rural Population for improving poverty related issues. It mentions that " Over ` 3 lakh crores are spent in rural areas every year, if we add up all the programmes meant for rural poor from the Central Budget, State Budgets, Bank linkage for self-help groups, etc. with a clear focus on improving accountability, outcomes and convergence, it will be possible to achieve Mission Antyodaya to bring one crore households out of poverty and to make 50,000 gram panchayats poverty free by 2019, the 150th birth anniversary of Gandhiji. The Government intends to utilise the existing resources more effectively along with annual increases. This mission will work with a focused micro plan for sustainable livelihood for every deprived household. A composite index for poverty free gram panchayats would be developed to monitor the progress from the baseline.

The Government has made a conscious effort to reorient MGNREGA to support the resolve to double farmers' income. While providing at least 100 days employment to every rural household, MGNREGA should create productive assets to improve farm productivity and incomes. Participation of women in MGNREGA has increased to 55% from less than 48% in the past. The Finance Minster of India also stressed that the focus of the Government next year will be on providing maximum livelihood opportunities in the rural areas by spending more on livelihood, agriculture and allied activities and construction of rural infrastructure. He said, in the year 2018-19, for creation of livelihood and infrastructure in rural areas, total amount to be spent by the Ministries will be Rs.14.34 lakh crore, including extra-budgetary and non-budgetary resources of Rs.11.98 lakh crore. Apart from employment due to farming activities and self employment, this expenditure will create employment of 321 crore person days, 3.17 lakh kilometers of rural roads, 51 lakh new rural houses, 1.88 crore toilets, and provide 1.75 crore new household electric connections besides boosting agricultural growth.

Are the initiatives adequate enough ?

Generally speaking, the SDG-1 is the most important goal asking for a lot of programme interventions to trigger the process of the remaining SDGs as well. The initiatives must be bold, big and visible and possibly completely new. The initiatives under SDG-1, till date, are, however, of the nature of continuing schemes and no new and big ticket programmes have come into being since the SDGs have become functional on 1 January,2016. Even the mapping of continuing schemes by NITI Aayog does not appear to be comprehensive for SDG-1 as the ongoing livelihood related schemes under Women, SC,ST and Weaker sections have not been captured therein nor financial institutions-sponsored livelihood programmes have been indicated there. Moreover, since eradication of poverty is connected with multipronged initiatives on associated areas, it would be useful to keep them in upfront and alongside to leverage with core poverty reduction programme for optimising possible convergence. That apart, people below poverty line are not homogeneous but belong to different layers of poverty groups. Dedicated schemes on them might be useful to make direct impact on them. Further, poverty in India is also due to big family size with large number of children in many geographical locations and more particularly in some religious community. A robust population control programme has to be in place in India to prevent un-controlled number of births and thereby adding number of BPL population in India.

Monitoring Indicators do have a role to signal the kind of schemes needed for obtaining better monitoring output. Monitoring under SDGs is subject-target specific e.g. proportion of population living on less than $1.25 a day,(or below the poverty line under national definitions) by sex, age, employment status and geographical location (urban/rural); proportion of population covered by social protection floors/systems, by sex, distinguishing children, unemployed persons, older persons, persons with disabilities, pregnant women, newborns, working injury victims and the poor and the vulnerable; proportion of population living in households with access to basic services; proportion of total adult population with secure tenure rights to land, etc. Consequently, schemes with universal application may not yield desired result. Schemes need to correspond with the volume and nature of poverty in a given location. Depending on the geographical diversity and cultural plurality, the schemes must be based on objective reality. In the given context, though the member countries of the UN system would be at liberty to design their country-specific monitoring indicators, it is only desirable that Monitoring Indicators of SDG-1, under process of finalisation in India, would take into considerations a good part of UN monitoring indicators to ensure that India is on course to reach SDG-1 goalpost by 2030.

The SDG's core philosophy of 'no one should be left behind' requires that the national government has to come up with an open and transparent poverty reduction strategy under SDG-1 for the Rural and Urban areas including the Women, the Children, the Physically and Mentally challenged and other vulnerable groups located both in the rural and urban areas having different age structure e.g.after the enactment of The Right of Persons with Disabilities Act, 2016, dedicated schemes on different categories of disabled persons is urgently called for. Incidentally, schemes per se are important for obtaining a defined outcome by a given date, but by itself, it cannot be taken as substitute for strategy nor can it qualify as a strategy. A strategy is a bigger concept which embodies plan of action designed to achieve a long-term or overall aim. Schemes are mere actionable parts of that strategy to achieve the given goal. The necessity of a poverty reduction strategy is thus very real. The central government is required to publish poverty reduction strategy for guidance for the nodal central government departments and also for the states of India for focus intervention in the best interest of achieving the SDG-1 in India.

Finally, the new SDG monitoring indicators requires periodical verification of poverty status of persons falling below SDG norms of $ 1.25 per day or under our country norms as set by the Rangarajan Committee. An institutional periodical report on poverty status is, therefore, needed for the country as a whole and also for the states of India. Needless to mention, series of poverty estimates in India by the erstwhile Planning Commission earlier, including the latest poverty estimates by the Rangarajan Committee, have not much relevance now after the Sustainable Development Summit,2015 and the launching of SDGs in 1 January,2016. Such poverty reports stand now as historical records of poverty journey in India. Consequently, there is a strong case for setting up an autonomous poverty estimation institution or in the alternative, an existing premier national institute need to be empowered to periodically update the poverty status in India. Incidentally, the Annual reports of related Ministry(s) do give us a lot of valuable data on the quantitative aspects of output of a given scheme or a number of schemes but it cannot indicate the impact of aggregated and cumulative effect on poverty status at different locations on different age groups and vulnerable. Besides, poverty is an outcome of several other variables, not linked with any particular scheme (s) alone. The institutional assessment on the poverty status, based on defined norms and its time format will enable the government to know the outcome of the poverty related strategy, its programme interventions, its adequacy, its strength and weakness, its relevance in different geographical and locational variations and the like. It is high time that central government put in place such a specialized institute for conducting poverty estimates at a shorter interval of time. Such periodical poverty estimate by an institute would enable the country to find the evolving poverty status for required course correction, when needed.

Chapter - 12

Sustainable Development Goal 2

End hunger, achieve food security and improved nutrition and promote sustainable agriculture

The UN Declaration on Sustainable Development Summit 2015 resolved to end hunger and to achieve food security as a matter of priority and to end all forms of malnutrition. In furtherance of this goal, it reaffirmed the important role and inclusive nature of the Committee on World Food Security and welcomed the Rome Declaration on Nutrition and the Framework for Action. Incidentally, the Rome Declaration on Nutrition and the Framework for Action ' made a pledge to eradicate hunger and prevent all forms of malnutrition worldwide – particularly under-nutrition in children, anaemia in women and children, and to other micronutrient deficiencies. It also called for increasing investments in food systems to improve people's diets and nutrition. The Framework also proposed the creation of an enabling environment for effective action and for strengthening sustainable food systems, including investments in pro-poor agriculture and smallholder agriculture to improve diets and raise levels of nutrition; nutrition education and information; social protection; strengthened health systems for addressing specific conditions; improved water, sanitation and hygiene; and improved food safety'.

The Goal 2 of Sustainable Development Summit aims at ending hunger and all forms of malnutrition by 2030. It also commits to universal access to safe, nutritious and sufficient food at all times of the year. This will require sustainable food production systems and resilient agricultural practices, equal access to land, technology and markets and international cooperation on investments in infrastructure and technology to boost agricultural productivity. An important factor that led to the broad formulation of goal 2 on traditional targets on hunger was the need to take into account cross -sector dialogue and greater policy coherence in explicit references to land management, agricultural production methods and ecosystems. Such connections may encourage development partners to make closer links between agriculture, nutrition, food security and ecosystems much more than in the past.

Before addressing this important goal for its adoption and implementation in our country situation, it would be relevant to understand the background to the formulation of Goal-2.Globally, the proportion of undernourished people in the developing regions has fallen by almost half since 1990, from 23.3% in 1990-1992 to 12.9% in 2014-2016. However, one in nine people in the world today (795 million) are still undernourished. The vast majority of the world's hungry people live in developing countries, Asia in particular accounting for two-thirds of the total. Incidentally, poor nutrition is instrumental to nearly half (45%) of deaths in children under five – 3.1 million children each year and resulted stunted growth in the range of one in four of the world's children, with one in three children in developing countries. As a result,66 million primary school-age children in developing countries attend classes hungry. Further, globally, Agriculture is the single largest employer, providing livelihoods for 40% of today's global population. It is the largest source of income and jobs for poor rural households. 500 million small farms worldwide, most still rain- fed, provide up to 80% of food consumed in a large part of the developing world. Investing in smallholder farmers is an important way to increase food security and nutrition for the poorest, as well as food production for local and global markets.

Understandably, Interactive Dialogues played crucial role in conceptualizing SDG-2 as poverty and hunger are interlinked issues; hunger exists because of inability to meet the food requirements because of poverty. Too many people are still poor and undernourished even after the MDG intervention. Ending poverty and hunger is a matter of human dignity and a responsibility of Mankind. Eradicating poverty and hunger, and leaving no one behind will require a multi-dimensional perspective that addresses their social, economic and environmental drivers. It also needs to address interconnected factors, such as: inclusive growth; livelihoods and employment; access to basic infrastructure and services; food security; nutrition; health; education; greater equality; improved agricultural productivity and the sustainable use of natural resources.. Additionally, building resilience to shocks and disasters and appropriate risk management plans and strategies is crucial along with strong social protection frameworks. Further, national ownership and political commitment to eradicate hunger need to be buttressed by effective fiscal policies, an integrated and coherent approach to policy making, adequate resources, monitoring of progress, and accountability and transparency. Finally, partnership for development in financing and investments from a range of actors, including national and regional development banks, the private sector and other institutional investors have to be roped in. In brief, Economic growth is necessary, but not sufficient, to accelerate the reduction of poverty and hunger. Future prosperity will also require that economic growth no longer degrades the environment. Climate change must be halted.

The UN Secretary-General, on his post "Progress towards the Sustainable Development Goals" vide, E/2016/75 has also mentioned that ending hunger and malnutrition relies heavily on sustainable food production systems and resilient agricultural practices. Genetic diversity in livestock breeds is crucial for agriculture and food production since it allows for the raising of farm animals in a wide range of environments and provides the basis for diverse products and services. To increase the productive capacity of agriculture, more investment is needed, both public and private, from domestic and foreign sources. However, recent trends in government spending are not favourable. The agriculture orientation index, defined as agriculture's share of government expenditures divided by the sector's share of gross domestic product (GDP), fell globally from 0.37 to 0.25 between 2001 and 2013. The decline in the index was interrupted only temporarily during the food price crisis of 2006 to 2008, when governments increased agricultural spending. Since the late 1990s, the percentage of aid for supporting agriculture in developing countries has been stable at around 8 per cent, when measured as a share of sector-allocable aid from member countries of the Development Assistance Committee of the Organization for Economic Cooperation and Development (OECD). This has decreased, from a peak of 20 per cent in the mid-1980s, as a result of donors beginning to focus more on improving governance, building social capital and bolstering fragile States.

The Secretary General also mentions that one of the targets for Goal 2 calls for correcting and preventing distortions in world agricultural markets, including the elimination of all forms of agricultural export subsidies. Those subsidies mask market signals, reduce competitiveness and can lead to environmental damage and the inequitable distribution of benefits. That said, some progress is being made, with members of the World Trade Organization adopting a ministerial decision, in December 2015, on eliminating export subsidies for agricultural products and restraining export measures that have an equivalent effect.

Based on the above observations, it would be appropriate to reiterate once again the Goal 2 of the Sustainable Development Summit, its targets and related indicators to keep it in the up-front, in sequential order, before addressing India's initiatives on ending hunger, achieve food security and improved nutrition and promote sustainable agriculture.

Goal 2. End hunger, achieve food security and improved nutrition and promote sustainable agriculture

2.1 By 2030, end hunger and ensure access by all people, in particular the poor and people in vulnerable situations, including infants, to safe, nutritious and sufficient food all year round

2.1.1 Prevalence of undernourishment

2.1.2 Prevalence of moderate or severe food insecurity in the population, based on the Food Insecurity Experience Scale (FIES)

2.2 By 2030, end all forms of malnutrition, including achieving, by 2025, the internationally agreed targets on stunting and wasting in children under 5 years of age,and address the nutritional needs of adolescent girls, pregnant and lactating women and older persons

2.2.1 Prevalence of stunting (height for age <-2 standard deviation from the median of the World Health Organization (WHO) Child Growth Standards) among children under 5 years of age

2.2.2 Prevalence of malnutrition (weight for height >+2 or <-2 standard deviation from the median of the WHO Child Growth Standards) among children under 5 years of age, by type (wasting and overweight)

2.3 By 2030, double the agricultural productivity and incomes of small-scale food producers, in particular women, indigenous peoples, family farmers, pastoralists and fishers, including through secure and equal access to land, other productive resources and inputs, knowledge, financial services, markets and opportunities for value addition and non-farm employment

2.3.1 Volume of production per labour unit by classes of farming/pastoral/forestry enterprise size

2.3.2 Average income of small-scale food producers,by sex and indigenous status

2.4 By 2030, ensure sustainable food production systems and implement resilient agricultural practices that increase productivity and production, that help maintain ecosystems, that strengthen capacity for adaptation to climate change, extreme weather, drought, flooding and other disasters and that progressively improve land and soil quality 2.4.1 Proportion of agricultural area under productive and sustainable agriculture

2.5 By 2020, maintain the genetic diversity of seeds,cultivated plants and farmed and domesticated animals and their related wild species, including through soundly managed and diversified seed and plant banks at the national, regional and international levels, and promote access to and fair and equitable sharing of benefits arising from the utilization of genetic resources and associated traditional knowledge, as internationally agreed

2.5.1 Number of plant and animal genetic resources for food and agriculture secured in either medium or long-term conservation facilities

2.5.2 Proportion of local breeds classified as being at risk, not-at-risk or at unknown level of risk of extinction

2.a Increase investment, including through enhanced international cooperation, in rural infrastructure, agricultural research and extension services, technology development and plant and livestock gene banks in order to enhance agricultural productive capacity in developing countries, in particular least developed countries

2.a.1 The agriculture orientation index for government expenditures

2.a.2 Total official flows (official development assistance plus other official flows) to the agriculture sector

2.b Correct and prevent trade restrictions and distortions in world agricultural markets, including through the parallel elimination of all forms of agricultural export subsidies and all export measures with equivalent effect, in accordance with the mandate of the Doha Development Round

2.b.1 Agricultural export subsidies

2.c Adopt measures to ensure the proper functioning of food commodity markets and their derivatives and facilitate timely access to market information, including on food reserves, in order to help limit extreme food price volatility

2.c.1 Indicator of food price anomalies:

The goals and targets per se are important from the angle of programme vision and intended outcome; however from the perspective of monitoring the performance, indicators do play critical role. Since indicator-design is essentially an expert professional skill- job requiring to keep harmony with overall goals and targets of the Sustainable Development Summit as embodied in paragraph 75 of Transforming our World: The 2030 Agenda for Sustainable Development mentioned : "the Goals and targets will be followed-up and reviewed using a set of global indicators. These will be complemented by indicators at the regional and national levels which will be developed by member states, in addition to the outcomes of work undertaken for the development of the baselines for those targets where national and global baseline data does not yet exist".

Needless to mention that purpose of SDG indicators is twofold; first it acts as a management tool to help countries develop implementation and monitoring strategies for achieving the SDGs and to monitor progress and secondly, it works as a report card, to measure progress towards achieving a target and ensure the accountability of governments to their citizens. As a matter of fact, Agenda 21 of the SD Summit also called on countries and the international community to develop indicators of sustainable development. Such indicators were needed to increase focus on sustainable development and assist decision-makers at all levels to adopt sound national sustainable development policies.

Be that as it may, the Global Indicator Framework as designed by the UN Statistical Commission at its 47th Session in March 2016 and adopted thereafter by the Economic and Social Council and the General Assembly, are as follows :

Indicators of Goal-2

2.1.1 Prevalence of undernourishment

2.1.2 Prevalence of moderate or severe food insecurity in the population, based on the Food Insecurity Experience Scale (FIES)

2.2.1 Prevalence of stunting (height for age <-2 standard deviation from the median of the World Health Organization (WHO) Child Growth Standards) among children under 5 years of age

2.2.2 Prevalence of malnutrition (weight for height >+2 or <-2 standard deviation from the median of the WHO Child Growth Standards) among children under 5 years of age, by type (wasting and overweight)

2.3.1 Volume of production per labour unit by classes of farming/pastoral/forestry enterprise size

2.3.2 Average income of small-scale food producers, by sex and indigenous status

2.4.1 Proportion of agricultural area under productive and sustainable agriculture

2.5.1 Number of plant and animal genetic resources for food and agriculture secured in either medium or long-term conservation facilities

2.5.2 Proportion of local breeds classified as being at risk, not-at-risk or at unknown level of risk of extinction

2.a.1 The agriculture orientation index for government expenditures

2.a.2 Total official flows (official development assistance plus other official flows) to the agriculture sector

2.b.1 Agricultural export subsidies

2.c.1 Indicator of food price anomalies

Based on the overarching goal of SDG-2, the national government of the country needs to take it forward to design appropriate programme and fructify them in ensuring commensurate outcome. In such efforts, the current scenario and revealed gaps need to be taken into consideration while drawing a roadmap for related goal. The validated data in the MDG Report, 2015 published by the United Nations on 6th July, 2015 are to be used as benchmark data on related indicators on hunger and its performance status over time in India, as indicated below:

- Series Name: Children under five moderately or severely under-weight percentage

  Goal 1. Eradicate extreme poverty and hunger

  Target 1.C Halve, between 1990 and 2015, the proportion of people who suffer from hunger

  Indicator 1.8 Prevalence of underweight children under five years of age

Last updated 6 July 2015

Country	1992	1993	1997	1999	2006
India	52.8	51.2	38.4	46.3	43.5

Source: unstat/Millennium Indicators.

- Series Name: Children under five severely under-weight, percentage

  Goal 1. Eradicate extreme poverty and hunger

  Target 1.C Halve, between 1990 and 2015, the proportion of people who suffer from hunger

  Indicator 1.8 Prevalence of underweight children under five years of age

Last updated 6 July 2015

Country	1992	1993	1997	1999	2006
India	-	24.3	-	20.6	17.4

Source: unstat/Millennium Indicators

- Series Name: Population under nourishment, percentage

  Goal 1. Eradicate extreme poverty and hunger

  Target 1.C Halve, between 1990 and 2015, the proportion of people who suffer from hunger

  Indicator 1.9 Proportion of population below minimum level of dietary energy consumption

Last updated 6 July 2015

Country	1991	1992	1993	1994	1995	1996	1997	1998	1999	2000	2001
India	23.7	22.2	22.4	22.1	21.6	20.5	19.2	18.0	17.3	17.0	17.5

contd...

2002	2003	2004	2005	2006	2007	2008	2009	2010	2011	2012	2013
18.6	19.9	20.9	21.2	20.5	18.9	17.2	16.2	17.2	15.7	15.6	15.4

Source: unstat/Millennium Indicators.

Another background data on nutrition status in India is to be located in NSS 540. As against the erstwhile Planning Commission's norm of energy requirement of 2400 kcal per person per day for the rural sector and 2100 kcal for the urban sector, the trend of All-India picture of the proportion of per capita calorie intake (kcal) for the rural and urban area for the states of India for 2004-05 and 2009-10 have been captured at Table -12.1.

Table 12.1: Estimated per capita calorie intake (kcal) per day in major states

States	*Rural*		*Urban*	
	2004-05	*2009-10*	*2004-05*	*2009-2010*
Andhra Pradesh	1995	2047	2000	1975
Assam	2067	1974	2143	2003
Bihar	2049	1931	2190	2013
Chhattisgarh	1942	1926	2087	1949
Gujarat	1923	1982	1991	1983
Haryana	2226	2180	2033	1940
Jharkhand 1	1961	1900	2458	2046
Karnataka	1845	1903	1944	1987
Kerala	2014	1964	1996	1941
Madhya Pradesh	1929	1939	1954	1854
Maharashtra	1933	2051	1847	1901
Orissa	2023	2126	2139	2096
Punjab	2240	2223	2150	2062
Rajasthan	2180	2191	2116	2014
Tamil Nadu	1842	1925	1935	1963
Uttar Pradesh	2200	2064	2124	1923
Uttarakhand	2160	2179	2205	1984
West Bengal	2070	1927	2011	1851

Source: NSS report 540, Nutritional intake in India.

Finally, the latest standing of India at the Global Hunger Index, a tool designed to comprehensively measure and track at the global, regional and national levels needs also to be revisited for reference. The 2017 Global Hunger Index (GHI), calculated for 119 countries based on four indicators, namely, the percentage of the population that is undernourished, the percentage of children under age five who suffer from wasting (low weight for height),the percentage of children under age five who suffer from stunting (low height for age), and the percentage of children who die before the age of five (child mortality), has been published. India ranked 100th position with a high proportion of malnourished children among 119 countries on Global Hunger

Index (GHI) 2017 report released by Washington-based International Food Policy Research Institute. Further, more than one-fifth of the Indian children under five years weigh too little for their height and over a third are too little for their age. The position is really alarming and calls for urgent policy and programme intervention.

SDG-2 and the initiatives in India

(a) The NITI Aayog and Mapping of Initiatives under SDG-2:

The roadmap for Sustainable development Goal 2 needs to be assessed in the broader framework of the basic approach and goal-specific initiatives undertaken in India. The NITI Aayog, as mentioned earlier, has been empowered to see the implementation of SDGs by the ministries of the Central Government and coordinate with States for the achievement of developmental targets as enshrined in the SDGs. The NITI Aayog tasked itself to prepare a initial draft based on mapping of the goals and targets proposed by Nodal and other Ministries in consultation with MoSPI. The schemes so mapped for Goal-2 include 6) National Food Security Mission (Core){2007}, 7) Mission for integrated Development of Horticulture{2014-15}, 8) National Mission on Sustainable Agriculture{2013}, 9) National Oilseed and Oil Palm Mission {2013}, 10) National Mission on Agriculture Extension and Technology {2014}, 11) Rashtriya Krishi Vikas Yojana (RKVY) (ACA) (Core) {2007}, 12) National Livestock Mission (Core) {2014-15}, 13) Livestock Health and Disease Control (Core){2013}, 14) National Programme for Bovine Breeding and Dairy Development {2013}, The said map also included Targeted Public Distribution System (TPDS) {1997}, National Nutrition Mission (NNM) (Core) {2018}, National Food Security Act (NFSA) {2013}, and Mid-Day Meal Scheme (2001}.

(b) The Voluntary National Review Report for United Nations High Level Political Forum 2017 on SDG-2

The outcomes of initiatives under SDG-2 are rather distant, farsighted and linked with several issues that do not bring immediate result overnight. It will take time for resolution of interlinked issues to reflect its final outcome. Be that as it may, the Voluntary National Review Report on Implementation of Sustainable Development Goals presented to the United Nations High Level Political Forum in 2017 is a good reference point for understanding the latest position on SDG-2 status in India. The report says that significant progress has been made in improving food and nutrition security. For instance, stunting among children less than 5 years has declined from 48% to 38.4% between 2005-06 and 2015-16. During the same period, the percentage of underweight children has declined from 42.5% to 35.7%.The absolute levels of stunted and underweight children, however, remain high. To address this, a number of schemes are being implemented. For instance, more than 800 million people are covered in India by providing the food grains at affordable prices through the Public Distribution System. The Mid-Day-Meal Programme is also providing nutritious cooked meals to 100 million children in primary schools. Additionally, food distribution governance is being strengthened through the digitization of ration cards and an online grievance redressal mechanism. Further, sustainable and climate-adaptive agriculture has been boosted by, inter alia, promoting organic farming and issuing of 62 million Soil Health Cards to farmers. A comprehensive plan is also being implemented for doubling farmers' income by 2022.

(c) The NITI Aayog, Three-Year Action Agenda and SDG-2

The NITI Aayog has recently released a Three-Year Action Agenda covering years 2017-18 to 2019-20 which begins with the objective of eliminating poverty in all its dimensions such that every citizen will have access to a minimum standard of food, education, health, clothing, shelter, transportation and energy. At chapter 5 of the said Three-Year Action Agenda, it is mentioned that Agriculture (inclusive of Animal Husbandry, Forestry and Fishing) is central to the nutrition needs of India and remains the largest sector of India's economy as a source of employment. It is also stipulated that immediate actions necessary to sustain and accelerate agricultural growth may be divided into four areas. At the first instance, it emphasized the need to reform agricultural produce, marketing policies and market interventions to receive remuneration prices. Secondly, productivity of both land and water resources are low for many crops when compared with other countries and has to be stepped up. Thirdly, tenancy laws in most of the states of India are no longer adequate to serve the interests of either the landlord or the tenants though a beginning of change has been taking place recently.Finally, relief measures in the event of natural disasters need to improve adequately.

(d) Economic Survey of India, 2017-18

The Government of India tabled the Economic Survey of India, 2017-18 in the Parliament in the Budget Session on 29th January,2018 to set the stage for the Government for the Annual Budget. The Survey contains an indepth analysis, serious research as well new policy ideas. The said Survey concludes in its report that 'the agriculture sector in India is experiencing structural changes which are opening up new challenges and opportunities. The Government has initiated reforms in the field of agricultural marketing, given a big push to the use of technology in agriculture, and also adopted Direct Benefit Transfer (DBT) mode for timely delivery of extension services, credit and other inputs to small and marginal farmers. The central priority of the government will be to provide opportunities for farmers to diversify their income generating opportunities to reduce the various risks by facilitating the development of agricultural sub-sectors like livestock and fisheries'.

The Survey reiterates that transformation of agriculture and allied sector is imminent as outcome of 'appropriate policy interventions related to prices, trade, adoption of Climate Smart Agriculture, increased focus on small, marginal and women farmers. Though the share of agriculture and allied sector in GVA is on the decline, in the quest for inclusive economic development in India, agriculture sector will remain an engine of broad based growth which will reduce inequalities and provide food security".

(e) Budget Initiatives of 2018-19

The Budget document embodies not only a financial statement on resources availability and its projected expenditure, it also expresses alongside overtly and covertly the policy statement of the Government of the day. The Budget Speech of the Finance Minister of India delivered on First February, 2018 is taken up to relate its relevance on SDGs. In so far as agriculture component of SDG-2 is concerned, the Budget Speech focuses extensively on Farmers. The Finance Minister said that Government has taken up programmes to direct the benefits of structural changes and good growth to reach farmers, poor and other vulnerable sections of our society and to uplift the under-developed regions. He said that this year's Budget will consolidate these gains and particularly focus on strengthening agriculture and rural economy among others.. He said that the Government has ensured that benefits reach eligible beneficiaries and are delivered to them directly and said that Direct Benefit Transfer mechanism of India is the biggest such exercise in the world and is a global success story.

Referring to the Government's commitment to the welfare of farmers and doubling farmers' income by 2022, as required under SDG-2 target, the Finance Minister announced a slew of new schemes and measures to ensure to keep Minimum Support Price (MSP) for all unannounced kharif crops at least one and half times of their production cost after declaring the same for the majority of rabi cops. The volume of institutional credit for agriculture sector from year-to-year increased from Rs.8.5 lakh crore in 2014-15 to Rs.10 lakh crore in 2017-18 and the Finance Minister proposed to raise this to Rs.11 lakh crore for the year 2018-19. After the establishment of Dairy Infrastructure Fund, the Finance Minister announced setting up a Fisheries and Aqua culture Infrastructure Development Fund (FAIDF) for fisheries sector and an Animal Husbandry Infrastructure Development Fund (AHIDF) for financing infrastructure requirement of animal husbandry sector with a total corpus of Rs.10,000 crore for the two new funds. On the lines of "Operation Flood" a new Scheme "Operation Greens" was announced with an outlay of Rs 500 Crore to address the challenge of price volatility of perishable commodities like tomato, onion and potato with the satisfaction of both the farmers and consumers. He also announced to develop and upgrade existing 22,000 rural haats into Gramin Agricultural Markets (GrAMs) to take care of the interests of more than 86% small and marginal farmers. These GrAMs, electronically linked to e-NAM and exempted from regulations of APMCs, will provide farmers facility to make direct sale to consumers and bulk purchasers. Moreover, an Agri-Market Infrastructure Fund with a corpus of Rs.2000 crore will be set up for developing and upgrading agricultural marketing infrastructure in the 22000 Grameen Agricultural Markets (GrAMs) and 585APMCs. He said, so far 470 APMCs have been connected to e-NAM network and rest will be connected by March, 2018. The Finance Minister announced Rs 200 crore for organized cultivation of highly specialized medicinal and aromatic plants and said that the organic farming by Farmer Producer Organizations (FPOs) and Village Producers' Organizations (VPOs) in large clusters, preferably of 1000 hectares each will be encouraged. Similarly, allocation of Ministry of Food Processing has been doubled from Rs.715 crore in 2017-18 to Rs.1400 crore in 2018-19. Terming Bamboo as 'Green Gold', the Finance Minister announced a Re-structured National Bamboo Mission with an outlay of Rs.1290 crore to promote bamboo sector in a holistic manner. Under Prime Minister Krishi Sinchai Yojna-Har Khet ko Pani, 96 deprived irrigation districts will be taken up with an allocation of Rs 2600 crore. The Centre will work with the state governments to facilitate farmers for installing solar water pumps to irrigate their fields. He also proposed to extend the facility of Kisan Credit Cards to fisheries and animal husbandry farmers to help them meet their working capital needs. the Finance Minister said India's agri-exports potential is as high as US $100 billion against current exports of US $30 billion and to realize this potential, export of agri-commodities will be liberalized. He also proposed to set up state-of-the-art testing facilities in all the forty two Mega Food Parks. He also announced a special Scheme to support the efforts of the governments of Haryana, Punjab, Uttar Pradesh and the NCT of Delhi to address air pollution in the Delhi-NCR region by subsidizing machinery required for in-situ management of crop residue.

Are the interventions adequate?

The SDG-2 is the second most important goal requiring ending hunger, boost up the nutrition standard of its citizens and put in place an infrastructure to supply nutrition by way of upgrading agricultural production system into its sustainable mode, and also by improving associated programme of live stocks and fisheries etc. Multiple other issues challenging the food system also belong to this area. Moreover, apart from poverty reduction, where agriculture and food has a key role to play, sustainable agriculture impacts substantially in achieving SDG 6 on water, SDG 12 on sustainable consumption and production, SDG 13 on climate change adaptation and mitigation and SDG 15 on land use and ecosystems. Consequently, interventions / initiatives under SDG-2 have to be bold, big, precise, interlinked, visible and possibly completely afresh. The initiatives under SDG-2 in India, till date, have been more and less continuing schemes till the budget declaration,2018-19 and no new and big ticket programmes came into being since the SDGs have become functional on 1January,2016 as would appear from the brackets mentioned earlier for the mapped-up schemes. Further, even the mapping of continuing schemes by NITI Aayog is not complete as only CSS /Mission mode programmes have been taken under consideration leaving a significant number of other ongoing and connected schemes out. Similarly, financial institution-sponsored agricultural programmes have remained non-represented. Additionally, hunger, per se does not indicate a homogeneous category of clients; it is inherently located in different layers of multiple poverty groups. Dedicated schemes on them would be useful to make direct impact on them.

Monitoring Indicators, like those of SDG-1, do have a role to signal the kind of schemes needed for obtaining better monitoring output. Monitoring under SDG-2 is subject/ target specific. Therefore, there is scope for inclusion of dedicated schemes of that subject area. The monitoring indicators under SDG-2 mention, among other things, Prevalence of under nourishment, Prevalence of moderate or severe food insecurity in the population, based on the Food Insecurity Experience Scale (FIES),Prevalence of stunting, Prevalence of malnutrition, Volume of production per labour unit by classes of farming/ pastoral/forestry enterprise size,, Average income of small-scale food producers, by sex and indigenous status, Proportion of agricultural area under productive and sustainable agriculture, Number of plant and animal genetic resources for food and agriculture secured in either medium or long-term conservation facilities, Proportion of local breeds classified as being at risk, not-at-risk or at unknown level of risk of extinction, the agriculture orientation index for government expenditures, Total official flows to the agriculture sector, Agricultural export subsidies etc.

Usually, schemes with multiple objectives and universal application do not yield desired outcome. Further, schemes need to correspond with the nature of hunger, nutrition gap etc of given location. Depending on the geographical diversity and cultural plurality, the schemes on sustainable agriculture with possible scope for adoption subsequent to climatic change and natural disasters need to be a part of the roadmap for SDG-2. Needless to mention that a roadmap need to be more focused, descript and detailed.

In so far the as the big push for sustainable agriculture is concerned, the country does have huge number of schemes individually addressing micro-components and numerous areas of big agricultural production system. The website of the Agricultural Ministry mentions several schemes, some of which have common features and overlapping in nature. It is a fact that agriculture is the most complex production system requiring dedicated service and care for its varied seasonal crops located at multiple soil conditions under different agro-climatic zones. The need for intensification of crops, its diversification and for taking care to adopt and adapt massive climatic change scenario also calls for individual schemes for focused intervention. Dedicated schemes are also required to take care on land diversity and soil health along with back-up support need for surface and under-ground irrigation and other inputs like marketing, credit etc. However, it is also a fact that there are commonalitities among various schemes in the Agriculture sector which need to be appropriately revisited and duplication of efforts avoided by way of pruning and rationalising number of schemes and refocusing them in the light of SDG-2 vision. It needs no reiteration to state that existence of common components among some schemes are rather wasteful and are usually soft areas of leakage. It would be useful to revisit all the schemes for focused interventions for enhancing SDG-2 outcome goal by 2030 for meeting hunger of a huge population galloping at a considerable speed, and in the process put in place sustainable agriculture at the same time.

As a general rule, the government schemes are target/client-specific. The implementing agencies follow only the scheme-specific guidelines of its own ministry/department without being least concerned about possible interconnectedness with related schemes with similar broad vision of other ministry/department of the government..In absence of convergence framework, existence of a good number of schemes by itself, under any goal or sub-goal, does not mean much since such schemes are not designed to be part of a framework to achieve an intended outcome. Needless to mention, schemes do not on its own move on to create an automatic convergence pathway to ensure better output. Further, since hunger is connected with life-cycle of an individual, abolition of hunger is linked with a number of interventions from a life-cycle approach/format. The current schemes do not appear to address Goal-2 from that life-cycle angle and definitely not converge-friendly in a strong sense.

The SDG-2 has been built on the premise that removal of hunger is linked with possible free flow of sustainable food basket from the agriculture sector. Indeed, the size of hunger is intricately linked with the size of population. The SDG Summit declaration is silent on role of burgeoning population in the areas of hunger and its removal, including the difficulty of having additional land for sustainable food production. As a matter of fact, population size has been taken as constant/neutral, and not a big factor to the cause either of hunger-size or sustainability of agriculture. India does not seem even to recognise the implication that we are replacing China to be the most populous country in the world by 2025 and the consequent burden of increased hunger-load. Be that as it may, the country needs to work out its roadmap with all given constraints. The Road-map for SDG-2 has necessarily to be more precise, pointed and comprehensive in addressing removal of hunger and critical issues on sustainable agricultural production.

The monitory indicators of SDG -2 require to measure proportion of population in different categories of malnutrition etc and verifiable norms of sustainable agriculture. The massive monitoring indicators have been designed to ensure end of hunger in all its forms everywhere and that nobody should be left behind. The designed monitoring indicators for sustainable agriculture is also to ensure whether due process is being followed in the agricultural front to support hunger initiative by way of ensuring required food basket. While the member countries of the UN system would be at liberty, to design their own country-specific monitoring indicators on each of the items of SDGs, including Goal-2, it is only desirable that Monitoring Indicators of SDG-2, now under process of finalisation in India, would take into considerations a good part of UN monitoring indicators to ensure that India is on course to reach SDG-2 goalpost by 2030 with robust performances.

Earlier, it has been mentioned at chapter 11 that the country needs a new empowered institute to assess poverty estimates at a period of interval. This is also equally applicable for periodical hunger estimates for SDG-2.Such an estimate or assessment, based on objective criteria, by an institute of excellence is accepted as creditable both by the government and the people at large including institutions abroad. Usually, Annual Reports of any nodal Ministry do give us a lot of valuable data on the quantitative aspects of a given scheme or a number of schemes but it cannot ipso facto reveal the impact of aggregated and cumulative effect on hunger at different locations on different age groups and the vulnerable. Besides, hunger is the outcome of failure of several linked schemes and factors. The institutional assessment on the hunger status, based on given norms and time frame will enable the government to know the outcome of the hunger related strategy, its programme interventions, its adequacy, its strength and weakness, its relevance in different geographical and locational variations and the like. It is high time that central government put in place such a specialized institute for conducting hunger estimates at a shorter interval of time. It would be all the more desirable if the hunger estimates and poverty estimates go together as those are intricately linked. Periodical hunger estimate by an institute would enable the country to find the evolving hunger status and the new challenges to effect required course correction, whenever needed.

The SDG's core philosophy of 'no one should be left behind' requires that the national government has to come up with an open and transparent Hunger Policy and Sustainable Agricultural Policy by way of revisiting existing approach and strategy under SDG-2. As is well known, a policy is a system of principles to guide and achieve rational outcomes; it is also a procedure or protocol. A policy assists in both subjective decision making and objective decision taking which are usually operational in nature. Till date, the country does not have either a National Hunger Policy or a Sustainable Agricultural Policy in the post-Sustainable Development Summit, 2015 era. Given the nature of importance of SDG-2, it is only desirable that based on objective reality in India, both in the hunger domain and also in the agricultural field scenario, fully baked policy in the related areas, having due regard to alarmingly rising population size, climatic change and damage limitation on post- disaster situation, is urgently called for.

Chapter - 13

Sustainable Development Goal 3

Ensure healthy lives and promote well-being for all at all ages

The Goal 3 of the Sustainable Development Goals is to ensure healthy lives and promote well-being for all at all ages. It seeks to ensure health and well-being for all, at every stage of life. The Goal encompasses all major health priorities, including reproductive, maternal and child health; communicable, non-communicable and environmental diseases; universal health coverage; and access for all to safe, effective, quality and affordable medicines and vaccines. It also calls for more research and development, increased health financing, and strengthened capacity of all countries in health risk reduction and management.

The macro health scenario that prevailed at the last leg of MDGs was instrumental in factoring the contents of Goal -3. The international concern principally veered around status on child health, maternal death and HIV/AIDS, among other areas. The Fact sheet on hand at the Sustainable Development Summit showed more than six million death of children before their fifth birthday each year. An estimated 5.9 million children under the age of 5 died in 2015, with a global under-five mortality rate being at 43 per 1,000 live births.The neonatal mortality rate declined from 31 deaths per 1,000 live births in 2000 to 19 deaths per 1,000 live births in 2015. Over that period, neonatal deaths represented a larger share (45 per cent) of all under-five deaths. As to the global maternal mortality ratio, which declined between 2000 and 2015, stood still at an estimated ratio of 216 per 100,000 live births in 2015. However, almost all maternal deaths occurred in low-resource settings and can be prevented.

The available data also mentioned that Non communicable diseases accounted for around 38 million deaths per year registering 68 per cent of all deaths worldwide, of which an estimated 52 per cent belong to persons under the age of 70, commonly referred to as premature deaths. Over three quarters of premature deaths were caused by cardiovascular disease, cancer, diabetes and chronic respiratory disease. Reducing tobacco stands critical for reducing premature mortality from non-communicable diseases by one third. Further, Non-communicable and infectious disease bred from unhealthy environmental conditions also resulted an estimated death of 889,000 in 2012 whereas household and ambient air pollution resulted in some 6.5 million deaths globally. Substance use and substance-use disorders have also created a significant public health burden. Worldwide, average alcohol consumption in 2015 was estimated at 6.3l of pure alcohol per person among those aged 15 or older, with wide variations across countries. Globally, mental disorders, anxiety and depression led suicide is the second leading cause of death among those between the ages of 15 and 29. Global deaths and injuries from road traffic accidents is around 1.25 million and it is intended to halve by 2020.

The HIV/AIDS scenario has not been less alarming. At the end of 2013, there were an estimated 35 million people living with HIV with new HIV infections accounting for around 2.1 million in 2013, including 240,000 children. Around 13.6 million people were accessing antiretroviral therapy in 2014.

In 2014, 9.6 million new cases of tuberculosis (133 cases per 100,000 people) were reported worldwide. Almost half the world's population is at risk of malaria and, in 2015, the incidence rate was 91 new cases per 1,000 people at risk, an estimated total of 214 million cases. In 2014, at least 1.7 billion people, in 185 countries, required treatment for at least one neglected tropical disease.

The core intention of Goal-3 is to build up the disease free-health of the international community in conjunction with other Goals, particularly to those of Goal-1 and Goal-2. Inter-linkages and inter-connectivity among other goals do play great role in ensuring the intended outcome. Further, while formulating the Goal-3 at the national level, it has to look at and address multiple sub-goals concurrently and in an integrated fashion. In other words, the Goal 3 covers /includes 13 targets, four of which relate to means of implementation. Additionally, Eight targets under goals 2, 6, 11 and 12 also explicitly refer to health in their wording. Those targets can be referred to as "extended "targets for goal 3, as opposed to the "core" targets listed under that goal. For that reason the national government while designing, implementing and monitoring policies on the health sector and operating within the framework of the sustainable development goals will have to consider both core and extended targets

The UN Secretary General, on his E/2016/75 on, "Progress towards the Sustainable Development Goals", has also observed the following:

- Goal 3 seeks to ensure health and well-being for all, at every stage of life. The Goal addresses all major health priorities, including reproductive, maternal and child health; communicable, non-communicable and environmental diseases; universal health coverage; and access for all to safe, effective, quality and affordable medicines and vaccines. It also calls for more research and development, increased health financing, and strengthened capacity of all countries in health risk reduction and management.
- Between 2000 and 2015, the global maternal mortality ratio, or number of maternal deaths per 100,000 live births, declined by 37 per cent, to an estimated ratio of 216 per 100,000 live births in 2015. Almost all maternal deaths occur in low-resource settings and can be prevented. Globally, 3 out of 4 births were assisted by skilled health-care personnel in 2015. Under-five mortality rates fell rapidly from 2000 to 2015, declining by 44 per cent globally. Nevertheless, an estimated 5.9 million children under the age of 5 died in 2015, with a global under-five mortality rate of 43 per 1,000 live births. The neonatal mortality rate, that is, the likelihood of dying in the first 28 days of life, declined from 31 deaths per 1,000 live births in 2000 to 19 deaths per 1,000 live births in 2015. Over that period, progress in the rate of child survival among children aged 1 to 59 months outpaced advances in reducing neonatal mortality; as a result, neonatal deaths now represent a larger share (45 per cent) of all under-five deaths.
- Preventing unintended pregnancy and reducing adolescent childbearing through universal access to sexual and reproductive health-care services are critical to further advances in the health of women, children and adolescents. Worldwide, in 2015, approximately 3 in 4 women of reproductive age (15 to 49 years of age) who were married or in union satisfied their need for family planning by using modern contraceptive methods; in sub-Saharan Africa and Oceania, however, the share was less than half. Childbearing in adolescence has steadily declined in almost all regions, but wide disparities persist: in 2015, the birth rate among adolescent girls aged 15 to 19 ranged from 7 births per 1,000 girls in Eastern Asia to 102 births per 1,000 girls in sub-Saharan Africa.
- The incidence of major infectious diseases, including HIV, tuberculosis and malaria, has declined globally since 2000. Globally in 2015, the number of new HIV infections among all people was 0.3 new infections per 1,000 uninfected people; 2.1 million people became newly infected that year. The incidence of HIV was highest

in sub-Saharan Africa, with 1.5 new cases per 1,000 uninfected people. In 2014, 9.6 million new cases of tuberculosis (133 cases per 100,000 people) were reported worldwide, with 58 per cent of them in South-Eastern Asia and the Western Pacific. Almost half the world's population is at risk of malaria and, in 2015, the incidence rate was 91 new cases per 1,000 people at risk, an estimated total of 214 million cases. Sub-Saharan Africa accounted for 89 per cent of all malaria cases worldwide, with an incidence rate of 235 cases per 1,000 people at risk. In 2014, at least 1.7 billion people, in 185 countries, required treatment for at least one neglected tropical disease.

- According to estimates from 2012, around 38 million deaths per year, accounting for 68 per cent of all deaths worldwide, were attributable to non communicable diseases. Of all deaths among persons under the age of 70, commonly referred to as premature deaths, an estimated 52 per cent were as a result of non-communicable diseases. Over three quarters of premature deaths were caused by cardiovascular disease, cancer, diabetes and chronic respiratory disease. Globally, premature mortality from those four main categories of non communicable disease declined by 15 per cent between 2000 and 2012. Reducing tobacco use will be critical for meeting the proposed target of reducing premature mortality from non-communicable diseases by one third. In 2015, over 1.1 billion people consumed tobacco, with far more male (945 million) than female (180 million) smokers.
- Unhealthy environmental conditions increase the risk of both non communicable and infectious diseases, which is reflected in the strong integrated nature of the Goals. In 2012, an estimated 889,000 people died from infectious diseases caused largely by faecal contamination of water and soil and by inadequate hand-washing facilities and practices resulting from poor or non-existent sanitation services. In 2012, household and ambient air pollution resulted in some 6.5 million deaths.
- Substance use and substance-use disorders have also created a significant public health burden. Worldwide, average alcohol consumption in 2015 was estimated at 6.3l of pure alcohol per person among those aged 15 or older, with wide variations across countries. Alcohol consumption was highest in the developed regions (10.4l per person) and lowest in Northern Africa (0.5l per person). In 2013, only about 1 in 6 people worldwide suffering from drug-use disorders received treatment. Approximately 1 in 18 people with drug-use disorders received treatment in Africa that year, compared with 1 in 5 in Western and Central Europe.

- Mental disorders occur in all regions and cultures. The most common are anxiety and depression, which, not infrequently, can lead to suicide. In 2012, an estimated 800,000 people worldwide committed suicide, and 86 per cent of them were under the age of 70. Globally, suicide is the second leading cause of death among those between the ages of 15 and 29.
- Around 1.25 million people died from road traffic injuries in 2013. Halving the number of global deaths and injuries from road traffic accidents by 2020 is an ambitious goal given the dramatic increase in the number of vehicles, which nearly doubled between 2000 and 2013.
- Total official flows from all providers for medical research and basic health sectors were $8.9 billion in 2014. Within this total, official development assistance (ODA) from DAC donors was $4.5 billion in 2014, an increase of 20 per cent in real terms since 2010, with the United Kingdom of Great Britain and Northern Ireland and the United States of America accounting for $2.6 billion of that total. In 2014, $1 billion was spent on malaria control and $1.2 billion was spent on other infectious diseases, excluding AIDS.

Based on the above observations, it would be appropriate to reiterate once again the Goal 3 of the SDGs, its targets and related indicators to keep it in the up-fronts, in sequential order, before addressing India's initiatives on ensuring healthy lives and promote well-being for all at all ages.

Goal 3. Ensure healthy lives and promote well-being for all at all ages

3.1 By 2030, reduce the global maternal mortality ratio to less than 70 per 100,000 live births

3.1.1 Maternal mortality ratio

3.1.2 Proportion of births attended by skilled health personnel

3.2 By 2030, end preventable deaths of newborns and children under 5 years of age, with all countries aiming to reduce neonatal mortality to at least as low as 12 per 1,000 live births and under-5 mortality to at least as low as 25 per 1,000 live births

3.2.1 Under-five mortality rate

3.2.2 Neonatal mortality rate

3.3 By 2030, end the epidemics of AIDS, tuberculosis,malaria and neglected tropical diseases and combat hepatitis, water-borne diseases and other communicable diseases

3.3.1 Number of new HIV infections per 1,000 uninfected population, by sex, age and key populations

3.3.2 Tuberculosis incidence per 100,000 population

3.3.3 Malaria incidence per 1,000 population

3.3.4 Hepatitis B incidence per 100,000 population

3.3.5 Number of peoplc requiring interventions against neglected tropical diseases

3.4 By 2030, reduce by one third premature mortality from non-communicable diseases through prevention and treatment and promote mental health and well-being

3.4.1 Mortality rate attributed to cardiovascular disease, cancer, diabetes or chronic respiratory disease

3.4.2 Suicide mortality rate

3.5 Strengthen the prevention and treatment of substance abuse, including narcotic drug abuse and harmful use of alcohol

3.5.1 Coverage of treatment interventions (pharmacological, psychosocial and rehabilitation and aftercare services) for substance use disorders

3.5.2 Harmful use of alcohol, defined according to the national context as alcohol per capita consumption (aged 15 years and older) within a calendar year in litres of pure alcohol

3.6 By 2020, halve the number of global deaths and injuries from road traffic accidents

3.6.1 Death rate due to road traffic injuries

3.7 By 2030, ensure universal access to sexual and reproductive health-care services, including for family planning, information and education, and the integration of reproductive health into national strategies and programmes

3.7.1 Proportion of women of reproductive age (aged 15-49 years) who have their need for family planning satisfied with modern methods

3.7.2 Adolescent birth rate (aged 10-14 years; aged 15-19 years) per 1,000 women in that age group

3.8 Achieve universal health coverage, including financial risk protection, access to quality essential health-care services and access to safe, effective, quality and affordable essential medicines and vaccines for all

3.8.1 Coverage of essential health services (defined as the average coverage of essential services based on tracer interventions that include reproductive, maternal, newborn and child health, infectious diseases, non-communicable diseases and service capacity and access, among the general and the most disadvantaged population)

3.8.2 Proportion of population with large household expenditures on health as a share of total household expenditure or income

3.9 By 2030, substantially reduce the number of deaths and illnesses from hazardous chemicals and air,water and soil pollution and contamination

3.9.1 Mortality rate attributed to household and ambient air pollution

3.9.2 Mortality rate attributed to unsafe water, unsafe sanitation and lack of hygiene (exposure to unsafe Water, Sanitation and Hygiene for All (WASH) services)

3.9.3 Mortality rate attributed to unintentional poisoning

3.a Strengthen the implementation of the World Health Organization Framework Convention on Tobacco Control in all countries, as appropriate

3.a.1 Age-standardized prevalence of current tobacco use among persons aged 15 years and older

3.b Support the research and development of vaccines and medicines for the communicable and non-communicable diseases that primarily affect developing countries, provide access to affordable essential medicines and vaccines, in accordance with the Doha Declaration on the TRIPS Agreement and Public Health, which affirms the right of developing countries to use to the full the provisions in the Agreement on Trade-Related Aspects of Intellectual Property Rights regarding flexibilities to protect public health, and, in particular, provide access to medicines for all

3.b.1 Proportion of the target population covered by all vaccines included in their national programme

3.b.2 Total net official development assistance to medical research and basic health sectors

3.b.3 Proportion of health facilities that have a core set of relevant essential medicines available and affordable on a sustainable basis

3.c Substantially increase health financing and the recruitment, development, training and retention of the health workforce in developing countries, especially in least developed countries and small island developing States

3.c.1 Health worker density and distribution

3.d Strengthen the capacity of all countries, in particular developing countries, for early warning, risk reduction and management of national and global health risks

3.d.1 International Health Regulations (IHR) capacity and health emergency preparedness

The goals and targets per se are important from the angle of programme vision and intended outcome; however from the perspective of monitoring the performance, indicators do play critical role. Since indicator-design is essentially an expert professional skill- job requiring to keep harmony with overall goals and targets of the Sustainable Development Summit as embodied in paragraph 75 of Transforming our World: The 2030 Agenda for Sustainable Development mentioned : "the Goals and targets will be followed-up and reviewed using a set of global indicators. These will be complemented by indicators at the regional and national levels which will be developed by member states, in addition to the outcomes of work undertaken for the development of the baselines for those targets where national and global baseline data does not yet exist".

Needless to mention that purpose of SDG indicators is twofold; first it acts as a management tool to help countries develop implementation and monitoring strategies for achieving the SDGs and to monitor progress and secondly, it works as a report card, to measure progress towards achieving a target and ensure the accountability of governments to their citizens.As a matter of fact, Agenda 21 of the SD Summit also called on countries and the international community to develop indicators of sustainable development. Such indicators were needed to increase focus on sustainable development and assist decision-makers at all levels to adopt sound national sustainable development policies.

Be that as it may, the Global Indicator Framework as designed by the UN Statistical Commission at its 47th Session in March 2016 and adopted thereafter by the Economic and Social Council and the General Assembly, are as follows :

Indicators of Goal-3:

3.1.1 Maternal mortality ratio

3.1.2 Proportion of births attended by skilled health personnel

3.2.1 Under-five mortality rate

3.2.2 Neonatal mortality rate

3.3.1 Number of new HIV infections per 1,000 uninfected population, by sex, age and key populations

3.3.2 Tuberculosis incidence per 100,000 population

3.3.3 Malaria incidence per 1,000 population

3.3.4 Hepatitis B incidence per 100,000 population

3.3.5 Number of people requiring interventions against neglected tropical diseases

3.4.1 Mortality rate attributed to cardiovascular disease, cancer, diabetes or chronic respiratory disease

3.4.2 Suicide mortality rate

3.5.1 Coverage of treatment interventions (pharmacological, psychosocial and rehabilitation and aftercare services) for substance use disorders

3.5.2 Harmful use of alcohol, defined according to the national context as alcohol per capita consumption (aged 15 years and older) within a calendar year in litres of pure alcohol

3.6.1 Death rate due to road traffic injuries

3.7.1 Proportion of women of reproductive age (aged 15-49 years) who have their need for family planning satisfied with modern methods

3.7.2 Adolescent birth rate (aged 10-14 years; aged 15-19 years) per 1,000 women in that age group

3.8.1 Coverage of essential health services (defined as the average coverage of essential services based on tracer interventions that include reproductive, maternal, newborn and child health, infectious diseases, non-communicable diseases and service capacity and access, among the general and the most disadvantaged population)

3.8.2 Proportion of population with large household expenditures on health as a share of total household expenditure or income

3.9.1 Mortality rate attributed to household and ambient air pollution

3.9.2 Mortality rate attributed to unsafe water, unsafe sanitation and lack of hygiene (exposure to unsafe Water, Sanitation and Hygiene for All (WASH) services)

3.9.3 Mortality rate attributed to unintentional poisoning

3.a.1 Age-standardized prevalence of current tobacco use among persons aged 15 years and older

3.b.1 Proportion of the target population covered by all vaccines included in their national programme

3.b.2 Total net official development assistance to medical research and basic health sectors

3.b.3 Proportion of health facilities that have a core set of relevant essential medicines available and affordable on a sustainable basis

3.c.1 Health worker density and distribution

3.d.1 International Health Regulations (IHR) capacity and health emergency preparedness

In the light of the overarching goal of SDG-3, the national government of the country needs to take it forward to design appropriate programme in ensuring commensurate outcome. In such efforts, the current scenario and revealed gaps need to be taken into consideration while drawing a roadmap for goal-3. The validated data in the MDG Report, 2015 published by the United Nations on 6th July, 2015 need to be used as benchmark reference for 'healthy lives and promote well-being for all at all ages' in India as indicated belw:

- Series Name: Children under five moderately or severely under-weight percentage

  Goal 1. Eradicate extreme poverty and hunger

  Target 1.C Halve, between 1990 and 2015, the proportion of people who suffer from hunger

  Indicator 1.8 Prevalence of underweight children under five years of age

  Last updated 6 July 2015

Country	1992	1993	1997	1999	2006
India	52.8	51.2	38.4	46.3	43.5

Source: unstat/Millennium Indicators.

- Series Name: Children under five severely under-weight, percentage

  Goal 1. Eradicate extreme poverty and hunger

  Target 1.C Halve, between 1990 and 2015, the proportion of people who suffer from hunger

  Indicator 1.8 Prevalence of underweight children under five years of age

  Last updated 6 July 2015

Country	1992	1993	1997	1999	2006
India	-	24.3	-	20.6	17.4

Source: unstat/Millennium Indicators

- Series Name: Population under nourishment, percentage

  Goal 1. Eradicate extreme poverty and hunger

  Target 1.C Halve, between 1990 and 2015, the proportion of people who suffer from hunger

  Indicator 1.9 Proportion of population below minimum level of dietary energy consumption

  Last updated 6 July 2015

Country	1991	1992	1993	1994	1995	1996	1997	1998	1999	2000	2001
India	23.7	22.2	22.4	22.1	21.6	20.5	19.2	18.0	17.3	17.0	17.5

contd...

2002	2003	2004	2005	2006	2007	2008	2009	2010	2011	2012	2013
18.6	19.9	20.9	21.2	20.5	18.9	17.2	16.2	17.2	15.7	15.6	15.4

Source: unstat/Millennium Indicators.

- Series Name: Children 1year old Immunization against measles

  Goal 4. Reduce Child mortality

  Target 4.A: Reduce by two-thirds, between 1990 and 2015, the under-five mortality

  Indicator 4.3 Proportion of 1 year old children immunized against measles

Last updated 6 July 2015

Country	1990	1991	1992	1993	1994	1995	1996	1997	1998	1999	2000	2001
India	56	43	51	59	67	72	66	55	57	58	99	57

contd....

2002	2003	2004	2005	2006	2007	2008	2009	2010	2011	2012	2013
56	62	68	59	71	69	74	74	74	74	74	74

Source: unstat/Millennium Indicators.

- Series Name: Children under five mortality rate per 1000 live births

  Goal 4. Reduce Child mortality

  Target 4.A: Reduce by two-thirds, between 1990 and 2015, the under- five mortality

  Indicator 4.1 Under five-mortality rate

Last updated 3,october 2014

Country	1990	1991	1992	1993	1994	1995	1996	1997	1998	1999	2000	2001
India	125.9	122.4	119	115.7	112.3	109	105.5	102	98.5	94.9	91.4	87.9

contd....

2002	2003	2004	2005	2006	2007	2008	2009	2010	2011	2012	2013
84.5	81.2	77.9	74.7	71.6	68.7	65.8	62.9	60.2	57.5	55	52.7

Source: unstat/Millennium Indicators.

- Series Name: Infant mortality rate (0-1) per 1000 live births

  Goal 4. Reduce Child mortality

  Target 4.A: Reduce by two thirds, between 1990 and 2015, the under- five mortality

  Indicator 4.2 Infant mortality rate

Last updated 3,october 2014

Country	1990	1991	1992	1993	1994	1995	1996	1997	1998	1999	2000	2001
India	88.4	86.2	84	81.9	79.8	77.7	75.5	75.3	71	68.7	66.5	64.3

contd....

2002	2003	2004	2005	2006	2007	2008	2009	2010	2011	2012	2013
62.1	60	57.9	55.9	53.9	52	50.1	48.3	46.4	44.7	42.9	41.4

Source: unstat/Millennium Indicators.

- Series Name: Maternal maternity ratio per 100000 live births

  Goal 5. Improve Maternal health

  Target: 5.A: Reduce by three quarter, from 1990 to 2015, maternal mortality ratio

  Indicator 5.1 Maternal mortality ratio

Country	1990	1995	2000	2005	2010	2015
India	560	460	370	280	220	190

Source: unstat/Millennium Indicators

The National Family Health Survey - 4, 2015 -16, also provides another background data which runs as follows:

India - Key Indicators	*NFHS-4 (2015-16)*			*NFHS-3 (2005-06)*
Population and Household Profile	***Urban***	***Rural***	***Total***	***Total***
1. Population (female) age 6 years and above who ever attended school (%)	80.6	63.0	68.8	58.3
2. Population below age 15 years (%)	24.9	30.5	28.6	34.9
3. Sex ratio of the total population (females per 1,000 males)	956	1,009	991	1,000
4. Sex ratio at birth for children born in the last five years (females per 1,000 males)	899	927	919	914
5. Children under age 5 years whose birth was registered (%)	88.8	76.1	79.7	41.2
6. Households with electricity (%)	97.5	83.2	88.2	67.9
7. Households with an improved drinking-water source[1] (%)	91.1	89.3	89.9	87.6
8. Households using improved sanitation facility[2] (%)	70.3	36.7	48.4	29.1
9. Households using clean fuel for cooking[3] (%)	80.6	24.0	43.8	25.5
10. Households using iodized salt (%)	96.5	91.4	93.1	76.1
11. Households with any usual member covered by a health scheme orhealth insurance (%)	28.2	29.0	28.7	4.8
Characteristics of Adults (age 15-49)				
12. Women who are literate (%)	81.4	61.5	68.4	55.1
13. Men who are literate (%)	90.8	82.6	85.7	78.1
14. Women with 10 or more years of schooling (%)	51.5	27.3	35.7	22.3
Marriage and Fertility				
15. Women age 20-24 years married before age 18 years (%)	17.5	31.5	26.8	47.4
16. Men age 25-29 years married before age 21 years (%)	14.1	24.4	20.3	32.3

(Contd...)

17. Total fertility rate (children per woman)	1.8	2.4	2.2	2.7
18. Women age 15-19 years who were already mothers or pregnant at the time of thesurvey (%)	5.0	9.2	7.9	16.0
Infant and Child Mortality Rates (per 1,000 live births)				
19. Infant mortality rate (IMR)	29	46	41	57
20. Under-five mortality rate (U5MR)	34	56	50	74
Current Use of Family Planning Methods (currently married women age 15–49 years)				
21. Any method[4] (%)	57.2	51.7	53.5	56.3
22. Any modern method[4] (%)	51.3	46.0	47.8	48.5
23. Female sterilization (%)	35.7	36.1	36.0	37.3
24. Male sterilization (%)	0.3	0.3	0.3	1.0
25. IUD/PPIUD (%)	2.4	1.1	1.5	1.7
26. Pill (%)	3.5	4.3	4.1	3.1
27. Condom (%)	9.0	3.9	5.6	5.2
Unmet Need for Family Planning (currently married women age 15–49 years)[5]				
28. Total unmet need (%)	12.1	13.2	12.9	13.9
29. Unmet need for spacing (%)	5.1	5.9	5.7	6.1
Quality of Family Planning Services				
30. Health worker ever talked to female non-users about family planning (%)	18.6	17.2	17.7	10.1
31. Current users ever told about side effects of current method[6] (%)	50.1	45.0	46.5	34.4
Maternity Care (for last birth in the 5 years before the survey)				
32. Mothers who had antenatal check-up in the first trimester (%)	69.1	54.2	58.6	43.9
33. Mothers who had at least 4 antenatal care visits (%)	66.4	44.8	51.2	37.0
34. Mothers whose last birth was protected against neonatal tetanus[7] (%)	89.9	88.6	89.0	76.3
35. Mothers who consumed iron folic acid for 100 days or more when theywere pregnant (%)	40.8	25.9	30.3	15.2
36. Mothers who had full antenatal care[8] (%)	31.1	16.7	21.0	11.6
37. Registered pregnancies for which the mother received Mother and Child Protection (MCP) card (%)	87.7	90.0	89.3	na
38. Mothers who received postnatal care from a doctor/nurse/LHV/ANM/mid wife/other health personnel within 2 days of delivery (%)	71.7	58.5	62.4	34.6
39. Mothers who received financial assistance under Janani Suraksha Yojana (JSY) for births delivered in an institution (%)	21.4	43.8	36.4	na

(Contd...)

40. Average out of pocket expenditure per delivery in public health facility (Rs.)	3,913	2,947	3,198	na
41. Children born at home who were taken to a health facility for check-up within 24hours of birth (%)	3.2	2.4	2.5	0.3
42. Children who received a health check after birth from a doctor/nurse/LHV/ ANM/midwife/other health personnel within 2 days of birth (%)	27.2	23.0	24.3	na
Delivery Care (for births in the 5 years before the survey)				
43. Institutional births (%)	88.7	75.1	78.9	38.7
44. Institutional births in public facility (%)	46.2	54.4	52.1	18.0
45. Home delivery conducted by skilled health personnel (out of total deliveries) (%)	3.0	4.9	4.3	8.2
46. Births assisted by a doctor/nurse/LHV/ ANM/other health personnel (%)	90.0	78.0	81.4	46.6
47. Births delivered by caesarean section (%)	28.3	12.9	17.2	8.5
48. Births in a private health facility delivered by caesarean section (%)	44.8	37.8	40.9	27.7
49. Births in a public health facility delivered by caesarean section (%)	19.9	9.3	11.9	15.2
Child Immunizations and Vitamin A Supplementation				
50. Children age 12-23 months fully immunized (BCG, measles, and 3 doses each of polio and DPT) (%)	63.9	61.3	62.0	43.5
51. Children age 12-23 months who have received BCG (%)	93.2	91.4	91.9	78.2
52. Children age 12-23 months who have received 3 doses of polio vaccine (%)	73.4	72.6	72.8	78.2
53. Children age 12-23 months who have received 3 doses of DPT vaccine (%)	80.2	77.7	78.4	55.3
54. Children age 12-23 months who have received measles vaccine (%)	83.2	80.3	81.1	58.8
55. Children age 12-23 months who have received 3 doses of Hepatitis B vaccine (%)	63.3	62.5	62.8	na
56. Children age 9-59 months who received a vitamin A dose in last 6 months (%)	62.9	59.1	60.2	16.5
57. Children age 12-23 months who received most of the vaccinations in public health facility (%)	82.1	94.2	90.7	82.0
58. Children age 12-23 months who received most of the vaccinations in private health facility (%)	16.7	3.4	7.2	10.5
Treatment of Childhood Diseases (children under age 5 years)				
59. Prevalence of diarrhoea (reported) in the last 2 weeks preceding the survey (%)	8.2	9.6	9.2	9.0

(Contd...)

60. Children with diarrhoea in the last 2 weeks who received oral rehydration salts(ORS) (%)	58.5	47.9	50.6	26.0
61. Children with diarrhoea in the last 2 weeks who received zinc (%)	23.7	19.1	20.3	na
62. Children with diarrhoea in the last 2 weeks taken to a health facility (%)	74.1	65.8	67.9	61.3
63. Prevalence of symptoms of acute respiratory infection (ARI) in the last 2 weeks preceding the survey (%)	2.3	2.9	2.7	5.8
64. Children with fever or symptoms of ARI in the last 2 weeks preceding the surveytaken to a health facility (%)	80.0	70.8	73.2	69.6
Child Feeding Practices and Nutritional Status of Children				
65. Children under age 3 years breastfed within one hour of birth[9] (%)	42.8	41.1	41.6	23.4
66. Children under age 6 months exclusively breastfed[10] (%)	52.1	56.0	54.9	46.4
67. Children age 6-8 months receiving solid or semi-solid food and breastmilk[10] (%)	50.1	39.9	42.7	52.6
68. Breastfeeding children age 6-23 months receiving an adequate diet[10,11] (%)	10.1	8.2	8.7	na
69. Non-breastfeeding children age 6-23 months receiving an adequate diet[10,11] (%)	16.9	12.7	14.3	na
70. Total children age 6-23 months receiving an adequate diet[10,11] (%)	11.6	8.8	9.6	na
71. Children under 5 years who are stunted (height-for-age)[12] (%)	31.0	41.2	38.4	48.0
72. Children under 5 years who are wasted (weight-for-height)[12] (%)	20.0	21.5	21.0	19.8
73. Children under 5 years who are severely wasted (weight-for-height)[13] (%)	7.5	7.4	7.5	6.4
74. Children under 5 years who are underweight (weight-for-age)[12] (%)	29.1	38.3	35.7	42.5

SDG-3 and the initiatives in India :

(a) The NITI Aayog and Mapping of Initiatives on SDG-3:

Given the above the factual position as obtained in India, it would be worthwhile to assess the roadmap for Sustainable development of Goal 3 of ensuring healthy lives and promote well-being for all at all ages with reference to the approach and goal-specific initiatives undertaken in India.The NITI Aayog has been empowered to oversee the implementation of SDGs by the ministries of the Central Government and coordinate with States for the achievement of developmental targets as enshrined in the SDGs. The NITI Aayog tasked itself to prepare a initial draft based on mapping of the goals and targets proposed by Nodal and other Ministries in consultation with MoSPI. The schemes so mapped for Goal-3 include National Health Mission including NRHM (Core) [2005], Human Resource in Health and Medical Education

(Core), National Mission on Ayush including Mission on Medical Plants (Core) [2014], National AIDS & STD Control Programme [1992], Integrated Child Development Service (ICDS) (Core) [1975]. It has also included 1) Pradhan Mantri Swasthya Suraksha Yojana (2006) (Core). Additionally, it has also mentioned 1) Pradhan Mantri Swasthya Suraksha Yojana (2006) *(Core)*

(b) National Review of SDG-3 for United Nations High Level Political Forum 2017

The outcomes of initiatives under SDG-3 would normally take a period of time to fructify as several other factors are also interlinked to reflect its final outcome. Be that as it may, the Voluntary National Review Report on Implementation of Sustainable Development Goals presented for United Nations High Level Political Forum 2017 is a good reference point for understanding the latest position on SDG-3 status in India. The report says " India has made significant strides in improving various health indicators. The Infant Mortality Rate has declined from 57 in 2005-06 to 41 in 2015-16. Similarly, Under-5 Mortality Rate has fallen from 74 to 50 over the same period. This has been enabled, at least partially, by a significant improvement in vaccination coverage for children between 12-23 months of age. Moreover, institutional deliveries have increased from 38.7% in 2005-06 to 78.9% in 2015-16. The country's strategy in health is focused on providing essential services to the entire population, with a special emphasis on the poor and vulnerable groups.

The National Health Policy, 2017 has specified targets for universalising primary health care, achieving further reductions in infant and under-5 mortality, preventing premature deaths due to non-communicable diseases as well as increasing government expenditure on health. A composite index is being used to monitor and incentivise improvements in health services delivery across states in the country. The government is aiming to immunize all immunized and partially immunized children against vaccine preventable diseases by 2020. Towards achieving universal health coverage, a health insurance cover of INR 100,000 (USD 1,563) is being extended to all poor families."

(c) The NITI Aayog, Three-Year Action Agenda and SDG-3

The NITI Aayog has recently released the Three-Year Action Agenda covering years 2017-18 to 2019-20 which begins with the objective of eliminating poverty in all its dimensions such that every citizen will have access to a minimum standard of food, education, health, clothing, shelter, transportation and energy. At chapter 21 of the Three-Year Action Plan Agenda, it is admitted that while India has made significant progress in outcomes over the past two decades, key indicators (Infant mortality Rate, Life Expectancy, Malnutrition and Maternal Mortality Rate) have remained below those of other countries and similar stages of development and levels of spending on health. Moreover, there are large disparities in outcomes and service coverage between different parts of the country.

The document further records that India faces the challenge of a double burden of disease, wherein communicable diseases still account for a significant proportion of disease burden In 2012,out of total number of Disability – Adjusted Life Years (DALYs) lost, 33% were attributable to those diseases.

Non-communicable diseases account for 55% of DALYs with injuries accounting for the remaining 12% in the same year. There is a rising morbidity and mortality cost attributable to non-communicable diseases. They are collectively responsible for an estimated 60% of premature deaths

The document diagnoses that for achieving the expected health outcome will require the following :

(1) Adequate investment of public financial resources on health;

(2) Efficient prioritization of spending with greater emphasis given to preventive health rather than curative cure

(3) Adequate attention by the government to the stewardship of organizing the health sector

(4) Reduce TFR to 2.1 (2013 actual 2.3)

(5) Reduce incidence of TB to 130/100,000 (2015 estimate 217/100,000

(6) Reduce incidence of Malaria (Annual Parasite Incidence) to less than 1/1000 in 90% of districts (2016 estimate 74% of districts have achieved as PPI of less than 1

(7) Estimate Kala Azar (2015 estimate :87% of endemic diseases were eliminated

(8) Reduce premature mortality from cardiovascular diseases, cancer, diabetes or chronic respiratory disease by $1/4^{th}$ of the National Family Survey-4 (NFHS-4) levels

(9) Reduce out of pockets spending (oops) to 50% of the total health expenditure (2014 estimate 62.4%)

(d) Economic Survey of India, 2017-18

The Government of India tabled the Economic Survey of India, 2017-18 in the Parliament in the Budget Session on 29th January,2018 to set the stage for the Government for the Annual Budget. The Survey contains an indepth analysis, serious research as well new policy ideas. The said Survey sums up the latest position on status on health. It states that the report 'India: Health of the Nation's States', 2017 has for the first time provided comprehensive set of findings on the distribution of diseases and risk factors across all States of the country from 1990 to 2016. Malnutrition still remains the most important risk factor (14.6 per cent) that results in disease burden in the country, though dropping substantially since 1990. Of the total disease burden in India, 33 per cent was due to communicable, maternal, neonatal, and nutritional diseases (termed infectious and associated diseases) in 2016. The contribution of non-communicable diseases has increased from 30 per cent of the total disease burden in 1990 to 55 per cent in 2016 and that of injuries from 9 per cent to 12 per cent. Around 5 per cent of health loss is attributable to unsafe water, sanitation, and hand-washing practices, which the government is trying to address through the Swachh Bharat Mission (SBM).

(e) Budget Inititives for 2018-19

The Budget document embodies not only a financial statement on resources availability and its projected expenditure, it also expresses alongside overtly and covertly the policy statement of the Government of the day. The Budget Speech of the Finance Minister of India delivered on First February,2018 is taken up to relate its relevance on SDGs. In so far as SDG-3 is concerned, the Union Finance Minister prefaced the linkage of Health sector with observations that the guiding principle of the Government is : Only Swasth Bharat can be a Samriddha Bharat. India cannot realize its demographic dividend without its citizens being healthy. The Finance Minister said that it is the poor who suffer the maximum from various chronic diseases. Government has therefore prepared an action plan to eliminate Kala-Azar and Filariasis by 2017, Leprosy by 2018 and Measles by 2020. Elimination of tuberculosis by 2025 is also targeted. Similarly, action plan has been prepared to reduce IMR from 39 in 2014 to 28 by 2019 and MMR from 167 in 2011-13 to 100 by 2018-2020. 1.5 lakh Health Sub Centres will be transformed into Health and Wellness Centres. He also mentioned that to ensure adequate availability of specialist doctors to strengthen Secondary and Tertiary levels of health care it has been decided to create additional 5,000 Post Graduate seats per annum and to roll out DNB courses in big District Hospitals; strengthen PG teaching in select ESI and Municipal Corporation Hospitals; and encourage reputed Private Hospitals to start DNB courses in collaboration with the State Governments to take these tasks forward. The Government is committed to take necessary steps for structural transformation of the Regulatory framework of Medical Education and Practice in India. Additionally, the Finance Minister proposed to amend the Drugs and Cosmetics Rules to ensure availability of drugs at reasonable prices and promote use of generic medicines. New rules for regulating medical devices will also be formulated. These rules will be internationally harmonised and attract investment into this sector. This will reduce the cost of such devices.

The Finance Minister also announced two major initiatives as part of "Ayushman Bharat" programme aimed at making path breaking interventions to address health holistically, in primary, secondary and tertiary care system covering both prevention and health promotion.

The National Health Policy, 2017 has envisioned Health and Wellness Centres as the foundation of India's health system. These 1.5 lakh centres will bring health care system closer to the homes of people. These centres will provide comprehensive health care, including for non-communicable diseases and maternal and child health services. These centres will also provide free essential drugs and diagnostic services. The Finance Ministe recommitted '1200 crore in this budget,2018-19 for this flagship programme. He also invited contribution of private sector through CSR and philanthropic institutions in adopting these centres.

Additionally, since the existing Rashtriya Swasthya Bima Yojana (RSBY) is too inadequate to provide healthl coverage of millions of poor families in the country, the Finance Minister announced announced another flagship National Health Protection Scheme, the world's largest government funded health care programme titled National Health Protection Scheme to cover over 10 crorc poor and vulnerable families (approximately 50 crore beneficiaries) providing coverage upto 5 lakh rupees per family per year for secondary and tertiary care hospitalization.Finally, in order to further enhance accessibility of quality medical education and health care, the Government will be setting up 24 new Government Medical Colleges and Hospitals by upgrading existing district hospitals in the country. This would ensure that there is at least 1 Medical College for every 3 Parliamentary Constituencies and at least 1 Government Medical College in each State of the country.

Chapter - 14

Sustainable Development Goal 4

Ensure inclusive and equitable quality education and promote lifelong learning opportunities for all

The Sustainable Development Goal-4 intends to ensure inclusive and equitable quality education and promote lifelong learning opportunities for all by putting in place inclusive and equitable quality education at all levels – early childhood, primary, secondary, tertiary, technical and vocational training. All people, irrespective of sex, age, race or ethnicity, and persons with disabilities, migrants, indigenous peoples, children and youth, especially those in vulnerable situations, need to have access to life-long learning opportunities to acquire the knowledge and skills to exploit opportunities and participate fully in society. The Goal-4 also seeks to provide children and youth with a nurturing environment for the full realization of their rights and capabilities.

The Fact sheet on educational scenario during the process of conceptualizing SDGs noted that globally Enrolment in primary education in developing countries has reached 91%.The Report of the Secretary-General, "Progress towards the Sustainable Development Goals" (E/2016/75) has mentioned that globally 59 million children of primary-school age were out of school. Of them, 1 in 5 of those children had dropped out and recent trends suggest that 2 in 5 of out-of-school children will never set foot in a classroom. Children in the poorest households are 4 times as likely to be out of school as children in the richest households. The Report further states that at the end of primary school, children should be able to read and write and to understand and use basic concepts in mathematics. However, in 2014, between

40 per cent and 90 per cent of children, failed to achieve even minimum levels of proficiency in reading. Additionally, the end of lower secondary education often coincides with the end of compulsory education. By this stage, young people should be able to master subject-related knowledge and skills and possess personal and social skills. However, data from 38 countries in the developed regions show that, in the majority of those countries, at least 75 per cent of young people achieved at least a minimum proficiency in reading and/ or mathematics; the same was true for only 5 out of 22 countries, in developing regions, for which data were available. Measuring learning achievement, starting in the early grades, will help to identify where schools are failing to meet their commitments to children and to formulate appropriate remedial action. The world has achieved equality in primary education between girls and boys, but few countries have achieved that target at all levels of education. Among youth aged 15 to 24, the literacy rate has improved globally from 83 per cent to 91 per cent between 1990 and 2015. The Sustainable Development Goals sets to ensure that this gap must be closed on ground of quality and equity.

Historically, the World Education Forum (26-28 April, 2000), Dakar adopted the Dakar Framework for Action, Education for All and adopted six Education for All (EFA) goals, namely, (1) expand early childhood care and education; (2) universalize primary education; (3) improve access to life-skill learning; (4) achieve 50 per cent improvement in adult literacy; (5) achieve gender equality; and (6) enhance the quality of education. Later, Millennium Development Goals (MDGs) took up universal access to primary education (MDG 2) and a target on gender parity in education, as part of the goal on gender equality and women's empowerment (MDG 3). In its aspirational vision for education in the post -2015 development agenda, the UNESCO and the UNICEF adopted the Muscat Agreement at the Global EFA Meeting in Oman in May 2014, which began a broad and intensive consultation to define the future education agenda. This extensive process culminated in the Muscat Agreement adopted at the Global EFA Meeting in Oman in May 2014, representing a shared vision of education for the future, which was closely aligned with SDG -4 and intended to pave the way for a transformative and sustainable future. It is also expected to meet UNESCO's stand that education is a fundamental human right inextricably linked to the realization of other rights and goal. As a matter of fact, sustainable development begins with education.

In order to realise the cherished goal -4,the statistical division of the UN have highlighted the desirability of additional care for enrolment and supervision to pre-empt drop-outs for the children in rural areas, who are poor or have parents with little or no education. Moreover, fundamental skills need to be provided to enrich a solid foundation to young people for further learning throughout their life. Incidentally, the FAO, sensitive to the needs of agricultural and rural communities, maintains that Worldwide, nearly 60 percent of child labour is found in agriculture, about 100 million boys and girls between 5 and 17 years are identified as child labourers in agriculture and that in Worldwide, the average out-of-school rate is twice as much in rural areas compared with urban areas. In that context the FAO favours a "whole school" approach to nutrition education, in which classroom learning is linked with practical activities, involving the participation of all school staff, families and the community.

In brief, the Sustainable Development Goal 4 aims to ensure access to quality education learning opportunities throughout life for all. The Goal focuses on the 'acquisition of foundational and higher-order skills at all stages of education and development; greater and more equitable access to quality education at all levels as well as technical and vocational education and training (TVET); and the knowledge, skills and values needed to function well and contribute to society'. As a matter of fact, obtaining a quality education is the foundation to improving people's lives and also in a way to all goals of sustainable development.

Based on the above perspective, it would be appropriate to reiterate the Goal 4 of the SDGs, its targets and related indicators to keep it in the up-front, in sequential order, before addressing India's initiatives on ensuring **inclusive and equitable quality education and promote lifelong learning opportunities for all.**

Goal 4. Ensure inclusive and equitable quality education and promote lifelong learning opportunities for all

4.1 By 2030, ensure that all girls and boys complete free, equitable and quality primary and secondary education leading to relevant and effective learning outcomes

4.2 By 2030, ensure that all girls and boys have access to quality early childhood development, care and pre-primary education so that they are ready for primary education

4.3 By 2030, ensure equal access for all women and men to affordable and quality technical, vocational and tertiary education, including university

4.4 By 2030, substantially increase the number of youth and adults who have relevant skills, including technical and vocational skills, for employment, decent jobs and entrepreneurship

4.5 By 2030, eliminate gender disparities in education and ensure equal access to all levels of education and vocational training for the vulnerable, including persons with disabilities, indigenous peoples and children in vulnerable situations

4.6 By 2030, ensure that all youth and a substantial proportion of adults, both men and women, achieve literacy and numeracy

4.7 By 2030, ensure that all learners acquire the knowledge and skills needed to promote sustainable development, including, among others, through education for sustainable development and sustainable lifestyles, human rights, gender equality, promotion of a culture of peace and non-violence, global citizenship and appreciation of cultural diversity and of culture's contribution to sustainable development

4.a Build and upgrade education facilities that are child, disability and gender sensitive and provide safe, non-violent, inclusive and effective learning environments for all

4.b By 2020, substantially expand globally the number of scholarships available to developing countries, in particular least developed countries, small island developing States and African countries, for enrolment in higher education, including vocational training and information and communications technology, technical, engineering and scientific programmes, in developed countries and other developing countries

4.c By 2030, substantially increase the supply of qualified teachers, including through international cooperation for teacher training in developing countries, especially least developed countries and small island developing States

The goals and targets per se are important from the angle of programme vision and intended outcome; however from the perspective of monitoring the performance, indicators do play critical role. Since indicator-design is essentially an expert professional skill- job requiring to keep harmony with overall goals and targets of the Sustainable Development Summit as embodied in paragraph 75 of Transforming our World: The 2030 Agenda for Sustainable Development mentioned : "the Goals and targets will be followed-up and reviewed using a set of global indicators. These will be complemented by indicators at the regional and national levels which will be developed by member states, in addition to the outcomes of work undertaken for the development of the baselines for those targets where national and global baseline data does not yet exist".

Needless to mention that purpose of SDG indicators is twofold; first it acts as a management tool to help countries develop implementation and monitoring strategies for achieving the SDGs and to monitor progress and secondly, it works as a report card, to measure progress towards achieving a target and ensure the accountability of governments to their citizens.As a matter of fact, Agenda 21 of the SD Summit also called on countries and the international community to develop indicators of sustainable development.

Such indicators were needed to increase focus on sustainable development and assist decision-makers at all levels to adopt sound national sustainable development policies.

Be that as it may, the Global Indicator Framework as designed by the UN Statistical Commission at its 47th Session in March 2016 and adopted thereafter by the Economic and Social Council and the General Assembly, are as follows:

Indicators of Goal-4

4.1.1 Proportion of children and young people: (a) in grades 2/3; (b) at the end of primary; and (c) at the end of lower secondary achieving at least a minimum proficiency level in (i) reading and (ii) mathematics, by sex

4.2.1 Proportion of children under 5 years of age who are developmentally on track in health, learning and psychosocial well-being, by sex

4.2.2 Participation rate in organized learning (one year before the official primary entry age), by sex

4.3.1 Participation rate of youth and adults in formal and non-formal education and training in the previous 12 months, by sex

4.4.1 Proportion of youth and adults with information and communications technology (ICT) skills, by type of skill

4.5.1 Parity indices (female/male, rural/urban, bottom/top wealth quintile and others such as disability status, indigenous peoples and conflict affected, as data become available) for all education indicators on this list that can be disaggregated

4.6.1 Proportion of population in a given age group achieving at least a fixed level of proficiency in functional (a) literacy and (b) numeracy skills, by sex

4.7.1 Extent to which (i) global citizenship education and (ii) education for sustainable development, including gender equality and human rights, are mainstreamed at all levels in: (a) national education policies; (b) curricula; (c) teacher education; and (d) student assessment

4.a.1 Proportion of schools with access to: (a) electricity; (b) the Internet for pedagogical purposes; (c) computers for pedagogical purposes;(d) adapted infrastructure and materials for students with disabilities; (e) basic drinking water; (f) singlesex basic sanitation facilities; and (g) basic handwashing facilities (as per the WASH indicator definitions)

4.b.1 Volume of official development assistance flows for scholarships by sector and type of study

4.c.1 Proportion of teachers in: (a) pre-primary; (b) primary; (c) lower secondary; and (d) upper secondary education who have received at least the minimum organized teacher training (e.g. pedagogical training) pre-service or in-service required for teaching at the relevant level in a given country

In the light of the overarching goal of SDG-4, the national government of the country needs to take it forward to design appropriate programme in ensuring commensurate outcome. In such efforts, the current scenario and revealed gaps need to be taken into consideration while drawing a roadmap for goal-4. The validated data in the MDG Report, 2015 published by the United Nations have to be used as benchmark data for roadmap on components of inclusive and equitable quality education and promote lifelong learning opportunities for all and its performance status over time in India as are indicated below:

MDG Country Report Snapshot August, 2015						*INDIA*		*Updated*	
Goal 2 Achieve Universal Primary Education									
Targets	*Indicators*	*First Year*		*Latest Year*		*Percentage*	*Country Progress*	*Latest Data*	
		Value	*Year*	*Value*	*Year*		*Level*	*Value*	*Year*
Universal Primary schooling	Net enrolment ratio in Primary education (enrolees per 100 children)	78.2	1990	98.6	2012	26	High enrolment	94.8	2015

Source: Unstat/MDG Report, 2015.

SDG-4 and the initiatives in India

(a) The NITI Aayog and Mapping of Initiatives on SDG-4

It is true that Goal-4 is more comprehensive and robust than erstwhile MDG-2, yet the factual position as obtained in India on MDG-2 would be important in preparing the roadmap for Sustainable development of **Goal 4** for revisiting the basic approach and goal-specific initiatives to be undertaken in India. The NITI Aayog has been empowered to oversee the implementation of SDGs by the ministries of the Central Government and coordinate with States for the achievement of developmental targets as enshrined in the SDGs. The NITI Aayog tasked itself to prepare a initial draft based on mapping of the goals and targets proposed by Nodal and other Ministries in consultation with MoSPI. The schemes so mapped for Goal-4 include 20)Sarva Shiksha Abhiyan (Core) [2001], 21) National Programme Nutritional Support to

Primary Education (MDM) (Core)22)Rashtriya Madhyamik Shiksha Abhiyan (RMSA)(Core)[2016],23)Support for Educational Development including Teachers Training & Adult Education(Core)[2015] 24)Scheme for providing education to Madrasas, Minorities and Disabled (Core of the Core)25)Rashtriya Uchhtar Shiksha Abhiyan (RUSA) (Core){2013}26)Umbrella scheme for Education of ST Students (Core of the Core)[2015]. It also included Padhe Bharat Badhe Bharat in its mapping[2014].

(b) National Review of SDG- 4 for United Nations High Level Political Forum 2017

The outcomes of initiatives under SDG-4 are dependent not only on right kind of programme selection but also on the quality of governance calling for effective convergence of all initiatives, both public and private, in a sequential platform to bring about envisaged result after a period of time. The Voluntary National Review Report on Implementation of Sustainable Development Goals presented for United Nations High Level Political Forum 2017 happens to be a good reference point for understanding the position on SDGs' status in India. The Voluntary National Review Report has not included SDG-4 as a separate item. However, it is noted therein that "given the interconnectedness of the SDGs, relevant strategies for enabling collaboration among different actors will be developed as part of the overall implementation process and that India will continue to pursue the implementation of the SDG agenda through close collaboration between the national and sub-national governments as well as active participation of all other relevant stakeholders".

(c) The NITI Aayog, Three-Year Action Agenda and SDG-4

NITI Aayog has recently released the Three-Year Action Agenda covering years 2017-18 to 2019-20 delineating ambitious proposals for changes in policy and strategy to improve outcome within a relatively shorter period. The Chapter 20 of Part VI of the Action Agenda deals with Education along with Skill development. It would be worthwhile to capture the Action Agenda for School Education and Higher Education. The Agenda begins with the admission that the youths in India need education and skills to be able to fulfil their promise and the current systems are ill-equipped to deliver them on a larger scale. The most important goal in the school education system today is to improve learning outcome. Though initiatives like the Sarva Siksha Abhiyan (SSA) and the Right of the Children to Free and Compulsory Education (RTE) Act, the Indian School System has focused on measuring and delivering inputs, and in this, it has largely succeeded. The Gross Enrolment Ratio (GER) in 2015-16 for Grades I-V was 99.2% and for all Grades VI-VIII was 92.8%. Unfortunately; however, this success in getting more children into schools with more teachers has not translated into more education. The Action Agenda, therefore, notes that the most critical missing pieces are pedagogy that focuses on teaching at the right level, outcome linked incentives, and governance that enables the system to operate smoothly. Accordingly three major goals have been thought of as action agenda, namely,

- Orient the system towards outcomes
- Provide tools to teachers and students for effective learning
- Improve existing governance mechanism and pilot new ones

The Action Agenda Report is also of the view that though India has made significant progress in increasing enrolment –the GER in tertiary education has risen from 20.3% in 2011-12 to 24.5% in 2015-16% and more than double what it was only 10 years ago, it has still to become a vibrant and successful higher education sector on ground of less regulation, a strategy to be followed for the three year period. The major actions to be completed over the next three years include the following:

- Designation of World Class University
- Autonomy of top colleges and universities
- Reform of the regulatory system-A tiered system of universities
- Establish system of Project/researcher specific research grants
- Increased focus on vocational and profession led education

(d) Economic Survey of India, 2017-18

The Government of India tabled the Economic Survey of India, 2017-18 in the Parliament in the Budget Session on 29th January,2018 to set the stage for the Government for the Annual Budget. The Survey contains an indepth analysis, serious research as well new policy ideas. The said Survey sums up the latest position on status on Education, as included in SDG-4, that as per the Right to Education (RTE) indicators, it reflects the effectiveness of universalization of education. Most of the States have registered an increase in the percentage of schools complying with the PTR (Pupil Teacher Ratio) norms. The GPI (Gender Parity Index) reflects disparity of girls vis-a-vis boys in access to education. With consistent efforts by the government through programmes like *Beti Padhao, Beti Bachao*, the GPI has improved substantially at the primary and secondary levels of enrolment. However, in higher education, gender disparities still prevail in enrolment, for which various programmes are being implemented by the Government to improve net intake rate of women in higher education.

(e) Budget Inititives for 2018-19

The Budget document embodies not only a financial statement on resources availability and its projected expenditure, it also expresses alongside overtly and covertly the policy statement of the Government of the day. The Budget Speech of the Finance Minister of India delivered on First February,2018 is taken up to relate its relevance on SDGs. In so far as SDG-4 is concerned, the Union Finance Minister observed that our Government's goal is to assist and provide opportunity to every Indian to realize her full potential capable of achieving her economic and social dreams. On school education, he stated that though the government have managed to get children to School but the quality of education is still a cause of serious concern. The Human Resources Development Ministry have now defined learning outcomes and National Survey of more than 20 lakh children has been conducted to assess the status on the ground. This will help in devising a district-wise strategy for improving quality of education. It is now looked upon education holistically without segmentation from pre-nursery to Class 12. For improvement in quality of teachers and consequent quality of education in the country, an integrated B.Ed. programme for teachers will be initiated and Training of teachers during service would also be strengthened. The Right to Education Act has been amended to enable more than 13 lakh untrained teachers to get trained. Moreover, Technology will be the biggest driver in improving the quality of education and accordingly, the government undertakes to increase the digital intensity in education and move gradually from "black board" to "digital board". Technology will also be used to upgrade the skills of teachers through the recently launched digital portal "DIKSHA".

The Finance Minister also announced setting up of Ekalavya Model Residential School on par with Navodaya Vidyalayas to provide the best quality education to the tribal children in their own environment by 2022 in every block with more than 50% ST population and at least 20,000 tribal persons with special facilities for preserving local art and culture besides providing training in sports and skill development. To step up investments in research and related infrastructure in premier educational institutions, including health institutions, a major initiative named "Revitalising Infrastructure and Systems in Education (RISE) by 2022" with a total investment of Rs.1,00,000 crore in next four years was announced. The Finance Minister said that the Government would launch the "Prime Minister's Research Fellows (PMRF)" Scheme this year. Under this, 1,000 best B.Tech students will be identified each year from premier institutions and provide them facilities to do Ph.D in IITs and IISc, with a handsome fellowship. He also said that the Government has taken major initiative of setting up Institutes of Eminence and that steps are being taken to set up a specialized Railways University at Vadodara, two new full-fledged Schools of Planning and Architecture and 18 new SPAs would be established in the IITs and NITs as autonomous Schools.

Are the initiatives enough ?

The Goal-4 is designed to shape the very foundation of sustainable development and demands robust intervention in programme front and its efficient implementation. The initiatives under SDG-4 in India, till date, have been more and less continuing schemes till the budget declaration,2018-19 and no new and big ticket programmes came into being since the SDGs have become functional on 1January,2016 as would appear from the brackets mentioned earlier for the mapped-up schemes. The seven important programmes mapped by NITI were taken up by the country before the Sustainable Development Summit, September, 2015 and are in that sense continuing schemes. The Declaration of Sustainable Development Summit and the new goals thereafter call for revisiting the continuing schemes with reference to the envisioned goal and its monitoring format. The short term Action agenda has diagnosed the grey areas of the continuing programmes and the need to revise the policy and strategy. Hopefully, new schemes tailored to outcome ensurance of Goal-4 in the Budget speech of the Finance Minister would be useful in this area. However, the country needs to relook the big grey area of educational and vocational needs of the Physically and Mentally challenged groups located both in the rural and urban areas having different age structure after the enactment of The Right of Persons with Disabilities Act, 2016. Dedicated new schemes on different categories of disabled persons are called for to ensure that nobody is left behind.

Chapter - 15

Sustainable Development Goal - 5

Achieve gender equality and empower all women and girls

In the historic declaration of Sustainable Development Summit, 2015, it has been put on record that Gender inequality remains still a key challenge even after 15 years of the Millennium Development Goals in place. It is a fact that hundreds of millions of people have emerged from extreme poverty and access to education greatly increased for both boys and girls, it remain off-track, in particular to those related to maternal, newborn and child health and to reproductive health. The Summit made a clarion call to recommit to the full realization of all off-track Millennium Development Goals. In this context the Summit, 2015 also reaffirmed that gender equality and the empowerment of women and girls will make a crucial contribution to progress across all the Goals and targets. The achievement of full human potential and of sustainable development is not possible if one half of humanity continues to be denied its full human rights and opportunities. Women and girls must enjoy equal access to quality education, economic resources and political participation as well as equal opportunities with men and boys for employment, leadership and decision-making at all levels. It will work for a significant increase in investments to close the gender gap and strengthen support for institutions in relation to gender equality and the empowerment of women at the global, regional and national levels. The systematic mainstreaming of a gender perspective in the implementation of the Agenda is crucial.

The Fact Sheet on Goal 5 and the Report of the Secretary General before the Sustinable Svelopment Summit mentioned that Gender equality and women's empowerment have relatively advanced in the MDGs era. Girls' access to education has improved, In Southern Asia region, 74 girls were enrolled in primary school for every 100 boys in 1990. By 2012, the enrolment ratios were the same for girls and for boys and in 46 countries. Substantial progress has also been made in the area of sexual and reproductive health and reproductive rights, including fewer maternal deaths. The rate of child marriage has declined, though it still remains a great obstacle to women empowerment. Globally the proportion of women aged between 20 and 24 who reported that they were married before their eighteenth birthday dropped from 32 per cent around 1990 to 26 per cent around 2015. However, in Southern Asia the rate is as high as 44 per cent. The political participation of women in elective posts has increased. There are no firm data on women participation of work. Women and girls usually do the bulk of unpaid work including care giving and household tasks in every region. On average, women spend 19 per cent of their time each day in unpaid activities, versus 8 per cent for men. The responsibilities of unpaid care and domestic work, combined with paid work, means greater total work burdens for women and girls and less time for rest, self-care, learning and other activities. Violence against women and girls is an indicator of social position enjoyed by them which infringes their human rights and hinders development. Surveys conducted between 2005 and 2015, in 52 countries, (including only one country from the developed regions) indicate that 21 per cent of girls and women aged between 15 and 49 experienced physical and/or sexual violence at the hands of an intimate partner in the previous 12 months. Further, human trafficking detected worldwide are disproportionately female and affects adversely women and girls. Globally, women's participation in parliament rose to 23 per cent in 2016, representing an increase by 6 percentage points over a decade. Slow progress in this area is in contrast with more women in parliamentary leadership positions. In 2016, the number of women speakers of national parliaments jumped from 43 to 49 (out of the 273 posts globally); women accounted for 18 per cent of all speakers of parliament in January 2016. However, gender equality remains a persistent challenge for countries worldwide and the lack of such equality is a major obstacle to sustainable development

The interactive Dialogue 2 preceding to the Sustainable Development Summit went through all connected issues of Goal 5. The Participants noted that the 2030 Agenda for Sustainable Development calls for unprecedented attention to the need to reduce inequalities both within and among nations. Only by doing so can we build a world that is more just, stable and peaceful. It also felt that for tackling inequalities national policies or laws and programmes need to be revisited, wherever required, to encompasses all human rights and eliminate all forms of discrimination. It is also needed capacity building at all levels, including the community level. The interactive Dialogue also emphasized that SDGs cannot be achieved unless progress includes all, especially women as half of the world's population. This marginalized section of our society must have equal opportunities and access to resources. They must also be given a voice. A sustainable world should give every person a fair chance. Gender equality was also highlighted to be the key to unlock multiplier effect on achieving all goals. It focused on four intervening actions, namely, universal access to quality education for girls by all means in the given timeframe, women to be given equal opportunities in the economic sphere, including at the workplace; more representation of women in political positions and leadership and finally violence against women must be eliminated.

In fine, the sustainable development goals seek to change the course of the 21st century, addressing key challenges such as poverty, inequality, and violence against women. Women's empowerment is a pre-condition for this. Empowering women and girls to reach their full potential requires that they have equal opportunities to those of men and boys. This means eliminating all forms of discrimination and violence against them, including violence by intimate partners, sexual violence and harmful practices, such as child marriage and female genital mutilation (FGM). Ensuring that women have better access to paid employment, sexual and reproductive health and reproductive rights, and real decision-making power in public and private spheres will further ensure that development is equitable and sustainable. Additionally, Women have a critical role to play in all of the SDGs, with many targets specifically recognizing women's equality and empowerment as both the objective, and as part of the solution. Goal 5 is known as the stand-alone gender goal because it is dedicated to achieving these ends.

Based on the above perspective, it would be appropriate to reiterate the Goal 5 of the SDGs, its targets and related indicators to keep it in the up-front, in sequential order, before addressing India's initiatives on ensuring 'Achieve gender equality and empower all women and girls'.

Goal 5. Achieve gender equality and empower all women and girls

5.1 End all forms of discrimination against all women and girls everywhere

5.2 Eliminate all forms of violence against all women and girls in the public and private spheres, including trafficking and sexual and other types of exploitation

5.3 Eliminate all harmful practices, such as child, early and forced marriage and female genital mutilation

5.4 Recognize and value unpaid care and domestic work through the provision of public services, infrastructure and social protection policies and the promotion of shared responsibility within the household and the family as nationally appropriate

5.5 Ensure women's full and effective participation and equal opportunities for leadership at all levels of decision-making in political, economic and public life

5.6 Ensure universal access to sexual and reproductive health and reproductive rights as agreed in accordance with the Programme of Action of the International Conference on Population and Development and the Beijing Platform for Action and the outcome documents of their review conferences

5.a Undertake reforms to give women equal rights to economic resources, as well as access to ownership and control over land and other forms of property, financial services, inheritance and natural resources, in accordance with national laws

5.b Enhance the use of enabling technology, in particular information and communications technology, to promote the empowerment of women

5.c Adopt and strengthen sound policies and enforceable legislation for the promotion of gender equality and the empowerment of all women and girls at all levels.

The goals and targets per se are important from the angle of programme vision and intended outcome; however from the perspective of monitoring the performance, indicators do play critical role. Since indicator-design is essentially an expert professional skill- job requiring to keep harmony with overall goals and targets of the Sustainable Development Summit as embodied in paragraph 75 of Transforming our World: The 2030 Agenda for Sustainable Development mentioned: "the Goals and targets will be followed-up and reviewed using a set of global indicators. These will be complemented by indicators at the regional and national levels which will be developed by member states, in addition to the outcomes of work undertaken for the development of the baselines for those targets where national and global baseline data does not yet exist".

Needless to mention that purpose of SDG indicators is twofold; first it acts as a management tool to help countries develop implementation and monitoring strategies for achieving the SDGs and to monitor progress and secondly, it works as a report card, to measure progress towards achieving a target and ensure the accountability of governments to their citizens. As a matter of fact, Agenda 21 of the SD Summit also called on countries and the international community to develop indicators of sustainable development. Such indicators were needed to increase focus on sustainable development and assist decision-makers at all levels to adopt sound national sustainable development policies.

Be that as it may, the Global Indicator Framework as designed by the UN Statistical Commission at its 47th Session in March 2016 and adopted

thereafter by the Economic and Social Council and the General Assembly, are as follows:

Indicators of Goal -5:

5.1.1 Whether or not legal frameworks are in place to promote, enforce and monitor equality and non-discrimination on the basis of sex

5.2.1 Proportion of ever-partnered women and girls aged 15 years and older subjected to physical, sexual or psychological violence by a current or former intimate partner in the previous 12 months, by form of violence and by age

5.2.2 Proportion of women and girls aged 15 years and older subjected to sexual violence by persons other than an intimate partner in the previous 12 months, by age and place of occurrence

5.3.1 Proportion of women aged 20-24 years who were married or in a union before age 15 and before age 18

5.3.2 Proportion of girls and women aged 15-49 years who have undergone female genital mutilation/cutting, by age

5.4.1 Proportion of time spent on unpaid domestic and care work, by sex, age and location

5.5.1 Proportion of seats held by women in (a) national parliaments and (b) local governments

5.5.2 Proportion of women in managerial positions

5.6.1 Proportion of women aged 15-49 years who make their own informed decisions regarding sexual relations, contraceptive use and reproductive health care

5.6.2 Number of countries with laws and regulations that guarantee full and equal access to women and men aged 15 years and older to sexual and reproductive health care, information and education

5.a.1 (a) Proportion of total agricultural population with ownership or secure rights over agricultural land,by sex; and (b) share of women among owners or rights-bearers of agricultural land, by type of tenure

5.a.2 Proportion of countries where the legal framework (including customary law) guarantees women's equal rights to land ownership and/or control

5.b.1 Proportion of individuals who own a mobile telephone, by sex

5.c.1 Proportion of countries with systems to track and make public allocations for gender equality and women's empowerment

In the light of the overarching goal of SDG-5, the national government of the country needs to take it forward to design appropriate programme in ensuring commensurate outcome. In such efforts, the current scenario and revealed gaps need to be taken into consideration while drawing a roadmap for SDG-5. The validated data in the MDG Report, 2015 published on MDG-3,Gender Equality and Empower Women, by the United Nations on 6th July, 2015 need to be used as benchmark data for SDG- **5.**

Table 15.1: MDG Report, 2015 on, Gender Equality and Empower Women

Series	*1990*	*2000*	*2010*	*2012*	*2013*	*2014*	*2015*
3.1 Ratio of Girls to Boys in Primary, Secondary and Tertiary Education							
MDG Gender Parity Index in Primary level enrolment Last updated 06 July, 2015	0.74	0.84	1.01	1.03			
MDG Gender Parity Index in Secondary level enrolment Last updated 06 July, 2015		0.71	0.93	0.95			
MDG Gender Parity Index in Tertiary level enrolment Last updated 06 July, 2015	0.52	0.66	0.72		0.92		
3.2 Share of Women in wage employment in the non-agricultural sector							
Percentage Last updated 06 July, 2015	12.7	16.6	19.3				
3.3 Proportion of seats held by Women in national parliament							
MDG Seats held by Women in national parliament, Percentage Last updated 06 July, 2015	5.0	9.0	10.8	11.0	11.0	11.4	12.0
MDG Seats held by Women in national parliament Last updated 06 July, 2015	26	49	59	60	60	62	65

SDG-5 and the initiatives in India :

(a) The NITI Aayog and Mapping of Initiatives on SDG-5

Given the above the factual position as obtained in India, it would be worthwhile to examine the roadmap for Sustainable development of Goal 5, revisit the basic approach and goal-specific initiatives undertaken in India. The NITI Aayog has been empowered to oversee the implementation of SDGs by the ministries of the Central Government and coordinate with States for the achievement of developmental targets as enshrined in the SDGs. The NITI Aayog tasked itself to prepare a initial draft based on mapping of the goals and targets proposed by Nodal and other Ministries in consultation with MoSPI. The schemes so mapped for Goal-5 include 27) National Mission for Empowerment of Women including Indira Gandhi Mattritav Sahyog Yojana (Core)[2010] 28)Rajiv Gandhi Scheme for Empowerment of Adolescent Girls (SABLA) (Core) [2011]. It also included related intervention like (1) Beti Bachao Beti Padhao[2015], (2) Sukanya Samridhi Yojana (Girl Child Prosperity Scheme) [2015], (3) Support to Training And Employment ProgrammeFor Women (STEP) 2014, (4) Janani Suraksha Yojana (JSY)[2015], (5) SWADHAR 2011 (A scheme for women in difficult circumstances) [2002] and 6) Kasturba Gandhi Balika Vidyalay (KGBV) [2004]. The NITI Aayog also put up a draft mapping on goal-5 on August, 2017 which mentions 1) Mission for Protection and Empowerment of Women (Beti Bachao Beti Padhao, One Stop Centre, Women Helpline, hostels, SWADHAR Greh, gender budgeting etc.) (Core). It also included related intervention like) Support to Training and Employment Programme (STEP), 2) PRAGATI (Providing Assistance for Girls' Advancement in Technical Education Initiative).

(b) National Review of SDG-5 for United Nations High Level Political Forum 2017

The outcomes of initiatives under SDG-5 would normally take a period of time to fructify as several other factors are also interlinked to reflect its final outcome. Be that as it may, the Voluntary National Review Report on Implementation of Sustainable Development Goals presented for United Nations High Level Political Forum 2017 is a good reference point for understanding the latest position on SDG-5 status in India. The report says that while much more progress remains to be made, a number of indicators pertaining to the status of women in India have moved in the right direction over the years. For instance, 68.4% of women were literate in 2015-16, as compared to 55.1% in 2005-06. Additionally, 53% of women were independently using a bank or savings account in 2015-16, which is a significant improvement from 15.1% in 2005-06.Numerous measures have been put in place for promoting gender equality. For example, the Beti Bachao Beti Padao (Save the Girl Child, Educate the Girl Child) initiative focuses on a comprehensive package of interventions for the girl child including those pertaining to education and protection. The Maternity Benefit Programme protects women from wage loss during the first six months after childbirth. Further, several programmes are being implemented for enabling greater participation of women in the work force

(c) The NITI Aayog, Three-Year Action Agenda and SDG-5

NITI Aayog has recently released the Three-Year Action Agenda covering years 2017-18 to 2019-20 which begins with the objective of eliminating poverty in all its dimensions such that every citizen will have access to a minimum standard of food, education, health, clothing, shelter, transportation and energy. The chapter 22 of the Three-Year Action Plan Agenda dwelt on Women under 'Towards Building a more Inclusive Society' where it has been noted that women encounter discriminatory practices throughout their life cycle as reflected in unfavourable sex ratio, high school drop-outs, and increasing incidence of violent crimes. The Agenda reiterates that women's economic empowerment plays a crucial role in talking gender inequality. The Report takes note of the fact that currently, the contribution of Indian women to the GDP (17%) is not only far below the global average (37%), but is less than China (41%) and Sub-Saharan Africa (35%). Further, the greater equality in educational attainment achieved through higher enrolment in schools has not translated into equal opportunities for women in the labour market. Despite acceleration in economic growth, labour market outcome for men far outweigh those for women reflecting at the same time extremely unequal participation of women across sectors and increasing gender wage gap in decision-making process.

The Agenda report affirms government's commitment in that during the next three years, the focus would be on promoting equal participation on women in the economy. Additionally, measures to protect women from all forms of violence will be prioritised. Further, Gender response Budgeting would be further improved to meet gender challenge by way of disaggregating gender data and integrating gender budget with outcome budget. Moreover, for enabling equal access to employment opportunity and financial services for women, it is designed to address financial literacy programme customised for women along with incentives for specific purposes. Pilot project like Bank Sakhis' would be scaled up to improve the integration of female bank agents into the community. Based on results of evaluation, priority sector lending would be made gender-friendly. The National Skill Development Corporation's policy of minimum reservation of 33% seats for women for skill development training would be monitored to see whether those trained are getting employed. Finally, a composite Women's Wellbeing Index to reflect the status of women in the country would be put in place.

(d) Economic Survey of India, 2017-18

The Government of India tabled the Economic Survey of India, 2017-18 in the Parliament in the Budget Session on 29th January,2018 to set the stage for the Government for the Annual Budget. The Survey contains an indepth analysis, serious research as well new policy ideas. The said Survey sums up the latest position on status of Women, as included in SDG-5. The Survey takes into account that Gender equality is an inherently multi-dimensional issue. Accordingly, assessments have been made based on three specific dimensions of gender, ie Agency (relates to women's ability to make decisions on reproduction, spending on themselves, spending on their households and their own mobility and health), Attitudes (relate to attitudes about violence against women/wives, and the ideal number of daughters preferred relative to the ideal number of sons) and Outcomes (relate to son preference' measured by sex ratio of last child, female employment, choice of contraception, education level, age at marriage, age at first birth and physical or sexual violence experienced by women) which aim to reflect the status, role and empowerment of women in the society. The key findings of the assessment made in the Survey include: Over the last 10-15 years, India's performance improved on 14 out of 17 indicators of women's agency, attitudes, and outcomes. On seven of them, the improvement has been such that India's situation is comparable to that of a cohort of countries after accounting for levels of development. The Survey encouragingly notes that gender outcomes exhibit a convergence pattern, improving with wealth to a greater extent in India than in similar countries so that even where it is lagging, it can expect to catch up over time. The Survey, however, cautions that on several other indicators, notably employment, use of reversible contraception, and son preference, India has some distance to traverse because development has not proved to be an antidote.

Economic Survey 2017-18 states that within India, there is significant heterogeneity, with the North-Eastern states (a model for the rest of the country) consistently out-performing others and not because they are richer; hinterland states are lagging behind but the surprise is that some southern states do less well than their development levels would suggest.

The Economic Survey 2017-18 notes the challenge of gender is long-standing, probably going back millennia, so all stakeholders are collectively responsible for its resolution.

The Survey thus recommends that India must confront the societal preference, even meta-preference for a son, which appears inoculated to development. The skewed sex ratio in favor of males led to the identification of 63 million missing? women. But there may be a meta-preference manifesting itself in fertility stopping rules contingent on the sex of the last child, which notionally creates unwanted girls, estimated at about 21 million, adds the Survey. Consigning these odious categories to history soon should be society's objective, opines the Survey.

The survey acknowledges that government's Beti Bachao, Beti Padhao and Sukanya Samridhi Yojana schemes, and mandatory maternity leave rules are all steps in the right direction. The Survey states that just as India has committed to moving up the ranks in 'Ease of Doing Business indicators', a similar commitment should be endeavoured on the gender front.

Another aspect related to the status of women and covered in the Economic Survey, 2017-18 is the Feminisation of Agriculture Sector with increasing number of women in multiple roles as cultivators, entrepreneurs, and labourers following growing migration by men. Towards this, Government has been implementing various schemes which help improve the entitlements of women farmers, which will prove to be advantageous in bridging the policy gaps which exits in the sector. The following measures have been taken to ensure mainstreaming of women in agriculture sector:

- Earmarking at least 30% of the budget allocation for women beneficiaries in all ongoing schemes/programmes and development activities.
- Initiating women centric activities to ensure benefits of various beneficiary-oriented programs/schemes reach them.
- Focusing on women self-help group (SHG) to connect them to micro-credit through capacity building activities and to provide information and ensuring their representation in different decision-making bodies.

- Recognizing the critical role of women in agriculture, the Ministry of Agriculture and Farmers Welfare has declared 15th October of every year as Women Farmer's Day.

With women predominant at all levels-production, pre-harvest, post-harvest processing, packaging, marketing – of the agricultural value chain, to increase productivity in agriculture, it is imperative to adopt gender specific interventions. An inclusive transformative agricultural policy' should aim at gender-specific intervention to raise productivity of small farm holdings, integrate women as active agents in rural transformation, and engage men and women in extension services with gender expertise.

(e) Budget Inititives for 2018-19

The Budget document embodies not only a financial statement on resources availability and its projected expenditure, it also expresses alongside overtly and covertly the policy statement of the Government of the day. The Budget Speech of the Finance Minister of India delivered on First February,2018 is taken up to relate its relevance on SDGs. In so far as SDG-5 is concerned, the Union Finance Minister observed that *Sabka Saath Sabka Vikas* begins with the girl child and women. *Mahila Shakti Kendra* will be set up at village level with an allocation of ' 500 crores in 14 lakh ICDS *Anganwadi* Centres. This will provide one stop convergent support services for empowering rural women with opportunities for skill development, employment, digital literacy, health and nutrition. A nationwide scheme for financial assistance to pregnant women has already been announced by the Prime Minister on 31st December, 2016. Under this scheme, Rs 6,000 will be transferred directly to the bank accounts of each pregnant woman who undergoes institutional delivery and vaccinate their children. On the loans to Self Help Groups of women, the Finance Minister said that it increased to about Rupees 42,500 crore in 2016-17, registering a growth of 37% over previous year and expressed confidence that loans to SHGs will increase to Rs.75,000 crore by March, 2019. The Finance Minister also substantially increased allocation of National Rural Livelihood Mission to Rs 5750 crore in 2018-19. Referring to the measures taken for the benefit of lower and middle class, the Finance Minister said, under Ujjwala Scheme, distribution of free LPG connections will be given to 8 crore poor women instead of the previous target of 5 crore women.

Chapter - 16

Sustainable Development Goal 6

Ensure availability and sustainable management of water and sanitation for all

Water and sanitation are at the very core of sustainable development and critical to the survival of people and the planet. Access to drinking water and sanitation is a human right and, together with water resources, a key determinant in all aspects of social, economic and environmental development. Clean, accessible water for all is an essential part of our living. Despite availability of sufficient fresh water on the planet, millions of people, most of them children, die every year from diseases associated with inadequate water supply, sanitation and hygiene. Moreover, water scarcity, poor water quality and inadequate sanitation negatively impact food security, livelihood choices and educational opportunities for poor families across the world. Drought afflicts some of the world's poorest countries, worsening hunger and malnutrition. Earlier, the MDGs incorporated targets on drinking water and sanitation but did not address other aspects crucial to sustainable development, such as water resources management, waste-water management, water quality and enhancing resilience to water-related disasters. The Goal 6 addresses the issues relating to drinking water, sanitation and hygiene along with the quality and sustainability of water resources worldwide.

The FAO has made a futuristic projection of possible water stress scenario in the world that by 2050 at least one in four people is likely to live in a country affected by chronic or recurring shortages of fresh water, and also evaluated the current status as below:

- 2.6 billion people have gained access to improved drinking water sources since 1990, but 663 million people are still without

- At least 1.8 billion people globally use a source of drinking water that is fecally contaminated
- Between 1990 and 2015, the proportion of the global population using an improved drinking water source has increased from 76 per cent to 91 per cent
- But water scarcity affects more than 40 per cent of the global population and is projected to rise. Over 1.7 billion people are currently living in river basins where water use exceeds recharge
- 2.4 billion people lack access to basic sanitation services, such as toilets or latrines
- More than 80 per cent of wastewater resulting from human activities is discharged into rivers or sea without any pollution removal
- Each day, nearly 1,000 children die due to preventable water and sanitation-related diarrhoeal diseases
- Hydropower is the most important and widely-used renewable source of energy and as of 2011, represented 16 per cent of total electricity production worldwide
- Approximately 70 per cent of all water abstracted from rivers, lakes and aquifers is used for irrigation
- Floods and other water-related disasters account for 70 per cent of all deaths related to natural disasters

The Fact sheet available before the Sustainable Development Summit, in September,2015 indicated that compared to 76% in 1990, the status of using an improved drinking water source in 2015 has improved to 91% of the global population. However, not all improved sources are safe. For instance, in 2012 it was estimated that at least 1.8 billion people were exposed to drinking water sources contaminated with faecal matter. Further, the global water stress condition (calculated as the ratio of total fresh water withdrawn by all major sectors to the total renewable fresh water resources) signals an alarming trend. The UN Secretary General has mentioned in its report" Progress towards the Sustainable Development Goals",E/2016/75 that currently, water stress affects more than 2 billion people around the world, a figure that is projected to rise. In fact, water stress has affected a number of countries on every continent and started hindering the sustainability of natural resources along with economic and social development. However, 65 per cent of the 130 countries reported that Integrated water resource management plans were in place at the national level in 2012. In the context of water for all in a national context, water fund /aid has to be better targeted to have access to water supply and/or sanitation

The Fact sheet also mentions that about 2.5 billion people lack access to basic sanitation services, such as toilets or latrines. On an average, about 5,000 children die on each day due to preventable water and sanitation-related diseases. The Fact sheet also says that approximately 70% of all available water is used for irrigation and that Floods account for 15% of all deaths related to natural disasters. The UN Secretary General has mentioned in its report that effective water and sanitation management also depends on the participation of stakeholders. In the Sustainable Development Goals, the focus is being refined to also include the participation of local communities, which will be captured in the next cycle of Global Analysis and Assessment of Sanitation and Drinking-Water monitoring.

Sustainable Development Goal 6 goes beyond drinking water, sanitation and hygiene to also address the quality and sustainability of water resources, critical to the survival of people and the planet. The 2030 Agenda recognizes the centrality of water resources to sustainable development, and the vital role that improved drinking water, sanitation and hygiene play in progress in other areas, including health, education and poverty reduction. Besides, Goal 6 also addresses additional targets such as protecting and restoring water-related ecosystems (including mountains, forests, wetlands, rivers and lakes). Goal 6 aims to improve water quality and reduce water pollution, especially the type caused by hazardous chemicals. It also advocates cross-border cooperation as the key to managing water resources in an integrated fashion at all levels.

Water and sanitation are at the very core of sustainable development, critical for thriving people, planet and prosperity. Water is needed for domestic purposes, for agricultural, industrial and energy production, and these uses are highly inter-linked, potentially in competition, and they generate wastewater that may cause pollution. Water is central to climate change, linking the climate system to the environmental and socio-economic systems; climate change severs water scarcity in some parts of the world, and the risk of flooding in others.

Water is a key factor in managing risks such as famine, epidemics, migration, inequalities and political instability. Integrated water resources management is essential to harness synergies as well as to manage potential trade-offs across sectors and regions, to ensure availability and sustainable management of water and sanitation for all. With water at the very core of sustainable development, SDG 6 does not only have strong linkages to all of the other SDGs, it also underpins them; meeting SDG 6 would go a long way towards achieving much of the 2030 Agenda.

Based on the above observations, it would be appropriate to reiterate the Goal 6 of the SDGs, its targets and related indicators to keep it in the up-fronts,in sequential order, before addressing India's initiatives on SDG 6 "Ensure availability and sustainable management of water and sanitation for all".

Goal 6. Ensure availability and sustainable management of water and sanitation for all

6.1 By 2030, achieve universal and equitable access to safe and affordable drinking water for all

6.2 By 2030, achieve access to adequate and equitable sanitation and hygiene for all and end open defecation, paying special attention to the needs of women and girls and those in vulnerable situations

6.3 By 2030, improve water quality by reducing pollution, eliminating dumping and minimizing release of hazardous chemicals and materials, halving the proportion of untreated wastewater and substantially increasing recycling and safe reuse globally

6.4 By 2030, substantially increase water-use efficiency across all sectors and ensure sustainable withdrawals and supply of freshwater to address water scarcity and substantially reduce the number of people suffering from water scarcity

6.5 By 2030, implement integrated water resources management at all levels, including through transboundary cooperation as appropriate

6.6 By 2020, protect and restore water-related ecosystems, including mountains, forests, wetlands, rivers, aquifers and lakes

6.a By 2030, expand international cooperation and capacity-building support to developing countries in water- and sanitation-related activities and programmes, including water harvesting, desalination, water efficiency, wastewater treatment, recycling and reuse technologies

6.b Support and strengthen the participation of local communities in improving water and sanitation management

It thus appears that SDG 6 contains six targets on outcomes across the entire water cycle, and two targets on the means of implementing the outcome targets. In addition, water-related issues are mentioned in many other goals across the 2030 Agenda, including target 11.5 on water-related disasters. Further, it is also noted the following:

- Targets 6.1 and 6.2 build on the MDG targets on drinking water and basic sanitation, providing continuity while expanding their scope and refining definitions.
- Targets 6.3 to 6.6 address the broader water context that was not explicitly included in the MDG framework, but whose importance was acknowledged at the Rio+20 Conference, such as water quality and wastewater management, water scarcity and water-use efficiency, integrated water resources management, and the protection and restoration of water-related ecosystems.

- Targets 6.a and 6.b acknowledge the importance of an enabling environment, addressing the means of implementation and aiming for international cooperation, capacity-building and the participation of local communities in water and sanitation management.

The goals and targets per se are important from the angle of programme vision and intended outcome; however from the perspective of monitoring the performance, indicators do play critical role. Since indicator-design is essentially an expert professional skill- job requiring to keep harmony with overall goals and targets of the Sustainable Development Summit as embodied in paragraph 75 of Transforming our World: The 2030 Agenda for Sustainable Development mentioned: "the Goals and targets will be followed-up and reviewed using a set of global indicators. These will be complemented by indicators at the regional and national levels which will be developed by member states, in addition to the outcomes of work undertaken for the development of the baselines for those targets where national and global baseline data does not yet exist".

Needless to mention that purpose of SDG indicators is twofold; first it acts as a management tool to help countries develop implementation and monitoring strategies for achieving the SDGs and to monitor progress and secondly, it works as a report card, to measure progress towards achieving a target and ensure the accountability of governments to their citizens. As a matter of fact, Agenda 21 of the SD Summit also called on countries and the international community to develop indicators of sustainable development. Such indicators were needed to increase focus on sustainable development and assist decision-makers at all levels to adopt sound national sustainable development policies.

Be that as it may, the Global Indicator Framework as designed by the UN Statistical Commission at its 47th Session in March 2016 and adopted thereafter by the Economic and Social Council and the General Assembly, are as follows:

Indicators of Goal 6

6.1.1 Proportion of population using safely managed drinking water services

6.2.1 Proportion of population using safely managed sanitation services, including a hand-washing facility with soap and water

6.3.1 Proportion of wastewater safely treated

6.3.2 Proportion of bodies of water with good ambient water quality

6.4.1 Change in water-use efficiency over time

6.4.2 Level of water stress: freshwater withdrawal as a proportion of available freshwater resources

6.5.1 Degree of integrated water resources management implementation (0-100)

6.5.2 Proportion of transboundary basin area with an operational arrangement for water cooperation

6.6.1 Change in the extent of water-related ecosystems over time

6.a.1 Amount of water- and sanitation-related official development assistance that is part of agovernment-coordinated spending plan

6.b.1 Proportion of local administrative units with established and operational policies and proceduresfor participation of local communities in water and sanitation management

Based on the overarching goal of SDG-6, the national government of the country needs to take it forward to design appropriate programme in ensuring commensurate outcome. In such efforts, the current scenario and revealed gaps need to be taken into consideration while drawing a roadmap for goal-6. The validated data in the MDG Report, 2015 published by the United Nations on 6th July, 2015 need to be used as benchmark data on a part of SDG 6 "Ensure availability and sustainable management of water and sanitation for all"and its performance status over time in India as are indicated below:

Table 16.1: MDG Goal 7: Ensure environmental sustainability relating to drinking water and sanitation

Series	*1990*	*2000*	*2011*	*2012*	*2013*	*2014*	*2015*
7.8 Proportion of population using improved water source							
Total percentage 27 July, 2015	71	83	91	92	93	94	94
Urban percentage 27 July, 2015	89	93	96	96	97	97	97
97Rural percentage 27 July, 2015	64	78	89	90	92	93	93
7.9 Proportion of population using a improved sanitation facility							
Total percentage 27 July, 2015	17	28	37	38	39	40	40
Urban percentage 27 July, 2015	49	56	61	61	62	63	63
Rura percentage 27 July, 2015	6	17	26	27	28	29	29

Source: unstat/MDG Report, 2015.

SDG-6 and the initiatives in India :

(a) The NITI Aayog and Mapping of Initiatives on SDG

Given the above the factual position as obtained in India it would be worthwhile to examine the roadmap for Sustainable development of SDG 6 with reference to the basic approach and goal-specific initiatives undertaken in India.The NITI Aayog has been empowered to oversee the implementation of SDGs by the ministries of the Central Government and coordinate with States for the achievement of developmental targets as enshrined in the SDGs. The NITI Aayog tasked itself to prepare a initial draft based on mapping of the goals and targets proposed by Nodal and other Ministries in consultation with MoSPI. The schemes so mapped for Goal-6 include 29) National Rural Drinking water Programme (Core) [2009] 30) Nirmal Bharat Abhiyan (Core)

[2012] {restructured as Swachh Bharat Mission in 2014} 31) Pradhan Mantri Krishi Sinchayee Yojana [2015] 32) National River Conservation Programme (NRCP) [2010]. It also included 1) Namami Gange - Integrated Ganga Conservation Mission [2016] and 2) Inter-linking of rivers.

(b) National Review of SDG- 6 for United Nations High Level Political Forum 2017

The outcomes of initiatives under SDG-6 would normally take a period of time to fructify as several other factors are also interlinked to reflect its final outcome. Be that as it may, the Voluntary National Review Report on Implementation of Sustainable Development Goals presented for United Nations High Level Political Forum 2017 is a good reference point for understanding the latest position on SDG-6 status in India. The report has not included SDG-6 as a separate item. However, it is noted that "given the interconnectedness of the SDGs, relevant strategies for enabling collaboration among different actors will be developed as part of the overall implementation process and that India will continue to pursue the implementation of the SDG agenda through close collaboration between the national and sub-national governments as well as active participation of all other relevant stakeholders. Further, a number of goals in the SDGs do not require the government to deliver public services, but instead to develop and enforce the necessary policy and regulatory frameworks. Given the interrelatedness of the goals and targets, the government is also considering setting up a high-level Committee headed by the Chief Statistician of India to oversee the monitoring framework for SDGs at the national-level"

(c) The NITI Aayog, Three-Year Action Agenda and SDG-6

The NITI Aayog has recently published the Three-Year Action Agenda covering years 2017-18 to 2019-20 which begins with the objective of eliminating poverty in all its dimensions such that every citizen will have access to a minimum standard of food, education, health, clothing, shelter, transportation and energy. The chapter 24 of the Agenda report deliberates on sustainable management of water resources where it mentions that out of annual precipitation (including snowfall) of 4000 billion cubic meters(BCM), the net utilizable water potential of India is 1223 BCM and as per the Central Water Commission, annual per capita availability dropped from 1816 cubic meters in 2001 to 1544 cubic meters in 2011 due to population change. The National Commission for Integrated Water Resources Development (NCIWRD) has worked out that the projected demand by the year 2050 would be 973 BCM for low demand scenario and 1180 BCM for high demand scenario, with break-up demand of Agriculture (70%), followed by households (9%) and industries (7%). In the given context, providing drinking water, through piped water supply, is a major challenge when Census 2011 revealed that only 30.8% of rural households and 70.6% of the total urban households were reportedly getting piped water supply.

India's vision for water sector is to ensure water security for economic prospects and environmental stability through sustainable management of available water resources with people's participation.

To achieve the above vision,India will have to adopt State-specific actions for each strategy:

(a) To provide irrigation to all farms (Har Khet Ko Pani) with improved on-fam water-use efficiency (Per drop More crop)

(b) Encourage industries to utilize recycled/treated water and ensure zero discharge of untreated effluents)

(c) To create additional water storage capacity to enhance utilization utilization of surface water reserves potential of 690 BCM

(d) Ensure long term sustainability of the limited ground water resources

(e) Water Governance

(f) Water footprint

(g) National Hydrology Project (NHP)

(h) Inter-linked Rivers (ILR)

(i) Namani Ganga

(d) Economic Survey of India, 2017-18

The Government of India tabled the Economic Survey of India, 2017-18 in the Parliament in the Budget Session on 29th January,2018 to set the stage for the Government for the Annual Budget. The Survey contains an indepth analysis, serious research as well new policy ideas. The said Survey sums up the latest position on status of Water and Sanitation, as included in SDG-6. The Economic Survey 2017-18 takes note of the basic fact that quality of hygiene and sanitation has significant impact on improving the health outcomes. With the launch of Swachh Bharat Mission (Gramin) on 2nd October, 2014, the sanitation coverage in rural India has increased substantially from 39 per cent in 2014 to 76 percent in January, 2018. The number of persons defecating in open in rural areas, which were 55 crore in October, 2014 declined to 25 crore in January, 2018. So far, 296 districts and 307,349 villages all over India have been declared Open Defecation Free (ODF). Eight states and two Union Territories. i.e., Sikkim, Himachal Pradesh, Kerala, Haryana, Uttarakhand, Chhattisgarh, Arunachal Pradesh, Gujarat, Daman & Diu and Chandigarh have been declared as ODF completely. The surveys conducted by the National Sample Survey Office (NSSO) and Quality Council of India (QCI) on usage of toilets by the individuals who have access to toilets reported more than 90 per cent of individuals using toilets in 2016 and 2017.

The Survey satisfactorily notes that there has been substantial reduction in the number of persons defecating in open in rural areas which has had positive health and economic impact in ODF areas. In a report, 'The Financial and Economic Impact of SBM in India', UNICEF estimated that a household in an ODF village in rural India saves Rs 50,000/- every year.

(e) Budget Initiatives for 2018-19

The Budget document embodies not only a financial statement on resources availability and its projected expenditure, it also expresses alongside overtly and covertly the policy statement of the Government of the day. The Budget Speech of the Finance Minister of India delivered on First February,2018 is taken up to relate its relevance on SDGs. In so far as SDG-6 is concerned, the Union Finance Minister stated that the Swachh Bharat Mission has benefited the poor. Under this mission, Government has already constructed more than 6 crore toilets. The positive effect of these toilets is being seen on the dignity of ladies, education of girls and the overall health of family. Government is planning to construct around 2 crore toilets. The Finance Minister also said that a total of 187 projects have been sanctioned under the Namami Gange programme for infrastructure development, river surface cleaning, rural sanitation and other interventions at a cost of Rs. 16,713 crore. 47 projects have been completed and remaining projects are at various stages of execution. All 4465 Ganga Grams – villages on the bank of river - have been declared open defecation free. The Finance Minister further said that the government has identified 115 aspirational districts taking various indices of development in consideration for making them model districts of development.

Chapter - 17

Sustainable Development Goal 7

Ensure access to affordable, reliable, sustainable and modern energy for all

Energy is the primary resource necessary for activating almost all initiatives for achieving the Sustainable Development Goals in some form or other. It is an essential input for major programmes in the eradication of poverty or for programmes for advancements in health, education, water supply and industrialization It has a key role to combating climate change.

The Fact sheet available before the Sustainable Development Summit, 2015 mentioned that 1.3 billion people –one in five globally –still lack access to modern electricity.3 billion people rely on wood, coal, charcoal or animal waste for cooking and heating. Energy is the dominant contributor to climate change, accounting for around 60% of total global greenhouse gas emissions. Energy from renewable resources –wind, water, solar, biomass and geothermal energy–is inexhaustible and clean. Renewable energy currently constitutes 15% of the global energy mix.

The Report of the Secretary-General, "Progress towards the Sustainable Development Goals", E/2016/75 captures the state of affairs on 'Energy for all' which state that the proportion of the global population with access to electricity has increased steadily, from 79 per cent in 2000 to 85 per cent in 2012. Still, 1.1 billion people –one in five globally - still lack access to modern electricity. Of those gaining access to electricity worldwide, 80 per cent are urban dwellers. The proportion of the world's population with access to clean fuels and technologies for cooking is limited to 58 per cent in 2014. About 3 billion people rely on polluting fuels such as wood, coal, charcoal or animal waste for cooking and heating.

Energy is the dominant contributor to climate change, accounting for around 60% of total global greenhouse gas emissions. The share of renewable energy derived from hydropower, solid and liquid biofuels, wind, the sun, biogas, geothermal and marine sources, and waste has increased from 17.4 per cent in 2000 to 18.1 per cent in 2012 in the world's total final energy consumption indicating a welcome trend, though slowly.. Globally, energy intensity decreased by 1.7 per cent per year from 2010 to 2012. This represents a considerable improvement over the period from 1990 to 2010, when it decreased by 1.2 per cent a year.

The proportion of the world's energy use covered by mandatory energy efficiency regulation, which has almost doubled over the past decade, from 14 per cent in 2005 to 27 per cent in 2014, was a factor. Still, current progress is only about two thirds of the pace needed to double the global rate of improvement in energy efficiency. Among end-use sectors, industry was the largest contributor to reduced energy intensity, followed closely by transportation. About 68 per cent of the savings in energy intensity between 2010 and 2012 came from developing regions, with Eastern Asia as the largest contributor.

Access to affordable, reliable and sustainable energy is crucial to achieving many of the Sustainable Development Goals –from poverty eradication via sustainable agriculture and advancements in health(in Goal-1, Goal-2 and in Goal-3), education (in Goal-4), water supply (in Goal-6)and industrialization(in Goal-9) to mitigating climate change(in Goal-13). Energy access, however, varies widely across countries and the current rate of progress falls short of what will be required to achieve the Goal. Redoubled efforts will be needed, particularly for countries with large energy access deficits and high energy consumption.

Energy is central to nearly every major challenge and opportunity the world faces today. Be it for jobs, security, climate change, food production or increasing incomes, access to energy for all is essential. Sustainable energy is opportunity – it transforms lives, economies and the planet. The UN Secretary is leading a Sustainable Energy for All initiative to ensure universal access to modern energy services, improve efficiency and increase use of renewable sources. Sustainable Energy for All – the global, multi-stakeholder platform that played a core role in putting universal access to modern energy services at the heart of the Sustainable Development Goals (SDGs) and Paris climate agreement – is shifting gear with a new five-year strategy that will drive action and deliver on those promises.

Based on the above facts and observations, it would be appropriate to reiterate the Goal 7 of the SDGs, its targets and related indicators to keep it in the up-fronts, in sequential order, before addressing India's initiatives on **Goal 7.**

Goal 7. Ensure access to affordable, reliable, sustainable and modern energy for all

7.1 By 2030, ensure universal access to affordable, reliable and modern energy services

7.2 By 2030, increase substantially the share of renewable energy in the global energy mix

7.3 By 2030, double the global rate of improvement in energy efficiency

7.a By 2030, enhance international cooperation to facilitate access to clean energy research and technology, including renewable energy, energy efficiency and advanced and cleaner fossil-fuel technology, and promote investment in energy infrastructure and clean energy technology

7.b By 2030, expand infrastructure and upgrade technology for supplying modern and sustainable energy services for all in developing countries, in particular least developed countries, small island developing States, and land-locked developing countries, in accordance with their respective programmes of support

The goals and targets per se are important from the angle of programme vision and intended outcome; however from the perspective of monitoring the performance, indicators do play critical role. Since indicator-design is essentially an expert professional skill- job requiring to keep harmony with overall goals and targets of the Sustainable Development Summit as embodied in paragraph 75 of Transforming our World: The 2030 Agenda for Sustainable Development mentioned : "the Goals and targets will be followed-up and reviewed using a set of global indicators. These will be complemented by indicators at the regional and national levels which will be developed by member states, in addition to the outcomes of work undertaken for the development of the baselines for those targets where national and global baseline data does not yet exist".

Needless to mention that purpose of SDG indicators is twofold; first it acts as a management tool to help countries develop implementation and monitoring strategies for achieving the SDGs and to monitor progress and secondly, it works as a report card, to measure progress towards achieving a target and ensure the accountability of governments to their citizens.As a matter of fact, Agenda 21 of the SD Summit also called on countries and the international community to develop indicators of sustainable development. Such indicators were needed to increase focus on sustainable development and assist decision-makers at all levels to adopt sound national sustainable development policies.

Be that as it may, the Global Indicator Framework as designed by the UN Statistical Commission at its 47th Session in March 2016 and adopted thereafter by the Economic and Social Council and the General Assembly, are as follows:

Indicators of SDG-7:

- 7.1.1 Proportion of population with access to electricity
- 7.1.2 Proportion of population with primary reliance on clean fuels and technology
- 7.2.1 Renewable energy share in the total final energy consumption
- 7.3.1 Energy intensity measured in terms of primary energy and GDP
- 7.a.1 International financial flows to developing countries in support of lean energy research and development and renewable energy production, including in hybrid systems
- 7.b.1 Investments in energy efficiency as a proportion of GDP and the amount of foreign direct investment in financial transfer for infrastructure and technology to sustainable development services

SDG-7 and the initiatives in India

(a) The NITI Aayog and Mapping of Initiatives on SDG-7

Based on the overarching goal of SDG-7, the national government of the country needs to take it forward to design appropriate programme in ensuring commensurate outcome. In such efforts, the current scenario and revealed gaps need to be taken into consideration while drawing a roadmap for goal-7. The NITI Aayog has been empowered in India to oversee the implementation of SDGs by the ministries of the Central Government and coordinate with States for the achievement of developmental targets as enshrined in the SDGs. The NITI Aayog tasked itself to prepare a initial draft based on mapping of the goals and targets proposed by Nodal and other Ministries in consultation with MoSPI. However, since there does not exit any centrally sponsored scheme in this area for Goal-7, the NITI Aayog's list does not include any. However, the list mentions other initiatives that are in place in India and those that will be put in place soon, such as Deen Dayal Upadhyaya Gram Jyoti Yojana, 2) National Solar Mission –providing continuous power supply to rural India, 3) India Energy Policy, 4) Power (2015) –Electrificiation of the remaining 20,000 villages including off- grid Solar Power by 2020, 5) Five new Ultra Mega Power Projects, each of 4000 MW (to be installed)..

(b) National Review of SDG-7 for United Nations High Level Political Forum 2017

The Voluntary National Review Report on Implementation of Sustainable Development Goals presented for United Nations High Level Political Forum 2017 is also a reference point from where current initiatives and achievemts could be seen. However, Goal -7 has also not included there. Needless to mention that it is noted therein that "given the interconnectedness of the SDGs, relevant strategies for enabling collaboration among different actors will be developed as part of the overall implementation process and that India will continue to pursue the implementation of the SDG agenda through close collaboration between the national and sub-national governments as well as active participation of all other relevant stakeholders.

(c) The NITI Aayog, Three-Year Action Agenda and SDG-7

The NITI Aayog has recently published the Three-Year Action Agenda covering years 2017-18 to 2019-20 which begins with the objective of eliminating poverty in all its dimensions such that every citizen will have access to a minimum standard of food, education, health, clothing, shelter, transportation and energy. Under the Section IV, Growth Enablers at chapter - 13, it is noted that the energy sector is fundamental to growth and development. Availability of electricity, petrol, diesel and gas at competitive prices is essential for the efficient functioning of energy users sector which include households, transportation, industries, Agriculture and the government, and comprises the entire economy. Presently, in India 304 million people do not have access to electricity and around 700 million Indians are dependent on solid biomass for cooking. Moreover, India's per capita consumption remains a fraction of major economies. As India proceeds towards its ambition of 8% plus growth in the coming 15 years, its energy needs will multiply manifold even taking into account enhanced energy efficiency. There is also a need to bring down energy intensity of the GDP to the level committed under the Paris Agreement..

The Three Year Action Agenda specifies the following Initiatives related to energy consumption of business, households, transportation and agriculture in India:

- Energy is one of the key inputs in raising standard of living of the citizens and is also linked with development indicator and Human Development Index(HDI).Per capita electric consumption is intended to be improved from 1010KWh4 to the world average of 3200KHw3
- India has already committed to bring electricity to every village by May 2018 and to every Households by 2022.An even more ambitious goal would be to provide electricity to all households on 24x7 basis
- India has already committed to bring LPG to 50 to 80 million households by 2019 under the Pradhan Mantri Ujjwala Yojana (PMUY). As of April,1917, 203 million connections had already been released under the Programme. Within the existing LPG network, efforts will be made to launch a campaign to bring LPG connections down to one per family. Efforts will also be made to target the 100 smart cities for the provision of gas via the City Gas Distribution (CGD)

- To bring additional relief against black carbon in cooking, the PMVY programme should be complemented by 1) Setting up of biomass palletizing units, and 2) launch of a scheme to distribute 'forced draft efficient biomass chullahs' supported by a modest subsidy for the vulnerable sections. Using the instruments, it intends to fully eliminate black carbon by 2022.
- For streamlining the demand in the industrial sector, the cross subsidy for the power sector must be reduced so that industry may receive electricity at competitive prices.
- On the agriculture sector, solar irrigation pump distribution targets must be stepped up and financed through credit support from NABAD and government subsidy. The option to connect irrigation pumps to feeder level small solar plants will be explored and if found cost effective, should be exercised.
- Finally, the government should explore the prospect of switching over to electric cooking in areas where reliable supply of electricity already exists. It must also study the costs and benefits of adoption of electric vehicle in the coming year.

The Government also aims at increasing Energy Efficiency (which refers to reduction of energy use for same product or services). The policy decision of the government is that energy efficiency must depend on cost-benefit analysis. De-carbonization alone cannot be justification for promoting a more energy efficient technology. The benefit from de-carbonization must outweigh its cost.

(d) Economic Survey of India, 2017-18

The Government of India tabled the Economic Survey of India, 2017-18 in the Parliament in the Budget Session on 29th January, 2018 to set the stage for the Government for the Annual Budget. The Survey contains an indepth analysis, serious research as well new policy ideas. The said Survey sums up the latest position on status of Energy, as included in SDG-7.As mentioned earlier, Access to affordable, reliable, sustainable and modern energy has deep inter-linkages with all the other goals. It is directly and indirectly linked to other sustainable development objectives such as good health and well-being, gender equality, industry, innovation and infrastructure, sustainable cities and communities. The burden of collecting fuel wood and water and cooking in India, however, falls disproportionately on the female members of households. The adverse impacts of indoor air pollution also fall disproportionately on women and children who are directly involved in cooking or spend a major portion of their time indoors. Although, over the years the country has made considerable progress in providing access to clean cooking options to households, a large number of people still lack access to clean cooking fuels. Access to modern energy sources is of paramount importance, as it can reduce the amount of time spent on collection of firewood thereby leading to a positive impact on girls' education and employment.

The Government of India had launched "Pradhan Mantri Ujjwala Yojana" (PMUY) in May, 2016 and upgraded it to provide 80 million LPG connections by 2020 to BPL households. Complementing the above scheme, Government has come out with other initiatives namely "Ujjawala Plus" which will address the cooking needs of deprived people who are not covered under the Socio-Economic Caste Census (SECC) 2011. During 2016-17, 3.25 crore new LPG connections were released that includes 2 crore connections released under PMUY.

In addition, Government of India is committed to provide 24X7 reliable and quality power supply to all its consumers by 2019. The Deen Dayal Upadhyaya Gram Jyoti Yojana (DDUGJY) scheme was launched in 2015 to achieve 100 per cent village electrification and Saubhagya scheme was launched on 25th September, 2017, to provide energy access to all by last mile connectivity and electricity connections to all remaining un-electrified households in rural and urban areas to achieve universal household electrification in the country. As per Saubhagya portal of Rural Electrification Corporation, out of 18.1 crore rural household in the country, 14.2 crore (78%) rural households have been electrified (as on January 16, 2018). Out of the total installed capacity of electricity in India, around 18 per cent was from renewable energy sources (as on November 30, 2017).

Further, International Solar Alliance (ISA), launched on November 30, 2015 in Paris, entered into force on December 6, 2017. ISA is a coalition of solar resource rich countries lying fully or partially between the Tropics of Cancer and Capricorn and aims to specifically address energy needs by harnessing solar energy. ISA is also the first International inter-governmental treaty-based organization headquartered in India. Currently, 46 countries have signed and out of these, 19 countries have ratified the ISA Framework Agreement. ISA is a trillion-dollar opportunity in solar energy. Economy and industry in turn can get benefitted by the business opportunities available across 121 ISA member countries".

The Economic Survey also captured the power generation status which states that All-India installed power generation capacity reached 330,861 MW as on November 30, 2017. As on April 1, 2015, there were 18,542 unelectrified census villages, of these electrification of 15,183 villages has been completed as on November 30, 2017. The Ujjawal DISCOM Assurance Yojana (UDAY) has focused on enhancing the financial health of DISCOMs by reducing interest burden, cost of power and aggregated technical and commercial losses. A new scheme, Saubhagya (Pradhan Mantri Sahaj Bijli Har Ghar Yojana), was launched in September 2017 to ensure electrification of all remaining willing households in the country in rural and urban areas

(e) Budget Inititives for 2018-19

The Budget document embodies not only a financial statement on resources availability and its projected expenditure, it also expresses alongside overtly and covertly the policy statement of the Government of the day. The Budget Speech of the Finance Minister of India delivered on First February,2018 is taken up to relate its relevance on SDGs. In so far as SDG-7 is concerned, the Union Finance Minister stated that the Government launched Prime Minister's Ujjwala Scheme to make poor women free from the smoke of wood. Initially the target was to provide free LPG connections to about 5 crore poor women. But in view of the pace of implementation of Ujjwala scheme and its popularity among the women, it has now been proposed to increase the target of providing free connection to 8 crore poor women. The Government has also launched Prime Minister Saubhagya Yojana for providing electricity to all households of the country. Under this scheme, four crores poor households are being provided with electricity connection free of charge and Rupees'16000 crore are being spent under this scheme.

Chapter - 18

Sustainable Development Goal 8

Promote sustained, inclusive and sustainable economic growth, full and productive employment and decent work for all

At para-27 of the declaration of the UN Summit on Sustainable Development it has been envisioned to build strong economic foundations for all countries. Sustained, inclusive and sustainable economic growth is essential for prosperity. This will only be possible if wealth is shared and income inequality is addressed. Accordingly, the Summit has take a pledge to help building dynamic, sustainable, innovative and people-centred economies, promoting youth employment and women's economic empowerment, in particular, and decent work for all. It has also pledged to eradicate forced labour and human trafficking and end child labour in all its forms. A healthy and well-educated workforce with the knowledge and skills needed for productive and fulfilling work and full participation in society will benefit all societies in real terms.

The UN document further notes that Sustained and inclusive economic growth is a prerequisite for sustainable development, which can contribute to improved livelihoods for people around the world. Economic growth can lead to new and better employment opportunities and provide greater economic security for all. Moreover, rapid growth, especially among the least developed and other developing countries, can help them reduce the wage gap relative to developed countries, thereby diminishing glaring inequalities between the rich and poor.

The Fact sheet available before the Sustainable Development Summit mentioned that Global unemployment increased from 170 million in 2007 to nearly 202 million in 2012, of which about 75 million were young women and men. Nearly 2.2 billion people live below the US$2 poverty line and that poverty eradication is only possible through stable and well-paid jobs. It was estimated that 470 million jobs are needed globally for new entrants to the labour market between 2016 and 2030. The UN Secretary General mentioned later vide Report on "Progress towards the Sustainable Development Goals", E/2016/75, that the global unemployment rate stood at 6.1 per cent in 2015, down from a peak of 6.6 per cent in 2009. Globally, women and youth (aged 15 to 24) are more likely to face unemployment than men and adults aged 25 and over. In all regions, the unemployment rate among women is higher than that of men. In almost all regions, the rate of youth unemployment is more than twice that of adults. An encouraging feature in the given global scenario is the decline of the number of child labour by one third from 2000 to 2012 (from 246 million to 168 million).However, more than half of child labourers in 2012 (85 million) were engaged in hazardous forms of work. Of all child labourers worldwide, 59 per cent were engaged in agricultural activities in 2012. Since access to financial services is a good indicator of inclusive growth, it is worth mentioning that the proportion of women who are account holders in 2014 is 9 percentage points lower than the proportion of men who are account holders. Moreover, the proportion of account holders among the poorest 40 per cent of households is 14 percentage points lower than among those living in the richest 60 per cent of households. The Fact Sheet also mentions that Small and medium -sized enterprises are typically the largest job creators. They make up over 90% of business worldwide and account for between 50-60% of employment.

In connection with Goal-8, the International Labour Organization (ILO), at its website, observed that more than 204 million people are unemployed as of 2015. About 470 million jobs are needed globally for new entrants to the labour market between 2016 and 2030, just to keep up with the growth of the global working age population. That is around 30 million per year for new entrants to the labour market to keep up with the growth of the global working age population. In addition to creating jobs, it is also needed to improve conditions for the some 780 million women and men who are working, but not earning enough to lift themselves and their families out of poverty. In addition, women and girls must enjoy equal access to equal opportunities with men and boys for employment. It has also mentioned that since Decent work means opportunities for every-one to get work that is productive and delivers a fair income, all women and men are to be given equal opportunities in the workplace along with security in the workplace and social protection for families, better prospects for personal development and social integration. When more people are being productive and contributing to their country's growth, productive employment and "decent work" takes place and are key elements to achieving fair globalization and poverty reduction. In other words, Promoting jobs and enterprise, guaranteeing rights at work, extending social protection and promoting social dialogue are the four pillars of the ILO Decent Work Agenda with gender as a cross-cutting theme. These are crucial to advancing the entire sustainable development agenda.

The FAO, at its website, observes that Sustainable economic growth will pave the way for societies to create the conditions that allow people to have quality jobs, stimulating the economy while not harming the environment. Quality jobs are particularly needed in rural areas where most of the world's poor live and work. Agriculture is the world's single largest employer, especially so in developing countries where it generates a sizeable share of GDP. Responsible investments in sustainable agriculture and food systems can contribute to major societal benefits, including reduced inequalities, inclusive growth, and the creation of decent jobs. However, agriculture cannot handle the employment challenge alone. In addition to farm jobs, there is significant potential for job creation through rural non-farm economic activities, including around agri-food chains linked to sustainable agriculture, agribusiness development and related support services.

Given this background, it would be worthwhile to see how the Sustainable Development Summit addressed the very important Goal-8 and the related targets. before addressing India's initiatives.

Goal 8. Promote sustained, inclusive and sustainable economic growth, full and productive employment and decent work for all

8.1 Sustain per capita economic growth in accordance with national circumstances and, in particular, at least 7 per cent gross domestic product growth per annum in the least developed countries

8.2 Achieve higher levels of economic productivity through diversification, technological upgrading and innovation, including through a focus on high-value added and labour-intensive sectors

8.3 Promote development-oriented policies that support productive activities, decent job creation, entrepreneurship, creativity and innovation, and encourage the formalization and growth of micro-, small- and medium-sized enterprises, including through access to financial services

8.4 Improve progressively, through 2030, global resource efficiency in consumption and production and endeavour to decouple economic growth from environmental degradation, in accordance with the 10-year framework of programmes on sustainable consumption and production, with developed countries taking the lead

8.5 By 2030, achieve full and productive employment and decent work for all women and men, including for young people and persons with disabilities, and equal pay for work of equal value

8.6 By 2020, substantially reduce the proportion of youth not in employment, education or training

8.7 Take immediate and effective measures to eradicate forced labour, end modern slavery and human trafficking and secure the prohibition and elimination of the worst forms of child labour, including recruitment and use of child soldiers, and by 2025 end child labour in all its forms

8.8 Protect labour rights and promote safe and secure working environments for all workers, including migrant workers, in particular women migrants, and those in precarious employment

8.9 By 2030, devise and implement policies to promote sustainable tourism that creates jobs and promotes local culture and products

8.10 Strengthen the capacity of domestic financial institutions to encourage and expand access to banking, insurance and financial services for all

8.a Increase Aid for Trade support for developing countries, in particular least developed countries, including through the Enhanced Integrated Framework for Trade-Related Technical Assistance to Least Developed Countries

8.b By 2020, develop and operationalize a global strategy for youth employment and implement the Global Jobs Pact of the International Labour Organization

The goals and targets per se are important from the angle of programme vision and intended outcome; however from the perspective of monitoring the performance, indicators do play critical role. Since indicator-design is essentially an expert professional skill- job requiring to keep harmony with overall goals and targets of the Sustainable Development Summit as embodied in paragraph 75 of Transforming our World: The 2030 Agenda for Sustainable Development, mentioned : "the Goals and targets will be followed-up and reviewed using a set of global indicators. These will be complemented by indicators at the regional and national levels which will be developed by member states, in addition to the outcomes of work undertaken for the development of the baselines for those targets where national and global baseline data does not yet exist".

Needless to mention that purpose of SDG indicators is twofold; first it acts as a management tool to help countries develop implementation and monitoring strategies for achieving the SDGs and to monitor progress and secondly, it works as a report card, to measure progress towards achieving a target and ensure the accountability of governments to their citizens. As a matter of fact, Agenda 21 of the SD Summit also called on countries and the international community to develop indicators of sustainable development. Such indicators were needed to increase focus on sustainable development and assist decision-makers at all levels to adopt sound national sustainable development policies.

Be that as it may, the Global Indicator Framework as designed by the UN Statistical Commission at its 47th Session in March 2016 and adopted thereafter by the Economic and Social Council and the General Assembly, as mentioned earlier,are as follows:

Indicators of Goal 8:

8.1.1 Annual growth rate of real GDP per capita

8.2.1 Annual growth rate of real GDP per employed person

8.3.1 Proportion of informal employment in non-agriculture employment, by sex

8.4.1 Material footprint, material footprint per capita, and material footprint per GDP

8.4.2 Domestic material consumption, domestic material consumption per capita, and domestic material consumption per GDP

8.5.1 Average hourly earnings of female and male employees, by occupation, age and persons with disabilities

8.5.2 Unemployment rate, by sex, age and persons with disabilities

8.6.1 Proportion of youth (aged 15-24 years) not in education, employment or training

8.7.1 Proportion and number of children aged 5-17 years engaged in child labour, by sex and age

8.8.1 Frequency rates of fatal and non-fatal occupational injuries, by sex and migrant status

8.8.2 Level of national compliance of labour rights (freedom of association and collective bargaining) based on International Labour Organization (ILO) textual sources and national legislation, by sex and migrant status

8.9.1 Tourism direct GDP as a proportion of total GDP and in growth rate

8.9.2 Proportion of jobs in sustainable tourism industries out of total tourism jobs

8.10.1 (a) Number of commercial bank branches per 100,000 adults and (b) number of automated teller machines (ATMs) per 100,000 adults

8.10.2 Proportion of adults (15 years and older) with an account at a bank or other financial institution or with a mobile-money-service provider

8.a.1 Aid for Trade commitments and disbursements

8.b.1 Existence of a developed and operationalized national strategy for youth employment, as a distinct strategy or as part of a national employment strategy

The Employment –Unemployment Scenario in India

In the light of the overarching goal of SDG-8, the national government of the country needs to take it forward to design appropriate programme in ensuring commensurate outcome. In such efforts, the current scenario and revealed gaps need to be taken into consideration while drawing a roadmap for goal-8.The Labour Bureau, Chandigarh, Government of India, Ministry of Labour & Employment publishes Annual Employment – Unemployment Survey Report which portrays the crucial unemployment situation in India. The Report on Fifth Annual Employment – Unemployment Survey (2015-16) Volume I summarises the situation as mentioned below:

'THE EMPLOYMENT-UNEMPLOYMENT SITUATION

- The unemployment rate was estimated to be 5.0 per cent at the All India level under the UPS approach or in other words 5.0 per cent of the persons aged 15 years and above who were available for work could not get work during the reference period.
- In rural sector, unemployment rate was 5.1 per cent whereas in urban sector, the unemployment rate was 4.9 per cent under the UPS approach.
- The unemployment rate was significantly higher among females as compared to males. At the All India level, the female unemployment rate was estimated to be 8.7 per cent, whereas for males it was 4.0 per cent (under the UPS approach).
- In urban areas, the female unemployment rate was estimated to be 12.1 per cent at the All India level under the UPS approach as compared to 3.3 per cent for males and 10.3 per cent for transgenders.
- The unemployment rate for different categories based on UPS approach is given below.

Sector	*Male*	*Female*	*Transgender*	*Person*
Rural	4.2	7.8	2.1	5.1
Urban	3.3	12.1	10.3	4.9
Rural + Urban	4.0	8.7	4.3	5.0

All India (in per cent)

To get a better picture about the Employment situation, it will be useful to look at the distribution of workers or employed persons according to the nature of their employment

- Majority of the employed persons were found to be self employed based on both the UPS and UPSS approach.
- At the All India level, 46.6 per cent of the workers were found to be self employed under the Usual Principal Status Approach followed by 32.8 per cent as casual labour. Only 17 per cent of the employed persons were wage/salary earners and the rest 3.7 per cent were contract workers.
- Employed persons are further classified on the basis of economic activity pursued by them. At the State/UT level, results are presented at Section level (Section A-U) based on National Industrial Classification, 2008.
- The survey results show that majority of the persons were employed in the primary sector. At the All India level, based on Usual Principal Status Approach, 46.1 per cent of the persons were estimated to be employed under Agriculture, Forestry and Fishing sector, followed by 32 percent in tertiary sector and 21.8 percent in the secondary sector.

It is pretty well-known that many of the persons who are reported as ‘ employed’ or ‘workers’ in official publications do not get work for the entire duration of their stay in the Labour Force. And even those who get some work or the other for the entire duration may be getting work for only a small fraction of the time they are available for work. This apart, some may be working on jobs which do not allow them to fully utilise their abilities or from which they earn very low incomes. All this constitutes under employment which remains a worrying aspect of the employment –unemployment scenario in the country. Fifth round of Annual Employment Unemployment survey also apart some important estimates for the under-employment, considering only the duration of work available to participants in the Labour Force.

- 60.6 per cent of the persons aged 15 years and above who were available for work for all the 12 months during the reference period were able to get work throughout the year, at the All India level. In rural areas, 52.7 per cent of the persons aged 15 years and above who were available for work for all the 12 months during the reference period were able to get work throughout the year at the All India level, whereas the corresponding figure for urban areas was 82.1 per cent.
- The present survey has also collected data on parameters like methods adopted to seek work by the unemployed, reasons for unemployment among graduates and post graduates, type of job

contract, availability of paid leave & social security benefits and social security benefits by different schemes.

- At the All India level, a majority 67.5 per cent of the self employed workers had average monthly earnings up to Rs 7500. Only 0.1 per cent of the self employed were estimated to have earnings above Rs 1 lakh.
- Similarly, 57.2 per cent i.e. more than half of the regular wage/ salaried workers had monthly average earnings up to Rs 10,000. At the All India level 38.5 per cent of the contract workers and 59.3 per cent of the casual workers had monthly earnings of up to Rs 5000.
- At the All India level, majority of unemployed persons (33.5 per cent) used more than two methods to seek work, followed by,through friends & relatives (24.1 per cent), application made in response to advertisement (23.7 per cent) and through employment exchange (4.3 per cent).
- At the All India level, 58.3 per cent of unemployed graduates and 62.4 per cent of unemployed post graduates cited non availability of jobs matching with education/skill and experience as the main reason for unemployment followed by non availability of adequate remuneration cited by 22.8 per cent of graduates and 21.5 per cent of post graduates.
- At the All India level, 64.9 per cent of the regular wage/ salaried workers, 67.8 per cent of the contract workers and 95.3 per cent of the casual workers do not have a written job contract. 27 per cent of the regular wage/salaried workers and 11.5 per cent of the contract workers had written job contract of more than three years.
- At the All India level, just 20.6 per cent of workers except self employed received paid leave and 21.6 per cent availed social security benefits. A majority 71.2 per cent of workers were not eligible for social security benefits'.

SDG-8 and the initiatives in India

(a) The NITI Aayog and Mapping of Initiatives on SDG-8

Based on the overarching goal of SDG-8 and the current status obtaining in the country, the national government of the country needs to take it forward to design appropriate programme in ensuring commensurate outcome..The NITI Aayog has been empowered to oversee the implementation of SDGs by the ministries of the Central Government and coordinate with States for the achievement of developmental targets as enshrined in the SDGs. The NITI Aayog tasked itself to prepare a initial draft based on mapping of the goals and targets proposed by Nodal and other Ministries in consultation with MoSPI. The schemes so mapped for Goal-8 include 33) National Service Scheme

(NSS) {1969} 34) Skill Development Mission {2015} 35) Social Security for Unorganised Workers including Rashtriya Swastya Bima Yojana (Core) {2009}. The NITI Aayog also mentioned related programmes like 1) Deendayal Upadhyaya Antodaya Yojana{2015}. 2) National Urban Development Mission (2016) which will also have bearing on Goal 8.

(b) National Review of SDG- 8 for United Nations High Level Political Forum 2017

The outcomes of initiatives under SDG-8 would normally take a period of time to fructify as several other factors are also interlinked to reflect its final outcome. Be that as it may, the Voluntary National Review Report on Implementation of Sustainable Development Goals presented for United Nations High Level Political Forum 2017 is a good reference point for understanding the latest position on SDG-8 status in India. The report has not included SDG-8 as a separate item. However, it is noted that "given the interconnectedness of the SDGs, relevant strategies for enabling collaboration among different actors will be developed as part of the overall implementation process and that India will continue to pursue the implementation of the SDG agenda through close collaboration between the national and sub-national governments as well as active participation of all other relevant stakeholders'.

(c) The NITI Aayog, Three-Year Action Agenda and SDG-8

The NITI Aayog has recently published the Three-Year Action Agenda covering years 2017-18 to 2019-20 which begins with the objective of eliminating poverty in all its dimensions such that every citizen will have access to a minimum standard of food, education, health, clothing, shelter, transportation and energy. In Part II of the Report, under section Economic Transformation in Major Sectors, and i sub-section Trade, Industry and Service :creates well-paid job, the action-approach on employment has been elucidated. It has been maintained that contrary to some assertions that India's growth has been jobless, the Employment Unemployment Survey (EUS) of the National Sample Survey Office (NSSO) has consistently reported low and stable rates of unemployment over more than three decades. Even under most demanding definition of employment, the unemployment rate consistently remains between 5% and 8%. Indeed, unemployment is the lesser of India's problems. The more serious problem, is severe unemployment... Three illustrations have been given. It has been mentioned in the first instance in that in 2011-12, as per the NSSO Employment Unemployment Survey, 49% of the workforce was employed in agriculture. But agriculture contributed only 17% of India's GDP at current prices. Second, in 2010-11, firms with less than 20 workers employed 72% of India's manufacturing work force but contributed only 12% of manufacturing output. Finally, services are no different. According to the 2006-7 NSSO Survey of service firms, 650 largest enterprise accounted for 38% of service output but employed 2% of service workers, Put another way, the remaining service firms employed 98% of the workforce but produced only 62% of the output. The NITI Aayog thereafter comments that what is needed is the creation of high productive, high-wage jobs. To this end, the focus has been given on some of the key manufacturing and service sectors, including apparel, electronics, gems and jewellery, financial services, tourism and cultural industries and real estate.

(d) Economic Survey of India, 2017-18:

The Government of India tabled the Economic Survey of India, 2017-18 in the Parliament in the Budget Session on 29th January,2018 to set the stage for the Government for the Annual Budget. The Survey contains an indepth analysis, serious research as well new policy ideas. The said Survey stated that the employment sector in India poses great challenge in terms of its structure which is dominated by informal workers, high levels of under employment, skill shortages and labour markets with rigid labour laws and institutions. In this context, the Government is in the process of rationalization of the 38 Labour Acts by framing relevant provisions of existing laws into 4 labour codes viz Code on Wages, Code on Industrial Relations, Code on Social Security & Welfare, and Code on Safety & Working conditions.

(e) Budget Initiatives for 2018-19

The Budget document embodies not only a financial statement on resources availability and its projected expenditure, it also expresses alongside overtly and covertly the policy statement of the Government of the day. The Budget Speech of the Finance Minister of India delivered on First February, 2018 is taken up to relate its relevance on SDGs. In so far as SDG-8 is concerned, the Union Finance Minister reiterated that creating job opportunities is at the core of Government policies. The Finance Minister cited an independent study as showing that 70 lakh formal jobs will be created this year. To carry forward the momentum created by the measures taken during the last 3 years to boost employment generation, he announced that the Government will contribute 12% of the wages of the new employees in the EPF for all the sectors for next three years. He proposed to make amendments in the Employees Provident Fund and Miscellaneous Provisions Act, 1952 to reduce women employees' contribution to 8% for first three years of their employment against existing rate of 12% or 10% with no change in employers' contribution.

The Finance Minister stressed that the focus of the Government next year will also be on providing maximum livelihood opportunities in the rural areas by spending more on livelihood, agriculture and allied activities and construction of rural infrastructure. He said, in the year 2018-19, for creation of livelihood and infrastructure in rural areas, total amount to be spent by the Ministries will be Rs. 14.34 lakh crore, including extra-budgetary and non-budgetary resources of Rs. 11.98 lakh crore. Apart from employment due to farming activities and self employment, this expenditure will create employment of 321 crore person days, 3.17 lakh kilometers of rural roads, 51 lakh new rural houses, 1.88 crore toilets, and provide 1.75 crore new household electric connections besides boosting agricultural growth.

The Finance Minister also stated that Medium, Small and Micro Enterprises (MSMEs) are a major engine of growth and employment in the country and have accordingly provided Rupees 3794 crore to MSME Sector for giving credit support, capital and interest subsidy and innovations.

Chapter - 19

Sustainable Development Goal 9

Build resilient infrastructure, promote inclusive and sustainable industrialization and foster innovation

The Sustainable Development Goal 9 deals with the economic foundation for sustainable development. Sustained investment in infrastructure and innovation are crucial drivers of economic growth and development. Investments in infrastructure – transportation, irrigation, storage facilities, energy, electrification and communication technology – are crucial to achieving sustainable development. It has been an established fact that growth in productivity and incomes, and improvements in food security, health and education require investment in infrastructure and market facilities. Investment in rural infrastructure also diversifies rural employment and improving rural-urban linkages and thereby creating opportunities for sustainable rural livelihoods and promoting inclusive and balanced society. Incidentally, Small-scale producers in rural communities are often the most isolated and vulnerable to food insecurity. Targeted interventions aimed at diversifying employment into non-agricultural activities, and providing smallholders with affordable access to technologies and infrastructure to sustainably transform food systems are essential to accelerating poverty reduction. Growth of non-farm activities is often driven by agricultural growth and can stimulate local employment creation. Technological progress is also key to finding lasting solutions to both economic and environmental challenges. Promoting sustainable industries, and investing in scientific research and innovation, are all important ways to facilitate sustainable development. As a matter of fact, inclusive and sustainable industrial development (ISID) is the primary source of income generation which triggers rapid and sustained increases in living standards for all people, and provides the technological solutions to environmentally sound industrialization. Technological progress is the foundation of efforts to achieve environmental objectives, such as increased resource and energy-efficiency. Without technology and innovation, industrialization will not happen, and without industrialization, development will not happen.

In brief, Sustainable Development Goal 9 addresses three important aspects of sustainable development: infrastructure, industrialization and innovation. Infrastructure provides the basic physical facilities essential to business and society; industrialization drives economic growth and job creation, thereby reducing income inequality; and innovation expands the technological capabilities of industrial sectors and leads to the development of new skills. Further, bridging the digital divide is also crucial to ensure equal access to information and knowledge, and as a consequence foster innovation and entrepreneurship. An integrated approach is crucial for progress across the multiple goals. Incidentally, the great scientist, Stephen Hawking cared much about Goal 9 as global goals.

The Fact sheet on hand on Goal 9 at the Sustainable Development Summit showed that about 2.6 billion people in the developing world are facing difficulties in accessing electricity full time and 2.5 billion people worldwide lack access to basic sanitation and almost 800 million people lack access to water. It also mentions that 1to 1.5 million people do not have access to reliable phone service. Moreover, Manufacturing is an important employer, accounting for around 470 million jobs worldwide in 2009 –or around 16% of the world's workforce of 2.9 billion. It is estimated that there were more than half a billion jobs in manufacturing in 2013.Industrialization's job multiplication effect has a positive impact on society. Every one job in manufacturing creates 2.2 jobs in other sectors. Further, in developing countries, barely 30% of agricultural production undergoes industrial processing. In high -income countries, 98% is processed. This suggests that there are great opportunities for developing countries in agribusiness.

The Report of the Secretary-General, "Progress towards the Sustainable Development Goals", E/2016/75 captures the state of affairs when he stated that Goal 9 encompasses three important aspects of sustainable development: infrastructure, industrialization and innovation. Infrastructure provides the basic physical systems and structures essential to the operation of a society or enterprise. Industrialization drives economic growth, creates job opportunities and thereby reduces income poverty. Innovation advances the technological capabilities of industrial sectors and prompts the development of new skills.

- An important component of physical infrastructure is air shipping and air travel. In 2014, 45 per cent of all air passengers originated from developing regions; 55 per cent originated from developed regions. However, in the least developed countries, landlocked developing countries and small island developing States, air passenger volume was extremely low, making up only 0.8 per cent, 0.8 per cent and 1.4 per cent, respectively, of the global total. Similar patterns are found for freight volumes in air transit: the least developed countries, landlocked developing countries and small island developing States made up only 1.1 per cent, 0.9 per cent and 2.6 per cent of the global total, respectively, in 2014.

- Manufacturing is a foundation of economic development, employment and social stability. In 2015, the share of manufacturing value added in terms of GDP of developed regions was estimated at 13 per cent, a decrease over the past decade owing largely to the increasing role of services in developed regions. In contrast, the share of manufacturing value added in GDP remained relatively stagnant for developing regions, increasing marginally from 19 per cent in 2005 to 21 per cent in 2015. Those values hide substantial differences, with manufacturing value added contributing over 31 per cent to GDP in Eastern Asia and 10 per cent or less in both sub-Saharan Africa and Oceania. The least developed countries face particular challenges in industrializing. Although those countries represent 13 per cent of the global population, they contribute less than 1 per cent of global manufacturing value added. Worldwide, about 500 million people are employed in manufacturing. While manufacturing job numbers have fallen in industrialized countries, they have steadily increased in developing countries. In the least developed countries, agricultural and traditional sectors remain the main sources of employment.
- In developing countries, small-scale industries accounted for an estimated 15 per cent to 20 per cent of value added and 25 per cent to 30 per cent of total industrial employment in 2015. However, access to financial services in those countries remains a problem. Globally, the credit gap for small and medium enterprises (defined as having between 5 and 99 employees) was estimated at $3.2 trillion to $3.9 trillion in 2012. In emerging markets, between 45 per cent and 55 per cent of all small and medium enterprises are unserved or underserved by financial services.
- As the structure of world economies shifts to less energy intensive industries and countries implement policies for enhanced energy efficiency, almost all regions have shown a reduction in carbon intensity of GDP. Global carbon dioxide emissions per unit of value added showed a steady decline between 1990 and 2013, a decrease of about 30 per cent.
- Innovation and the creation of new and more sustainable industries are spurred by investments in research and development. Global

expenditure on research and development as a proportion of GDP stood at 1.7 per cent in 2013. However, this figure masks wide disparities. expenditure on research and development was 2.4 per cent of GDP for developed regions, 1.2 per cent for developing regions, and below 0.3 per cent for the least developed countries and landlocked developing countries. The number of researchers per 1 million inhabitants showed a similar pattern. While the global average was 1,083 researchers per 1 million inhabitants, the ratio ranged from 65 per 1 million in the least developed countries to 3,641 per 1 million in developed regions.

- Total official flows for economic infrastructure in developing regions reached $59.5 billion in 2014. The main sectors receiving assistance were transport and energy.
- Infrastructure and economic development also rely on information and communications technology. Mobile cellular services have spread rapidly around the world, allowing people in previously unconnected areas to join the global information society. By 2015, the percentage of the population living in areas covered by mobile broadband networks stood at 69 per cent globally. In rural areas, the share was only 29 per cent.

Based on the above facts and observations, it would be appropriate to reiterate the Goal 9 of the SDGs, its targets and related indicators to keep it in the up-fronts, in sequential order, before addressing India's initiatives on Goal 9.

Goal 9. Build resilient infrastructure, promote inclusive and sustainable industrialization and foster innovation

9.1 Develop quality, reliable, sustainable and resilient infrastructure, including regional and transborder infrastructure, to support economic development and human well-being, with a focus on affordable and equitable access for all

9.2 Promote inclusive and sustainable industrialization and, by 2030, significantly raise industry's share of employment and gross domestic product, in line with national circumstances, and double its share in least developed countries

9.3 Increase the access of small-scale industrial and other enterprises, in particular in developing countries, to financial services, including affordable credit, and their integration into value chains and markets

9.4 By 2030, upgrade infrastructure and retrofit industries to make them sustainable, with increased resource-use efficiency and greater adoption of clean and environmentally sound technologies and industrial processes, with all countries taking action in accordance with their respective capabilities

9.5 Enhance scientific research, upgrade the technological capabilities of industrial sectors in all countries, in particular developing countries, including, by 2030, encouraging innovation and substantially increasing the number of research and development workers per 1 million people and public and private research and development spending

9.a Facilitate sustainable and resilient infrastructure development in developing countries through enhanced financial, technological and technical support to African countries, least developed countries, landlocked developing countries and small island developing States

9.b Support domestic technology development, research and innovation in developing countries, including by ensuring a conducive policy environment for, inter alia, industrial diversification and value addition to commodities

9.c Significantly increase access to information and communications technology and strive to provide universal and affordable access to the Internet in least developed countries by 2020

The goals and targets per se are important from the angle of programme vision and intended outcome; however from the perspective of monitoring the performance, indicators do play critical role. Since indicator-design is essentially an expert professional skill- job requiring to keep harmony with overall goals and targets of the Sustainable Development Summit as embodied in paragraph 75 of Transforming our World: The 2030 Agenda for Sustainable Development, mentioned: "the Goals and targets will be followed-up and reviewed using a set of global indicators. These will be complemented by indicators at the regional and national levels which will be developed by member states, in addition to the outcomes of work undertaken for the development of the baselines for those targets where national and global baseline data does not yet exist".

Needless to mention that purpose of SDG indicators is twofold; first it acts as a management tool to help countries develop implementation and monitoring strategies for achieving the SDGs and to monitor progress and secondly, it works as a report card, to measure progress towards achieving a target and ensure the accountability of governments to their citizens. As a matter of fact, Agenda 21 of the SD Summit also called on countries and the international community to develop indicators of sustainable development. Such indicators were needed to increase focus on sustainable development and assist decision-makers at all levels to adopt sound national sustainable development policies.

Be that as it may, the Global Indicator Framework as designed by the UN Statistical Commission at its 47th Session in March 2016 and adopted thereafter by the Economic and Social Council and the General Assembly, as mentioned earlier,are as follows:

Indicators of Goal 9

9.1.1 Proportion of the rural population who live within 2 km of an all-season road

9.1.2 Passenger and freight volumes, by mode of transport9.2.1 Manufacturing value added as a proportion of GDP and per capita

9.2.2 Manufacturing employment as a proportion of total employment

9.3.1 Proportion of small-scale industries in total industry value added

9.3.2 Proportion of small-scale industries with a loan or line of credit9.4.1 CO2 emission per unit of value added

9.5.1 Research and development expenditure as a proportion of GDP

9.5.2 Researchers (in full-time equivalent) per million inhabitants

9.a.1 Total official international support (official development assistance plus other official flows) toinfrastructure

9.b.1 Proportion of medium and high-tech industry value added in total value added

9.c.1 Proportion of population covered by a mobile network, by technology

SDG-9 and the initiatives in India

Based on the overarching goal of SDG-9, the national government of the country needs to take it forward to design appropriate programme in ensuring commensurate outcome. In such efforts, the current scenario and revealed gaps need to be taken into consideration while drawing a roadmap for goal-9

(a) The NITI Aayog and Mapping of Initiatives on SDG-9

The NITI Aayog has been empowered to oversee the implementation of SDGs by the ministries of the Central Government and coordinate with States for the achievement of developmental targets as enshrined in the SDGs. The NITI Aayog tasked itself to prepare a initial draft based on mapping of the goals and targets proposed by Nodal and other Ministries in consultation with MoSPI. The schemes so mapped for Goal-9 include 36) Border Area Development Programme (BADP) (ACA) (MHA/M/o Finance){1994} 37) National Handloom Development Programme{12th Plan} 38) Catalytic Development Programme under Sericulture {9th Plan} 39) Pradhan Mantri Gram Sadak Yojana (PMGSY) Core) {2000} including programmes like (1) Pt. Deendayal Upadhyaya Shramev Jayate Karyakram (2014) (2) Minimum Government Maximum Governance (3) Make in India (2014) (4) Start Up

India (2016) (5) Ease of doing business initiative (2017) (6) FDI Policy, which will effect on Goal-9.

(b) National Review of SDG- 9 for United Nations High Level Political Forum 2017

The outcomes of initiatives under SDG-9 would normally take a period of time to fructify as several other factors are also interlinked to reflect its final outcome. Be that as it may, the Voluntary National Review Report on Implementation of Sustainable Development Goals presented for United Nations High Level Political Forum 2017 is a good reference point for understanding the latest position on SDG-9 status in India. It has been noted therein that 'all forms of transportation - roads, railways, civil aviation and waterways - are being rapidly expanded. Road connectivity and electricity are being brought to all villages. The Bharat Broadband Network Ltd. initiative is aiming to provide high-speed broadband connectivity to all village councils in the country.

Over the last five years, there has been a consistent growth in installed electricity generation capacity. The installed capacity in fuel sectors has grown by 51.3% and more than doubled in the renewable energy sector (solar, wind, bio- and small hydro power). Further, India is making efforts to become an Information Technology and manufacturing hub through its 'Make in India' campaign. These efforts have greatly accelerated Foreign Direct Investment (FDI) inflows and helped the country sustain an average growth of 7.5% during the last three financial years (2014-15 to2016-17). Employment-intensive manufacturing segments are being boosted by providing easy credit to small-scale business entrepreneurs. Additionally, the 'Start-up India' programme promotes entrepreneurship and labour-intensive economic growth'.

(c) The NITI Aayog, Three-Year Action Agenda and SDG-9

The NITI Aayog has recently released the Three-Year Action Agenda covering years 2017-18 to 2019-20 which begins with the objective of eliminating poverty in all its dimensions such that every citizen will have access to a minimum standard of food, education, health, clothing, shelter, transportation and energy. In chapter 10 of the Agenda report *the NITI Aayog, in its 3-year Action Agenda addressed in depth various infrastucral challenges* It mentions that Infrastructure development is one of the most crucial elements of economic transformation. The development of transport and connectivity infrastructure, including the roadways, railways, shipping & ports, in-land waterways and civil aviation contribute immensely in this economic transformation.. The challenges faced in this sector include physical capacity constraints, severe modal imbalances and a lack of holistic planning, maintenance and safety. Action Agenda of the NITI Aayog have been briefly covered hereunder:

(a) In the Transport and Connectivity area The NITI Aayog could locate following six major gaps that needed to be addressed, namely,

- *The transport network is not planned holistically.*
- *Maintenance of different modes of transport infrastructure is poor.*
- *The capacity of physical transport infrastructure is limited.*
- *The transport network has severe modal imbalances.*
- *Transport safety, particularly road safety, remains poor.*
- *The transport sector remains highly dependent on conventional sources of energy.*

The Action Agenda intends to ensure that in the next three years, it should enhance the transport and connectivity network such that it facilitates the efficient movement of people and goods, is accessible, affordable, safe, environmentally sustainable and develops in a manner that is aligned with industry demands.

(b) In the Roadways, The NITI Aayog observes that India happens to be the second largest road network in the world with over 4.24 million km of roads in 2013-14, consisting of National Highways, Expressways, State Highways, major district roads, other district roads and village roads. In 2014-15, national highways alone made up 97,958 km, a 50% increase in length since 2004-05. The National Highways Development Program (NHDP), the Bharatmala Project and Special Accelerated Road Development Programme-North East (SARDP-NE) focus on the development and improvement of national highways. The Pradhan Mantri Gram Sadak Yojana (PMGSY) and Bharat Nirman focus on the construction and maintenance of rural roads. The development of secondary road networks falls under the purview of state governments and is being addressed by them.

(c) In the Road Connectivity and Mobility area, the NITI Aayog has suggested the following initiatives in the Action Agenda :

- *Increase connectivity, especially in Rural India and with Ports by expanding the road network.*
- *Enhance Public Transport in the road segment through allowing private providers.*
- *Increase the coverage of Electronic Toll Collection (ETC) in National and State Highway*

(d) On Road Maintenance, the NITI Aayog has programmed to address the following:

- *Improve maintenance of highways and expressways.*
- *Allocate additional funds for maintenance of all roads.*
- *Define criteria for converting state to national highways.*

(e) On the Road Safety area, the NITI Aayog intends to cover the following:

- *Strengthen rules governing road safety by passing the Motor Vehicles (Amendment) Bill, 2016.*
- *Create Road Safety Boards to reduce accidents.*
- *Use data to monitor accidents.*
- *Standardize reporting of accidents and enhance preparedness through better logistics.*
- *Create supporting infrastructure and economic models to support better safety and efficiency.*

(f) On Railways, *the NITI Aayog notes that,* the Indian Railways transported in 2014-15 1,140 billion-passenger km and 682 billion net-tonne km, making it the largest passenger and fourth largest freight transporting railway system globally. Despite its extensive reach and scale, the share of railways in the total surface freight carried has declined from 86.2% to 35.5% between 1950-51 and 2011-12. The railways also suffer from low capacity, poor utilization of existing capacity, safety issues and lack of quality service delivery in the passenger segment. While the merging of the railway budget with the union budget in 2017-18 will help increase funding for the railways, improving financing to address several of these challenges will require specific actions.

As to Freight Segment, Connectivity, Service Delivery and Efficiency and Railway Safety, the NITI Aayog included the following action agenda:

Freight Segment

- *Rationalize railway fares to increase capacity utilization along non-major routes in the freight segment.*
- *Implement and plan DFCs.*

Connectivity

- *Build additional infrastructure for railways to augment capacity and connectivity.*
- *Fast track the development of the Mumbai-Ahmadabad High Speed Rail (MAHSR).*
- *Develop semi high-speed trains to enhance connectivity.*

Service Delivery and Efficiency

- *Enhance service quality in passenger railways.*
- *Improve efficiency of freight railways.*
- *Improve the quality of railway stations and trains.*
- *Redevelop and modernize railway stations..*
- *Improve the punctuality of trains.*

Railway Safety

- *Achieve zero fatalities in railways by 2019 by upgrading infrastructure.*
- *Improve safety by adopting new technologies.*
- *Strengthen the institutional framework to ensure safety.*

(g) Shipping and Ports

India currently has 12 major and 205 non-major ports located across about 7,500 km of coast. Coastal shipping remains largely underutilised, accounting for only 6.5% of the total freight traffic in India in 2014-15, relative to 30% by rail and 57% by road. The total export-import (EXIM) trade handled at all ports increased from 815 MT in 2010-11 to 1,052 MT in 2014-15, registering a Compound Annual Growth Rate (CAGR) of 4.4 %. During the period, the growth in volume of cargo traffic handled at non-major ports has been much higher at 10% than that at major ports (0.5%). The non-major ports in Gujarat and Andhra Pradesh account for a large share of increase in traffic.

*The NITI Aayog considers that t*he key challenges faced by the sector include a strict regulatory regime, lack of infrastructure and investment and the absence of a competitive ship building industry. By 2020,the country has to improve the standards in Indian ports to improve logistics and boost export efficiency. It can be done by easing the regulatory environment, digitizing the customs process, improving the technology used in the tracking of consignments and adopting additional technology systems to ensure timely deliveries. A uniform Goods and Services Tax (GST) will reduce internal barriers to trade. The improvement of standards and infrastructure in Indian ports will also be crucial in the functioning of the proposed CEZs. Further, the following action agenda need also to carried forward :

- *Increase competition through easing cabotage.*
- *Increase the capacity of and eliminate discriminatory provisions for Indian vessels.*
- *Explore creating deep-water ports or barges for ports with low drafts.*
- *Facilitate minor/non-major port connectivity to hinterland areas.*

(h) Inland Waterways

India has about 14,500 km of navigable inland waterways, including rivers, canals, backwaters, and creeks. Despite its potential to transport large volumes of goods and connectivity to rural areas, inland water transport accounts for a small amount of freight movement relative to other modes. The NITI Aayog took up the the following Action Agenda:

Currently, the bulk of freight traffic is carried on three national waterways, NWs I, II, and III, and the Mumbai and Goa waterways. The traffic on the

Mumbai and Goa waterways, which is mostly short lead, is heavier than the traffic on the national waterways. Traffic on NW-I is long lead. Traffic on the National Waterways is dominated by over-dimensional cargo and coal. There has been a significant push towards improving the traffic on inland waterways. The "Jal Marg Vikas" project involves the development of River Ganga stretch between Allahabad to enable commercial navigation of at least 1,500 tonne vessels. Multi-modal terminals are currently being developed at Varanasi, Haldia and Sahebganj, and a new navigational lock at Farraka is also planned. The Inland Waterways Authority of India (IWAI) has a target of achieving 9,286 km of National and State Waterways as well as feeder routes by 2020. The following action points will help increase the connectivity and efficiency of inland waterways in India.

- *Streamline the governance of inland waterways.*
- *Develop measures for year-round navigation.*
- *Ease restrictions on river-sea movement.*
- *Develop inland waterways transport to facilitate movement of goods to neighbouring countries and the Northeast.*

(i) Civil Aviation

The Civil Aviation sector transported 85 million passengers and 590,793 tonnes of freight in India in 2015-16. The NITI Aayog suggested the following Action Agenda:

- *High costs of flying through metropolitan airports, traffic rights and high aeronautical charges hinder the development of Indian airports as major hubs and slow down the sector's growth. Four key policy actions can facilitate the development of the civil aviation sector: (1) Aligning the excise duty on Aviation Turbine Fuel (ATF) with international levels (2) adopting a consistent model for tariff determination, (3) removing bottlenecks for theimplementation of the second control period in Delhi and Mumbai, (4) allowing credit for aviation infrastructure under the GST and (5) including provisions for domestic hub development while auctioning traffic rights. These actions will help reduce aviation costs, thereby promoting the sector's growth and help develop hub airports.*
- *Align excise duties on ATF to international levels to bring down its cost.*
- *Adopt a consistent model for tariff determination.*
- *Although airports in the US, Australia, Belgium and New Zealand currently do not include non-aeronautical charges in the calculation of their tariffs, it is important to note that these countries already have well-established hub airports.Australia started out with a single till model and only now has it moved to a dual till structure.*

India could also move to a hybrid or dual till structure once its hub and spoke model is established. This would also encourage further infrastructure investments to expand airports in line with increases in demand.. Further, the following action agenda need also to carried forward

- *Remove bottlenecks for the second control period to be implemented in Delhi and Mumbai.*
- *Allow credit for aviation infrastructure under the GST.*
- *Include provisions for domestic hub development while auctioning traffic rights.*

Cross-cutting Issues

The NITI Aayog has also included the following Cross-cutting Issues:

(i) Seamless Transport across Modes

- Increasing Intermodal Connectivity. For each mode of transport, we need to design plans for achieving complete and seamless access from start to end point. This would also ensure intermodal connectivity. We should shift the coverage of public transport systems to clusters rather than individual locations (cities, towns or villages). By 2020, we also need to develop plans for feeder services such that they connect remote places to main transit routes.
- Explore the feasibility of logistics parks and expedite the completion of these parks. The MoRTH has already announced its intention to adopt an integrated transport and logistics framework. As part of this policy, a number of logistics parks around existing industrial clusters are to be built. The master planning for these parks should be expedited and construction on the initially identified parks should begin by 2018.

(ii) Logistics and Technology Adoption

- By 2020, we should improve our logistics performance and witness an improvement in our ranking in the Logistics Performance Index (LPI). I
- The adoption of an integrated systems-based approach for logistics along with increased technology-use will help improve efficiency.

(iii) International Connectivity

- To enhance transport connectivity with neighbouring countries through various modes, we should work on streamlining standards, technologies and improving the transportation infrastructure.

(iv) Access to Finance

- Since the transport sector has direct and indirect effects on economic growth, we should work to ensure increasing investment in the sector. Because public investment is constrained by limited revenues available, we need to explore avenues to mobilizing private investment in a major way.

Digital Connectivity

Digital connectivity has become an important driver of economic growth. In order to leverage efficiencies promised by the adoption of digital technologies, we need to develop a physical digital infrastructure network that is accessible to all. The Action Agenda discusses the Digital India campaign and the actions related to enhancing digital connectivity.

(d) Economic Survey of India, 2017-18

The Government of India tabled the Economic Survey of India, 2017-18 in the Parliament in the Budget Session on 29th January,2018 to set the stage for the Government for the Annual Budget. The Survey contains an indepth analysis, serious research as well new policy ideas. The said Survey sums up the latest position on status of building resilient infrastructure, promote inclusive and sustainable industrialization and foster innovation, as included in SDG-9. The Economic Survey observed that promoting inclusive employment-intensive industry, and building resilient infrastructure are vital factors for economic and development and the Government is taking several sector- specific measures and investment over time in this direction to support India's long-term growth. Apart from structural reforms like Goods and Services Tax, Insolvency and Bankruptcy Code and measures to facilitate Ease of Doing Business, the Survey highlights that the Government has initiated sector specific reforms in Steel, Apparel, Leather and Power sectors to address specific challenges associated with each of these sectors. Various reforms undertaken by the Government over the last 3 years, have been recognized by international rating agencies such as Moody's Investor Service and up-gradation in the ranking of Ease of Doing Business of the World Bank Report 2018, the Survey further adds.

The Economic Survey 2017-18 further says that the Index of Industrial Production (IIP) which is a volume index with base year 2011-12, shows that the industrial output increased by 3.2 percent during April-November 2017-18. This was a composite effect of robust growth in electricity generation at 5.2 percent and moderate growth in both mining and manufacturing sectors at 3.0 percent and 3.1 percent respectively. The Index of Industrial Production (IIP) registered a 25-month high growth of 8.4 per cent with manufacturing growing at 10.2 per cent.

The Economic Survey 2017-18 also states that the Eight Core Infrastructure Supportive Industries, viz. Coal, Crude Oil, Natural Gas, Petroleum, Refinery Products, Fertilizers, Steel, Cement and Electricity attained a cumulative growth of 3.9 percent during April-November, 2017-18. The production growth of Coal, Natural Gas, Refinery Products, Steel, Cement and Electricity was positive during this period. The steel production increased substantially, while the production of crude oil and fertilizers fell marginally during the period.The Survey notes that nominal outstanding credit growth to industry turned positive to 1 per cent in November 2017 for the first time after witnessing negative growth since October 2016. Demand for funds by Indian firms, in the wake of the credit slowdown, has been somewhat met by alternative sources such as corporate bonds and commercial paper.

According to the Survey, the Government is investing massively on building infrastructure to support Indias long term growth. India is far ahead than many emerging economies in terms of providing qualitative transportation related infrastructure as indicated below:

Roads: The primary agenda of the Government in this sector has been building new National Highways (NHs) and also converting State Highways (SHs) into NHs. As of September 2017, the length of roadways comprises 115,530 km of NHs along with 1,76,166 km of state highways and 53,26,166 km of other roads. In order to expedite completion of delayed projects, various steps have been taken for streamlining of land acquisition & environment clearances. The new umbrella program 'Bharatmala Pariyojana' aims to achieve optimal resource allocation for a holistic highway development.

Railways: During April-September 2017, Indian Railways carried 558.1 million tonnes of revenue earning freight traffic as against 531.2 million tonnes during the corresponding period of previous year, showing an increase of 5.1 per cent during this period. The Government has emphasized on railways infrastructure development. The pace of commissioning Broad Gauge (BG) lines and completion of electrification have been accelerated. With financial assistance from Government of India, 425 km of metro rail systems are operational and about 684 km are under construction in various cities across India as in December 2017.

Ports: In 2017-18 (till 31.12.2017), cargo traffic handled at Major Ports has been 499.4 million tonnes, as compared to 481.8 million tonnes handled during the corresponding period of 2016-17. Under the Sagarmala Programme which aims to promote port-led development along Indian coast line, 289 projects worth Rs. 2.17 lakh crore are under various stages of implementation and development.

Telecom: The programmes including 'Bharat Net' and 'Digital India' aim at converting India into a digital economy. At the end of September 2017, the number of subscribers stood at 1207 million, out of which 502 million connections were in the rural areas and 705 million in the urban areas.

Civil Aviation: In April–September 2017, domestic airlines carried 57.5 million passengers, showing a growth rate of 16 per cent over the corresponding period of previous year. Government is taking initiatives like liberalization of air services, airport development and regional connectivity through UDAN scheme.

Power: All-India installed power generation capacity reached 330,861 MW as on November 30, 2017. As on April 1, 2015, there were 18,542 unelectrified census villages, of these electrification of 15,183 villages has been completed as on November 30, 2017. The Ujjawal DISCOM Assurance Yojana (UDAY) has focused on enhancing the financial health of DISCOMs by reducing interest burden, cost of power and aggregated technical and commercial losses. A new scheme, Saubhagya (Pradhan Mantri Sahaj Bijli Har Ghar Yojana), was launched in September 2017 to ensure electrification of all remaining willing households in the country in rural and urban areas".

According to the Survey, the Indian logistics industry worth around US$ 160 Billion has grown at a compound annual growth rate (CAGR) of 7.8 per cent during last five years. Logistics sector provides employment to more than 22 million people. The Global Ranking of the World Bank's 2016 Logistics Performance Index shows that India jumped to 35th rank in 2016 from 54th rank in 2014 in terms of overall logistics performance. India has improved its rank in all the six components of logistics performance index.

India's housing policies have been mostly focused on building more homes and on home ownership. The Economic Survey suggests that a more holistic approach is required that takes into account rentals and vacancy rates. In turn, this needs to pay more attention to contract enforcement, property rights and spatial distribution of housing supply vs. demand.

The Economic Survey also notes that the Global Infrastructure Outlook forecasts around US$ 4.5 trillion worth of investments is required by India till 2040 to develop infrastructure to improve economic growth and community wellbeing.

(e) Budget Initiatives for 2018-19

The Budget document embodies not only a financial statement on resources availability and its projected expenditure, it also expresses alongside overtly and covertly the policy statement of the Government of the day. The Budget Speech of the Finance Minister of India delivered on First February, 2018 is taken up to relate its relevance on SDGs. In so far as SDG-9 is concerned, the Union Finance Minister mentioned at chapter V which is summarised as below: Emphasising that infrastructure is the growth driver of economy, the Finance Minister estimated that investment in excess of Rs. 50 lakh crore is needed to increase growth of GDP and connect the nation with a network of roads, airports, railways, ports and inland waterways. He announced increase of budgetary allocation on infrastructure for 2018-19 to Rs. 5.97 lakh crore against estimated expenditure of Rs. 4.94 lakh crore in 2017-18.

The Government has made an all-time high allocation to rail and road sectors and is committed to further enhance public investment. The Prime Minister personally reviews the targets and achievements in infrastructure sectors on a regular basis. Using online monitoring system of PRAGATI alone, projects worth 9.46 lakh crore have been facilitated and fast tracked. To further boost tourism, the Budget proposes to develop ten prominent tourist sites into Iconic Tourism destinations by following a holistic approach involving infrastructure and skill development, development of technology, attracting private investment, branding and marketing. Under the Bharatmala Pariyojana, about 35000 kms road construction in Phase-I at an estimated cost of Rs. 5,35,000 crore has been approved. The Budget proposes to expand the airport capacity more than five times to handle a billion trips a year under a new initiative - NABH Nirman. Under the Regional connectivity scheme of UDAN (Ude Desh ka Aam Nagrik) initiated by the Government last year, 56 unserved airports and 31 unserved helipads would be connected. The Budget has given a big thrust to Medium, Small and Micro Enterprises (MSMEs) to boost employment and economic growth. A sum of Rs. 3794 crore has been provided for giving credit support, capital and interest subsidy and for innovations. MUDRA Yojana launched in April, 2015 has led to sanction of Rs. 4.6 lakh crore in credit from 10.38 crore MUDRA loans. 76% of loan accounts are of women and more than 50% belong to SCs, STs and OBCs. It is proposed to set a target of Rs.3 lakh crore for lending under MUDRA for 2018-19 after having successfully exceeded the targets in all previous years.

The Finance Minister stressed that the focus of the Government next year will be on providing maximum livelihood opportunities in the rural areas by spending more on livelihood, agriculture and allied activities and construction of rural infrastructure. The Finance Minister also said that in the year 2018-19, for creation of livelihood and infrastructure in rural areas, total amount to be spent by the Ministries will be Rs. 14.34 lakh crore, including extra-budgetary and non-budgetary resources of Rs.11.98 lakh crore. Apart from employment due to farming activities and self employment, this expenditure will create employment of 321 crore person days, 3.17 lakh kilometers of rural roads, 51 lakh new rural houses, 1.88 crore toilets, and provide 1.75 crore new household electric connections besides boosting agricultural growth.

Chapter - 20

Sustainable Development Goal 10

Reduce inequality within and among countries

Inequality poses a serious threat to social and political stability. It is also a serious stumbling block for sustained growth. The Open Working Group (OWG) of the General Assembly on Sustainable Development Goals, while addressing among the member states, commented that inequality jeopardizes the achievement of the overarching economic goals, such as eliminating extreme poverty, boosting decent work and transforming economic structures. Inequality is, however, not a matter of fate or chance and can be reversed through policies and reforms. While solutions for inequality per se rests with national and regional policy makers, collective actions and measures at the international level also have a crucial role to play for inequality among the countries of the world. Incidentally, the Rio+20 negotiations, the starting platform on the initiation of the Sustainable Development Summit, took place amidst the fallout from the 2008 financial crisis that revealed that the economic, social and environmental imbalances around the world could no longer be tackled separately or by countries acting alone. It was recognized that the sustainable development goals (SDGs) would have to be more universal and more inclusive than the Millennium Development Goals (MDGs), to address a wider range of socioeconomic differences around which inequalities had emerged and grown.

The Fact-sheet on Goal 1 that was placed at the time of Sustainable Development Summit, 2015 says 'On average – and taking into account population size –income inequality increased by 11% in developing countries between 1990 and 2010.A significant majority of households in developing countries –more than 75%–are living today in societies where income is more unequally distributed than it was in the 1990s. Children in the poorest 20% of the population are still up to three times more likely to die before their fifth birthday than children in the richest quintiles. Social protection has been significantly extended globally, yet persons with disabilities are up to five times more likely than average to incur catastrophic health expenditures. Despite overall declines in maternal mortality in the majority of developing countries, women in rural areas are still up to three times more likely to die while giving birth than women living in urban centres.

The UN Secretary General's observation on "Progress towards the Sustainable Development Goals" vide E/2016/75 stated that Goal 10 calls for reducing inequalities in income as well as those based on age, sex, disability, race, ethnicity, origin, religion or economic or other status within a country. The Goal also addresses inequalities among countries, including those related to representation, migration and development assistance. It emphasizes that Target 10.1 seeks to ensure that income growth among the poorest 40 per cent of the population in every country is more rapid than its national average. This was true in 56 of 94 countries with data available from 2007 to 2012. However, this does not necessarily imply greater prosperity, since nine of those countries experienced negative growth rates over that period. Further, the labour share of GDP, which represents the proportion of wages and social protection transfers in an economy, provides an aggregate measure of primary income inequality. A shift of income away from labour towards capital has contributed to rising inequality. Globally, the labour share of GDP decreased from 57 per cent in 2000 to 55 per cent in 2015, mainly owing to stagnating wages and a decline in employers' social contributions in developed regions, while the trend was stable or slightly upward in developing regions. Preferential treatment for developing countries and the least developed countries in trade can help reduce inequalities by creating more export opportunities. Major developed country markets already offer duty-free market access to the least developed countries on most of their tariff lines. But even when they do not, as in the case of some agricultural products, the average applied tariff rate is often close to zero per cent. The share of exports from the least developed countries and developing regions that benefitted from duty-free treatment increased from 2000 to 2014, reaching 79 per cent for developing countries and 84 per cent for the least developed countries. The comparative advantage of the least developed countries in duty-free access varies depending on the product groups analysed. Almost all agricultural products from the least developed countries (98 per cent) were exempt from duties by developed countries, versus 74 per cent of products from developing countries. Shares of exports exempt from duties diverged even more for textiles and clothing: the rate for both product groups for the least developed countries was around 70 per cent, while for developing countries it was 41 per cent for textiles and 34 per cent for clothing. It also notes that Official development assistance and financial flows contribute to reducing inequalities within and among countries. In 2014, total resource flows for development to the least developed countries totalled $55.2 billion, and eight donor countries met the target of 0.15 per cent of gross national income (GNI) for ODA to the least developed countries. Preliminary ODA figures for 2015 show that bilateral net ODA to the least developed countries increased by 4 per cent in real terms, compared to 2014. The report also says that People migrate for many reasons, including better employment opportunities and higher wages. When successful, many migrants send money back to their country of origin to care of family members. Remittances to developing countries have increased slightly, rising to $431.6 billion in 2015, up 0.4 per cent from 2014. In contrast, global remittances (including those to developed countries) were estimated at $582 billion in 2015, a decline of 1.7 per cent from 2014. Even with the global contraction in remittance flows in 2015, the longer term trend is upward. However, the cost of sending money across national borders is significant, averaging 7.5 per cent of the amount remitted in 2015, down from 10 per cent in 2008 but still above the 3 per cent called for in target 10.c.

The prevalence of such widening disparities call for action that require the adoption of sound policies to empower the bottom percentile of income earners and promote economic inclusion of all regardless of sex, race or ethnicity, and also responding to the 2030 Agenda's mandate of leaving no one behind, the Goal 10 of Sustainable Development came into being. Before addressing India's initiatives on ensuring Goal 10, it would be appropriate to reiterate once again the Goal 10, its targets and related indicators to keep it in the up-fronts, in sequential order.

Goal 10. Reduce inequality within and among countries

10.1 By 2030, progressively achieve and sustain income growth of the bottom 40 per cent of the population at a rate higher than the national average

10.2 By 2030, empower and promote the social, economic and political inclusion of all, irrespective of age, sex, disability, race, ethnicity, origin, religion or economic or other status

10.3 Ensure equal opportunity and reduce inequalities of outcome, including by eliminating discriminatory laws, policies and practices and promoting appropriate legislation, policies and action in this regard

10.4 Adopt policies, especially fiscal, wage and social protection policies, and progressively achieve greater equality

10.5 Improve the regulation and monitoring of global financial markets and institutions and strengthen the implementation of such regulations

10.6 Ensure enhanced representation and voice for developing countries in decision-making in global international economic and financial institutions in order to deliver more effective, credible, accountable and legitimate institutions

10.7 Facilitate orderly, safe, regular and responsible migration and mobility of people, including through the implementation of planned and well-managed migration policies

10.a Implement the principle of special and differential treatment for developing countries, in particular least developed countries, in accordance with World Trade Organization agreements

10.b Encourage official development assistance and financial flows, including foreign direct investment, to States where the need is greatest, in particular least developed countries, African countries, small island developing States and landlocked developing countries, in accordance with their national plans and programmes

10.c By 2030, reduce to less than 3 per cent the transaction costs of migrant remittances and eliminate remittance corridors with costs higher than 5 per cent

The goals and targets per se are important from the angle of programme vision and intended outcome; however from the perspective of monitoring the performance, indicators do play critical role. Since indicator-design is essentially an expert professional skill- job requiring to keep harmony with overall goals and targets of the Sustainable Development Summit as embodied in paragraph 75 of Transforming our World: The 2030 Agenda for Sustainable Development mentioned: "the Goals and targets will be followed-up and reviewed using a set of global indicators. These will be complemented by indicators at the regional and national levels which will be developed by member states, in addition to the outcomes of work undertaken for the development of the baselines for those targets where national and global baseline data does not yet exist".

Needless to mention that purpose of SDG indicators is twofold; first it acts as a management tool to help countries develop implementation and monitoring strategies for achieving the SDGs and to monitor progress and secondly, it works as a report card, to measure progress towards achieving a target and ensure the accountability of governments to their citizens.As a matter of fact, Agenda 21 of the SD Summit also called on countries and the international community to develop indicators of sustainable development. Such indicators were needed to increase focus on sustainable development and assist decision-makers at all levels to adopt sound national sustainable development policies.

Be that as it may, the Global Indicator Framework as designed by the UN Statistical Commission at its 47th Session in March 2016 and adopted

thereafter by the Economic and Social Council and the General Assembly, are as follows:

Indicators of Goal 10

10.1.1 Growth rates of household expenditure or income per capita among the bottom 40 per cent of thepopulation and the total population

10.2.1 Proportion of people living below 50 per cent of median income, by sex, age and persons withdisabilities

10.3.1 Proportion of population reporting having personally felt discriminated against or harassed in theprevious 12 months on the basis of a ground of discrimination prohibited under international humanrights law

10.4.1 Labour share of GDP, comprising wages and social protection transfers

10.5.1 Financial Soundness Indicators10.6.1 Proportion of members and voting rights of developing countries in international organizations

10.7.1 Recruitment cost borne by employee as a proportion of yearly income earned in country ofdestination

10.7.2 Number of countries that have implemented well-managed migration policies

10.a.1 Proportion of tariff lines applied to imports from least developed countries and developingcountries with zero-tariff

10.b.1 Total resource flows for development, by recipient and donor countries and type of flow (e.g. official development assistance, foreign direct investment and other flows)

10.c.1 Remittance costs as a proportion of the amount Remitted

The Goal 10 is a big challenge of the international community. It has many interlinked role and policy dimensions at the global, regional, national and sub-national level. While the global and regional level interventions relate to adopting policies regulation and monitoring of global financial markets and institutions, it also includes, among others, long-standing issue of fair representation and voice of developing countries in the global governance system. However, 'reduction of inequality within' is most critical from practical life point of view for which national policy and sub-national programme performances are very relevant.

SDG-10 and the initiatives in India

(a) The NITI Aayog and Mapping of Initiatives on SDG-10

Given the above the above premises, it would be worthwhile to examine the roadmap for Sustainable development of 'Goal 10 in India with reference to the basic approach and goal-specific initiatives. The NITI Aayog has been empowered to oversee the implementation of SDGs by the ministries of the Central Government and coordinate with States for the achievement of developmental targets as enshrined in the SDGs. The NITI Aayog tasked itself to prepare a initial draft based on mapping of the goals and targets proposed by Nodal and other Ministries in consultation with MoSPI. The schemes so mapped for Goal-10 covered 40) Multi Sectoral Development Programme for Minorities (2013) 41) Backward Regions Grant Fund (District Component) (ACA) (M/o PR/M/o Finance) {2007},42) Scheme for Development of Scheduled Castes (Core of the Core) 43) Scheme for Development of Other Backward Classes and Denotified, Nomadic and Semi-nomadic Tribes. (Core of the Core) 44) Scheme for development of Economically Backward Classes (EBCs) 45) Backward Regions Grant Fund (BRGF) (State Component) (ACA) including related interventions{2007} (1) Grants from Central Pool of Resources for North Eastern Region and Sikkim{2016}, (2) Udaan Scheme for youth of Jammu & Kashmir{2016}, (3) PAHAL- Direct Benefit s Transfer for LPG (DBTL consumers scheme(2014), (4) Give it Up Campaign (for LPG subsidy{2016}) and (5) Mudra Yojana (2016)

(b) National Review of SDG- 10 for United Nations High Level Political Forum 2017

The outcomes of initiatives under SDG-10 would normally take a period of time to fructify as several other factors are also interlinked to reflect its final outcome. Be that as it may, the Voluntary National Review Report on Implementation of Sustainable Development Goals presented for United Nations High Level Political Forum 2017 is a good reference point for understanding the latest position on SDG-10 status in India. The report has not included SDG-10 as a separate item. However, it is noted that "given the interconnectedness of the SDGs, relevant strategies for enabling collaboration among different actors will be developed as part of the overall implementation process and that India will continue to pursue the implementation of the SDG agenda through close collaboration between the national and sub-national governments as well as active participation of all other relevant stakeholders.

(c) The NITI Aayog, Three-Year Action Agenda and SDG-10

The NITI Aayog has recently released a draft Three-Year Action Agenda covering years 2017-18 to 2019-20 which begins with the objective of eliminating poverty in all its dimensions such that every citizen will have access to a minimum standard of food, education, health, clothing, shelter, transportation and energy. The Three-Year Action Agenda does not include any separate chapter to dwell on SDG-10. However, the interventions under 'Towards building a More Inclusive Society' as covered in chapter -22 along with those included in other chapters covering several SDGs will also go a long way in improving quality changes of life of the least privileged and remove the economic disparities within a period of time.

(d) Economic Survey of India, 2017-18

The Government of India tabled the Economic Survey of India, 2017-18 in the Parliament in the Budget Session on 29th January,2018 to set the stage for the Government for the Annual Budget. The Survey contains an indepth analysis, serious research as well new policy ideas. The guiding principle is the 'Sabke Sath Sabke Vikas which implies that development should include every citizen.

The Government has taken up programmes to direct the benefits of structural changes and good growth to reach farmers, poor and other vulnerable sections of our society and to uplift the under-developed regions. The Government has also ensured that benefits reach eligible beneficiaries and are delivered to them directly. The Direct Benefit Transfer mechanism of India is the biggest such exercise in the world and is a global success story.

(e) Budget Inititives, 2018-19

The Budget document embodies not only a financial statement on resources availability and its projected expenditure, it also expresses alongside overtly and covertly the policy statement of the Government of the day. The Budget Speech of the Finance Minister of India delivered on First February, 2018 is taken up to relate its relevance on SDGs. In so far as SDG-10 is concerned, the Union Finance Minister mentioned that to give focused attention and to achieve our vision of an inclusive society, the Government has identified 115 aspirational districts taking various indices of development in consideration. The Government aims at improving the quality of life in these districts by investing in social services like health, education, nutrition, skill upgradation, financial inclusion and infrastructure like irrigation, rural electrification, potable drinking water and access to toilets at an accelerated pace and in a time bound manner. It is expected that these 115 districts would become model of development. Further, the Finance Minister also stated that Economic and social advancement of hard working people of Scheduled Castes (SCs) and Scheduled Tribes (STs) has received core attention of Government. Accordingly, the Government increased total earmarked allocation for SCs in 279 programmes from '34,334 crore in 2016-17 to '52,719 crore in RE 2017-18. Likewise, for STs, earmarked allocation was increased from '21,811 crore in 2016-17 to '32,508 crore in RE 2017-18 in 305 programmes. The Finance Minister proposed an earmarked allocation of '56,619 crore for SCs and '39,135 crore for STs in BE 2018-19.

The Budget, 2018-19 also said that Pradhan Mantri Jeevan Jyoti Beema Yojana (PMJJBY) has benefitted 5.22 crore families with a life insurance cover of '2 lakh on payment of a premium of only '330/- per annum. Likewise, under Pradhan Mantri Suraksha Bima Yojana, 13 crore 25 lakh persons have been insured with personal accident cover of '2 lakh on payment of a premium of only '12 per annum. The Government will work to cover all poor households, including SC/ST households, under these in a mission mode. Further, the Government will expand the coverage under Prime Minister Jan Dhan Yojana by bringing all sixty crore basic accounts within its fold and undertake measures to provide services of micro insurance and unorganized sector pension schemes through these accounts.

Chapter - 21

Sustainable Development Goal 11

Make cities and human settlements inclusive, safe, resilient and sustainable

More than half the world's population lives in cities. It is projected that by 2030 out of 10 people 6 will be urban dwellers. Almost a third of the urban population in developing regions still live in slums. In 2014, 30 per cent of the urban population in developing regions lived in conditions categorized as slums. Concerted action will be needed to address this challenge and enhance resilience because cities remain magnets for people seeking greater opportunities and a better life. Moreover, in many burgeoning cities around the world, growing populations are moving outwards, far beyond administrative boundaries. Urban sprawl has come into being in such places. Unplanned urban sprawl is associated with increased per capita emissions of carbon dioxide and hazardous pollution and often drives housing prices up, all of which hamper sustainable development. In aggregate terms, however, cities in every part of the world have dangerously high levels of air pollution. Be that as it may, cities offer more efficient economics of scale on many levels, including the provision of goods, services and transportation for a better quality of life. Overcoming numerous planning challenges and management, cities often become incubators for innovation and growth and drivers of sustainable development. National policies and regional development plans that take into account the specific needs and characteristics of urban areas are essential to sustainable development. Nearly three-quarters of countries have implemented or are working to implement national-level urban policies. The vast majority of these urban policies need to be aligned with SDGs and validated through sustainability radar. Indeed, this is a way to connect national policy to local action. The SDG-11 is about to make cities and human settlements inclusive, safe, resilient and sustainable.

The Fact-sheet on Goal 11 that was placed at the time of Sustainable Development Summit, 2015 says that half of humanity – 3.5 billion people – lives in cities today. By 2030, almost 60% of the world's population will live in urban areas. 828 million people live in slums today and the number keeps rising. The world's cities occupy just 2% of the Earth's land, but account for 60 – 80% of energy consumption and 75% of carbon emissions. Rapid urbanization is exerting pressure on fresh water supplies, sewage, the living environment, and public health. But the high density of cities can bring efficiency gains and technological innovation while reducing resource and energy consumption. Cities have the potential to either dissipate the distribution of energy or optimise their efficiency by reducing energy consumption and adopting green – energy systems. For instance, Rizhao, China has turned itself into a solar – powered city; in its central districts, 99% of households already use solar water heaters.

The UN Secretary General's observation on "Progress towards the Sustainable Development Goals" vide E/2016/75 stated that Goal 11 underpins the fact that 'more than half the world's population lives in cities. By 2030, it is projected that 6 out of 10 people will be urban dwellers. Despite numerous planning challenges, well-managed cities and other human settlements can be incubators for innovation and ingenuity and key drivers of sustainable development. However, as more people migrate to cities in search of a better life and urban populations grow, housing issues intensify. Already in 2014, 30 per cent of the urban population lived in slum-like conditions; in sub-Saharan Africa, the proportion was 55 per cent, the highest of any region. Globally, more than 880 million people were living in slums in 2014. This estimate does not include people in inadequate or unaffordable housing (defined as costing more than 30 per cent of total monthly household income). Further, as population growth outpaces available land, cities expand far beyond their formal administrative boundaries. This urban sprawl can be seen in many cities around the world, and not only in developing regions. From 2000 to 2015, the ratio of the land consumption rate to the population growth rate in Eastern Asia and the Oceania was the highest in the world, with developed regions second. Other regions, such as South-Eastern Asia and Latin America and the Caribbean, showed a decrease in that indicator over the same time period. Unfortunately, a low value for this ratio is not necessarily an indication that urban dwellers are faring well, as this can indicate a prevalence of overcrowded slums. Unplanned urban sprawl undermines other determinants of sustainable development. For example, for every 10 per cent increase in sprawl, there is a 5.7 per cent increase in per capita carbon dioxide emissions and a 9.6 per cent increase in per capita hazardous pollution. This illustrates the important interlinkages across the goals and targets.Likewise, managing solid waste is often problematic in densely populated areas. In fact, in many developing regions, less than half of solid waste is safely disposed of. As per capita waste generation continues to rise, the collection and safe disposal of solid waste will continue to require serious attention. Moreover, Urban air pollution also challenged cities around the world, causing illness and millions of premature deaths annually. In 2014, around half the global urban population was exposed to air pollution levels at least 2.5 times higher than maximum standards set by the World Health Organization.The quest for sustainable and coordinated urban development starts with national policies and regional development plans. As of 2015, 142 countries had a national urban policy in place or under development. Those countries are home to 75 per cent of the world's urban population.

Based on the above facts and observations, it would be appropriate to reiterate the Goal 11 of the SDGs, its targets and related indicators to keep it in the up-fronts, in sequential order, before addressing India's initiatives on Goal 11.

Goal 11. Make citics and human settlements inclusive, safe, resilient and sustainable

11.1 By 2030, ensure access for all to adequate, safe and affordable housing and basic services and upgrade slums

11.2 By 2030, provide access to safe, affordable, accessible and sustainable transport systems for all, improving road safety, notably by expanding public transport, with special attention to the needs of those in vulnerable situations, women, children, persons with disabilities and older persons

11.3 By 2030, enhance inclusive and sustainable urbanization and capacity for participatory, integrated and sustainable human settlement planning and management in all countries

11.4 Strengthen efforts to protect and safeguard the world's cultural and natural heritage

11.5 By 2030, significantly reduce the number of deaths and the number of people affected and substantially decrease the direct economic losses relative to global gross domestic product caused by disasters, including water-related disasters, with a focus on protecting the poor and people in vulnerable situations

11.6 By 2030, reduce the adverse per capita environmental impact of cities, including by paying special attention to air quality and municipal and other waste management

11.7 By 2030, provide universal access to safe, inclusive and accessible, green and public spaces, in particular for women and children, older persons and persons with disabilities

11.a Support positive economic, social and environmental links between urban, peri-urban and rural areas by strengthening national and regional development planning

11.b By 2020, substantially increase the number of cities and human settlements adopting and implementing integrated policies and plans towards inclusion, resource efficiency, mitigation and adaptation to climate change, resilience to disasters, and develop and implement, in line with the Sendai Framework for Disaster Risk Reduction 2015-2030, holistic disaster risk management at all levels

11.c Support least developed countries, including through financial and technical assistance, in building sustainable and resilient buildings utilizing local materials

The goals and targets per se are important from the angle of programme vision and intended outcome; however from the perspective of monitoring the performance, indicators do play critical role. Since indicator-design is essentially an expert professional skill- job requiring to keep harmony with overall goals and targets of the Sustainable Development Summit as embodied in paragraph 75 of Transforming our World: The 2030 Agenda for Sustainable Development mentioned: "the Goals and targets will be followed-up and reviewed using a set of global indicators. These will be complemented by indicators at the regional and national levels which will be developed by member states, in addition to the outcomes of work undertaken for the development of the baselines for those targets where national and global baseline data does not yet exist".

Needless to mention that purpose of SDG indicators is twofold; first it acts as a management tool to help countries develop implementation and monitoring strategies for achieving the SDGs and to monitor progress and secondly, it works as a report card, to measure progress towards achieving a target and ensure the accountability of governments to their citizens.As a matter of fact, Agenda 21 of the SD Summit also called on countries and the international community to develop indicators of sustainable development. Such indicators were needed to increase focus on sustainable development and assist decision-makers at all levels to adopt sound national sustainable development policies.

Be that as it may, the Global Indicator Framework as designed by the UN Statistical Commission at its 47th Session in March 2016 and adopted thereafter by the Economic and Social Council and the General Assembly, are as follows:

Indicators of Goal -11

11.1.1 Proportion of urban population living in slums, informal settlements or inadequate housing

11.2.1 Proportion of population that has convenient access to public transport, by sex, age and persons with disabilities

11.3.1 Ratio of land consumption rate to population growth rate

11.3.2 Proportion of cities with a direct participation structure of civil society in urban planning and management that operate regularly and democratically

11.4.1 Total expenditure (public and private) per capita spent on the preservation, protection and conservation of all cultural and natural heritage, by type of heritage (cultural, natural, mixed and World Heritage Centre designation), level of government (national, regional and local/municipal), type of expenditure (operating expenditure/investment) and type of private funding (donations in kind, private non-profit sector and sponsorship)

11.5.1 Number of deaths, missing persons and directly affected persons attributed to disasters per 100,000 population

11.5.2 Direct economic loss in relation to global GDP,damage to critical infrastructure and number of disruptions to basic services, attributed to disasters

11.6.1 Proportion of urban solid waste regularly collected and with adequate final discharge out of total urban solid waste generated, by cities

11.6.2 Annual mean levels of fine particulate matter (e.g. PM2.5 and PM10) in cities (population weighted)

11.7.1 Average share of the built-up area of cities that is open space for public use for all, by sex, age and persons with disabilities

11.7.2 Proportion of persons victim of physical or sexual harassment, by sex, age, disability status and place of occurrence, in the previous 12 months

11.a.1 Proportion of population living in cities that implement urban and regional development plans integrating population projections and resource needs,by size of city

11.b.1 Number of countries that adopt and implement national disaster risk reduction strategies in line with the Sendai Framework for Disaster Risk Reduction 2015-2030

11.b.2 Proportion of local governments that adopt and implement local disaster risk reduction strategies in line with national disaster risk reduction strategies

11.c.1 Proportion of financial support to the least developed countries that is allocated to the construction and retrofitting of sustainable, resilient and resource-efficient buildings utilizing local materials

SDG-11 and the initiatives in India

(a) The NITI Aayog and Mapping of Initiatives on SDG-11

Based on the overarching goal of SDG-11, the national government of the country needs to take it forward to design appropriate programme in ensuring commensurate outcome. In such efforts, the current scenario and revealed gaps need to be taken into consideration while drawing a roadmap for goal-11.The NITI Aayog has been empowered to oversee the implementation of SDGs by the ministries of the Central Government and coordinate with States for the achievement of developmental targets as enshrined in the SDGs. The NITI Aayog tasked itself to prepare a initial draft based on mapping of the goals and targets proposed by Nodal and other Ministries in consultation with MoSPI. The schemes so mapped for Goal-11 covered 46) Rajiv Awas Yojana (including BSUP & IHSDP){2009) 47) Indira Awas Yojana (IAY) {1985} 48) Pradhan Mantri Adarsh Gram Yojana (PMAGY) {2010} 49) National Programme for Persons with Disabilities {2011} 50) Jawaharlal Nehru National Urban Renewal Mission (JNNURM) (ACA){2005} including Smart Cities Mission *(Core) {2015}*, (2) Pradhan Mantri Awas Yojana (Housing for All-2022) *(Core) {2015}*, (3) Atal Mission for Rejuvenation and Urban Transformation (AMRUT) *(Core) {2015} and* (4) Heritage City Development and Augmentation Yojana (HRIDAY) {2015}

(b) National Review of SDG-11 for United Nations High Level Political Forum 2017

The outcomes of initiatives under SDG-11 would normally take a period of time to fructify as several other factors are also interlinked to reflect its final outcome. Be that as it may, the Voluntary National Review Report on Implementation of Sustainable Development Goals presented for United Nations High Level Political Forum 2017 is a good reference point for understanding the latest position on SDG-11 status in India. The report has not included SDG-11 as a separate item. However, it is noted that "given the interconnectedness of the SDGs, relevant strategies for enabling collaboration among different actors will be developed as part of the overall implementation process and that India will continue to pursue the implementation of the SDG agenda through close collaboration between the national and sub-national governments as well as active participation of all other relevant stakeholders. Further, a number of goals in the SDGs do not require the government to deliver public services, but instead to develop and enforce the necessary policy and regulatory frameworks."

(c) The NITI Aayog, Three Year Action Agenda and SDG-11

The NITI Aayog has recently released the Three-Year Action Agenda covering years 2017-18 to 2019-20 which begins with the objective of eliminating poverty in all its dimensions such that every citizen will have access to a minimum standard of food, education, health, clothing, shelter, transportation and energy. The chapter 22 of the 3-year Action Agenda affirms government's commitment in that during the next three years the focus would be on...transformation process of facilitating urbanization in the country. Key challenges faced by the urban sector include affordable housing, infrastructure development, public transport, promotion of Swachh Bharat, reform of urban land markets and waste management.

(d) Economic Survey of India, 2017-18

The Government of India tabled the Economic Survey of India, 2017-18 in the Parliament in the Budget Session on 29th January,2018 to set the stage for the Government for the Annual Budget. The Survey contains an indepth analysis, serious research as well new policy ideas. The said Survey sums up the latest position on the SDG 11. It states that India is now embarking on a fast rural to urban transition. The need of the hour is the provision of public services by the cities to its residents. However, raising resources of the magnitude that is required for a sustainable urban transformation is going to be a daunting challenge. The average cost recovery is less than 50 per cent in most of the Urban Local Bodies (ULBs). The way forward is to encourage the ULBs to raise resources through various innovative financial instruments such as municipal bonds, PPPs, credit risk guarantees, etc".

(e) Budget Initiatives for 2018-19

The Budget document embodies not only a financial statement on resources availability and its projected expenditure, it also expresses alongside overtly and covertly the policy statement of the Government of the day. The Budget Speech of the Finance Minister of India delivered on First February, 2018 is taken up to relate its relevance on SDGs. In so far as SDG-11 is concerned, the Union Finance Minister reiterated that Urbanization is our opportunity and priority. The Government has rolled out two interlinked programmes – Smart Cities Mission and the AMRUT.

Smart Cities Mission aims at building 100 Smart Cities with state-of-the-art amenities. And that 99 Cities have been selected with an outlay of '2.04 lakh crore. These Cities have started implementing various projects like Smart Command and Control Centre, Smart Roads, Solar Rooftops, Intelligent Transport Systems, Smart Parks. Projects worth '2350 crore have been completed and works of '20,852 crore are under progress. To preserve and revitalize soul of the heritage cities in India, National Heritage City Development and Augmentation Yojana (HRIDAY) has been taken up in a major way. The AMRUT programme focuses on providing water supply to all households in 500 cities. State level plans of '77,640 crore for 500 cities have been approved. Water supply contracts for 494 projects worth '19,428 crore and sewerage work contract for 272 projects costing '12,429 crore has been awarded.

Chapter - 22

Sustainable Development Goal 12

Ensure sustainable consumption and production patterns

Sustainable Development Goals are multi-dimensional. All possible areas relevant to ensuring sustainable development have been identified by the Sustainable Development Summit for its possible contribution towards Sustainable development. The Goal-12 is one of such areas where national governments of the world at large have to take care of balance between production and consumption. During Interactive Dialogue stage, preceding to Sustainable Development Summit, it was noted that prosperity has risen and many people have been lifted out of poverty. But, much more needs to be done, especially for the most vulnerable. Further reducing poverty levels, addressing the structural causes of inequality, ensuring access to justice and respecting human rights remain critical priorities. Economic growth must be decoupled from environmental degradation and combat climate change to protect future generations. Accelerating a real shift towards more sustainable lifestyles will require changing how we consume and use valuable resources. In real terms Sustainable consumption and production is about promoting resource and energy efficiency, sustainable infrastructure, and providing access to basic services, green and decent jobs and a better quality of life for all. Its implementation helps to achieve overall development plans, reduce future economic, environmental and social costs, strengthen economic competitiveness and reduce poverty.

The UN document mentions that Sustainable consumption and production aims at "doing more and better with less," increasing net welfare gains from economic activities by reducing resource use, degradation and pollution along the whole lifecycle, while increasing quality of life. It involves different stakeholders, including business, consumers, policy makers, researchers, scientists, retailers, media, and development cooperation agencies, among others. It also requires a systemic approach and cooperation among actors operating in the supply chain, from producer to final consumer. It involves engaging consumers through awareness-raising and education on sustainable consumption and lifestyles, providing consumers with adequate information through standards and labels and engaging in sustainable public procurement, among others.

The facts and figures incorporated in the UN website also state as follows:

- Each year, an estimated one third of all food produced – equivalent to 1.3 billion tonnes worth around $1 trillion – ends up rotting in the bins of consumers and retailers, or spoiling due to poor transportation and harvesting practices
- If people worldwide switched to energy efficient lightbulbs the world would save US$120 billion annually
- Should the global population reach 9.6 billion by 2050, the equivalent of almost three planets could be required to provide the natural resources needed to sustain current lifestyles

Water

- Less than 3 per cent of the world's water is fresh (drinkable), of which 2.5 per cent is frozen in the Antarctica, Arctic and glaciers. Humanity must therefore rely on 0.5 per cent for all of man's ecosystem's and fresh water needs.
- Man is polluting water faster than nature can recycle and purify water in rivers and lakes.
- More than 1 billion people still do not have access to fresh water.
- Excessive use of water contributes to the global water stress.
- Water is free from nature but the infrastructure needed to deliver it is expensive.

Energy

- Despite technological advances that have promoted energy efficiency gains, energy use in OECD countries will continue to grow another 35 per cent by 2020. Commercial and residential energy use is the second most rapidly growing area of global energy use after transport.
- In 2002 the motor vehicle stock in OECD countries was 550 million vehicles (75 per cent of which were personal cars). A 32 per cent increase in vehicle ownership is expected by 2020. At the same time, motor vehicle kilometres are projected to increase by 40 per cent and global air travel is projected to triple in the same period.

- Households consume 29 per cent of global energy and consequently contribute to 21 per cent of resultant CO_2 emissions.
- One-fifth of the world's final energy consumption in 2013 was from renewables.

Food

- While substantial environmental impacts from food occur in the production phase (agriculture, food processing), households influence these impacts through their dietary choices and habits. This consequently affects the environment through food-related energy consumption and waste generation.
- 1.3 billion tonnes of food is wasted every year while almost 1 billion people go undernourished and another 1 billion hungry.
- Overconsumption of food is detrimental to our health and the environment.
- 2 billion people globally are overweight or obese.
- Land degradation, declining soil fertility, unsustainable water use, overfishing and marine environment degradation are all lessening the ability of the natural resource base to supply food.
- The food sector accounts for around 30 per cent of the world's total energy consumption and accounts for around 22 per cent of total Greenhouse Gas emissions.

The Fact sheet on hand on Goal 12 at the Sustainable Development Summit showed that 1.3 billion tonnes of food are wasted every year. If people worldwide switched to energy-efficient light bulbs, the world would save US$120 billion annually. Should the global population reach 9.6 billion by 2050, the equivalent of almost three planets could be required to provide the natural resources needed to sustain current lifestyles. More than 1 billion people still do not have access to fresh water

The Report of the Secretary-General, "Progress towards the Sustainable Development Goals", E/2016/75 mentioned with reference to Goal 12 that Economic growth and development require the production of goods and services that improve the quality of life. Sustainable growth and development require minimizing the natural resources and toxic materials used, and the waste and pollutants generated, throughout the entire production and consumption process. Two measures, material footprint and domestic material consumption, provide an accounting of global material extraction and use, as well as flows of consumption of materials in countries. The material footprint reflects the amount of primary materials required to meet a country's needs. It is an indicator of the material standard of living or level of capitalization of an economy. Domestic material consumption measures the amount of natural resources used in economic processes. In 2010, the total material footprint in developed regions was significantly higher than that of developing regions, 23.6 kg per unit of GDP versus 14.5 kg per unit of GDP, respectively. The material footprint of developing regions increased from 2000 to 2010, with non-metallic minerals showing the largest increase. Domestic material consumption in developed regions has diminished slightly, from 17.5 tonnes per capita in 2000 to 15.3 tonnes per capita in 2010. It remains significantly higher than the value for developing regions, which stood at 8.9 tonnes per capita in 2010. Domestic material consumption per capita increased in almost all developing regions from 2000 to 2010, except in Africa, where it remained relatively stable (around 4 tonnes per capita), and Oceania, where it decreased from around 10.7 to 7.7 tonnes per capita. The rise in domestic material consumption per capita in Asia during that period is primarily a result of rapid industrialization. The Basel Convention on the Control of Transboundary Movements of Hazardous Wastes and Their Disposal, the Rotterdam Convention on the Prior Informed Consent Procedure for Certain Hazardous Chemicals and Pesticides in International Trade and the Stockholm Convention on Persistent Organic Pollutants established international frameworks to achieve the environmentally sound management of hazardous wastes, chemicals and persistent organic pollutants. With six exceptions, all Member States are party to at least one of those conventions. The number of parties to those conventions rose significantly from 2005 to 2015, particularly in Africa and Oceania. There are now 183 parties to the Basel Convention, 180 to the Stockholm Convention and 155 to the Rotterdam Convention.

With this broad framework in view the Sustainable Development Summit declared as follows:

> "28. We commit to making fundamental changes in the way that our societies produce and consume goods and services. Governments, international organizations, the business sector and other non-State actors and individuals must contribute to changing unsustainable consumption and production patterns, including through the mobilization, from all sources, of financial and technical assistance to strengthen developing countries' scientific, technological and innovative capacities to move towards more sustainable patterns of consumption and production. We encourage the implementation of the 10-Year Framework of Programmes on Sustainable Consumption and Production Patterns. All countries take action, with developed countries taking the lead, taking into account the development and capabilities of developing countries'.

Based on the above observations, it would be appropriate to reiterate the Goal 12 of the SDGs, its targets and related indicators to keep it in the up-fronts,in sequential order, before addressing India's initiatives on ensuring sustainable consumption and production patterns.

Goal 12. Ensure sustainable consumption and production patterns

12.1 Implement the 10-year framework of programmes on sustainable consumption and production, all countries taking action, with developed countries taking the lead, taking into account the development and capabilities of developing countries

12.2 By 2030, achieve the sustainable management and efficient use of natural resources

12.3 By 2030, halve per capita global food waste at the retail and consumer levels and reduce food losses along production and supply chains, including post-harvest losses

12.4 By 2020, achieve the environmentally sound management of chemicals and all wastes throughout their life cycle, in accordance with agreed international frameworks, and significantly reduce their release to air, water and soil in order to minimize their adverse impacts on human health and the environment

12.5 By 2030, substantially reduce waste generation through prevention, reduction, recycling and reuse

12.6 Encourage companies, especially large and transnational companies, to adopt sustainable practices and to integrate sustainability information into their reporting cycle

12.7 Promote public procurement practices that are sustainable, in accordance with national policies and priorities

12.8 By 2030, ensure that people everywhere have the relevant information and awareness for sustainable development and lifestyles in harmony with nature

12.a Support developing countries to strengthen their scientific and technological capacity to move towards more sustainable patterns of consumption and production

12.b Develop and implement tools to monitor sustainable development impacts for sustainable tourism that creates jobs and promotes local culture and products

12.c Rationalize inefficient fossil-fuel subsidies that encourage wasteful consumption by removing market distortions, in accordance with national circumstances, including by restructuring taxation and phasing out those harmful subsidies, where they exist, to reflect their environmental impacts, taking fully into account the specific needs and conditions of developing countries and minimizing the possible adverse impacts on their development in a manner that protects the poor and the affected communities.

The goals and targets per se are important from the angle of programme vision and intended outcome; however from the perspective of monitoring the performance, indicators do play critical role. Since indicator-design is essentially an expert professional skill- job requiring to keep harmony with overall goals and targets of the Sustainable Development Summit as embodied in paragraph 75 of Transforming our World: The 2030 Agenda for Sustainable Development, mentioned: "the Goals and targets will be followed-up and reviewed using a set of global indicators. These will be complemented by indicators at the regional and national levels which will be developed by member states, in addition to the outcomes of work undertaken for the development of the baselines for those targets where national and global baseline data does not yet exist".

Needless to mention that purpose of SDG indicators is twofold; first it acts as a management tool to help countries develop implementation and monitoring strategies for achieving the SDGs and to monitor progress and secondly, it works as a report card, to measure progress towards achieving a target and ensure the accountability of governments to their citizens.As a matter of fact, Agenda 21 of the SD Summit also called on countries and the international community to develop indicators of sustainable development. Such indicators were needed to increase focus on sustainable development and assist decision-makers at all levels to adopt sound national sustainable development policies.

Be that as it may, the Global Indicator Framework as designed by the UN Statistical Commission at its 47th Session in March 2016 and adopted thereafter by the Economic and Social Council and the General Assembly, are as follows:

Indicators of Goal 12

12.1.1 Number of countries with sustainable consumption and production (SCP) national action plans or SCP mainstreamed as a priority or a target into national policies

12.2.1 Material footprint, material footprint per capita, and material footprint per GDP

12.2.2 Domestic material consumption, domestic material consumption per capita, and domestic material consumption per GDP

12.3.1 Global food loss index

12.4.1 Number of parties to international multilateral environmental agreements on hazardous waste, and other chemicals that meet their commitments and obligations in transmitting information as required by each relevant agreement

12.4.2 Hazardous waste generated per capita and proportion of hazardous waste treated, by type of treatment

12.5.1 National recycling rate, tons of material recycled

12.6.1 Number of companies publishing sustainability reports

12.7.1 Number of countries implementing sustainable public procurement policies and action plans

12.8.1 Extent to which (i) global citizenship education and (ii) education for sustainable development (including climate change education) are mainstreamed in (a) national education policies; (b) curricula; (c) teacher education; and (d) student assessment

12.a.1 Amount of support to developing countries on research and development for sustainable consumption and production and environmentally sound technologies

12.b.1 Number of sustainable tourism strategies or policies and implemented action plans with agreed monitoring and evaluation tools

12.c.1 Amount of fossil-fuel subsidies per unit of GDP (production and consumption) and as a proportion of total national expenditure on fossil fuels

SDG-12 and the initiatives in India

(a) The NITI Aayog and Mapping of Initiatives on SDG-12

Based on the overarching goal of SDG-12, the national government of the country needs to take it forward to design appropriate programme in ensuring commensurate outcome. In such efforts, the current scenario and revealed gaps need to be taken into consideration while drawing a roadmap for goal-12. The NITI Aayog has been empowered to oversee the implementation of SDGs by the ministries of the Central Government and coordinate with States for the achievement of developmental targets as enshrined in the SDGs. The NITI Aayog tasked itself to prepare a initial draft based on mapping of the goals and targets proposed by Nodal and other Ministries in consultation with MoSPI. The draft so mapped, however, does not include any programme for Goal-12 presumably because Goal 12 is an outcome effect of initiatives taken in other areas. However, it mentioned that related interventions like (1) National Policy on bio-fuels {2018}, (2) National Clean India Fund, (3) National Clean Energy Fund (NCEF) {2011}, (4) Renewable Energy: Renewable Energy Global Investment Promotion Meet and Expo (RE-INVEST), Feb-2015 and (5) Soil Health Card Scheme {2015} would address goal-12.

(b) National Review of SDG 12 for United Nations High Level Political Forum 2017

The outcomes of initiatives under SDG-12 would normally take a period of time to fructify as several other factors are also interlinked to reflect its final outcome. Be that as it may, the Voluntary National Review Report on Implementation of Sustainable Development Goals presented for United Nations High Level Political Forum 2017 is a good reference point for understanding the latest position on SDG-12 status in India. The report has not included SDG-12 as a separate item. However, it is noted that "given the interconnectedness of the SDGs, relevant strategies for enabling collaboration among different actors will be developed as part of the overall implementation process and that India will continue to pursue the implementation of the SDG agenda through close collaboration between the national and sub-national governments as well as active participation of all other relevant stakeholders.

(c) The NITI Aayog, Three-Year Action Agenda and SDG-12

The NITI Aayog has recently released the Three-Year Action Agenda covering years 2017-18 to 2019-20 which begins with the objective of eliminating poverty in all its dimensions such that every citizen will have access to a minimum standard of food, education, health, clothing, shelter, transportation and energy. The Three-Year Action Agenda does not include any separate chapter to dwell on SDG-12. However, the interventions on Economic Transformations in Major Sectors under Part II along with action agenda on other SDGs therein, will also go a long way in improving sustainable consumption and production patterns within a period of time.

(d) Economic Survey of India, 2017-18

The Government of India tabled the Economic Survey of India, 2017-18 in the Parliament in the Budget Session on 29th January,2018 to set the stage for the Government for the Annual Budget. The Survey contains an indepth analysis, serious research as well new policy ideas. The said Survey however, did not cover anything on SDG-12.

(e) Budget Initiatives for 2018-19

The Budget document embodies not only a financial statement on resources availability and its projected expenditure, it also expresses alongside overtly and covertly the policy statement of the Government of the day. The Budget Speech of the Finance Minister of India delivered on First February,2018 did not incorporate specifically with reference to any item relating to SDG- 12. It is a fact that budget document provides annual outlay for all connected programmes/schemes for the concerned financial year as it did for items falling under SDG-12 for 2018-19; however, the inclusion of any subject in the Budget Speech endows it due recognition and importance in the area of programme management. It also reflects priority focus of the government and the country. The absence any focus on improving sustainable consumption and production patterns in the budget speech of the Finance Minister has to that extent diminished the importance of SDG-12 in the perception of general public.

An observation

The sustainable Development Goal-12 stands on a very strong platform of moral, philosophical, economic and sustainable framework in ensuring waste-free balanced economic journey of a country. There are targets and monitoring indicators as well to ensure whether the country moves in the right path on its development trajectory. It was wished by the Sustainable Development Summit that the business sector and other non-State actors and individuals must contribute to changing unsustainable consumption and production patterns, including through the mobilization, from all sources, of financial and technical assistance to strengthen developing countries' scientific, technological and innovative capacities to move towards more sustainable patterns of consumption and production. It was also reiterated that in real terms Sustainable consumption and production is about promoting resource and energy efficiency, sustainable infrastructure, and providing access to basic services, green and decent jobs and a better quality of life for all. Its implementation helps to achieve overall development plans, reduce future economic, environmental and social costs, strengthen economic competitiveness and reduce poverty. The country is under obligation to take up the implementation of the Framework of Programmes on Sustainable Consumption and Production Patterns taking into account its development and capabilities. It is worth mentioning, however, that the monitoring indicator 12.1.1 require that the country has to map out its sustainable consumption and production (SCP) national action plan and that SCP needs to be mainstreamed as a priority or a target into national policies. Neither the NITI Aayog nor the nodal ministry has come up as yet with such an initiative till date.

Chapter - 23

Sustainable Development Goal 13

Take urgent action to combat climate change and its impacts

Climate change has been emerging as the single most threat to human civilisation. The growth story of bygone years at various locations on this earthly heaven, years of hard work in building up structural base of livelihood and the silent contribution of years of love in shaping a character of its civilisation are now vulnerable to the whims of nature-the climatic change vulnerability. The formidable impact of nature usually causes widespread and unprecedented effects on burden of the poorest and the most vulnerable in a disproportionate manner. Goal 13 calls for urgent action not only to combat climate change and its impacts, but also to build resilience in responding to climate-related hazards and natural disasters.

The fact-sheet available to the international community before the Sustainable Development Summit is the real story of the domain situation reflecting the kind of concern that the Sustainable Development Summit introspected and subsequently addressed to resolve the monostriety of climatic change as would be evident from below :

'The greenhouse gas emissions from human activities are driving climate change and continue to rise. They are now at their highest levels in history. Global emissions of carbon dioxide have increased by almost 50% since 1990. Moreover, the atmospheric concentrations of carbon dioxide, methane, and nitrous oxide have increased to levels unprecedented in at least the last 800,000 years. Carbon dioxide concentrations have increased by 40% since pre-industrial times, primarily from fossil fuel emissions and secondarily from net land use change emissions. The ocean has absorbed about 30% of the emitted anthropogenic carbon dioxide, causing ocean acidification. Further, each of the last three decades has been successively warmer at the Earth's surface than any preceding decade since 1850. In the Northern Hemisphere, 1983-2012 was likely the warmest 30-year period of the last 1,400 years. Additionally, from 1880 to 2012, average global temperature increased by 0.85°C. Without action, the world's average surface temperature is projected to rise over the 21st century and is likely to surpass 3 degrees Celsius this century – with some areas of the world, including in the tropics and subtropics, expected to warm even more. The poorest and most vulnerable people are being affected the most. Further, the rate of sea level rise since the mid-19th century has been larger than the mean rate during the previous two millennia. Over the period 1901 to 2010, global mean sea level rose by 0.19 [0.17 to 0.21] meters. Moreover, from 1901 to 2010, the global average sea level rose by 19 cm as oceans expanded due to warming and melted ice. The Arctic's sea ice extent has shrunk in every successive decade since 1979, with 1.07 million km2 of ice loss every decade." The fact sheet also mentioned that it is still possible, using an array of technological measures and changes in behaviour, to limit the increase in global mean temperature to two degrees Celsius above preindustrial levels. Additionally, there are multiple mitigation pathways to achieve the substantial emissions reductions over the next few decades necessary to limit, with a greater than 66% chance, the warming to 2°C – the goal set by governments. However, delaying additional mitigation to 2030 will substantially increase the technological, economic, social and institutional challenges associated with limiting the warming over the 21stcentury to below 2 °C relative to pre-industrial levels'.

Earlier, the Intergovernmental Panel on Climate Change has also observed on similar lines which are noted below:

- **From 1880 to 2012, average global temperature increased by 0.85°C**. To put this into perspective, for each 1 degree of temperature increase, grain yields decline by about 5 per cent. Maize, wheat and other major crops have experienced significant yield reductions at the global level of 40 megatonnes per year between 1981 and 2002 due to a warmer climate.
- **Oceans have warmed, the amounts of snow and ice have diminished and sea level has risen.** From 1901 to 2010, the global average sea level rose by 19 cm as oceans expanded due to warming and ice melted. The Arctic's sea ice extent has shrunk in every successive decade since 1979, with 1.07 million km^2 of ice loss every decade
- **Given current concentrations and on-going emissions of greenhouse gases, it is likely that by the end of this century, the increase in global temperature will exceed 1.5°C compared to 1850 to 1900 for all but one scenario**. The world's oceans will

warm and ice melt will continue. Average sea level rise is predicted as 24 – 30cm by 2065 and 40-63cm by 2100. Most aspects of climate change will persist for many centuries even if emissions are stopped

- Global emissions of carbon dioxide (CO2) have increased by almost 50 per cent since 1990
- Emissions grew more quickly between 2000 and 2010 than in each of the three previous decades
- It is still possible, using a wide array of technological measures and changes in behaviour, to limit the increase in global mean temperature to two degrees Celsius above pre-industrial levels

The UN Secretary-General, while addressing Progress of goal 13, in its Report, E/2016/75, on "Progress towards the Sustainable Development Goals" observed that "Climate change presents the single biggest threat to development, and its widespread, unprecedented impacts disproportionately burden the poorest and most vulnerable. Urgent action to combat climate change and minimize its disruptions is integral to the successful implementation of the Sustainable Development Goals. The global nature of climate change calls for broad international cooperation in building resilience and adaptive capacity to its adverse effects, developing sustainable low-carbon pathways to the future, and accelerating the reduction of global greenhouse gas emissions. On 22 April 2016, 175 Member States signed the Paris Agreement under the United Nations Framework Convention on Climate Change. The new agreement aims to reduce the pace of climate change and to accelerate and intensify the actions and investments needed for a sustainable low-carbon future.

Climate change often exacerbates disasters. Between 1990 and 2013, more than 1.6 million people died in internationally reported disasters, with annual deaths trending upwards. As a result, more countries are acting on the imperative to implement national and local disaster risk reduction strategies. In 2015, 83 countries had legislative and/or regulatory provisions in place for managing disaster risk. Parties to the United Nations Framework Convention on Climate Change are responsible for providing a range of national reports on their efforts to implement the agreement. As of 4 April 2016, 161 intended nationally determined contributions, from 189 of the 197 Parties to the Framework Convention (the European Commission submitted one joint intended determined contribution) had been recorded by the secretariat of the Framework Convention, providing insights into the efforts many countries are taking to integrate climate change measures into national policies, strategies and planning. Among those countries, 137 parties included an adaptation component in their intended nationally determined contributions. Some countries stressed that adaptation was their main climate change priority, with strong linkages to other aspects of national development, sustainability and security. In order to help countries move forward on climate action, a global stocktaking was established, in the context of the Paris Agreement, to assess collective progress every five years. The process will begin in 2018, with a facilitative dialogue to review the efforts of parties towards emissions reductions and to inform the preparation of final nationally determined contributions.

As parties scale up climate change action, enhanced cooperation, capacity-building and access to financial and technical support will be needed to help many countries realize their priorities, including those identified in intended nationally determined contributions and national adaptation plans. Developed countries have committed to mobilizing, by 2020, $100 billion a year in climate financing from a wide variety of sources to help address the needs of developing countries. By 2025, parties to the United Nations Framework Convention on Climate Change will set a new collective goal of at least $100 billion per year. The Green Climate Fund, a mechanism within the Framework Convention created to assist developing countries in adaptation and mitigation practices, is an important delivery vehicle for this financing. As of May 2016, the Green Climate Fund had mobilized $10.3 billion.

Climate change is already affecting the most vulnerable countries and populations, in particular the least developed countries and the small island developing States. The preparation of national adaptation programmes of action under the United Nations Framework Convention on Climate Change is helping the least developed countries address urgent and immediate needs, with support from the Least Developed Countries Fund and the Least Developed Countries Expert Group. In addition, the implementation of national adaptation programmes of action will help the least developed countries prepare and seek funding for comprehensive national adaptation plans, thereby reducing their risk of being left behind".

The study of Climate change and its various dimensions is also a frontier area of scientific research. As per analyses by NASA and the National Oceanic and Atmospheric Administration (NOAA), Earth's 2016 surface temperatures were the warmest since modern recordkeeping began in 1880.Globally-averaged temperatures in 2016 were 1.78 degrees Fahrenheit (0.99 degrees Celsius) warmer than the mid-20th century mean. The 2016 temperatures continue a long-term warming trend and makes 2016 the third year in a row to set a new record for global average surface temperatures. Incidentally, Most of the warming occurred in the past 35 years, a change driven largely by increased carbon dioxide and other human-made emissions into the atmosphere.

Before the Goal 13 and the associated targets are enumerated, it would be desirable and worthwhile to capture the visionary statement at para 31 and 32 of the Outcome document of the SD Summit which runs as follows:

"31. We acknowledge that the United Nations Framework Convention on Climate Change is the primary international, intergovernmental forum for negotiating the global response to climate change. We are determined to address decisively the threat posed by climate change and environmental degradation. The global nature of climate change calls for the widest possible international cooperation aimed at accelerating the reduction of global greenhouse gas emissions and addressing adaptation to the adverse impacts of climate change. We note with grave concern the significant gap between the aggregate effect of parties' mitigation pledges in terms of global annual emissions of greenhouse gases by 2020 and aggregate emission pathways consistent with having a likely chance of holding the increase in global average temperature below 2 °C or 1.5 °C above pre-industrial levels.

32. Looking ahead to the twenty-first session of the Conference of the Parties in Paris, we underscore the commitment of all States to work for an ambitious and universal climate agreement. We reaffirm that the protocol, another legal instrument or agreed outcome with legal force under the Convention applicable to all parties shall address in a balanced manner, inter alia, mitigation, adaptation, finance, technology development and transfer and capacity-building; and transparency of action and support."

The Goal 13 as finally emerged from the SDG Summit and its associated targets are as follows:

Goal 13. Take urgent action to combat climate change and its impacts*

13.1 Strengthen resilience and adaptive capacity to climate-related hazards and natural disasters in all countries

13.2 Integrate climate change measures into national policies, strategies and planning

13.3 Improve education, awareness-raising and human and institutional capacity on climate change mitigation, adaptation, impact reduction and early warning

13.a Implement the commitment undertaken by developed-country parties to the United Nations Framework Convention on Climate Change to a goal of mobilizing jointly $100 billion annually by 2020 from all sources to address the needs of developing countries in the context of meaningful mitigation actions and transparency on implementation and fully operationalize the Green Climate Fund through its capitalization as soon as possible

13.b Promote mechanisms for raising capacity for effective climate change-related planning and management in least developed countries and small island developing States, including focusing on women, youth and local and marginalized communities

* Acknowledging that the United Nations Framework Convention on Climate Change is the primary international, intergovernmental forum for negotiating the global response to climate change.

The goals and targets per se are important from the angle of programme vision and intended outcome; however from the perspective of monitoring the performance, indicators do play critical role. Since indicator-design is essentially an expert professional skill- job requiring to keep harmony with overall goals and targets of the Sustainable Development Summit as embodied in paragraph 75 of Transforming our World: The 2030 Agenda for Sustainable Development mentioned: "the Goals and targets will be followed-up and reviewed using a set of global indicators. These will be complemented by indicators at the regional and national levels which will be developed by member states, in addition to the outcomes of work undertaken for the development of the baselines for those targets where national and global baseline data does not yet exist".

Needless to mention that purpose of SDG indicators is twofold; first it acts as a management tool to help countries develop implementation and monitoring strategies for achieving the SDGs and to monitor progress and secondly, it works as a report card, to measure progress towards achieving a target and ensure the accountability of governments to their citizens.As a matter of fact, Agenda 21 of the SD Summit also called on countries and the international community to develop indicators of sustainable development. Such indicators were needed to increase focus on sustainable development and assist decision-makers at all levels to adopt sound national sustainable development policies.

Be that as it may, the Global Indicator Framework as designed by the UN Statistical Commission at its 47th Session in March 2016 and adopted thereafter by the Economic and Social Council and the General Assembly, are as follows:

Indicators for Goal 13

13.1.1 Number of deaths, missing persons and directly affected persons attributed to disasters per 100,000 population

13.1.2 Number of countries that adopt and implement national disaster risk reduction strategies in line with the Sendai Framework for Disaster Risk Reduction 2015-2030

13.1.3 Proportion of local governments that adopt and implement local disaster risk reduction strategies in line with national disaster risk reduction strategies

13.2.1 Number of countries that have communicated the establishment or operationalization of an integrated policy/strategy/plan which increases their ability to adapt to the adverse impacts of climate change, and foster climate resilience and low greenhouse gas emissions development in a manner that does not threaten food production (including a national adaptation plan, nationally determined contribution, national communication, biennial update report or other)

13.3.1 Number of countries that have integrated mitigation, adaptation, impact reduction and early warning into primary, secondary and tertiary curricula

13.3.2 Number of countries that have communicated the strengthening of institutional, systemic and individual capacity-building to implement adaptation,mitigation and technology transfer, and development actions

13.a.1 Mobilized amount of United States dollars per year between 2020 and 2025 accountable towards the $100 billion commitment

13.b.1 Number of least developed countries and small island developing States that are receiving specialized support, and amount of support, including finance, technology and capacity-building, for mechanisms for raising capacities for effective climate change-related planning and management, including focusing on women, youth and local and marginalized communities

The International conference on climatic change

It has been mentioned earlier in the Sustainable Development Summit Declaration at paragraph 31 and 32 that the Goal-13 is interlinked with International conference on climatic change at Paris. Before the status and actionable points on climatic change for India is taken up, it would be appropriate to touch upon, in brief, the Paris Conference on climate change. The Paris UN Climate Conference, also known as COP 21,represents an historic opportunity to put the world on course to meet the climate change challenge. The world has been in search of a new model of growth that is safe, durable and beneficial to all. The COP21 seeks to deliver a clear pathway with short and long term milestones, and a system to help measure and increase progress over time until the agreed goals are met. The French President Francois Hollande summed up the COP21 as: "In Paris, there have been many revolutions over the centuries. Today it is the most beautiful and the most peaceful revolution that has just been accomplished – a revolution for climate change."

The Paris Agreement in brief, reached the following decisions:

- Reaffirm the goal of limiting global temperature increase well below

2 degrees Celsius, while urging efforts to limit the increase to 1.5 degrees;

- Establish binding commitments by all parties to make "nationally determined contributions" (NDCs), and to pursue domestic measures aimed at achieving them;
- Commit all countries to report regularly on their emissions and "progress made in implementing and achieving" their NDCs, and to undergo international review;
- Commit all countries to submit new NDCs every five years, with the clear expectation that they will "represent a progression" beyond previous ones;
- Reaffirm the binding obligations of developed countries under the UNFCCC to support the efforts of developing countries, while for the first time encouraging voluntary contributions by developing countries too;
- Extend the current goal of mobilizing $100 billion a year in support by 2020 through 2025, with a new, higher goal to be set for the period after 2025;
- Extend a mechanism to address "loss and damage" resulting from climate change, which explicitly will not "involve or provide a basis for any liability or compensation;"
- Require parties engaging in international emissions trading to avoid "double counting;" and
- Call for a new mechanism, similar to the Clean Development Mechanism under the Kyoto Protocol, enabling emission reductions in one country to be counted toward another country's NDC.

The climate change accord agreed by nearly 200 countries in December 2015, came into force on 4 November 2016. The agreement commits world leaders to keeping global warming below 2C, seen as the threshold for safety by scientists, and pursuing a tougher target of 1.5C. The carbon emission curbs put forward by countries under Paris are not legally-binding but the framework of the accord, which includes a mechanism for periodically cranking those pledges up, is binding. The agreement also has a long-term goal for net zero emissions which would effectively phase out fossil fuels

India and the Paris Climatic Conference

In this section, it would be endeavoured to limit the narration under two broad items:

(a) the status of Climate scenario of India as presented by the Government at the said conference.

(b) The fall-outs of the Paris Conference on India

(a) the status of Climate scenario of India as presented by the Government at the said conference.

The Union Environment Ministry submitted its Intended Nationally Determined Contributions (INDCs) to the UN Framework Convention on Climate Change (UNFCCC), committing to cut the emissions intensity of GDP by 33-35 per cent by 2030 from 2005 levels. It has also pledged to increase the share of non-fossil fuels-based electricity to 40 per cent by 2030. It has agreed to enhance its forest cover which will absorb 2.5 to 3 billion tonnes of carbon dioxide ($CO_{2,}$ the main gas responsible for global warming) by 2030.India has accepted the huge impact that climate change is exerting and will exert on different sectors of its economy and has agreed to enhance investments to adapt in vulnerable sectors like agriculture, water resources, coastal regions, health and disaster management. India has also reiterated its need for international finance and technology support to meet its climate goals. In this regard, it has said it would require at least US $ 2.5 trillion (at 2014-15 prices) to meet its climate change actions between now and 2030.

The Union Minister for Environment, Forests and Climate Change referred India's INDCs, as "balanced and comprehensive" and that for a developing nation, India's goals for tackling climate change were far more ambitious when compared to that of other developed countries.

(b) The fall-outs of the Paris Conference on India:

The Paris accord sets the architecture for carbon emission reduction after 2020. It safeguards the principle of common but differentiated responsibility that has remained a non-negotiable aspect of India's climate position. This principle squarely puts the major responsibility on developed nations to drastically cut their carbon emissions and provide the necessary finance, technology and capacity building for developing economies to mitigate and adapt to climate change.

The agreement on pursuing long-term efforts to limit global average temperature rise to 1.5 degrees Celsius above pre-industrial levels invites the Intergovernmental Panel of Climate Change (IPCC) to produce a special report by 2018 on the potential impacts of crossing 1.5 degrees and drawing emission pathways to avoid these impacts. India is likely to be badly hit as it would impose severe restrictions on the lives of millions along its coastline and those dependent directly on agricultural yields and thus affecting in the process SDG-1 and SDG-2 as well

On the issue of carbon mitigation targets, India's approach has been the principle of equity and fair distribution of the remaining carbon space. However, the Paris accord requires voluntary commitments or Intended Nationally Determined Commitments (INDCs) from both developed and developing countries to enhance their pre-2020 emission cuts The Countries are also expected to submit revised INDCs by 2020, and every five years thereafter. In other words, the carbon reductions from the developed countries post 2020 still remain voluntary and the scope for a fair carbon budgeting is a distant dream. This will also impact India hard, requiring to mobilise more financial resources and enhanced capacity building initiatives in the renewable energy sector.

At the Paris Conference, Climate finance failed to see any overwhelming agreement. Developed nations agreed to raise $100 billion annually by 2020 for climate finance, with a commitment. To enhanced financing thereafter. India, however, took the position that $ 2.5 trillion would be needed in climate finance for achieving its INDC by 2030. The global commitment of $100 billion would be too little to make any positive impact. The variety of public and private channels has to come in a big way for meeting the gap for climate finance.

The then Minister in Charge of Environment, Government of India commented that India signed the final agreement in a spirit of compromise. Its significance lies in the fact that India accounts for over 4% of global emissions and is crucial for crossing the threshold mark of 55%. United States and China which together account for 40% of global carbon emissions have already ratified the agreement. Once the 55% barrier is crossed, the climate regime will become legally binding on all signatories after a period of 30 days.

It is a fact that India tried to balance its carbon emissions with its economic growth objectives by not setting an outright pollution reduction goal. However, being a part of the global climate change regime, India would now have obligations to reduce its carbon footprint by 33-35% from its 2005 levels. This has to be achieved by 2030.

Another fall-out is in the form of the reduction of emission intensity targets {i.e the volume of emissions per unit of gross domestic product (GDP)}. India will have to diversify its power generation sources and shift them significantly towards renewable energy sources to reduce volumes of emissions per unit of GDP. In numbers, by 2025, India will need a 175 gigawatt-power production capacity from non-fossil fuel sources.

Under the treaty India would also require to increase its forest cover by five million hectares along with an improvement in the quality of green cover of an equal measure to absorb massive carbon emissions from the atmosphere.

The Paris accord isn't legally binding on two key aspects. There is no obligation on developed nations to enhance mitigation targets or increase climate finance. The legally-binding nature of the agreement is on developed nations to report progress on the climate finance being delivered to developing countries on a biennial basis, and mitigation targets with a five-year review mechanism starting in 2018.

Climate change initiatives in India

It is with this background that the roadmap for Sustainable development of Goal 13(Take urgent action to combat climate change and its impacts) need to be examined with reference to the basic approach and goal-specific initiatives undertaken in India. As mentioned earlier, NITI Aayog has been empowered to oversee the implementation of SDGs by the ministries of the Central Government and coordinate with States for the achievement of developmental targets as enshrined in the SDGs. The NITI Aayog tasked itself to prepare a initial draft based on mapping of the goals and targets proposed by Nodal and other Ministries in consultation with MoSPI. The schemes so mapped for Goal-13 include National Action Plan on climate Change, National Mission for a Green India, National Solar Mission, National Mission for Enhanced Energy Efficiency, National Mission for Sustainable Habitat, National Water Mission, National Mission for Sustaining the Himalayan Ecosystem, National Mission for Sustainable Agriculture and National Mission on Strategic Knowledge for Climate Change.

For understanding the initiatives and outcome under SDG-13, it is incumbent to understand that Climate is the "average weather" in a place and includes patterns of temperature, precipitation (rain or snow), humidity, wind and seasons and that climate patterns play a fundamental role in shaping natural ecosystems, and the human economies and cultures that depend on them. Indeed, while Some short-term climate variation is normal, longer-term trends indicate a changing climate. In other words, the outcomes of initiatives under SDG-13 are bound to be long term and linked with several issues that do not bring immediate result overnight. For the same reason, the Voluntary National Review Report on Implementation of Sustainable Development Goals presented for United Nations High Level Political Forum 2017 did not include any initiatives under SDG-13. However, it is beyond understanding why the Thee Year Action Plan Agenda,prepared by NITI Aayog did not project the issue of climatic change directly as a focused item; instead it intends to cover it indirectly when it mentions " the need to address high level of air pollution in the cities black carbon pollution indoor from the use of biomass fuels in cooking, massive volume of solid wastes in urban areas and deforestation. Also that we must strengthen and streamline regulatory structures governing sustainability of environment. While on the other hand we must remove hurdles that adversely impact growth without protecting our environment."

Monitoring Indicators, like those of other SDGs, do have role to signal the kind of schemes needed for obtaining better monitoring output. Monitoring under SDGs is subject/ target specific. It would, however, be worthwhile to look at the monitoring indicators before commenting on inclusion of dedicated schemes in this subject area. The monitoring indicators under SDG-13 mentions.

Number of deaths, missing persons and directly affected persons attributed to disasters per 100,000 Population, Number of countries that adopt and implement national disaster risk reduction strategies in line with the Sendai Framework for Disaster Risk Reduction 2015-2030,, Proportion of local governments that adopt and implement local disaster risk reduction strategies in line with national disaster risk reduction strategies, Number of countries that have communicated the establishment or operationalization of an integrated policy/strategy/plan which increases their ability to adapt to the adverse impacts of climate change, and foster climate resilience and low greenhousc gas emissions development in a manner that does not threaten food production (including a national adaptation plan, nationally determined contribution, national communication, biennial update report or other), Number of countries that have integrated mitigation, adaptation, impact reduction and early warning into primary, secondary and tertiary curricula, Number of countries that have communicated the strengthening of institutional, systemic and individual capacity-building to implement adaptation, mitigation and technology transfer, and development actions, Mobilized amount of United States dollars per year between 2020 and 2025 accountable towards the $100 billion commitment, Number of least developed countries and small island developing States that are receiving specialized support, and amount of support, including finance, technology and capacity-building, for mechanisms for raising capacities for effective climate change-related planning and management, including focusing on women, youth and local and marginalized communities. The monitoring indicators, to all intents and purposes, relate to policy framework and components connected therewith. It is also linked with raw data on consequences of climatic change in the country and fund mobilisation efforts on mitigation actions, including transparency on implementation and operationalization of the Green Climate Fund. There is a good scope for India to include such monitoring indicators in policy and implementation of programme design.

A new report prepared jointly by the New Climate Institute, Netherlands Environmental Assessment Agency, and the International Institute for Applied Systems Analysis and released at the UN Climate Change Conference in Bonn, Germany says that ' India is among the small group of countries that are on track to achieve their self-declared climate targets under the Paris Agreement with their current policies in place. The report says that only nine of the 25 top emitting countries it surveyed were in line with achieving their targets mentioned in their respective 'nationally-determined contributions (NDCs)' that every country had submitted in the run-up to the 2015 climate change conference in Paris.

In its NDC, India had promised to reduce its emissions intensity — greenhouse gas emissions per unit of GDP — by 33 to 35 per cent below 2005 levels by the year 2030. It had also promised to ensure that at least 40 per cent of its energy in 2030 would be generated from non-fossil fuel sources, like solar, wind or bio-fuels. In addition, it had said it would rapidly increase its forest cover so that an additional carbon sink of 2.5 to 3 billion tonne of carbon dioxide equivalent is created by the year 2030.

The new report also says India was "likely to overachieve" its target for 2020 and on course to achieve the promises made in the NDC for the year 2030. It also says that the projections made in India's draft National Electricity Plan of 2016 — which talks about stabilisation of coal-powered electricity to 250 GW over the next decade and an expansion of renewable energy to 275 GW by 2026/27 — would, if implemented, were "expected to have substantial impact on (its) emissions".

Economic Survey of India, 2017-18

The Government of India tabled the Economic Survey of India, 2017-18 in the Parliament in the Budget Session on 29th January,2018 to set the stage for the Government for the Annual Budget. The Survey contains an indepth analysis, serious research as well new policy ideas. The said Survey sums up the latest initiatives on Climatic Change. India has launched various policies and set up institutional mechanisms to advance its climate actions. The survey notes India's commitment to environment and climate change that is reflected in the number of actions in supporting sustainable development goals while retaining reliance on cleaner energy, including cleaner, greener coal. It states that India has strengthened its response to the threat of climate change in accordance with the principles of equity and Common But Differentiated Responsibilities and in the light of national circumstances with the Paris Pledge to reduce the emission intensity of GDP by 33-35 percent over 2005 levels by the year 2030.The Government of India is implementing the National Action Plan on Climate Change (NAPCC), which includes eight national missions covering solar, energy efficiency, agriculture, water, sustainable habitat, forestry, Himalayan eco system and knowledge, apart from various other initiatives. These actions reflect its commitment to address climate change. Further, on Current Multilateral Negotiations on Climate Change, the Economic Survey went on to state that currently, the multilateral climate change negotiations are primarily focused on framing the rules and regulations for implementing the Paris Agreement. At the 23rd session of the Conference of Parties to the UNFCCC (COP 23), the Parties advanced the work programme under Paris Agreement. Key takeaways for India from COP 23 have been that the agenda of pre-2020 climate change commitments and implementation has found a significant place in COP 23 outcome in the form of a decision with steps for future action on pre-2020 action and ambition. This decision emphasizes that enhanced pre-2020 actions can lay a solid foundation for enhanced post-2020 ambitions. India has been able to preserve differentiation in informal notes/texts on various elements of Paris Agreement work programme including nationally determined contributions, adaptation communication, transparency framework, compliance, technology framework, finance and capacity building prepared for further work on rules, modalities and guidelines for Paris Agreement.

On the issue of sustainable development, the Survey says that India's urban population is projected to grow to about 600 million by 2031. It suggests that Urban Local Bodies generate resources through financial instruments such as municipal bonds, PPPs and credit risk guarantees. The Survey says that access to sustainable, modern and affordable energy is the basis of achieving Sustainable Development Goals. Stating that as on 30th November 2017, the share of renewable energy sources was 18 percent in the total installed capacity of electricity in the country and that the increasing share of renewables has trebled in the last 10 years. Outlining India's commitment to address Climate Change, the Survey mentions establishment of 8 Global Technology Watch Groups, extending Climate Change Action Programme launched in 2014 for the period 2017-18 to 2019-20 with a budget outlay of Rs. 132.4 crore and continuation of National Adaption Fund on Climate Change till 31st March 2020 with financial implication of Rs. 364 crore.

Budget Inititives, 2018-19

The Budget document embodies not only a financial statement on resources availability and its projected expenditure, it also expresses alongside overtly and covertly the policy statement of the Government of the day. The Budget Speech of the Finance Minister of India delivered on First February,2018, though addressed broader issues connected with SDGs, did not specifically mention about climatic change related intervention under SDG-13. It is a fact that budget document provides annual outlay for all connected programmes/ schemes for the concerned financial year as it did for 2018-19; however being a part of budget speech surely highlights the priority of the government and also for the country. The absence of any focus on climatic change in the budget speech of the Finance Minister has to that extent diminished the. importance of climatic change to the general public.

Chapter - 24

Sustainable Development Goal 14

Conserve and sustainably use the oceans, seas and marine resources for sustainable development

Elizabeth Thompson, Co-Executive Coordinator for the Rio+20 Conference, at Oceans Day at Rio+20, 16 June 2012 made a telling comment:

> *Oceans are the point at which planet, people, and prosperity come together. And that is what sustainable development is about. It is about all of us as shareholders of Earth, incorporated, acknowledging and acting on our responsibility to the planet, to the people, and to its bloodstream, the oceans.*

Oceans, seas and other marine resources are essential to human well-being and social and economic development worldwide. Their conservation and sustainable use are central to achieving the 2030 Agenda, especially for small island developing States. Marine resources are particularly important for people living in coastal communities, who represented 37 per cent of the world population in 2010. Oceans provide livelihoods, subsistence and benefits from fisheries, tourism and other sectors. They also help regulate the global ecosystem by absorbing heat and carbon dioxide (CO2) from the atmosphere. However, oceans and coastal areas are extremely vulnerable to environmental degradation, overfishing, climate change and pollution.

In the parlance of sustainable development literature, three Pillars approach are often mentioned as necessary requirements to put in place Sustainable Development, namely, economic, social and environmental. When oceans development are taken up, it addresses all the three parameters of sustainable development simultaneously as the UN Chronicle has put it wonderfully that 'the oceans are the most prominent feature on the planet, covering nearly three quarters of the Earth, and are essential for planetary survival. Just as a person cannot live without a healthy heart and lungs, the Earth cannot survive without healthy oceans and seas. They serve as the Earth's respiratory system, producing oxygen for life and absorbing carbon dioxide and waste. The oceans provide storage and absorb 30 per cent of the world's carbon dioxide, while marine phytoplankton generates 50 per cent of the oxygen needed for survival. The oceans regulate the climate and temperature, making the planet hospitable to diverse forms of life.

The oceans and seas are essential for national and global economic well-being. The global ocean economic activity is estimated to be between US $3 trillion to US $6 trillion, contributing to the world economy in many important ways, such as:

- 90 per cent of global trade moves by marine transport.
- Submarine cables carry 95 per cent of all global telecommunications.
- Fisheries and aquaculture supply 4.3 billion people with more than 15 per cent of annual consumption of animal protein.
- Over 30 per cent of global oil and gas produced is extracted offshore.
- Coastal tourism is the largest market segment in the world economy, comprising 5 per cent of the global gross domestic product (GDP) and 6 to 7 per cent of global employment.
- Expanding knowledge on marine biodiversity has provided breakthrough advances in sectors such as pharmaceuticals, food production, and aquaculture.
- 13 of the world's 20 megacities are coastal.
- Tides, waves, currents, and offshore wind are emerging sources of energy that have significant potential to contribute to low-carbon energy in many coastal countries.

The oceans and seas are essential for social well-being. Over 40 per cent, or 3.1 billion, of the world's population lives within 100 kilometres of the ocean or sea in about 150 coastal and island nations. Regardless of whether a country is landlocked, or has a coastline, all nations are directly connected to the oceans and seas through rivers, lakes and streams. Nations have placed significant importance on the benefits that are provided by the oceans and seas, comprising over 60 per cent of the global gross national product (GNP). In particular, coastal economic activity is the lifeblood of coastal and island nations'.

The world's oceans – their temperature, chemistry, currents and life – drive global systems that make the Earth habitable for humankind. Our rainwater, drinking water, weather, climate, coastlines, much of our food, and even the oxygen in the air we breathe, are all ultimately provided and regulated by the sea. Throughout history, oceans and seas have been vital conduits for trade and transportation. Careful management of this essential global resource is a key feature of a sustainable future.

The Fact sheet available to the Sustainable Development Summit in September,2015 noted that Oceans cover three-quarters of the Earth's surface, contain 97% of the Earth's water, and represent 99% of the living space on the planet by volume. Globally, the market value of marine and coastal resources and industries is estimated at $3 trillion per year or about 5% of global GDP. Globally, the levels of capture fisheries are near the ocean's productive capacity, with catches on the order of 80 million tons. Oceans contain nearly 200,000 identified species, but actual numbers may lie in the millions. Oceans absorb about 30% of carbon dioxide produced by humans, buffering the impacts of global warming. Oceans serve as the world's largest source of protein, with more than 3 billion people depending on the oceans as their primary source. Marine fisheries directly or indirectly employ over 200 million people. Subsidies for fishing are contributing to the rapid depletion of many fish species and are preventing efforts to save and restore global fisheries and related jobs, causing ocean fisheries to generate US$ 50 billion less per year. As much as 40% of world oceans are heavily affected by human activities, including pollution, depleted fisheries, and loss of coastal habitats.

The UN Secretary-General in its Report of "Progress towards the Sustainable Development Goals", E/2016/75 on Goal-14 observed as follows:

- Oceans, along with coastal and marine resources, play an essential role in human well-being and social and economic development worldwide. They are particularly crucial for people living in coastal communities, who represented 37 per cent of the global population in 2010. Oceans provide livelihoods and tourism benefits, as well as subsistence and income. They also help regulate the global ecosystem by absorbing heat and carbon dioxide from the atmosphere and protecting coastal areas from flooding and erosion. In fact, coastal and marine resources contribute an estimated $28 trillion to the global economy each year through ecosystem services. However, those resources are extremely vulnerable to environmental degradation, overfishing, climate change and pollution. The sustainable use and preservation of marine and coastal ecosystems and their biological diversity is essential to achieving the 2030 Agenda, in particular for small island developing States.
- Pollution of both land and seas is a threat in many coastal regions. In addition, since river basins, marine ecosystems and the atmosphere are all part of hydrological systems, the effects of such pollution are often felt far from their source. In many coastal communities, pollution and eutrophication, which is the presence of excessive

nutrients in water, frequently owing to runoff from the land, causing dense plant growth and the death of animal life, are driving detrimental changes. The five large marine ecosystems most at risk from coastal eutrophication, according to a global comparative assessment undertaken in 2016 as part of the Transboundary Water Assessment Programme, are the Bay of Bengal, the East China Sea, the Gulf of Mexico, the North Brazil Shelf and the South China Sea.

- Since the beginning of the industrial revolution, the ocean has absorbed about one third of the carbon dioxide released by human activities, thereby mitigating the full impact of climate change. However, this comes at a steep ecological price, as dissolved carbon dioxide in seawater lowers the pH level of oceans, thereby increasing acidity and changing the biogeochemical carbonate balance. Concerns about ocean acidification, first expressed in the early 1980s, have now been confirmed, and the extent of its impact on marine ecosystems is being investigated.
- Fisheries contribute significantly to global food security, livelihoods and the economy. However, if not sustainably managed, fishing can damage fish habitats. Ultimately, overfishing impairs the functioning of ecosystems and reduces biodiversity, with negative repercussions for sustainable social and economic development. In order to achieve a healthy balance, fish stocks must be maintained within biologically sustainable limits, at or above the abundance level that can produce maximum sustainable yields. Based on an analysis of assessed stocks, the percentage of world marine fish stocks within biologically sustainable levels declined from 90 per cent in 1974 to 69 per cent in 2013. Fortunately, the downward trend has slowed and appears to have stabilized since 2008.
- Biodiverse marine sites require safeguarding to ensure sustainable long-term use of their precious natural resources. Globally, in 2014, 8.4 per cent of the marine environment under national jurisdiction (up to 200 nautical miles from shore) and 0.25 per cent of the marine environment beyond national jurisdiction were under protection. From 2000 to 2016, the share of marine sites around the world that are designated as key biodiversity areas and are completely covered by protected areas increased from 15 per cent to 19 per cent.

An oceans goal for planetary survival and for global and national economic and social well-being as adopted by the Sustainable Development Summit onGoal-14, is as follows:

Goal 14. Conserve and sustainably use the oceans, seas and marine resources for sustainable development

14.1 By 2025, prevent and significantly reduce marine pollution of all kinds, in particular from land-based activities, including marine debris and nutrient pollution

14.2 By 2020, sustainably manage and protect marine and coastal ecosystems to avoid significant adverse impacts, including by strengthening their resilience, and take action for their restoration in order to achieve healthy and productive oceans

14.3 Minimize and address the impacts of ocean acidification, including through enhanced scientific cooperation at all levels

14.4 By 2020, effectively regulate harvesting and end overfishing, illegal, unreported and unregulated fishing and destructive fishing practices and implement science-based management plans, in order to restore fish stocks in the shortest time feasible, at least to levels that can produce maximum sustainable yield as determined by their biological characteristics

14.5 By 2020, conserve at least 10 per cent of coastal and marine areas, consistent with national and international law and based on the best available scientific information

14.6 By 2020, prohibit certain forms of fisheries subsidies which contribute to overcapacity and overfishing, eliminate subsidies that contribute to illegal, unreported and unregulated fishing and refrain from introducing new such subsidies, recognizing that appropriate and effective special and differential treatment for developing and least developed countries should be an integral part of the World Trade Organization fisheries subsidies negotiation

14.7 By 2030, increase the economic benefits to Small Island developing States and least developed countries from the sustainable use of marine resources, including through sustainable management of fisheries, aquaculture and tourism

14.a Increase scientific knowledge, develop research capacity and transfer marine technology, taking into account the Intergovernmental Oceanographic Commission Criteria and Guidelines on the Transfer of Marine Technology, in order to improve ocean health and to enhance the contribution of marine biodiversity to the development of developing countries, in particular small island developing States and least developed countries

14.b Provide access for small-scale artisanal fishers to marine resources and markets

14.c Enhance the conservation and sustainable use of oceans and their resources by implementing international law as reflected in UNCLOS, which provides the legal framework for the conservation and sustainable use of oceans and their resources, as recalled in paragraph 158 of The Future We Want

The goals and targets per se are important from the angle of programme vision and intended outcome; however from the perspective of monitoring the performance, indicators do play critical role. Since indicator-design is essentially an expert professional skill- job requiring to keep harmony with overall goals and targets of the Sustainable Development Summit as embodied in paragraph 75 of Transforming our World: The 2030 Agenda for Sustainable Development mentioned: "the Goals and targets will be followed-up and reviewed using a set of global indicators. These will be complemented by indicators at the regional and national levels which will be developed by member states, in addition to the outcomes of work undertaken for the development of the baselines for those targets where national and global baseline data does not yet exist".

Needless to mention that purpose of SDG indicators is twofold; first it acts as a management tool to help countries develop implementation and monitoring strategies for achieving the SDGs and to monitor progress and secondly, it works as a report card, to measure progress towards achieving a target and ensure the accountability of governments to their citizens. As a matter of fact, Agenda 21 of the SD Summit also called on countries and the international community to develop indicators of sustainable development. Such indicators were needed to increase focus on sustainable development and assist decision-makers at all levels to adopt sound national sustainable development policies.

Be that as it may, the Global Indicator Framework as designed by the UN Statistical Commission at its 47th Session in March 2016 and adopted thereafter by the Economic and Social Council and the General Assembly, are as follows:

Indicators of SDG-14

14.1.1 Index of coastal eutrophication and floating plastic debris density

14.2.1 Proportion of national exclusive economic zones managed using ecosystem-based approaches

14.3.1 Average marine acidity (pH) measured at agreed suite of representative sampling stations

14.4.1 Proportion of fish stocks within biologically sustainable levels

14.5.1 Coverage of protected areas in relation to marine areas

14.6.1 Progress by countries in the degree of implementation of international instruments aiming tocombat illegal, unreported and unregulated fishing

14.7.1 Sustainable fisheries as a proportion of GDP in small island developing States, least developedcountries and all countries

14.a.1 Proportion of total research budget allocated to research in the field of marine technology

14.b.1 Progress by countries in the degree of application of a legal/regulatory/policy/institutional framework which recognizes and protects access rights for small-scale fisheries

14.c.1 Number of countries making progress in ratifying, accepting and implementing through legal,policy and institutional frameworks, ocean-related instruments that implement international law, asreflected in the United Nation Convention on the Law of the Sea, for the conservation and sustainable use ofthe oceans and their resources

In fine, it would be worthwhile to note that several other SDGs have strong bearing on achieving SDG -14 on oceans and seas such as SDG- 1 (on poverty), SDG -2 (on food security), SDG- 6 (on water and sanitation), SDG -7 (on energy), SDG -8 (on economic growth), SDG- 9 (on infrastructure), SDG- 10 (on reduction of inequality), SDG -11 (on cities and human settlements), SDG -12 (on sustainable consumption and production), SDG -13 (on climate change), SDG -15 (on biodiversity), and SDG- 17 (on means of implementation and partnerships). This fact points to very basis of sustainable development goals that "these goals constitute an integrated, indivisible set of global priorities for sustainable development...The goals and targets integrate economic, social, and environmental aspects and recognize their interlinkages in achieving sustainable development in all of its dimensions".

SDG-14 and the initiatives in India

(a) The NITI Aayog and Mapping of Initiatives on SDG-14

It is with this background that the roadmap for Sustainable development of SDG-14 Conserve and sustainably use the oceans, seas and marine resources for sustainable development need to be examined with reference to basic approach and goal-specific initiatives undertaken in India. As mentioned earlier that the NITI Aayog has been tasked to oversee the implementation of SDGs by the ministries of the Central Government and coordinate with States for the achievement of developmental targets as enshrined in the SDGs. The NITI Aayog took upon itself to prepare a initial draft based on mapping of the goals and targets proposed by Nodal and other Ministries in consultation with MoSPI. The schemes so mapped for Goal-14 include 51) Conservation of Natural Resources and Eco-Systems{PIB 1.8.2016}. The NITI Aayog also took into consideration1)National Plan for Conservation of Aquatic Eco –System(2013) 2) Sagarmala Project (Blue Revolution){2015}.

(b) National Review of SDG- 14 for United Nations High Level Political Forum 2017

The outcomes of initiatives under SDG-14 are time taking linked with several issues that do not bring immediate result overnight. It will take time for resolution of interlinked issues to reflect its final outcome. Be that as it may, the Voluntary National Review Report on Implementation of Sustainable Development Goals presented for United Nations High Level Political Forum 2017 is a good reference point for understanding the position on SDG-14 status in India. The report says that a clear agenda has been formulated for promoting the 'Blue Revolution'. For tracking the levels of marine pollution along the coastline, the country has developed the Coastal Ocean Monitoring and Prediction System. Additionally, an oil spill management system has been put in place for responding to emergencies arising out of oil spills. Further, the Integrated National Fisheries Action Plan, 2016 is being implemented to promote the livelihoods of fishing communities as well as the ecological integrity of the marine environment. Giving new impetus to port-led development, the Sagarmala programme is improving port connectivity, port-linked industrialization and coastal community development.

The said Report further elaborated that India has taken various steps to protect and enhance the coastal and marine ecosystem. The first Maritime Summit was organized in the country in April 2016. More than 4,500 delegates from across 40 countries participated in the Summit. Further, on Mangroves and Coral Reefs, the Report has noted that India has a long history of mangrove forest management. The Sundarbans mangroves, located in the Bay of Bengal, were the first in the world to be put under scientific management. Government of India supports research and development activities with an emphasis on mangrove biodiversity. There has been a net increase of 112 square km in the mangrove cover of the country as compared to the previous assessment. In fact, more than 15,000 ha. of mangroves has been planted in the state of Gujarat alone through active participation of local communities under the Integrated Coastal Zone Management project. Further, India is a part of the regional initiative 'Mangroves for the Future', being coordinated by the United Nations Development Programme and the International Union for Conservation of Nature. Four major coral reefs have also been identified in the country for intensive conservation and management. India has 25 Marine Protected Areas in the peninsular region and 106 in islands, collectively covering approximately 10,000 square km of the country's geographical areas.

As to ensuring Sustainability of Fisheries, the Report says that India has the highest population of fishing communities globally. These communities are spread over 3,600 fishing villages. More than 14.50 million people depend on fisheries for their livelihood. In order to ensure sustainable development of the sector, a number of measures have been taken by the government, with an emphasis on livelihood creation as well as resource conservation. Some of the measures include establishment of a Potential Fishing Zone Advisory programme, modernization and upgradation of fishing centres as well as banning of mechanized fishing in certain areas.

The Prime Minister of India has also emphasized the need for a "Blue Revolution". In alignment with his vision, a central plan, the Integrated Development and Management of Fisheries, has been formulated. A detailed Integrated National Fisheries Action Plan, 2016 has also been formulated. The plan envisages connecting 15 million beneficiaries for livelihood opportunities through various interventions. Further, the government has emphasized maintenance of the ecological integrity of the marine environment, in order to ensure that there are no adverse effects on endangered marine species.

On Protection of Coastal Ecosystems, various national and sub-national legislations are in place for the management and protection of the coastal and marine environment. India has also ratified numerous international conventions related to the use of oceans and their resources, including the United Nations Convention on the Law of the Sea. An online mechanism for predicting the movement of oil spills, the Online Oil Spill Advisory System, was launched in 2015. In addition, the revised National Oil Spill Disaster Contingency Plan, 2015 reflects the important national regulations as well as the current international norms. Further, levels of marine pollution are being monitored by the government at various locations along the country's coastline through the Coastal Ocean Monitoring and Prediction System. India is also setting up a Marine Observation System along the Coast to gain a better understanding of coastal processes and monitor water quality.

Additionally, on Holistic Development of Islands and Coastal Areas, the Prime Minister of India launched a flagship programme, Sagarmala in 2016 for promoting port connectivity, development and industrialization, in a phased manner during 2015 to 2025. Holistic and sustainable development of coastal communities, especially the population engaged in fishing, is one of the key pillars of the programme. Coastal tourism is also being promoted under the programme for enabling access to better livelihood opportunities.

(c) The NITI Aayog, Three-Year Action Agenda and SDG-14

NITI Aayog has recently released the Three-Year Action Agenda covering years 2017-18 to 2019-20 which begins with the objective of eliminating poverty in all its dimensions such that every citizen will have access to a minimum standard of food, education, health, clothing, shelter, transportation and energy. The Three-Year Action Agenda does not include any separate chapter to dwell on SDG-14

(d) Economic Survey of India, 2017-18

The Government of India tabled the Economic Survey of India, 2017-18 in the Parliament in the Budget Session on 29th January,2018 to set the stage for the Government for the Annual Budget. The Survey contains an indepth analysis, serious research as well new policy ideas. The said Survey sums up the latest approach on sustainability of which goal-14 is also an important component.The Economic Survey notes that India's commitment to environment and climate change is reflected in the number of actions in supporting sustainable development goals while retaining reliance on cleaner energy, including cleaner, greener coal. It states that India has strengthened its response to the threat of climate change in accordance with the principles of equity and Common But Differentiated Responsibilities and in the light of national circumstances with the Paris Pledge to reduce the emission intensity of GDP by 33-35 percent over 2005 levels by the year 2030.

Outlining India's commitment to address Climate Change, the Survey mentions establishment of 8 Global Technology Watch Groups, extending Climate Change Action Programme launched in 2014 for the period 2017-18 to 2019-20 with a budget outlay of Rs. 132.4 crore and continuation of National Adaption Fund on Climate Change till 31st March 2020 with financial implication of Rs. 364 crore.

(e) Budget Inititives, 2018-19

The Budget document embodies not only a financial statement on resources availability and its projected expenditure, it also expresses alongside overtly and covertly the policy statement of the Government of the day. The Budget Speech of the Finance Minister of India delivered on First February, 2018 did not incorporate specifically of any item relating to SDG- 14. It is a fact that budget document provides annual outlay for all connected programmes/ schemes for the concerned financial year as it did for items falling under SDG-14 for 2018-19; however, the inclusion of any subject in the Budget Speech endows it due recognition and importance in the area of programme management. It also reflects priority focus of the government and the country. The absence any specific mention of items falling under SDG-14 in the budget speech of the Finance Minister on conservation and to the sustainably use the oceans, seas and marine resources for sustainable development has to an extent diminished the importance of oceans and seas for sustainable development to the general public.

Chapter - 25

Sustainable Development Goal 15

Protect, restore and promote sustainable use of terrestrial ecosystems, sustainably manage forests, combat desertification, and halt and reverse land degradation and halt biodiversity loss

The Sustainable Development Goal 15 aims at preserving diverse forms of life and also on protection, restoration, conservation and sustainable use of terrestrial ecosystem. It focuses on managing forests sustainably halting and reversing land and natural habitat degradation, successfully combating desertification and stopping biodiversity loss. The vision is to bequeath the benefits of land-based ecosystems, including sustainable livelihoods for generations to come.

Before dwelling on the importance of ecosystem, it would be worth mentioning to capture some facts and figures on components of the ecosystems. The FAO website mentions the following:

- **Forests:** Forests cover 31 percent of global land area, and shelter about 18 percent of the world's population. It contains over 80 percent of the world's terrestrial biodiversity. Over half of all wood produced in the world is used for energy; a third of all households use wood as their main fuel for cooking.
- **Mountains:** Mountains cover almost a quarter of the earth's land area. They are home to more than one tenth of the world's population.They are also the major storehouses of the freshwater

that sustains life on earth, providing 70 percent of the world's freshwater resources for domestic, agricultural and industrial consumption.

- **Land:** The grassland system, including mosaics of grasslands and shrub lands,are estimated to cover about 32 percent of the world's land area, and tree covered areas cover another 28 percent. In 40 countries, grasslands cover more than 50 percent of the land area.About 20 percent of grasslands around the world are degraded. Grassland cover can potentially capture 50 to 80 percent more water compared to uncovered soils, reducing the risk of drought and floods.The biodiversity of rangelands is rich. For flora, around 750 general and 12000 grass species occur across all climatic zones. For fauna, grasslands contain 11 percent of the world's endemic bird areas, and contribute to the maintenance of pollinators and other insects important for regulating ecosystem functions.
- **Soils:** Soils contain nearly three times as much carbon as is stored in all terrestrial plants. A third of the planet's soils are degraded. Erosion carries away 25 to 40 billion tonnes of topsoil every year, significantly reducing crop yields and soil's ability to store and cycle carbon, nutrients and water.An estimated 760,000 km2 of land worldwide is affected by human-induced salinity, caused mainly by large-scale irrigation projects.

These healthy ecosystems protect the planet and sustain livelihoods. Terrestrial and inland freshwater ecosystems, in particular forests, wetlands, mountains and drylands, make vital contributions to biodiversity and provide myriad environmental goods and services. They contribute to decent livelihoods while providing clean air and water, conserving biodiversity and mitigating climate change. Forests and rangelands sustain a range of industries, generate jobs and income and act as a source of food, medicine and fuel for more than a billion people.

However, across the globe, natural resources are deteriorating, ecosystems are stressed and biological diversity is being lost. 60% of the world's ecosystem services have been degraded over the past 50 years Land use changes, including deforestation, result in a loss of valuable habitats, a decrease in clean water, land degradation, soil erosion and the release of carbon into the atmosphere. Incidentally, between 1990 and 2015, the world's forest area diminished from 31.7 per cent of the world's total land mass to 30.7 per cent. This loss was mainly due to the conversion of forests to other uses, such as agriculture and infrastructure development. They contribute to the loss of valuable economic assets and livelihood opportunities'. Further, in every region of the world, the survival of species is increasingly threatened. As of 2015, over 23,000 species of plants, fungi and animals were known to face a high probability of extinction.

The UN Secretary-General, while addressing Progress of goal 15, in its Report, E/2016/75, on "Progress towards the Sustainable Development Goals" observed that

- Preserving diverse forms of life on land requires targeted efforts to protect, restore and promote the conservation and sustainable use of terrestrial and other ecosystems. Goal 15 focuses specifically on managing forests sustainably, restoring degraded lands and successfully combating desertification, reducing degraded natural habitats and ending biodiversity loss.
- Between 1990 and 2015, the world's forest area diminished from 31.7 per cent of the world's total land mass to 30.7 per cent. The loss was mainly attributable to the conversion of forest to other land uses, such as agriculture and infrastructure development. Meanwhile, other areas were transformed into forests through planting, landscape restoration or the natural expansion of forest. Owing to the balance of the two processes and efforts to slow deforestation, the global net loss of forest area declined from 7.3 million hectares per year in the 1990s to 3.3 million hectares per year during the period from 2010 to 2015.
- To safeguard places that contribute significantly to global biodiversity, protected areas have been established and identified as key biodiversity areas. In 2014, 15.2 per cent of the world's terrestrial and freshwater environments were covered by protected areas. The percentage of terrestrial key biodiversity areas covered by protected areas has increased, from 16.5 per cent in 2000 to 19.3 per cent in 2016. Over the same period, the share of freshwater key biodiversity areas that are protected has increased from 13.8 per cent to 16.6 per cent, and the share of mountain key biodiversity areas under protection has grown from 18.1 per cent to 20.1 per cent.
- The focus in Goal 15 on halting biodiversity loss comes at a critical time, since many species of amphibians, birds and mammals are sliding towards extinction. According to the International Union for Conservation of Nature's Red List Index, amphibians are declining most rapidly in Latin America and the Caribbean, primarily as a result of the chytrid fungal disease, one of numerous wildlife diseases on the rise worldwide. The greatest extinction risks for birds and mammals are found in South-Eastern Asia, mainly owing to the conversion of lowland forests. However, their decline is not inevitable, with extinction risks for vertebrate species having been reversed in five small island developing States (the Cook Islands, Fiji, Mauritius, Seychelles and Tonga) as a result of conservation actions over the past several decades.

- Conservation efforts can also be thwarted by poaching and the trafficking of wildlife. Since 1999, at least 7,000 species of animals and plants have been detected in illegal trade, and the list of species under international protection continues to grow. Comparing the size of legal trade in wildlife products (about 900,000 transactions per year) to the quantity of wildlife seized (about 16,000 seizures per year) provides an indication of the scope of illicit wildlife trafficking. The value of legal and illicit wildlife products can also be compared. For example, the value of recorded seizures of Crocodylus genus represents between 0.4 per cent and 0.6 per cent of the value of legal protected exports of this species between 2009 and 2013, with no clear trend discernible.
- In 2014, bilateral ODA to support biodiversity amounted to $7 billion, an increase of 16 per cent in real terms over 2013. The two largest recipients of biodiversity assistance were the Philippines and India, which together received about $1 billion of the total aid.

The SDG-15 moves beyond pure conservation to recognising the importance of sustainable management of natural resources in ensuring the long-term survival of our planet. Accordingly, the Goal 15 as adopted in the SDG Summit and its associated targets are as follows:

Goal 15. Protect, restore and promote sustainable use of terrestrial ecosystems, sustainably manage forests, combat desertification, and halt and reverse land degradation and halt biodiversity loss

15.1 By 2020, ensure the conservation, restoration and sustainable use of terrestrial and inland freshwater ecosystems and their services, in particular forests, wetlands, mountains and drylands, in line with obligations under international agreements

15.2 By 2020, promote the implementation of sustainable management of all types of forests, halt deforestation, restore degraded forests and substantially increase afforestation and reforestation globally

15.3 By 2030, combat desertification, restore degraded land and soil, including land affected by desertification, drought and floods, and strive to achieve a land degradation-neutral world

15.4 By 2030, ensure the conservation of mountain ecosystems, including their biodiversity, in order to enhance their capacity to provide benefits that are essential for sustainable development

15.5 Take urgent and significant action to reduce the degradation of natural habitats, halt the loss of biodiversity and, by 2020, protect and prevent the extinction of threatened species

15.6 Promote fair and equitable sharing of the benefits arising from the utilization of genetic resources and promote appropriate access to such resources, as internationally agreed

15.7 Take urgent action to end poaching and trafficking of protected species of flora and fauna and address both demand and supply of illegal wildlife products

15.8 By 2020, introduce measures to prevent the introduction and significantly reduce the impact of invasive alien species on land and water ecosystems and control or eradicate the priority species

15.9 By 2020, integrate ecosystem and biodiversity values into national and local planning, development processes, poverty reduction strategies and accounts

15.a Mobilize and significantly increase financial resources from all sources to conserve and sustainably use biodiversity and ecosystems

15.b Mobilize significant resources from all sources and at all levels to finance sustainable forest management and provide adequate incentives to developing countries to advance such management, including for conservation and reforestation

15.c Enhance global support for efforts to combat poaching and trafficking of protected species, including by increasing the capacity of local communities to pursue sustainable livelihood opportunities

The goals and targets per se are important from the angle of programme vision and intended outcome; however from the perspective of monitoring the performance, indicators do play critical role. Since indicator-design is essentially an expert professional skill- job requiring to keep harmony with overall goals and targets of the Sustainable Development Summit as embodied in paragraph 75 of Transforming our World: The 2030 Agenda for Sustainable Development mentioned: "the Goals and targets will be followed-up and reviewed using a set of global indicators. These will be complemented by indicators at the regional and national levels which will be developed by member states, in addition to the outcomes of work undertaken for the development of the baselines for those targets where national and global baseline data does not yet exist".

Needless to mention that purpose of SDG indicators is twofold; first it acts as a management tool to help countries develop implementation and monitoring strategies for achieving the SDGs and to monitor progress and secondly, it works as a report card, to measure progress towards achieving a target and ensure the accountability of governments to their citizens.As a matter of fact, Agenda 21 of the SD Summit also called on countries and the international community to develop indicators of sustainable development. Such indicators were needed to increase focus on sustainable development and assist decision-makers at all levels to adopt sound national sustainable development policies.

Be that as it may, the Global Indicator Framework as designed by the UN Statistical Commission at its 47th Session in March 2016 and adopted

thereafter by the Economic and Social Council and the General Assembly, are as follows:

Indicators of SDG-15

15.1.1 Forest area as a proportion of total land area

15.1.2 Proportion of important sites for terrestrial and freshwater biodiversity that are covered by protected areas, by ecosystem type

15.2.1 Progress towards sustainable forest management

15.3.1 Proportion of land that is degraded over total land area

15.4.1 Coverage by protected areas of important sites for mountain biodiversity

15.4.2 Mountain Green Cover Index

15.5.1 Red List Index

15.6.1 Number of countries that have adopted legislative, administrative and policy frameworks to ensure fair and equitable sharing of benefits

15.7.1 Proportion of traded wildlife that was poached or illicitly trafficked

15.8.1 Proportion of countries adopting relevant national legislation and adequately resourcing the prevention or control of invasive alien species

15.9.1 Progress towards national targets established in accordance with Aichi Biodiversity Target 2 of the Strategic Plan for Biodiversity 2011-2020

15.a.1 Official development assistance and public expenditure on conservation and sustainable use of biodiversity and ecosystems

15.b.1 Official development assistance and public expenditure on conservation and sustainable use of biodiversity and ecosystems

15.c.1 Proportion of traded wildlife that was poached or illicitly trafficked

SDG-15 and the initiatives in India

(a) The NITI Aayog and Mapping of Initiatives on SDG-15

It is with this background that the roadmap for Sustainable development of SDG-15 need to be examined with reference to the basic approach and goal-specific initiatives as undertaken in India. As mentioned earlier, NITI Aayog has been tasked to oversee the implementation of SDGs by the ministries of the Central Government and coordinate with States for the achievement of developmental targets as enshrined in the SDGs. The NITI Aayog undertook to itself to prepare a initial draft based on mapping of the goals and targets proposed by Nodal and other Ministries in consultation with MoSPI. The schemes so mapped for Goal-15 include (1) National Afforestation Programme (National Mission for a Green India) (Core){2014}, (2) Integrated Development of Wild Life Habitats (Core) {11th Plan} and (3) Project Tiger (Core) {1973}. The NITI Aayog also took into consideration other programmes like. (1) Project Elephant {1992} (2)National Environmental Policy 2006 (3) National Agroforestry Policy (2014) (4) National Action Programme to Combat Desertification (2001)

(b) National Review of SDG- 15 for United Nations High Level Political Forum 2017

The outcomes of initiatives under SDG-15 are rather distant, farsighted and linked with several issues that do not bring immediate result overnight. It will take time for resolution of interlinked issues to reflect its final outcome.The Voluntary National Review Report on Implementation of Sustainable Development Goals presented for United Nations High Level Political Forum 2017 is,however, a good reference point for understanding the position on SDG-15 status in India. The report has not included SDG-15 as a separate item. However, it is noted that "given the interconnectedness of the SDGs, relevant strategies for enabling collaboration among different actors will be developed as part of the overall implementation process and that India will continue to pursue the implementation of the SDG agenda through close collaboration between the national and sub-national governments as well as active participation of all other relevant stakeholders. Further, a number of goals in the SDGs do not require the government to deliver public services, but instead to develop and enforce the necessary policy and regulatory frameworks.

(c) The NITI Aayog, Three-Year Action Agenda and SDG-15

NITI Aayog has recently released the Three-Year Action Agenda covering years 2017-18 to 2019-20 delineating ambitious proposals for policy changes within a relatively shorter period, Part 7 of which deals with overarching area of sustainability, capturing Environment and Forestry and sustainable management of water resources. These are meant to ensure that growth is not at the expense of the wealth that nature has bestowed upon India..It has also required the government to address the high level of air pollution in the cities, black carbon pollution indoor from biomass fuels in cooking, massive volume of solid waste in urban areas and deforestation. It also requires the government to strengthen and streamline regulatory structures governing sustainability of environment and remove hurdles that adversely impact growth without protecting the environment.

(d) Economic Survey of India, 2017-18

The Government of India tabled the Economic Survey of India, 2017-18 in the Parliament in the Budget Session on 29th January,2018 to set the stage for the Government for the Annual Budget. The Survey contains an indepth analysis, serious research as well new policy ideas. The said Survey sums up the latest approach on sustainability of which goal-15 is also an important component.The Economic Survey notes that India's commitment to environment and climate change is reflected in the number of actions in supporting sustainable development goals while retaining reliance on cleaner energy, including cleaner, greener coal. It states that India has strengthened its response to the threat of climate change in accordance with the principles of equity and Common But Differentiated Responsibilities and in the light of national circumstances with the Paris Pledge to reduce the emission intensity of GDP by 33-35 percent over 2005 levels by the year 2030.

On the issue of sustainable development, the Survey says that India's urban population is projected to grow to about 600 million by 2031. It suggests that Urban Local Bodies generate resources through financial instruments such as municipal bonds, PPPs and credit risk guarantees. The Survey says that access to sustainable, modern and affordable energy is the basis of achieving Sustainable Development Goals. Stating that as on 30th November 2017, the share of renewable energy sources was 18 percent in the total installed capacity of electricity in the country and that the increasing share of renewables has trebled in the last 10 years. Outlining India's commitment to address Climate Change, the Survey mentions establishment of 8 Global Technology Watch Groups, extending Climate Change Action Programme launched in 2014 for the period 2017-18 to 2019-20 with a budget outlay of Rs. 132.4 crore and continuation of National Adaption Fund on Climate Change till 31st March 2020 with financial implication of Rs. 364 crore.

(e) Budget Inititives, 2018-19

The Budget document embodies not only a financial statement on resources availability and its projected expenditure, it also expresses alongside overtly and covertly the policy statement of the Government of the day. The Budget Speech of the Finance Minister of India delivered on First February,2018 did not incorporate specifically of any item relating to SDG- 15. It is a fact that budget document provides annual outlay for all connected programmes/ schemes for the concerned financial year as it did for items falling under SDG-15 for 2018-19; however, the inclusion of any subject in the Budget Speech endows it due recognition and importance in the area of programme management. It also reflects priority focus of the government and the country. The absence any focus on protection, restoration and promotion of sustainable use of terrestrial ecosystems, for sustainable development in the budget speech of the Finance Minister has to that extent diminished the importance of sustainable use of terrestrial ecosystems and halting biodiversity loss for sustainable development to the perception of general public.

Chapter - 26

Sustainable Development Goal 16

Promote peaceful and inclusive societies for sustainable development, provide access to justice for all and build effective, accountable and inclusive institutions at all levels

The UN document says that central to the 2030 Agenda for Sustainable Development is the need to promote peaceful and inclusive societies based on respect for human rights, the rule of law and transparent, effective and accountable institutions. A number of regions have enjoyed increased and sustained levels of peace and security in recent decades. But many countries still face protracted violence and armed conflict, and far too many people are poorly supported by weak institutions and lack access to justice, information and other fundamental freedoms. It also states that the SDGs, particularly SDG 16, tackle another omission of the MDGs, that of governance, inclusion, participation, rights and security. The SDG 16 aims to "*Promote peaceful and inclusive societies for sustainable development, provide access to justice for all and build effective, accountable and inclusive institutions at all levels*". It is held that SDG 16 is both an end in itself, and a crucial part of delivering sustainable development in all countries. It has in fact been seen by many commentators as being *the* transformational goal and key to ensuring that the Agenda can be accomplished. The inclusion of Goal 16 is one of the innovative aspects of the new development framework.

The Fact sheet on hand on Goal 16 before the Sustainable Development Summit showed that the number of refugees registered to the United Nations

High Commissioner for Refugees (UNHCR) stood at 13 million in mid-2014, up from a year earlier. Corruption, bribery, theft and tax evasion cost some US $1.26 trillion for developing countries per year. The rate of children leaving primary school in conflict-affected countries reached 50% in 2011,which amounts to 28.5 million children.

The Report of the Secretary-General, "Progress towards the Sustainable Development Goals", E/2016/75 mentioned with reference to Goal 16 that Peace, justice and effective, accountable and inclusive institutions are at the core of sustainable development. Several regions have enjoyed increased and sustained levels of peace and security in recent decades. But many countries still face protracted armed conflict and violence, and far too many people struggle as a result of weak institutions and the lack of access to justice, information and other fundamental freedoms. The number of victims of intentional homicide worldwide remained relatively stable from 2008 to 2014. The worldwide number of victims of intentional homicide was estimated to be between 4.6 and 6.8 per 100,000 people in 2014, a slight decrease with respect to previous years. Yet during that period, the homicide rate in developing countries was twice that in developed countries, and increased in the least developed countries. Moreover, despite the lack of harmonized data, fatalities and injuries related to armed conflict appear to be increasing in some countries, causing unprecedented population displacements and enormous humanitarian needs. Various forms of violence against children are pervasive, including discipline that relies on physical punishment and psychological aggression. In all but 7 of 73 countries and areas with available survey data from 2005 to 2015, more than half of children between the ages of 1 and 14 were subjected to some form of psychological aggression and/or physical punishment at home. In Northern Africa, the share was more than 90 per cent. Globally, the share of girls and boys among victims of human trafficking (21 per cent and 13 per cent, respectively) peaked in 2011. By 2014, the figures had dropped to 18 per cent and 7 per cent, respectively, but were still almost twice the levels recorded for 2004. Sexual violence is one of the most unsettling of children's rights violations. Yet underreporting and the lack of comparable data limit understanding of the full extent of the problem. Survey data from 31 low- and middle-income countries suggest that the proportion of women aged between 18 and 29 who experienced sexual violence for the first time before the age of 18 varies widely, ranging from zero to 16 per cent. Comparable data on the experiences of men are only available for five countries, but values are lower than those reported among women in the same countries. Progress with respect to the rule of law and access to justice is mixed. Globally, the proportion of people held in detention without sentencing decreased slightly, from 32 per cent of total detainees in 2003-2005 to 30 per cent in 2012-2014. However, the percentage for developing regions has consistently been more than two times that of developed regions. In Southern Asia, for instance, more than 2 out of 3 prisoners remained unsentenced in 2012-2014, despite some improvement over the data available for the period 2003 to 2005. Among victims of robbery, between one quarter and one half reported the crime to the police, in 27 countries with available data. The data suggest a significant gap in citizens' access to and trust in authorities. Although official data on the prevalence of bribery are limited, figures from 19 countries indicate that the rate of prevalence of bribery may reach as high as 50 per cent among citizens who had contact with public officials, undermining trust in state institutions.Registering children at birth is a first step in securing recognition before the law and safeguarding individual rights and access to justice. Despite recent progress, the births of more than 1 in 4 children under the age of 5 worldwide have not been recorded. In sub-Saharan Africa, over half (54 per cent) of children have not been registered by their fifth birthday. Globally, children living in urban areas are around 1.5 times more likely to be registered than their rural counterparts. In most regions, birth registration rates tend to be highest among the richest 20 per cent of the population. Efforts are under way to make national and international institutions more effective, inclusive and transparent. Over the past 10 years, nearly two thirds of 144 countries with available data were able to plan their national budgets effectively (where final expenses remained within 10 per cent of original budgets). Voting rights assigned to various groups of countries in international institutions is one indication of inclusivity at the international level. For example, while developing countries account for 63 per cent of voting rights in the African Development Bank, this figure is only 35 per cent in the International Monetary Fund and 38 per cent in the International Bank for Reconstruction and Development of the World Bank Group. A free press is closely linked to access to information and the protection of human rights, but the trend in this regard is discouraging. The number of journalists killed increased from 65 in 2010 to 114 in 2015, despite the fact that, by 2013, 90 States had adopted laws on freedom of and/or access to information.The proportion of countries with national human rights institutions has doubled over the past 15 years, reaching 35.5 per cent by the end of 2015. The share of such institutions that are compliant with the principles relating to the status of national institutions for the promotion and protection of human rights (Paris Principles) (adopted by the General Assembly in its resolution 48/134) was highest in developed regions (46 per cent) and in Latin America and the Caribbean (41 per cent).

Earlier, having regard to the importance of goal -16 in the broader framework of SDGs, the Sustainable Development Summit resolved as follows:

35. Sustainable development cannot be realized without peace and security; and peace and security will be at risk without sustainable development. The new Agenda recognizes the need to build peaceful,

just and inclusive societies that provide equal access to justice and that are based on respect for human rights (including the right to development), on effective rule of law and good governance at all levels and on transparent, effective and accountable institutions. Factors which give rise to violence, insecurity and injustice, such as inequality, corruption, poor governance and illicit financial and arms flows, are addressed in the Agenda. We must redouble our efforts to resolve or prevent conflict and to support post-conflict countries, including through ensuring that women have a role in peace-building and State-building.We call for further effective measures and actions to be taken, in conformity with international law, to remove the obstacles to the full realization of the right of self-determination of peoples living under colonial and foreign occupation, which continue to adversely affect their economic and social development as well as their environment."

With the above perspective in mind, it would be appropriate to look into the Goal 16 of the SDGs, its targets and related indicators to keep it in the up-fronts, in sequential order, before addressing India's initiatives under Goal-16.

Goal 16. Promote peaceful and inclusive societies for sustainable development, provide access to justice for all and build effective, accountable and inclusive institutions at all levels

16.1 Significantly reduce all forms of violence and related death rates everywhere

16.2 End abuse, exploitation, trafficking and all forms of violence against and torture of children

16.3 Promote the rule of law at the national and international levels and ensure equal access to justice for all

16.4 By 2030, significantly reduce illicit financial and arms flows, strengthen the recovery and return of stolen assets and combat all forms of organized crime

16.5 Substantially reduce corruption and bribery in all their forms

16.6 Develop effective, accountable and transparent institutions at all levels

16.7 Ensure responsive, inclusive, participatory and representative decision-making at all levels

16.8 Broaden and strengthen the participation of developing countries in the institutions of global governance

16.9 By 2030, provide legal identity for all, including birth registration

16.10 Ensure public access to information and protect fundamental freedoms, in accordance with national legislation and international agreements

16.a Strengthen relevant national institutions, including through international cooperation, for building capacity at all levels, in particular in developing countries, to prevent violence and combat terrorism and crime

16.b Promote and enforce non-discriminatory laws and policies for sustainable development

The goals and targets per se are important from the angle of programme vision and intended outcome; however from the perspective of monitoring the performance, indicators do play critical role. Since indicator-design is essentially an expert professional skill- job requiring to keep harmony with overall goals and targets of the Sustainable Development Summit as embodied in paragraph 75 of Transforming our World: The 2030 Agenda for Sustainable Development mentioned: "the Goals and targets will be followed-up and reviewed using a set of global indicators. These will be complemented by indicators at the regional and national levels which will be developed by member states, in addition to the outcomes of work undertaken for the development of the baselines for those targets where national and global baseline data does not yet exist".

Needless to mention that purpose of SDG indicators is twofold; first it acts as a management tool to help countries develop implementation and monitoring strategies for achieving the SDGs and to monitor progress and secondly, it works as a report card, to measure progress towards achieving a target and ensure the accountability of governments to their citizens. As a matter of fact, Agenda 21 of the SD Summit also called on countries and the international community to develop indicators of sustainable development. Such indicators were needed to increase focus on sustainable development and assist decision-makers at all levels to adopt sound national sustainable development policies.

Be that as it may, the Global Indicator Framework as designed by the UN Statistical Commission at its 47th Session in March 2016 and adopted thereafter by the Economic and Social Council and the General Assembly, are as follows:

Indicators of Goal 16

16.1.1 Number of victims of intentional homicide per 100,000 population, by sex and age

16.1.2 Conflict-related deaths per 100,000 population, by sex, age and cause

16.1.3 Proportion of population subjected to physical, psychological or sexual violence in the previous 12 months

16.1.4 Proportion of population that feel safe walking alone around the area they live

16.2.1 Proportion of children aged 1-17 years who experienced any physical punishment and/or psychological aggression by caregivers in the past month

16.2.2 Number of victims of human trafficking per 100,000 population, by sex, age and form of exploitation

16.2.3 Proportion of young women and men aged 18-29 years who experienced sexual violence by age 18

16.3.1 Proportion of victims of violence in the previous 12 months who reported their victimization to competent authorities or other officially recognized conflict resolution mechanisms

16.3.2 Unsentenced detainees as a proportion of overall prison population

16.4.1 Total value of inward and outward illicit financial flows (in current United States dollars)

16.4.2 Proportion of seized, found or surrendered arms whose illicit origin or context has been traced or established by a competent authority in line with international instruments

16.5.1 Proportion of persons who had at least one contact with a public official and who paid a bribe to a public official, or were asked for a bribe by those public officials, during the previous 12 months

16.5.2 Proportion of businesses that had at least one contact with a public official and that paid a bribe to a public official, or were asked for a bribe by those public officials during the previous 12 months

16.6.1 Primary government expenditures as a proportion of original approved budget, by sector (or by budget codes or similar)

16.6.2 Proportion of population satisfied with their last experience of public services

16.7.1 Proportions of positions (by sex, age, persons with disabilities and population groups) in public institutions (national and local legislatures, public service, and judiciary) compared to national distributions

16.7.2 Proportion of population who believe decisionmaking is inclusive and responsive, by sex, age, disability and population group

16.8.1 Proportion of members and voting rights of developing countries in international organizations

16.9.1 Proportion of children under 5 years of age whose births have been registered with a civil authority, by age

16.10.1 Number of verified cases of killing,kidnapping, enforced disappearance, arbitrary detention and torture of journalists, associated media personnel, trade unionists and human rights advocates in the previous 12 months

16.10.2 Number of countries that adopt and implement constitutional, statutory and/or policy guarantees for public access to information

16.a.1 Existence of independent national human rights institutions in compliance with the Paris Principles

16.b.1 Proportion of population reporting having personally felt discriminated against or harassed in the previous 12 months on the basis of a ground of discrimination prohibited under international human rights law

SDG-16 and the initiatives in India

- ***The NITI Aayog and Mapping of Initiatives on SDG-16***

Based on the overarching goal of SDG-16, the national government of the country needs to take it forward to design appropriate programme in ensuring commensurate outcome. The NITI Aayog has been empowered to oversee the implementation of SDGs by the ministries of the Central Government and coordinate with States for the achievement of developmental targets as enshrined in the SDGs. The NITI Aayog tasked itself to prepare a initial draft based on mapping of the goals and targets proposed by Nodal and other Ministries in consultation with MoSPI. The schemes so mapped for Goal-16 include 55) Panchayat Yuva Krida aur Khel Abhiyan (PYKKA) {2008} 56) Development of Infrastructure Facilities for Judiciary including Gram Nyayalayas (Core) {2017} 57) Integrated Child Protection Scheme (ICPS) (Core){2009}. It has also included related schemes like (1) Digital India{2015}, (2) Pragati Platform (Public Grievance Redressal System){2015} and (3) RTI (Right to Information Act) {2005}

- ***National Review of SDG- 16 for United Nations High Level Political Forum 2017***

The outcomes of initiatives under SDG-16 would normally take a period of time to fructify as several other factors are also interlinked to reflect its final outcome. Be that as it may, the Voluntary National Review Report on Implementation of Sustainable Development Goals presented for United Nations High Level Political Forum 2017 is a good reference point for understanding the latest position on SDG-16 status in India. The report has not included SDG-16 as a separate item. However, it is noted that "given the interconnectedness of the SDGs, relevant strategies for enabling collaboration among different actors will be developed as part of the overall implementation process and that India will continue to pursue the implementation of the SDG agenda through close collaboration between the national and sub-national governments as well as active participation of all other relevant stakeholders.

- ***The NITI Aayog, Three-Year Action Agenda and SDG-16***

The NITI Aayog has recently released the Three-Year Action Agenda covering years 2017-18 to 2019-20 which begins with the objective of eliminating poverty in all its dimensions such that every citizen will have access to a minimum standard of food, education, health, clothing, shelter, transportation and energy. The Three-Year Action Agenda does not include any separate chapter to dwell on SDG-16. However, the interventions under ' Towards building a More Inclusive Society' as covered in chapter -22 along with action agenda on other SDGs therein, will also go a long way in improving quality changes of life of the least privileged and remove the economic disparities within a period of time.

- ***Economic Survey of India, 2017-18***

The Government of India tabled the Economic Survey of India, 2017-18 in the Parliament in the Budget Session on 29th January,2018 to set the stage for the Government for the Annual Budget. The Survey contains an indepth analysis, serious research as well new policy ideas. The said Survey sums up the latest approach on SDG-16 when the Finance Minister said that Government has taken up programmes to direct the benefits of structural changes and good growth to reach farmers, poor and other vulnerable sections of our society and to uplift the under-developed regions. He said that this year's Budget will consolidate these gains and particularly focus on strengthening agriculture and rural economy, provision of good health care to economically less privileged, taking care of senior citizens, infrastructure creation and working with the States to provide more resources for improving the quality of education in the country. He said that the Government has ensured that benefits reach eligible beneficiaries and are delivered to them directly and said that Direct Benefit Transfer mechanism of India is the biggest such exercise in the world and is a global success story.

- ***Budget Inititives,2018-19***

The Budget document embodies not only a financial statement on resources availability and its projected expenditure, it also expresses alongside overtly and covertly the policy statement of the Government of the day. The Budget Speech of the Finance Minister of India delivered on First February,2018 did not incorporate specifically with reference to any item relating to SDG- 16. It is a fact that budget document provides annual outlay for all connected programmes/schemes for the concerned financial year as it did for items falling under SDG-16 for 2018-19; however, the inclusion of any subject in the Budget Speech endows it due recognition and importance in the area of programme management. It also reflects priority focus of the government and the country. The absence any focus on protection, restoration and promotion of sustainable use of terrestrial ecosystems, for sustainable development in the budget speech of the Finance Minister has to that extent diminished the importance of sustainable use of terrestrial ecosystems and halting biodiversity loss for sustainable development to the perception of general public.

Chapter - 27

Sustainable Development Goal 17

Strengthen the means of implementation and revitalize the global partnership for sustainable development

At the Preamble of the Outcome document, under caption Partnership, it has been vouched to mobilize the means required to implement this Agenda through a revitalised Global Partnership for Sustainable Development, based on a spirit of strengthened global solidarity, focussed in patlicular on the needs of the poorest and most vulnerable and with the participation of all countries, all stakeholders and all people. The interlinkages and integrated nature of the Sustainable Development Goals are of crucial importance in ensuring that the purpose of the new Agenda is realised. If the full extent of the Agenda is realized, the lives of all will be profoundly improved and our world will be transformed for the better.

A major challenge will now be to ensure that all countries build on the momentum created by the Summit and truly undertake to adapt the 2030 Agenda to their national situations by reviewing policies, plans and institutions. Developed countries acknowledged that the Agenda extends beyond development cooperation, and are considering relevant reforms in their domestic policies to address its provisions. Much emphasis was placed at the Summit on the need to forge innovative partnerships between governments, businesses and civil society. Regional and national development challenges were stressed by many, with emphasis on countries in special situations.

The Fact-sheet on Goal 17 that was placed at the time of Sustainable Development Summit, 2015 says that Official development assistance (ODA) stood at approximately $135 billion in 2014. In 2014, 79% of imports from developing countries entered developed countries duty-free. The debt burden on developing countries remains stable at about 3% of export revenue. The number of internet users in Africa almost doubled in the past four years. As of 2015, 95% of the world's population is covered by a mobile-cellular signal. 30% of the world's youth are digital natives, active online for at least five years. Internet penetration has grown from just over 6% of the world's population in 2000 to 43% in 2015. But more than four billion people do not use the Internet, and 90% of them are from the developing world.

The Report of the Secretary-General, "Progress towards the Sustainable Development Goals", E/2016/75 mentioned with reference to Goal 17 that achieving the ambitious targets of the 2030 Agenda requires a revitalized and enhanced global partnership that brings together Governments, civil society, the private sector, the United Nations system and other actors and mobilizes all available resources. Enhancing support to developing countries, in particular the least developed countries and the small island developing States, is fundamental to equitable progress for all.

It further addressed all the components of Goal-17 as below:

Finance

- In 2015, net ODA from member countries of the Development Assistance Committee of OECD totalled $131.6 billion. Taking account of inflation and the rise in the value of the dollar in 2015, this was 6.9 per cent higher in real terms than in 2014, and represented the highest level ever reached. Total ODA from those countries as a share of their gross national income was 0.30 per cent, on par with 2014. Most of the increase was owing to higher expenditures for costs associated with refugees. However, even if those costs are excluded, ODA still rose by 1.7 per cent. Seven countries met the United Nations target for ODA of 0.7 per cent of gross national income in 2015: Denmark, Luxembourg, the Netherlands, Norway, Sweden, the United Arab Emirates and the United Kingdom.

Information and communications technology

- Fixed-broadband services remain largely unaffordable and unavailable across much of the population in developing regions, highlighting digital divides in access to high-speed, high-capacity Internet services. By 2015, fixed-broadband penetration had reached 29 per cent in developed regions, but only 7.1 per cent and 0.5 per cent, respectively, in developing regions and the least developed countries. Major disparities are also found in Internet use. In developing regions, one third of the population is online versus 1 in 10 people in the least developed countries. Data also reveal that more men than women are online. In 2015, globally, the Internet user penetration rate was about 11 per cent lower for women than for men. The gender gap is even higher in developing regions (15 per cent) and highest in the least developed countries (29 per cent).

Capacity-building

- Net ODA for capacity-building and national planning amounted to $23 billion in 2014; of that total, sub-Saharan Africa received $6 billion and Southern and Central Asia received $4.6 billion. The main sectors receiving assistance were public administration, environment and energy, which together were allocated a total of $9.3 billion.

Trade

- The weighted average of applied tariffs has been decreasing over time, but still varies widely across regions and country groups on main product sectors. Average agricultural tariffs on imports coming into Asia, for instance, are the highest in the world, at around 27 per cent for Southern Asia and 20 per cent for Eastern Asia in 2015, under most-favoured nation status.
- In 14 years, the least developed countries' share in world merchandise exports nearly doubled, from 0.6 per cent in 2000 to 1.1 per cent in 2014. The key driver of export growth during that period was a massive rise in the price of fuel, ores and metals, reflecting a high demand in developing countries, notably China. In services, the least developed countries increased their share of world exports to 0.8 per cent in 2014 ($40 billion), up from 0.5 per cent in 2005.

Data, monitoring and accountability

- The requirements of the indicators developed in the context of the Millennium Development Goals have fostered stronger national statistical plans and systems. The number of countries with a national statistical plan increased in some regions between 2010 and 2015, including in sub-Saharan Africa and the least developed countries. However, the overall number of plans declined from 56 to 54 among the countries being observed, since the time period of some existing plans expired.
- Financial support for statistical capacity amounted to $325 million in 2013, compared with $379 million in 2010. However, assistance to the least developed countries, in this regard, tripled during the period and reached $265 million. Despite an increasing awareness of the importance of statistics for evidence-based policymaking and development, the share of ODA dedicated to statistics hovered at around 0.3 per cent between 2010 and 2013.

- Population and housing censuses are a primary source of the disaggregated data needed for formulating, implementing and monitoring development policies and programmes. During the 10-year period spanning from 2006 to 2015, 90 per cent of countries or areas around the world conducted at least one population and housing census.
- Over the period 2005-2014, birth registration data were available for 183 out of 230 countries or areas, whereas death registration data were available for 157. Only 58 per cent of developing countries with available data have birth registration coverage of 90 per cent or more; 71 per cent of developing countries with available data have death registration coverage of 75 per cent or more. Sub-Saharan Africa has the lowest levels of complete birth and death registration.

With the above perspective in mind, it would be appropriate to look into the Goal 17 of the SDGs, its targets and related indicators to keep it in the up-fronts, in sequential order, before addressing India's initiatives under Goal-16.

Goal 17. Strengthen the means of implementation and revitalize the global partnership for sustainable development

Finance

17.1 Strengthen domestic resource mobilization, including through international support to developing countries, to improve domestic capacity for tax and other revenue collection

17.2 Developed countries to implement fully their official development assistance commitments, including the commitment by many developed countries to achieve the target of 0.7 per cent of ODA/GNI to developing countries and 0.15 to 0.20 per cent of ODA/GNI to least developed countries; ODA providers are encouraged to consider setting a target to provide at least 0.20 per cent of ODA/GNI to least developed countries

17.3 Mobilize additional financial resources for developing countries from multiple sources

17.4 Assist developing countries in attaining long-term debt sustainability through coordinated policies aimed at fostering debt financing, debt relief and debt restructuring, as appropriate, and address the external debt of highly indebted poor countries to reduce debt distress

17.5 Adopt and implement investment promotion regimes for least developed countriesTechnology17.6 Enhance North-South, South-South and triangular regional and international cooperation on and access to science, technology and innovation and enhance knowledge sharing on mutually agreed terms, including through improved coordination among existing mechanisms, in particular at the United Nations level, and through a global technology facilitation mechanism

17.7 Promote the development, transfer, dissemination and diffusion of environmentally sound technologies to developing countries on favourable terms, including on concessional and preferential terms, as mutually agreed

17.8 Fully operationalize the technology bank and science, technology and innovation capacity-building mechanism for least developed countries by 2017 and enhance the use of enabling technology, in particular information and communications technologyCapacity-building

17.9 Enhance international support for implementing effective and targeted capacity-building in developing countries to support national plans to implement all the sustainable development goals, including through North-South, South-South and triangular cooperationTrade

17.10 Promote a universal, rules-based, open, non-discriminatory and equitable multilateral trading system under the World Trade Organization, including through the conclusion of negotiations under its Doha Development Agenda

17.11 Significantly increase the exports of developing countries, in particular with a view to doubling the least developed countries' share of global exports by 2020

17.12 Realize timely implementation of duty-free and quota-free market access on a lasting basis for all least developed countries, consistent with World Trade Organization decisions, including by ensuring that preferential rules of origin applicable to imports from least developed countries are transparent and simple, and contribute to facilitating market accessSystemic issuesPolicy and institutional coherence17.13 Enhance global macroeconomic stability, including through policy coordination and policy coherence

17.14 Enhance policy coherence for sustainable development

17.15 Respect each country's policy space and leadership to establish and implement policies for poverty eradication and sustainable developmentMulti-stakeholder partnerships

17.16 Enhance the global partnership for sustainable development, complemented by multi-stakeholder partnerships that mobilize and share knowledge, expertise, technology and financial resources, to support the achievement of the sustainable development goals in all countries, in particular developing countries

17.17 Encourage and promote effective public, public-private and civil society partnerships, building on the experience and resourcing strategies of partnershipsData, monitoring and accountability

17.18 By 2020, enhance capacity-building support to developing countries, including for least developed countries and small island developing States, to increase significantly the availability of high-quality, timely and reliable data disaggregated by income, gender, age, race, ethnicity, migratory status, disability, geographic location and other characteristics relevant in national contexts

17.19 By 2030, build on existing initiatives to develop measurements of progress on sustainable development that complement gross domestic product, and support statistical capacity-building in developing countries

The goals and targets per se are important from the angle of programme vision and intended outcome; however from the perspective of monitoring the performance, indicators do play critical role. Since indicator-design is essentially an expert professional skill- job requiring to keep harmony with overall goals and targets of the Sustainable Development Summit as embodied in paragraph 75 of Transforming our World: The 2030 Agenda for Sustainable Development, mentioned: "the Goals and targets will be followed-up and reviewed using a set of global indicators. These will be complemented by indicators at the regional and national levels which will be developed by member states, in addition to the outcomes of work undertaken for the development of the baselines for those targets where national and global baseline data does not yet exist".

Needless to mention that purpose of SDG indicators is twofold; first it acts as a management tool to help countries develop implementation and monitoring strategies for achieving the SDGs and to monitor progress and secondly, it works as a report card, to measure progress towards achieving a target and ensure the accountability of governments to their citizens. As a matter of fact, Agenda 21 of the SD Summit also called on countries and the international community to develop indicators of sustainable development. Such indicators were needed to increase focus on sustainable development and assist decision-makers at all levels to adopt sound national sustainable development policies.

Be that as it may, the Global Indicator Framework as designed by the UN Statistical Commission at its 47th Session in March 2016 and adopted thereafter by the Economic and Social Council and the General Assembly, are as follows:

Indicators of Goal 17

Finance

17.1.1 Total government revenue as a proportion of GDP, by source

17.1.2 Proportion of domestic budget funded by domestic taxes

17.2.1 Net official development assistance, total and to least developed countries, as a proportion of theOrganization for Economic Cooperation and Development (OECD) Development Assistance Committee donors' gross national income (GNI)

17.3.1 Foreign direct investments (FDI), official development assistance and South-South Cooperationas a proportion of total domestic budget

17.3.2 Volume of remittances (in United States dollars) as a proportion of total GDP

17.4.1 Debt service as a proportion of exports of goods and services

17.5.1 Number of countries that adopt and implement investment promotion regimes for least developedCountries

Technology

17.6.1 Number of science and/or technology cooperation agreements and programmes betweencountries, by type of cooperation

17.6.2 Fixed Internet broadband subscriptions per 100 inhabitants, by speed1

7.7.1 Total amount of approved funding for developing countries to promote the development,transfer, dissemination and diffusion of environmentally sound technologies

17.8.1 Proportion of individuals using the Internet

Capacity-building

17.9.1 Dollar value of financial and technicalassistance (including through North-South, South-South and triangular cooperation) committed todeveloping countries

Trade

17.10.1 Worldwide weighted tariff-average

17.11 Significantly increase the exports of developing countries, in particular with a view to doubling the leastdeveloped countries' share of global exports by 2020

17.11.1 Developing countries' and least developed countries' share of global exports

17.12.1 Average tariffs faced by developingcountries, least developed countries and small islanddeveloping States **Systemic issues** *Policy and institutional coherence*

17.13.1 Macroeconomic Dashboard

17.14.1 Number of countries with mechanisms in place to enhance policy coherence of sustainabledevelopment

17.15.1 Extent of use of country-owned resultsframeworks and planning tools by providers ofdevelopment cooperation *Multi-stakeholder partnerships*

17.16.1 Number of countries reporting progress inmulti-stakeholder development effectivenessmonitoring frameworks that support the achievementof the sustainable development goals

17.17.1 Amount of United States dollars committedto public-private and civil society partnerships *Data, monitoring and accountability*

17.18.1 Proportion of sustainable development indicators produced at the national level with fulldisaggregation when relevant to the target, in accordance with the Fundamental Principles of Official Statistics

17.18.2 Number of countries that have national statistical legislation that complies with theFundamental Principles of Official Statistics

17.18.3 Number of countries with a national statistical plan that is fully funded and underimplementation, by source of funding

17.19.1 Dollar value of all resources made available to strengthen statistical capacity in developingcountries

17.19.2 Proportion of countries that (a) have conducted at least one population and housing censusin the last 10 years; and (b) have achieved 100 per cent birth registration and 80 per cent deathregistration

SDG-17 and the initiatives in India

(a) The NITI Aayog and Mapping of Initiatives on SDG-17

Based on the overarching goal of SDG-17, the national government of the country needs to take it forward to design appropriate programme in ensuring commensurate outcome. The NITI Aayog has been empowered to oversee the implementation of SDGs by the ministries of the Central Government and coordinate with States for the achievement of developmental targets as enshrined in the SDGs. The NITI Aayog tasked itself to prepare a initial draft based on mapping of the goals and targets proposed by Nodal and other Ministries in consultation with MoSPI. The scheme that has been so mapped for Goal-17 is 58) Support for Statistical Strengthening (2015). Further related programmes, such as (1) South-South Cooperation, (2) India Africa Summit, (3) SCO (Shanghai Cooperation Organisation), (4) BRICS (Brazil, Russia, India, China, and South Africa), (5) NDB (New Development Bank – BRICS) and (6) SAARC Satellite (South Asian Association for Regional Cooperation would also be relevant for implementation of Goal-17.

(b) National Review of SDG- 17 for United Nations High Level Political Forum 2017

The outcomes of initiatives under SDG-17 would normally take a period of time to fructify as several other factors are also interlinked to reflect its final outcome. Be that as it may, the Voluntary National Review Report on Implementation of Sustainable Development Goals presented for United Nations High Level Political Forum 2017 is a good reference point for understanding the latest position on SDG-17 status in India. The report mentions that 'while working towards revitalising the global partnership for the achievement of the SDGs, India reaffirms the principle of common but differentiated responsibilities. Despite significant efforts for domestic resource mobilisation, India is unlikely to gather sufficient revenues for achieving the SDGs. Therefore, India reiterates that the developed countries have an essential obligation to provide financial assistance to the developing countries, especially for global public goods such as climate change mitigation and control of pandemics, so that they can fully achieve the SDGs. India also highlights the need for international cooperation for curbing illicit financial flows, defining aid unambiguously and establishing robust systems for monitoring commitments made by donor countries.

A path-breaking tax reform agenda is being readied in the country to optimise domestic resourcemobilization. This includes direct tax reforms as well as the Goods and Services Tax (GST), a uniform and simplified form of indirect taxation. An innovative tax like the Swachh Bharat Cess (Clean India Cess) has also been levied for mobilizing resources for the Clean India Mission. Additionally, implementation of the budget responsibility legislation is ensuring predictable and sustainable budgeting as well as long-term debt sustainability. Proactive policy reforms have boosted the FDI flows during the last three fiscal years to USD 156 billion including a record-breaking USD 56 billion in the latest fiscal year.

To enable the implementation of development interventions by sub-national governments, the fiscal devolution to states has been increased substantially (from 32 to 42% of the central pool of tax proceeds). Initiatives are also being undertaken to enhance development cooperation with neighbouring and other countries of the global South. For instance, the South Asia Satellite was launched in May 2017 for sharing data with neighbours.

Lastly, efforts are underway at the national-level for finalizing the indicators that will enable monitoring of the progress made on the SDGs. The government is also considering setting up a high-level Committee headed by the Chief Statistician of India to oversee the monitoring framework for SDGs at the national level. While national efforts are paramount, global technical support is important in various areas including developing methodologies for data collection as well as monitoring and evaluation'.

(c) The NITI Aayog, Three-Year Action Agenda and SDG-17

The NITI Aayog has recently released the Three-Year Action Agenda covering years 2017-18 to 2019-20 which begins with the objective of eliminating poverty in all its dimensions such that every citizen will have access to a minimum standard of food, education, health, clothing, shelter, transportation and energy. The Three-Year Action Agenda does not include any separate chapter to dwell on SDG-17. However, the interventions under ' Towards building a More Inclusive Society' as covered in chapter -22 along with those included in other chapters covering several SDGs, will also go a long way in improving quality changes of life of the least privileged and remove the economic disparities within a period of time.

(d) Economic Survey of India, 2017-18

The Government of India tabled the Economic Survey of India, 2017-18 in the Parliament in the Budget Session on 29th January,2018 to set the stage for the Government for the Annual Budget. The Survey contains an indepth analysis, serious research as well new policy ideas. The said Survey sums up the latest approach on SDG-17 when the Finance Minister said that Government has taken up programmes to direct the benefits of structural changes and good growth to reach farmers, poor and other vulnerable sections of our society and to uplift the under-developed regions. The Finance Minister said that this year's Budget will consolidate these gains and particularly focus on strengthening agriculture and rural economy, provision of good health care to economically less privileged, taking care of senior citizens, infrastructure creation and working with the States to provide more resources for improving the quality of education in the country. The Finance Minister also said that the Government has ensured that benefits reach eligible beneficiaries and are delivered to them directly and said that Direct Benefit Transfer mechanism of India is the biggest such exercise in the world and is a global success story.

(e) Budget Inititives, 2018-19

The Budget document embodies not only a financial statement on resources availability and its projected expenditure, it also expresses alongside overtly and covertly the policy statement of the Government of the day. The Budget Speech of the Finance Minister of India delivered on First February,2018 did not incorporate specifically with reference to any item relating to SDG- 17. It is a fact that budget document provides annual outlay for all connected programmes/schemes for the concerned financial year as it did for items falling under SDG-17 for 2018-19; however, the inclusion of any subject in the Budget Speech endows it due recognition and importance in the area of programme management. It also reflects priority focus of the government and the country. The absence any focus on protection, restoration and promotion of sustainable use of terrestrial ecosystems, for sustainable development in the budget speech of the Finance Minister has to that extent diminished the importance of sustainable use of terrestrial ecosystems and halting biodiversity loss for sustainable development to the perception of general public.

Chapter - 28

The concluding scenario at 2030 – a robust optimism missing the goalpost

One world, one human species and common sustainable goal posts for all countries are the hallmarks of the clarion call on the march ahead towards the new journey of our civilization green-lighted from high pedestal of philosophical and moral values; the leaving no one left behind is anything but a signal of the seriousness in which the roadmap for achieving such a huge task has to be achieved. The 17 goals and 169 targets have been designed to play critical role in reshaping the destiny of people around the world without causing much damage to our natural assets. The onus of this great task is as much to the world community as it is to a particular country. Through collaborative efforts, the national government of the day has to undertake the shared responsibility to implement them in totality. The final outcome of national efforts would be known at 2030 only.

India is an important participant to the historic Sustainable Development Summit,2015 and a signatory to the Declaration of Sustainable Development Goals. India, which occupies 2.3% of the geographical space and 17.74% of the world population, is a front ranking country and an important global player and has therefore, to assume commensurate responsibility to ensure that the nation reaches the lofty targets rather honourably in 2030.

Sustainable development initiatives in India have been discussed, goal-wise, in great details in section IV from chapter 11 to chapter 27, delineating the current interventions and its existing status. It is a fact that conceptualising such a big tasks takes time; it is also a fact that a democratic country like India has to rope in its federal state units to carry out this onerous tasks through a process of consultations, motivation and its implementations, and that this process itself has its own time requirement. However, in this fast-spaced world, the scope for repeating the MDGs experience of time slippage is no more acceptable; the country has yet to see the take off the SDG mode of implementing the tasks.

As a general observation, it would not be unfair to state that the NITI Aayog, the principal coordinator of SDGs in India, has merely mapped out continuing programmes/schemes in a given goal-area without examining goal-wise gaps and deficits either for the states or for the country as a whole. The kind of intervention needed in bridging the gap between the target and the gaps, and its time planning do not appear to have been adequately covered. It is true that ongoing programmes/schemes are likely to contribute immensely in reaching the SDGs and targets; but it is also true that such existing programmes/schemes are needed to be revisited and re-tailored to fit in the new and bigger SDG challenges, its targets and meeting the monitoring indicators. Since most of the mapped-out programmes/schemes were introduced in pre-SDG Summit era and lacked the vision of SDG in terms of its content and implementation, the outcome of the destination target for 2030 would be really suspect and uncertain unless the national and state governments take measures to refocus them with SDG perspective.

It would be appropriate to admit that, given the federal functioning system in our country, the success of SDGs would depend ultimately on efforts made by the states of India. The current state of preparedness of the SDGs in the states of India does not inspire enough confidence to state that SDGs are being implemented with mission-mode zeal and that the spirit of SDG has been a strong motivating commitment in the implementation of development programme. Such a mission-mode zeal has neither percolated down, in required scale to the departments of the state governments nor among the rural and urban local bodies down below. As a result, the mission of accelerating inclusive and equitable economic growth and sustainable development, including full, productive employment and decent work for all has not registered as a strong point in the overall focus of development initiatives and related efforts.

In brief, the primary requirement of State-specific identification of gaps on each of the SDGs, the kind of programme intervention required over a period of time, the availability of central government programmes on each of the areas, assessment of adequacy of such schemes in the context of identified gaps, additional interventions required by the state government on each of the SDGs etc. are also not in place in general though some state governments have been making sporadic efforts in particular areas. The efforts of the state governments, by and large, have not generated enough public enthusiasm to feel that take-off of SDGs at the state level has been in place for the outcome journey.

As a result with each passing time, the work-load at hand would be increasing bigger and bigger. Consequently, the related targets on hand for each of the SDGs, per year, would correspondingly increase making the implementation more challenging. At the same time,the size of clientele /

beneficiaries would also move up. Since the huge size of population is never considered as a threat to development on ground of 'politics over population' in India, the incremental big size of annual growth (along with disproportionately higher growth of a particular religious faith) would pose difficult situations to outreach SDGs in general and for some SDGs in particular. The projection of population size of India by the UN Population Division to move up from 1311 million in 2015 to 1354 million in 2018 and 1526 million in 2030 bears testimony to the magnitude of load of increasing population and its increased target of coverage. While diversity is a distinguishing feature of the richness of the natural assets in India, diversity of human values and ownership of national cause has surfaced as a factor that will also be impacting adversely and negatively in any efforts to reach out SDGs agenda in time.

The demise of the Planning Commission and the no more necessity of State Annual Plans to follow norms of guidance on national priorities has opened up altogether a new dimension to work together in carrying forward national agenda, including the agenda of Sustainable Development Goals. The State Plans are no longer required to be presented, discussed and vetted at the apex planning body of the country. The states have virtually no obligation to follow any directive of the NITI Aayog in the annual plan exercise as it remains unconnected with funding linkage either indirectly through the various ministries or directly by way of awarding additional central assistance for certain purposes.. The Lassie fare approach of the state governments to fix its own priorities, based on perceived felt-needs of the state along with vote-bank considerations, may not always correspond with the high valued objectives of the SDGs. The website of the NITI Aayog on state-specific SDGs is anything but encouraging to the huge task at hand in the SDG areas. Further, the institution of Five Year Plan, which refocused the priorities of the country at an interval of five years, is no longer in place. The vision document along with new sectoral priorities in a plan document ceases to exist. The NITI Aayog's three year action agenda does not appear to be good substitute as it has not even addressed all the areas of SDGs.

The absence of robust SDG vision along with the data availability on the current status of the SDGs in India in general and the states in particular is likely to play considerable strain in designing appropriate programme intervention, in setting national and state-specific targets and its phasing, apart from surveillance of monitoring indicators. The high-level Committee headed by the Chief Statistician of India working for the monitoring framework for SDGs at the national-level need to work out state specific gaps on each of SDGs as well to enable focused intervention by them.

A vision document incorporating the high valued agenda of SDGs need to be put in place in public domain. Such a document would enable productive interactions, education and guidance among all the stake holders and prepare the social-mind sets to participate in the great task of economic transformation..The academic body needs to take it up as a subject of serious study and discipline, the way they had hitherto discussed the national five year plans of the country among the students and the researchers earlier. Since the perceived transformational change would course through generations of students and others, it is imperative that SDGs become part of the regular syllabus of the appropriate faculty. The UNESCO's stand that education is a fundamental human right is also inextricably linked to the realization of other rights including all Sustainable Development Goals. In a word, sustainable development begins with education.

A corollary to role of students of sustainable development is also the emergence of a new role for the youths in shaping the SDGs outcome in any location. Incidentally, at the biggest gathering of young people in the implementation of the 2030 Agenda for Sustainable Development at the United Nations, the President of the UN Economic and Social Council (ECOSOC) pointed out "By having a large amount of people coming into the UN, we give a visual impact that we are here. Our voices count and our voices should be heard," Indeed in the journey of SDGs right up to 2030, today's youths of 1.8 billion population in the world as a whole and 42.19 crore youths in India (representing 34.8% of total population) would have to be key partners of implementation of SDGs and in reshaping the destiny of mankind. It would be apt to conclude by quoting para 52 of the Sustainable Development Summit Declaration : "The future of humanity and of our planet lies in our hands. It lies also in the hands of today's younger generation who will pass the torch to future generations. We have mapped the road to sustainable development; it will be for all of us to ensure that the journey is successful and its gains irreversible."

Acronyms

AHIDF-Animal Husbandry Infrastructure Development Fund
AIDS- Acquired immune deficiency syndrome
ART- Antiretroviral therapy
ATF-Aviation Turbine Fuel
BCG- Bacillus Calmette–Guérin vaccine
BPL-Below the Poverty Line
COP21 –Conference of Paties in Paris
DBT-Direct Benefit Transfer
DALYs-Disability –Adjusted Life Years
DDUGJY-Deen Dayal Upadhyaya Gram Jyoti Yojana
DPT- Diphtheria-Pertussis-Tetanus vaccine
FAIDF -Fisheries and Aqua culture Infrastructure Development Fund
FGM-Female genital mutilation
FIES-Food Insecurity Experience Scale
FPO-Farmer Producer Organizations
GA-General Assembly
GDI- Gender Development Index
GDP – Gross Domestic Product
GEM- Gender Empowerment Measurement
GII - Gender Inequality Index
GNI- Gross national income
GPI-Gender Parity Index
GrAMs- Gramin Agricultural Markets
GVA- Gross Value Added
HDI- Human Development Index
HIV/AIDS- Human immunodeficiency virus / Acquired immune deficiency syndrome

HLPF - High-level Political Forum
ICDS-Integrated Child Development Scheme
IIP-Industrial Production
ISID-**inclusive and sustainable industrial development**
IMR-Infant Mortality Rate
IUD-Intrauterine device
INDC-Intended Nationally Determined Contributions
IPCC-Intergovernmental Panel of Climate Change
ISA-International Solar Alliance
IWAI-Inland Waterways Authority of India
JSY- Janani Suraksha Yojana
MDGs- Millennium Development Goals
MoSPI-Ministry of Statistics and Programme Implementation
MSP-Minimum Support Price
ORS- Oral Rehydration Solution
NAPCC- National Action Plan on Climate Change
NDCs-Nationally-determined contributions
NFHS- National Family Health Survey
NPP- National Population Policy
OECD- Organization for Economic Cooperation and Development
OWG-Open Working Group
PHCR-Poverty Head Count Ratio
PMJDY -Pradhan Mantri Jan Dhan Yojana)
PMRF-Prime Minister's Research Fellows
PMUY-Pradhan Mantri Ujjwala Yojana
PTR-Pupil Teacher Ratio
RISE-Revitalising Infrastructure and Systems in Education
SD- Sustainable development
SDGs-Sustainable Development Goals
SDM-Sustainable Development Summit
SECC-Socio-Economic Caste Census
SHG-Self-help group
STD-Sexually transmitted disease
TVET- - Technical and vocational education and training
UDAN-Ude Desh ka Aam Nagrik
UDAY-Ujjawal DISCOM Assurance Yojana)
UN- United Nations

UNCSD- United Nations Conference on Sustainable Development
UNDP-United Nations Development Programme
UNFCCC- UN Framework Convention on Climate Change
UNGA- United Nations General Assembly
UNSC-United Nations Statistical Commission
U5MR-Under Five Mortality Rate
VNR- Voluntary National Review Report
VPOs-Village Producers' Organizations
WASH-Water, Sanitation and Hygeine
WHO-World Health Organization

Appendix-1

FAQs on Sustainable Development Summit, 2015

(Press Kit for the Sustainable Development Summit 2015: Time for Global Action for People and Planet)

FREQUENTLY ASKED QUESTIONS

What is sustainable development?

- Sustainable development has been defined as development that meets the needs of the present without compromising the ability of future generations to meet their own needs.
- Sustainable development calls for concerted efforts towards building an inclusive, sustainable and resilient future for people and planet.
- For sustainable development to be achieved, it is crucial to harmonize three core elements: economic growth, social Inclusion and environmental protection. These elements are interconnected and all are crucial for the wellbeing of individualsand societies.
- Eradicating poverty in all its forms and dimensions is an indispensable requirement for sustainable development. To this end,there must be promotion of sustainableinclusive and equitable economic growth, creating greater opportunities for all, reducing inequalities, raising basic standards of living, fostering equitable social development and inclusion, and promoting integrated and sustainable management of natural resources and ecosystems

What are the Sustainable Development Goals?

- The193 MemberStates of the United Nations reached consensus on the outcome document of a new sustainable development agenda entitled, "Transforming Our World: The 2030 Agenda for Sustainable Development".

This agenda contains 17 goals and 169 targets. The complete list of goals and targets are available at: http://www.un.org/sustainabledevelopment/sustainable–developmentgoals/The outcome document is available at: https://sustainabledevelopment.un.org/post2015/transformingourworld

- World leaders will officially adopt this universal, integratedand transformative agenda inSeptember to spur actions that will end poverty and build a more sustainable world over the next 15 years.
- This agenda builds on the achievements of the Millennium Development Goals (MDGs), which were adopted in 2000 and guided development action for thelast 15 years. The MDGs have proven that global goals can lift millions out of poverty.
- The new goals are part of an ambitious, boldsustainable development agenda that will focus on the three interconnected elements of sustainable development: economic growth, social inclusion and environmental protection
- The Sustainable Development Goals (SDGs) and targets are global in nature and universally applicable, taking into account different national realities, capacities and levels of development and respecting national policies and priorities. They are notindependent from each other—they need to be implemented in an integrated manner.
- The SDGs are the result of a threeyearlong transparent, participatory process inclusive of all stakeholders and people's voices. They represent an unprecedented agreement around sustainable development priorities among 193 Member States. They have received worldwide support from civil society, business, Parliamentariansand other actors. The decision to launch a process to develop a set of SDGs was made by UN Member States at the United Nations Conference on Sustainable Development (Rio+20), held in Rio de Janeiro in June 2012.

What are the elementsunderpinningthe Sustainable DevelopmentGoals?

- The Goals and targets will stimulate action over the next 15years in areas of critical importance: people, planet, prosperity, peace and partnership.
- People, as we are determined to end poverty and hunger, in all their forms and dimensions, and to ensure that all human beings can fulfil their potential in dignity and equality and in a healthy environment.
- Planet,to protect the planet from degradation, including through sustainableconsumption and production, sustainably managing its

natural resources and taking urgent action on climate change, so that it can support the needs of the present and future generations.

- Prosperity,to ensure that all human beings can enjoy prosperous and fulfilling lives and that economic, social and technological progress occurs in harmony with nature.
- Peace, to foster peaceful, just and inclusive societies free from fear and violence. There can be no sustainable development without peace and no peace without sustainable development.
- Partnership,tomobilize the means required to implement this agenda through a revitalised global partnership for sustainable development, based on a spirit of strengthened global solidarity, focussed in particular on the needs of the poorest and most vulnerable and withthe participation of all countries, all stakeholders and all people.

Why are new goals being adopted this year?

- The Millennium Development Goals thatwere launchedin 2000 set 2015 as the target year. Recognizing the success of the Goals–and the fact that a new development agenda was needed beyond 2015–countries agreed in 2012 at Rio+20, the UN Conference on Sustainable Development,to establish an open working group to develop a set of sustainable development goals for consideration andappropriate action.
- After more than a year of negotiations, the Open Working Group presented its recommendation for the 17 sustainable development goals.
- In early August 2015, the 193 member states of the United Nations reached consensus on the outcomedocument of the new agenda "Transforming Our World: The 2030 Agenda for Sustainable Development".
- Member States decided that the UN summit for the adoption of new sustainable developmentagenda with its 17 goals will be held from 25 to 27 September 2015,in New York and convened as a highlevel plenary meeting of the General Assembly.

Why are theSustainable DevelopmentGoals so broad in comparison to the MillenniumDevelopmentGoals which were very specific?

- There are 17 sustainable development goals with 169 targets,in contrast to the 8 Millennium Development Goals with 21 targets. The complex challenges that exist in the world today demand that a wide range of issues becovered. It is, also, critical to addresstheroot causes of the problemsand not only the symptoms.
- The Sustainable Development Goals are the result of a negotiation process that involved the 193 UN MemberStates and also saw unprecedented participation of civil society and other stakeholders

This ledto the representation of a wide range of interestsand perspectives. On the other hand, theMDGs were produced by a group of experts behind closeddoors.

- The SDGs are broad in scope because they will address the interconnected elements of sustainable development: economic growth, social inclusionand environmental protection. The MDGs focused primarily on the social agenda.
- The MDGs targeted developing countries, particularly the poorest, while the Sustainable Development Goals will apply tothe entire world, developed and developing countries.

Aren't 17 SDGs and 169 targets too many, too ambiguous and unrealistic?

- Poverty eradication, shared prosperity and planetary sustainability cannot be reduced to a simple formula.
- The SDGs represent the shared global goals and targets that will be tailored at the country level, informed by context–based evidence.

Howare theSDGs different from the MDGs?

- The 17 Sustainable Development Goalswith 169 targets are broaderin scope and will go further than the MDGs by addressing the root causes of poverty and the universal need for development that works for all people.These goals will cover the three dimensions of sustainable development: economic growth, social inclusionand environmental protection.
- Building on the success and momentum of the MDGs, the new global goals will cover more ground with ambitions to addressin equalities, economic growth, decent jobs, cities and human settlements, industrialization, energy, climate change, sustainable consumption and production, peace and justice.
- The new goals are universal and apply to all countries, whereas the MDGs were intended for action in developing countriesonly
- A core featureof the SDGs has been the means of implementation– the mobilization of financial resourcesas well as capacitybuilding and the transfer of environmentally sound technologies
- The new goals recognize that tackling climate change is essential for sustainabledevelopmentand poverty eradication. SDG 13 aimsto promoteurgent action to combat climate change and its impacts.

Civil society has participated in the process of negotiations for the new sustainable development agenda. How can we quantify their contribution to the final document?

- The negotiating process on the sustainable development goals involved the unprecedentedparticipation of civil societyand other stakeholders, such as the private sector and mayors

- During the negotiations,civil societyand other stakeholders were able to speakdirectly to government representatives.
- Many young people werealsoinvolved from the beginning on social media platformsand the UN's global My World survey that received more than 7 million votes from around the world, with approximately 75% of participants under 30 years of age
- How much will the implementation of this new sustainable development agenda cost?
- The means of implementation –how to mobilize the financial resources to achieve the sustainable development agenda is a core feature of the new agenda.
- This ambitious agenda will require the mobilization of significant resources—in the trillions of dollars. But these resourcesalready exist. There are far more than enough savings in the world to finance the new agenda.
- Resources need to be mobilized from domestic and international sources, as well as fromthe public and private sectors.
- Official development assistance is still necessary to help finance sustainable development to assistthe least developed countries.
- The agenda can be met within the framework of a revitalized global partnership for sustainable development, supported by the concrete policies and actions as outlined in the Addis Ababa Action Agenda, the outcome document of the Third International Conference on Financing for Development held in July.

How will the new development agenda be implemented?

- Implementation and success will rely on countries' own sustainable development policies, plans and programmes, andwill beled by countries. The SDGs will be a compass for aligning countries' plans with theirglobal commitments.
- Nationally ownedand country–led sustainable development strategies will require equivalent resource mobilization and financing strategies.
- The 17 SDGs and 169 targets of the new agenda will be Monitoredand reviewed using a set of global indicators. The global indicator framework, to be developed by the Inter Agency and Expert Group on SDG Indicators, will be agreed on by the UN Statistical Commission by March 2016.
- Governments will also develop their own national indicators to assist in monitoring progress made on thegoals and targets
- The follow–up and review process will be undertaken on an annual basis by the High Level Political Forum on Sustainable development

through a SDG Progress Report to be prepared by the Secretary General.

- The means of implementation of the SDGs will be monitored and reviewed as outlined in the Addis Ababa Action Agenda, the outcome document of the Financing for Development Conference, to ensure that financial resources are effectively mobilizedto support the new sustainable development agenda.
- A Technology Facilitation Mechanism, to be launched at the September Summit, will address the technology needs of developing countries, the options to address thoseneeds and capacity building. Recognizing the central role of technological cooperation for the achievement of sustainable development, countries agreed on this mechanism at the Financing for Development Conference

How does climate change relate to sustainable development?

- We are already seeing that climate change is impacting publichealth, food and water security, migration, peace and security. Investments in sustainable development will help address climate change by reducing emissions and building climate resilience. Action on climate change will drive sustainable developmentand viceversa.
- Climate change, left unchecked, will roll back the development gains we have made over the last decadesand will make further gains impossible.
- Tackling climate change and fostering sustainable development are two mutually reinforcing sides ofthe same coin; sustainable development cannot be achieved without climate action, asmany of the SDGs are actually addressing the core drivers of climate change.

How does the climate component of the SDGs influence the debate on climate change and the upcoming climate change conference in Paris later this year?

- The consensus reached on the outcomedocument of the new sustainable development agendadoes not aim to anticipate or usurp the role of the United Nations Framework Convention on Climate Change, the body responsible for the Climate Change Conference in Paris in December.
- Nevertheless, the agreement willsend a strong signal that the world has high expectationsthat the time has come for decisive positive outcomes on matters of climate change.
- Given that many of the SDGs guide action on the core drivers of climate change, their implementation, beginningon 1 January 2016,will accelerate transition towards the implementation of the climate agreement that will enter into force in 2020.

What have the MDGsaccomplished?

- The MDGs have produced the most successful anti–poverty movement in history and will serve as the springboard for the new sustainable development agenda.
- Poverty and hunger: only two short decades ago, nearly half of the developing world lived in extreme poverty. The number of people now living in extreme poverty has declined by more than half, fallingfrom 1.9 billion in 1990 to 836 million in 2015.
- Gender equality: The world has also witnessed dramatic improvement in gender equality in schooling since the MDGs, and gender parity in primary school has been achieved in the majority of countries. More girls are now in school, and women have gained ground in parliamentary representation over the past 20 years in nearly 90% of the 174 countries with data.
- Child mortality: globally, the under–five mortality rate dropped from 90 to 43 deaths per 1,000 live birthsbetween 1990 and 2015.
- Maternal health: the maternal mortality ratio shows a decline of 45% worldwide, with most of the reduction occurring since 2000.
- Fighting diseases: new infection ratesfromHIV fell approximately by 40% between 2000 and 2013. Over 6.2 million malaria deaths were averted between 2000 and 2015, while tuberculosis prevention, diagnosis and treatment interventions saved an estimated 37 million lives between 2000 and 2013.
- Sanitation: Worldwide, 2.1 billion have gained access to improved sanitation and the proportion of people practicing open defecation has fallen almost by half since 1990.
- Global partnership: official development assistance from developed countries saw an increase of 66% in real terms from 2000 and 2014, reaching $135.2 billion.

What are the remaining gaps left by the MDGs?

- About 800 million people still live in extreme poverty and 795 million still suffer from hunger.
- Between 2000 and 2015, the number of children out of school declined by almost half. However, there are still 57 million children who are denied the right to primary education.
- Gender inequality persists in spite of more representation of women in parliament and more girls going to school. Women continue to face discrimination in access to work, economic assets and participation in private and public decision–making.
- Economic gaps still existbetween the poorest and richest households and rural and urban areas.Children from the poorest 20% of

households are more than twice as likely to be stunted as those from the wealthiest 20% and are also four times as likely to be out of school. Improved sanitation facilities are only covering half of rural population, as opposed to 82% in urban areas.

- While the mortality rate for children under five dropped by 53 per cent between 1990 and 2015, child deaths continue to be increasingly concentrated in the poorest regions and in the first month of life.

How will progress of the SDGs be measured? How many indicators will be developed forthe 169 targets of the Sustainable Development Goals?

- The 17 goals and 169 targets will be monitoredand reviewed using a set of global indicators. These will be complemented by indicators at the regional and national levels,which will be developed by Member States.
- The Inter Agency and Expert Group on SDG Indicators will develop the global indicator framework which the UN Statistical Commission will subsequently agree on in March 2016. Thereafter,the Economic and Social Council and the General Assemblywill adopt these indicators
- Chief statisticians from Member States are working on the identification of the targetswith the aim to have 2 indicators for each target. There will beapproximately 300 indicators for all the targets. Where the targets cover cross–cutting issues,however,the number of indicators may be reduced.

When are the SDGs expected to start and end?

- The SDGs are expected to start on 1 January 2016 and to be achieved by 31December 2030. However, some targets that build on pre–set international agreements are expected to be achieved even earlier than the end of 2030.

Appendix - 2

The Paris Agreement: Turning Point for a Climate Solution

(by David Waskow and Jennifer Morgan - December 12, 2015)

[*WRI experts YamideDagnet, Eliza Northrop, Heather McGray, Athena Ballesteros, Joe Thwaites and Niranjali Amerasinghe contributed to this post.*]

'Today marks an historic turning point in global action on climate change. At the UN Climate Conference in Paris, known as COP21, 196 countries joined together in theParis Agreement, a universal pact that sets the world on a course to a zero-carbon, resilient, prosperous and fair future. While the Agreement is not enough by itself to solve the problem, it places us clearly on the path to a truly global solution.

Building on the foundation of national climate plans from 187 countries, the Paris Agreement is a reflection of the remarkable momentum from cities, companies, civil society groups and others that complement the global will to act that has grown over the years since the first international conference on climate change in 1992.

The Paris Agreement will maintain and accelerate that momentum. It offers clear direction with:

- long-term goals and signals,
- a commitment to return regularly to make climate action stronger,
- a response to the impact of extreme climate events on the most vulnerable,
- the transparency needed to ensure action takes place and
- finance, capacity building and technology to enable real change.

But the Agreement does even more: it marks a new type of international cooperation where developed and developing countries are united in a common framework, and all are involved, engaged contributors. It reflects the growing recognition that climate action offers tremendous opportunities and benefits, and that climate impacts can be tackled effectively, with the unity of purpose that has brought us to this moment.

The moment in Paris extended far beyond the Agreement itself. Cities and forests, business and finance – all these were part of the many initiatives and commitments that were launched or strengthened over the past two weeks. And they will be key to the solution as action moves forward with the energy generated by Paris.

Key Provisions

Long-Term Mitigation Goals

The Paris Agreement sets landmark goals for taking action on climate change, aiming to keep temperature rise to well below 2 degrees C (3.6 degrees F) and to pursue efforts to keep it to limit temperature increase to 1.5 degrees C (2.7 degrees F). To achieve this, countries will aim to peak global emissions as soon as possible and – remarkably – countries agreed to reduce emissions rapidly to reach net-zero greenhouse gas (GHG) emissions in the second half of the century. They will do that taking equity, sustainable development and poverty into account.

Five-Year Cycles of Action

To build on the momentum from countries' national climate plans put forward for Paris, countries have agreed to a process to ramp up action on emissions every five years. By 2020, countries have agreed to come back and either submit new or updated national climate plans (known as nationally determined contributions). Every five years after that, countries will submit new contributions. Countries have also agreed that their mitigation plans will represent a progression beyond their previous efforts.

Five-Year Comprehensive Global Stocktake

The Agreement establishes a strong process for countries to regularly assess implementation and take stock of climate action every five years, called the Global Stocktake. This will assess implementation of action on mitigation, adaptation and support, including finance, and inform implementation of countries' climate plans. Assessment will start in 2023, but countries have agreed to return in 2018 to review implementation of mitigation measures to inform their 2020 mitigation contributions.

Adaptation

Adaptation to climate change is a central issue for global climate action in this Agreement, where it is on par with mitigation. It establishes a global goal of enhancing adaptive capacity, strengthening resilience and reducing vulnerability, including an adequate adaptation response given the Agreement's temperature goal. The Agreement creates a cycle of action for strengthening adaptation efforts regularly, similar to the mitigation cycle. Countries will have flexibility on the timing and methods for communicating information about their adaptation activities or efforts. Support will be provided to developing countries for planning, implementation and communication of adaptation activities.

Loss and Damage

The Agreement addresses the important issue of loss and damage, referring to the serious impacts of climate change when mitigation and adaptation fail. Those people who are affected by climate change may face damage to their property or health, or in worse cases, permanent loss of land or livelihoods, or even loss of life. The Agreement acknowledges the issue of loss and damage as separate from adaptation, and makes permanent the Warsaw International Mechanism (WIM) on Loss and Damage, established two years ago to find ways to address these issues. The outcome also establishes a task force on climate change-related displacement within the WIM, and makes clear that the loss and damage provision does not create new legal liability for emitting countries.

Finance

Finance will provide the needed power to turn the world toward a zero-carbon, climate-resilient future, and the purpose of the Agreement states that all financial flows – both public and private – need to be shifted from high to low emissions activities and risky to resilient investments. The Agreement makes clear that developed countries will continue to provide and mobilize finance to support developing countries, and developed countries agreed to continue their 2020 commitment of mobilizing $100 billion a year until 2025. For the period after that, governments will adopt a new, higher, collective goal, though the extent to which finance will increase, and who will mobilize it, is a significant outstanding question. The Agreement opens the door for developing countries to provide support to their peers, recognizing that some developing countries are already doing so.

In addition, governments agreed to balance public funding between adaptation and mitigation, and agreed to significantly increase support for adaptation before 2020, which is of vital importance for the most vulnerable countries dealing with the impacts of a warmer world. Countries also committed to improve reporting on finance, with everyone providing information about finance provided or received, as appropriate.

Transparency

The Agreement establishes a common system for transparency for all countries. Through an enhanced transparency framework all countries will be required to report on their emissions and track progress on achieving their nationally determined contributions regularly. The information provided by all parties will be subject to an expert review and facilitative multilateral consideration of progress. The framework provides flexibility and support that takes account of different countries' capacities. Developed countries will report on the finance and support they provide, and developing countries will report on the finance and support needed and received.

Capacity Building

For the new international climate agreement to be universal, countries acknowledged that effective capacity building is vital to enable developing countries to take strong climate action. To elevate this issue, countries established the new Paris Committee on Capacity Building to oversee a work plan to enhance capacity building. The Committee will identify capacity gaps and needs, foster international cooperation and identify opportunities to strengthen capacity for climate action.

Legal Form

The Paris Agreement is a universal, legal agreement under the UNFCCC, with the participation of all countries. It will be open for signature next April, and will come into force in January 2020. Notably, the Agreement contains a strong, legally binding framework for reporting, transparency and review of implementation capable of driving greater ambition to tackle climate change. The establishment of a mechanism to facilitate implementation and promote compliance will provide further assurance of Parties' actions.

Climate Conference Highlights

COP21's outcome fulfilled the promise of its opening day, when more than 150 heads of state and government converged in Paris to express their commitment to climate action and a viable agreement. On the same day, 20 countries and 27 representatives from the private sector announced a multi-billion dollar clean energy fund and commitment to increase R&D investments, a major boost to the talks. This set the stage for more progress on climate action across a wide spectrum of areas.

Forests and Restoration

Opening day, November 30, also saw significant government commitments to protect forests, including $5 billion in funding from Germany, Norway and the United Kingdom. Global Forest Watch Climate, launched during the conference, offers the potential to shift the debate on monitoring forest-based emissions. TheAfrican Forest and Landscapes Restoration Initiative (AFR100) seeks to restore 100 million hectares (nearly 250 million acres) of degraded and deforested land in Africa by 2030.Initiative 20x20 is landscape restoration effort in Latin America and the Caribbean that has now reached nearly 28 million hectares (nearly 70 million acres) and $730 million in investment.

Cities

Building efficiency, sustainable mobility and interactive tools were among the city-level solutions advanced to prevent carbon-intensive congestion, sprawl and inefficiencies from locking in for decades to come. WRI announced 25 new partnersto the Building Efficiency Accelerator as part of the UN SE4All initiative and presented the New Climate Economy message of better transport, better climate. A coalition including WRI advanced the Paris Process on Mobility and Climate to position mitigation and adaptation contributions from transport sector. Along with UK DECC, WRI demonstrated the 2050 Global Calculator, an interactive model – WRI contributed the transport section that allows users to explore 2 degrees C pathways. Looking ahead, the UN announced the Climate Action 2016 conference to deepen and expand action in six focus areas—with cities and transport being key.

Business

More than 114 companies committed to set emissions reduction targets in line withScience Based Targets, using what scientists say is necessary to keep global warming below 2 degrees C. Participating companies have combined annual carbon dioxide emissions equivalent to what125 coal-fired power plants emit in a year. Goldman Sachs announced plans to invest $150 billion in clean energy projects and technology.The investment bank previously had a target to invest $40 billion in clean energy technologies by 2012, and will now almost quadruple that by 2025. Google added 842 megawatts of renewable energy capacity around the world, nearly doubling the amount of renewables it has purchased to 2 gigawatts, equivalent to taking nearly 1 million cars off the road.

Investment

Institutional investors and banks signaled their plans to build climate change considerations into their decisions. Allianz and ABP officially joined the Portfolio Carbon Initiative, bringing the value of the Coalition's assets under management to $600 billion. Five Principles for Mainstreaming Climate Action within Financial Institutions also launched, with more than two dozen financial institutions indicating their intent to incorporate climate change into strategies and operations. An alliance of global investors, development banks, financial sector associations and NGOs launched the Green Infrastructure

Investment Coalition to support the accelerated financing of green infrastructure through investor-government global and regional dialogues, and 27 global investors issued the Paris Green Bonds Statement to support policies that drive the development of long term, sustainable global markets in green bonds.Bottom of Form

Appendix-3 Revised list of global Sustainable Development Goal indicators (General Assembly resolution 68/261)

Appendix - 3

Revised list of global Sustainable Development Goal indicators

(General Assembly resolution 68/261)

Sustainable Development Goal indicators should be disaggregated, where relevant, by income, sex, age, race, ethnicity, migratory status, disability and geographic location, or other characteristics, in accordance with the Fundamental Principles of Official Statistics

Goals and targets (from the 2030 Agenda) Indicators

Goal 1. End poverty in all its forms everywhere

1.1 By 2030, eradicate extreme poverty for all people everywhere, currently measured as people living on less than $1.25 a day

1.1.1 Proportion of population below the international poverty line, by sex, age, employment status and geographical location (urban/rural)

1.2 By 2030, reduce at least by half the proportion of men, women and children of all ages living in poverty in all its dimensions according to national definitions

1.2.1 Proportion of population living below the national poverty line, by sex and age

1.2.2 Proportion of men, women and children of all ages living in poverty in all its dimensions according to national definitions

1.3 Implement nationally appropriate social protection systems and measures for all, including floors, and by 2030 achieve substantial coverage of the poor and the vulnerable

1.3.1 Proportion of population covered by social protection floors/ systems, by sex, distinguishing children, unemployed persons, older persons, persons with disabilities, pregnant women, newborns, working jury victims and the poor and the vulnerable

1.4 By 2030, ensure that all men and women, in particular the poor and the vulnerable, have equal rights to economic resources, as well as access to basic services, ownership and control over land and other forms of property, inheritance, natural resources, appropriate new technology and financial services, including microfinance

1.4.1 Proportion of population living in households with access to basic services

1.4.2 Proportion of total adult population with secure tenure rights to land, with legally recognized documentation and who perceive their rights to land as secure, by sex and by type of tenure

1.5 By 2030, build the resilience of the poor and those in vulnerable situations and reduce their exposure and vulnerability to climate-related extreme events and other economic, social and environmental shocks and disasters

1.5.1 Number of deaths, missing persons and directly affected persons attributed to disasters per 100,000 population

1.5.2 Direct economic loss attributed to disasters in relation to global gross domestic product (GDP)

Note: The present annex contains the revised list of global Sustainable Development Goal indicators, including refinements, modifications to several indicators to reflect the agreements on the Sendai Framework for Disaster Risk Reduction 2015-2030 and editorial changes. These changes are based on the final list of proposed Sustainable Development Goal indicators contained in annex IV to E/CN.3/2016/2/Rev.1, agreed by the Statistical Commission at its forty seventh session, in March 2016.

Report of the Inter-Agency and Expert Group on Sustainable Development Goal Indicators (E/CN.3/2017/2)

3/26

Goals and targets (from the 2030 Agenda) Indicators

1.5.3 Number of countries that adopt and implement national disaster risk reduction strategies in line with the Sendai Framework for Disaster Risk Reduction 2015-2030

1.5.4 Proportion of local governments that adopt and implement local disaster risk reduction strategies in line with national disaster risk reduction strategies

1.a Ensure significant mobilization of resources from a variety of sources, including through enhanced development cooperation, in order to provide adequate and predictable means for developing countries, in particular least developed countries, to implement programmes and policies to end poverty in all its dimensions

1.a.1 Proportion of domestically generated resources allocated by the government directly to poverty reduction programmes

1.a.2 Proportion of total government spending on essential services (education, health and social protection)

1.a.3 Sum of total grants and non-debt-creating inflows directly allocated to poverty reduction programmes as a proportion of GDP

1.b Create sound policy frameworks at the national,regional and international levels, based on pro-poor and gender-sensitive development strategies, to support accelerated investment in poverty eradication actions

1.b.1 Proportion of government recurrent and capital spending to sectors that disproportionately benefit women, the poor and vulnerable groups

Goal 2. End hunger, achieve food security and improved nutrition and promote sustainable agriculture

2.1 By 2030, end hunger and ensure access by all people, in particular the poor and people in vulnerable situations, including infants, to safe, nutritious and sufficient food all year round

2.1.1 Prevalence of undernourishment

2.1.2 Prevalence of moderate or severe food insecurity in the population, based on the Food Insecurity Experience Scale (FIES)

2.2 By 2030, end all forms of malnutrition, including achieving, by 2025, the internationally agreed targets on stunting and wasting in children under 5 years of age,and address the nutritional needs of adolescent girls,pregnant and lactating women and older persons 2.2.1 Prevalence of stunting (height for age <-2 standard deviation from the median of the World Health Organization (WHO) Child Growth Standards) among children under 5 years of age

2.2.2 Prevalence of malnutrition (weight for height >+2 or <-2 standard deviation from the median of the WHO Child Growth Standards) among children under 5 years of age, by type (wasting and overweight)

2.3 By 2030, double the agricultural productivity and incomes of small-scale food producers, in particular women, indigenous peoples, family farmers, pastoralists and fishers, including through secure and equal access to land, other productive resources and inputs, knowledge, financial services, markets and opportunities for value addition and non-farm employment

2.3.1 Volume of production per labour unit by classes of farming/ pastoral/forestry enterprise size

2.3.2 Average income of small-scale food producers,by sex and indigenous status

Report of the Inter-Agency and Expert Group on Sustainable Development Goal Indicators (E/CN.3/2017/2)

4/26

Goals and targets (from the 2030 Agenda) Indicators

2.4 By 2030, ensure sustainable food production systems and implement resilient agricultural practices that increase productivity and production, that help maintain ecosystems, that strengthen capacity for adaptation to climate change, extreme weather, drought,flooding and other disasters and that progressively improve land and soil quality

2.4.1 Proportion of agricultural area under productive and sustainable agriculture

2.5 By 2020, maintain the genetic diversity of seeds, cultivated plants and farmed and domesticated animals and their related wild species, including through soundly managed and diversified seed and plant banks at the national, regional and international levels, and promote access to and fair and equitable sharing of benefits arising from the utilization of genetic resources and associated traditional knowledge, as internationally agreed

2.5.1 Number of plant and animal genetic resources for food and agriculture secured in either medium or long-term conservation facilities

2.5.2 Proportion of local breeds classified as being at risk, not-at-risk or at unknown level of risk of extinction

2.a Increase investment, including through enhanced international cooperation, in rural infrastructure, agricultural research and extension services, technology development and plant and livestock gene banks in order to enhance agricultural productive capacity in developing countries, in particular least developed countries

2.a.1 The agriculture orientation index for government expenditures

2.a.2 Total official flows (official development assistance plus other official flows) to the agriculture sector

2.b Correct and prevent trade restrictions and distortions in world agricultural markets, including through the parallel elimination of all forms of agricultural export subsidies and all export measures with equivalent effect, in accordance with the mandate of the Doha Development Round

2.b.1 Agricultural export subsidies

2.c Adopt measures to ensure the proper functioning of food commodity markets and their derivatives and facilitate timely access to market information, including on food reserves, in order to help limit extreme food price volatility

2.c.1 Indicator of food price anomalies

Goal 3. Ensure healthy lives and promote well-being for all at all ages

3.1 By 2030, reduce the global maternal mortality ratio to less than 70 per 100,000 live births

3.1.1 Maternal mortality ratio

3.1.2 Proportion of births attended by skilled health personnel

3.2 By 2030, end preventable deaths of newborns and children under 5 years of age, with all countries aiming to reduce neonatal mortality to at least as low as 12 per 1,000 live births and under-5 mortality to at least as low as 25 per 1,000 live births

3.2.1 Under-five mortality rate

3.2.2 Neonatal mortality rate

Report of the Inter-Agency and Expert Group on Sustainable Development Goal Indicators (E/CN.3/2017/2) 5/26

Goals and targets (from the 2030 Agenda) Indicators

3.3 By 2030, end the epidemics of AIDS, tuberculosis, malaria and neglected tropical diseases and combat hepatitis, water-borne diseases and other communicable diseases

3.3.1 Number of new HIV infections per 1,000 uninfected population, by sex, age and key populations

3.3.2 Tuberculosis incidence per 100,000 population

3.3.3 Malaria incidence per 1,000 population

3.3.4 Hepatitis B incidence per 100,000 population

3.3.5 Number of people requiring interventions against neglected tropical diseases

3.4 By 2030, reduce by one third premature mortality from non-communicable diseases through prevention and treatment and promote mental health and well-being

- 3.4.1 Mortality rate attributed to cardiovascular disease, cancer, diabetes or chronic respiratory disease
- 3.4.2 Suicide mortality rate

3.5 Strengthen the prevention and treatment of substance abuse, including narcotic drug abuse and harmful use of alcohol

- 3.5.1 Coverage of treatment interventions (pharmacological, psychosocial and rehabilitation and aftercare services) for substance use disorders
- 3.5.2 Harmful use of alcohol, defined according to the national context as alcohol per capita consumption (aged 15 years and older) within a calendar year in litres of pure alcohol

3.6 By 2020, halve the number of global deaths and injuries from road traffic accidents

- 3.6.1 Death rate due to road traffic injuries

3.7 By 2030, ensure universal access to sexual and reproductive health-care services, including for family planning, information and education, and the integration of reproductive health into national strategies and programmes

- 3.7.1 Proportion of women of reproductive age (aged 15-49 years) who have their need for family planning satisfied with modern methods
- 3.7.2 Adolescent birth rate (aged 10-14 years; aged 15-19 years) per 1,000 women in that age group

3.8 Achieve universal health coverage, including financial risk protection, access to quality essential health-care services and access to safe, effective, quality and affordable essential medicines and vaccines for all

- 3.8.1 Coverage of essential health services (defined as the average coverage of essential services based on tracer interventions that include reproductive,maternal, newborn and child health, infectious diseases, non-communicable diseases and service capacity and access, among the general and the most disadvantaged population)
- 3.8.2 Proportion of population with large household expenditures on health as a share of total household expenditure or income

3.9 By 2030, substantially reduce the number of deaths and illnesses from hazardous chemicals and air, water and soil pollution and contamination

- 3.9.1 Mortality rate attributed to household and ambient air pollution

Report of the Inter-Agency and Expert Group on Sustainable Development Goal Indicators (E/CN.3/2017/2)

6/26

Goals and targets (from the 2030 Agenda) Indicators

3.9.2 Mortality rate attributed to unsafe water, unsafe sanitation and lack of hygiene (exposure to unsafe Water, Sanitation and Hygiene for All (WASH) services)

3.9.3 Mortality rate attributed to unintentional poisoning

3.a Strengthen the implementation of the World Health Organization Framework Convention on Tobacco Control in all countries, as appropriate

3.a.1 Age-standardized prevalence of current tobacco use among persons aged 15 years and older

3.b Support the research and development of vaccines and medicines for the communicable and non-communicable diseases that primarily affect developing countries, provide access to affordable essential medicines and vaccines, in accordance with the Doha Declaration on the TRIPS Agreement and Public Health, which affirms the right of developing countries to use to the full the provisions in the Agreement on Trade-Related Aspects of Intellectual Property Rights regarding flexibilities to protect public health, and, in particular, provide access to medicines for all

3.b.1 Proportion of the target population covered by all vaccines included in their national programme

3.b.2 Total net official development assistance to medical research and basic health sectors

3.b.3 Proportion of health facilities that have a core set of relevant essential medicines available and affordable on a sustainable basis

3.c Substantially increase health financing and the recruitment, development, training and retention of the health workforce in developing countries, especially in least developed countries and small island developing States

3.c.1 Health worker density and distribution

3.d Strengthen the capacity of all countries, in particular developing countries, for early warning, risk reduction and management of national and global health risks

3.d.1 International Health Regulations (IHR) capacity and health emergency preparedness

Goal 4. Ensure inclusive and equitable quality education and promote lifelong learning opportunities for all

4.1 By 2030, ensure that all girls and boys complete free, equitable and quality primary and secondary education leading to relevant and effective learning outcomes

4.1.1 Proportion of children and young people:

(a) in grades 2/3; (b) at the end of primary; and (c) at the end of lower secondary achieving at least a minimum proficiency level in (i) reading and (ii) mathematics, by sex

4.2 By 2030, ensure that all girls and boys have access to quality early childhood development, care and pre-primary education so that they are ready for primary education

4.2.1 Proportion of children under 5 years of age who are developmentally on track in health, learning and psychosocial well-being, by sex

4.2.2 Participation rate in organized learning (one year before the official primary entry age), by sex

Report of the Inter-Agency and Expert Group on Sustainable Development Goal Indicators (E/CN.3/2017/2)

7/26

Goals and targets (from the 2030 Agenda) Indicators

4.3 By 2030, ensure equal access for all women and men to affordable and quality technical, vocational and tertiary education, including university

4.3.1 Participation rate of youth and adults in formal and non-formal education and training in the previous 12 months, by sex

4.4 By 2030, substantially increase the number of youth and adults who have relevant skills, including technical and vocational skills, for employment, decent jobs and entrepreneurship

4.4.1 Proportion of youth and adults with information and communications technology (ICT) skills, by type of skill

4.5 By 2030, eliminate gender disparities in education and ensure equal access to all levels of education and vocational training for the vulnerable, including persons with disabilities, indigenous peoples and children in vulnerable situations

4.5.1 Parity indices (female/male, rural/urban,bottom/top wealth quintile and others such as disability status, indigenous peoples and conflict affected,as data become available) for all education indicators on this list that can be disaggregated

4.6 By 2030, ensure that all youth and a substantial proportion of adults, both men and women, achieve literacy and numeracy

4.6.1 Proportion of population in a given age group achieving at least a fixed level of proficiency in functional (a) literacy and (b) numeracy skills, by sex

4.7 By 2030, ensure that all learners acquire the knowledge and skills needed to promote sustainable development, including, among others, through education for sustainable development and sustainable lifestyles, human rights, gender equality, promotion of a culture of peace and non-violence, global citizenship and appreciation of cultural diversity and of culture's contribution to sustainable development

4.7.1 Extent to which (i) global citizenship education and (ii) education for sustainable development, including gender equality and human rights, are mainstreamed at all levels in: (a) national education policies; (b) curricula; (c) teacher education; and (d) student assessment

4.a Build and upgrade education facilities that are child, disability and gender sensitive and provide safe,non-violent, inclusive and effective learning environments for all

4.a.1 Proportion of schools with access to:

(a) electricity; (b) the Internet for pedagogical purposes; (c) computers for pedagogical purposes; (d) adapted infrastructure and materials for students with disabilities; (e) basic drinking water; (f) single sex basic sanitation facilities; and (g) basic handwashing facilities (as per the WASH indicator definitions)

4.b By 2020, substantially expand globally the number of scholarships available to developing countries, in particular least developed countries, small island developing States and African countries, for enrolment in higher education, including vocational training and information and communications technology, technical,engineering and scientific programmes, in developed countries and other developing countries

4.b.1 Volume of official development assistance flows for scholarships by sector and type of study

Report of the Inter-Agency and Expert Group on Sustainable Development Goal Indicators (E/CN.3/2017/2)

8/26

Goals and targets (from the 2030 Agenda) Indicators

4.c By 2030, substantially increase the supply of qualified teachers, including through international cooperation for teacher training in developing countries,especially least developed countries and small island developing States

4.c.1 Proportion of teachers in: (a) pre-primary;(b) primary; (c) lower secondary; and (d) upper secondary education who have received at least the minimum organized teacher training (e.g. pedagogical training) pre-service or in-service required for teaching at the relevant level in a given country

Goal 5. Achieve gender equality and empower all women and girls

5.1 End all forms of discrimination against all women and girls everywhere

5.1.1 Whether or not legal frameworks are in place to promote, enforce and monitor equality and non-discrimination on the basis of sex

5.2 Eliminate all forms of violence against all women and girls in the public and private spheres, including trafficking and sexual and other types of exploitation

5.2.1 Proportion of ever-partnered women and girls aged 15 years and older subjected to physical, sexual or psychological violence by a current or former intimate partner in the previous 12 months, by form of violence and by age

5.2.2 Proportion of women and girls aged 15 years and older subjected to sexual violence by persons other than an intimate partner in the previous 12 months, by age and place of occurrence

5.3 Eliminate all harmful practices, such as child, early and forced marriage and female genital mutilation

5.3.1 Proportion of women aged 20-24 years who were married or in a union before age 15 and before age 18

5.3.2 Proportion of girls and women aged 15-49 years who have undergone female genital mutilation/cutting,by age

5.4 Recognize and value unpaid care and domestic work through the provision of public services, infrastructure and social protection policies and the promotion of shared responsibility within the household and the family as nationally appropriate

5.4.1 Proportion of time spent on unpaid domestic and care work, by sex, age and location

5.5 Ensure women's full and effective participation and equal opportunities for leadership at all levels of decision-making in political, economic and public life

5.5.1 Proportion of seats held by women in (a) national parliaments and (b) local governments

5.5.2 Proportion of women in managerial positions

5.6 Ensure universal access to sexual and reproductive health and reproductive rights as agreed in accordance with the Programme of Action of the International Conference on Population and Development and the Beijing Platform for Action and the outcome documents of their review conferences

5.6.1 Proportion of women aged 15-49 years who make their own informed decisions regarding sexual relations, contraceptive use and reproductive health care

Report of the Inter-Agency and Expert Group on Sustainable Development Goal Indicators (E/CN.3/2017/2)

9/26

Goals and targets (from the 2030 Agenda) Indicators

5.6.2 Number of countries with laws and regulations that guarantee full and equal access to women and men aged 15 years and older to sexual and reproductive health care, information and education

5.a Undertake reforms to give women equal rights to economic resources, as well as access to ownership and control over land and other forms of property, financial services, inheritance and natural resources, in accordance with national laws

5.a.1 (a) Proportion of total agricultural population with ownership or secure rights over agricultural land, by sex; and (b) share of women among owners or rights-bearers of agricultural land, by type of tenure

5.a.2 Proportion of countries where the legal framework (including customary law) guarantees women's equal rights to land ownership and/or control

5.b Enhance the use of enabling technology, in particular information and communications technology,to promote the empowerment of women

5.b.1 Proportion of individuals who own a mobile telephone, by sex

5.c Adopt and strengthen sound policies and enforceable legislation for the promotion of gender equality and the empowerment of all women and girls at all levels

5.c.1 Proportion of countries with systems to track and make public allocations for gender equality and women's empowerment

Goal 6. Ensure availability and sustainable management of water and sanitation for all

6.1 By 2030, achieve universal and equitable access to safe and affordable drinking water for all

6.1.1 Proportion of population using safely managed drinking water services

6.2 By 2030, achieve access to adequate and equitable sanitation and hygiene for all and end open defecation, paying special attention to the needs of women and girls and those in vulnerable situations

6.2.1 Proportion of population using safely managed sanitation services, including a hand-washing facility with soap and water

6.3 By 2030, improve water quality by reducing pollution, eliminating dumping and minimizing release of hazardous chemicals and materials, halving the proportion of untreated wastewater and substantially increasing recycling and safe reuse globally

6.3.1 Proportion of wastewater safely treated

6.3.2 Proportion of bodies of water with good ambient water quality

6.4 By 2030, substantially increase water-use efficiency across all sectors and ensure sustainable withdrawals and supply of freshwater to address water scarcity and substantially reduce the number of people suffering from water scarcity

6.4.1 Change in water-use efficiency over time

6.4.2 Level of water stress: freshwater withdrawal as a proportion of available freshwater resources

6.5 By 2030, implement integrated water resources management at all levels, including through transboundary cooperation as appropriate

6.5.1 Degree of integrated water resources management implementation (0-100)

6.5.2 Proportion of transboundary basin area with an operational arrangement for water cooperation

Report of the Inter-Agency and Expert Group on Sustainable Development Goal Indicators (E/CN.3/2017/2)

10/26

Goals and targets (from the 2030 Agenda) Indicators

6.6 By 2020, protect and restore water-related ecosystems, including mountains, forests, wetlands, rivers, aquifers and lakes

6.6.1 Change in the extent of water-related ecosystems over time

6.a By 2030, expand international cooperation and capacity-building support to developing countries in water- and sanitation-related activities and programmes, including water harvesting, desalination, water efficiency, wastewater treatment, recycling and reuse technologies

6.a.1 Amount of water- and sanitation-related official development assistance that is part of a government-coordinated spending plan

6.b Support and strengthen the participation of local communities in improving water and sanitation management

6.b.1 Proportion of local administrative units with established and operational policies and procedures for participation of local communities in water and sanitation management

Goal 7. Ensure access to affordable, reliable, sustainable and modern energy for all

7.1 By 2030, ensure universal access to affordable,reliable and modern energy services

7.1.1 Proportion of population with access to electricity

7.1.2 Proportion of population with primary reliance on clean fuels and technology

7.2 By 2030, increase substantially the share of renewable energy in the global energy mix

7.2.1 Renewable energy share in the total final energy consumption

7.3 By 2030, double the global rate of improvement in energy efficiency

7.3.1 Energy intensity measured in terms of primary energy and GDP

7.a By 2030, enhance international cooperation to facilitate access to clean energy research and technology, including renewable energy, energy efficiency and advanced and cleaner fossil-fuel technology, and promote investment in energy infrastructure and clean energy technology

7.a.1 International financial flows to developing countries in support of clean energy research and development and renewable energy production,including in hybrid systems

7.b By 2030, expand infrastructure and upgrade technology for supplying modern and sustainable energy services for all in developing countries, in particular least developed countries, small island developing States and landlocked developing countries, in accordance with their respective programmes of support

7.b.1 Investments in energy efficiency as a proportion of GDP and the amount of foreign direct investment in financial transfer for infrastructure and technology to sustainable development services

Report of the Inter-Agency and Expert Group on Sustainable Development Goal Indicators (E/CN.3/2017/2)

11/26

Goals and targets (from the 2030 Agenda) Indicators

Goal 8. Promote sustained, inclusive and sustainable economic growth, full and productive employment and decent work for all

8.1 Sustain per capita economic growth in accordance with national circumstances and, in particular, at least 7 per cent gross domestic product growth per annum in the least developed countries

8.1.1 Annual growth rate of real GDP per capita

8.2 Achieve higher levels of economic productivity through diversification, technological upgrading and innovation, including through a focus on high-value added and labour-intensive sectors

8.2.1 Annual growth rate of real GDP per employed person

8.3 Promote development-oriented policies that support productive activities, decent job creation, entrepreneurship, creativity and innovation, and encourage the formalization and growth of micro-, small- and medium-sized enterprises, including through access to financial services

8.3.1 Proportion of informal employment in non-agriculture employment, by sex

8.4 Improve progressively, through 2030, global resource efficiency in consumption and production and endeavour to decouple economic growth from environmental degradation, in accordance with the 10-Year Framework of Programmes on Sustainable Consumption and Production, with developed countries taking the lead

8.4.1 Material footprint, material footprint per capita, and material footprint per GDP

8.4.2 Domestic material consumption, domestic material consumption per capita, and domestic material consumption per GDP

8.5 By 2030, achieve full and productive employment and decent work for all women and men, including for young people and persons with disabilities, and equal pay for work of equal value

8.5.1 Average hourly earnings of female and male employees, by occupation, age and persons with disabilities

8.5.2 Unemployment rate, by sex, age and persons with disabilities

8.6 By 2020, substantially reduce the proportion of youth not in employment, education or training

8.6.1 Proportion of youth (aged 15-24 years) not in education, employment or training

8.7 Take immediate and effective measures to eradicate forced labour, end modern slavery and human trafficking and secure the prohibition and elimination of the worst forms of child labour, including recruitment and use of child soldiers, and by 2025 end child labour in all its forms

8.7.1 Proportion and number of children aged 5-17 years engaged in child labour, by sex and age

8.8 Protect labour rights and promote safe and secure working environments for all workers, including migrant workers, in particular women migrants, and those in precarious employment

8.8.1 Frequency rates of fatal and non-fatal occupational injuries, by sex and migrant status

Report of the Inter-Agency and Expert Group on Sustainable Development Goal Indicators (E/CN.3/2017/2)

12/26

Goals and targets (from the 2030 Agenda) Indicators

8.8.2 Level of national compliance of labour rights (freedom of association and collective bargaining) based on International Labour Organization (ILO) textual sources and national legislation, by sex and migrant status

8.9 By 2030, devise and implement policies to promote sustainable tourism that creates jobs and promotes local culture and products

8.9.1 Tourism direct GDP as a proportion of total GDP and in growth rate

8.9.2 Proportion of jobs in sustainable tourism industries out of total tourism jobs

8.10 Strengthen the capacity of domestic financial institutions to encourage and expand access to banking,insurance and financial services for all

8.10.1 (a) Number of commercial bank branches per 100,000 adults and (b) number of automated teller machines (ATMs) per 100,000 adults

8.10.2 Proportion of adults (15 years and older) with an account at a bank or other financial institution or with a mobile-money-service provider

8.a Increase Aid for Trade support for developing countries, in particular least developed countries, including through the Enhanced Integrated Framework for Trade-related Technical Assistance to Least Developed Countries

8.a.1 Aid for Trade commitments and disbursements

8.b By 2020, develop and operationalize a global strategy for youth employment and implement the Global Jobs Pact of the International Labour Organization

8.b.1 Existence of a developed and operationalized national strategy for youth employment, as a distinct strategy or as part of a national employment strategy

Goal 9. Build resilient infrastructure, promote inclusive and sustainable industrialization and foster innovation

9.1 Develop quality, reliable, sustainable and resilient infrastructure, including regional and trans-border infrastructure, to support economic development and human well-being, with a focus on affordable and equitable access for all

9.1.1 Proportion of the rural population who live within 2 km of an all-season road

9.1.2 Passenger and freight volumes, by mode of transport

9.2 Promote inclusive and sustainable industrialization and, by 2030, significantly raise industry's share of employment and gross domestic product, in line with national circumstances, and double its share in least developed countries

9.2.1 Manufacturing value added as a proportion of GDP and per capita

9.2.2 Manufacturing employment as a proportion of total employment

9.3 Increase the access of small-scale industrial and other enterprises, in particular in developing countries, to financial services, including affordable credit, and their integration into value chains and markets

9.3.1 Proportion of small-scale industries in total industry value added

9.3.2 Proportion of small-scale industries with a loan or line of credit

Report of the Inter-Agency and Expert Group on Sustainable Development Goal Indicators (E/CN.3/2017/2)

13/26

Goals and targets (from the 2030 Agenda) Indicators

9.4 By 2030, upgrade infrastructure and retrofit industries to make them sustainable, with increased resource-use efficiency and greater adoption of clean and environmentally sound technologies and industrial processes, with all countries taking action in accordance with their respective capabilities

9.4.1 CO2 emission per unit of value added

9.5 Enhance scientific research, upgrade the technological capabilities of industrial sectors in all countries, in particular developing countries, including, by 2030, encouraging innovation and substantially increasing the number of research and development workers per 1 million people and public and private research and development spending

9.5.1 Research and development expenditure as a proportion of GDP

9.5.2 Researchers (in full-time equivalent) per million inhabitants

9.a Facilitate sustainable and resilient infrastructure development in developing countries through enhanced financial, technological and technical support to African countries, least developed countries, landlocked developing countries and small island developing States

9.a.1 Total official international support (official development assistance plus other official flows) to infrastructure

9.b Support domestic technology development, research and innovation in developing countries, including by ensuring a conducive policy environment for, inter alia, industrial diversification and value addition to commodities

9.b.1 Proportion of medium and high-tech industry value added in total value added

9.c Significantly increase access to information and communications technology and strive to provide universal and affordable access to the Internet in least developed countries by 2020

9.c.1 Proportion of population covered by a mobile network, by technology

Goal 10. Reduce inequality within and among countries

10.1 By 2030, progressively achieve and sustain income growth of the bottom 40 per cent of the population at a rate higher than the national average

10.1.1 Growth rates of household expenditure or income per capita among the bottom 40 per cent of the population and the total population

10.2 By 2030, empower and promote the social, economic and political inclusion of all, irrespective of age, sex, disability, race, ethnicity, origin, religion or economic or other status

10.2.1 Proportion of people living below 50 per cent of median income, by sex, age and persons with disabilities

10.3 Ensure equal opportunity and reduce inequalities of outcome, including by eliminating discriminatory laws, policies and practices and promoting appropriate legislation, policies and action in this regard

10.3.1 Proportion of population reporting having personally felt discriminated against or harassed in the previous 12 months on the basis of a ground of discrimination prohibited under international human rights law

Report of the Inter-Agency and Expert Group on Sustainable Development Goal Indicators (E/CN.3/2017/2)

14/26

Goals and targets (from the 2030 Agenda) Indicators

10.4 Adopt policies, especially fiscal, wage and social protection policies, and progressively achieve greater equality

10.4.1 Labour share of GDP, comprising wages and social protection transfers

10.5 Improve the regulation and monitoring of global financial markets and institutions and strengthen the implementation of such regulations

10.5.1 Financial Soundness Indicators

10.6 Ensure enhanced representation and voice for developing countries in decision-making in global international economic and financial institutions in order to deliver more effective, credible, accountable and legitimate institutions

10.6.1 Proportion of members and voting rights of developing countries in international organizations

10.7 Facilitate orderly, safe, regular and responsible migration and mobility of people, including through the implementation of planned and well-managed migration policies

10.7.1 Recruitment cost borne by employee as a proportion of yearly income earned in country of destination

10.7.2 Number of countries that have implemented well-managed migration policies

10.a Implement the principle of special and differential treatment for developing countries, in particular least developed countries, in accordance with World Trade Organization agreements

10.a.1 Proportion of tariff lines applied to imports from least developed countries and developing countries with zero-tariff

10.b Encourage official development assistance and financial flows, including foreign direct investment, to States where the need is greatest, in particular least developed countries, African countries, small island developing States and landlocked developing countries, in accordance with their national plans and programmes

10.b.1 Total resource flows for development, by recipient and donor countries and type of flow (e.g. official development assistance, foreign direct investment and other flows)

10.c By 2030, reduce to less than 3 per cent the transaction costs of migrant remittances and eliminate remittance corridors with costs higher than 5 per cent

10.c.1 Remittance costs as a proportion of the amount remitted

Goal 11. Make cities and human settlements inclusive, safe, resilient and sustainable

11.1 By 2030, ensure access for all to adequate, safe and affordable housing and basic services and upgrade slums

11.1.1 Proportion of urban population living in slums, informal settlements or inadequate housing

11.2 By 2030, provide access to safe, affordable, accessible and sustainable transport systems for all, improving road safety, notably by expanding public transport, with special attention to the needs of those in vulnerable situations, women, children, persons with disabilities and older persons

11.2.1 Proportion of population that has convenient access to public transport, by sex, age and persons with disabilities

Report of the Inter-Agency and Expert Group on Sustainable Development Goal Indicators (E/CN.3/2017/2)

15/26

Goals and targets (from the 2030 Agenda) Indicators

11.3 By 2030, enhance inclusive and sustainable urbanization and capacity for participatory, integrated and sustainable human settlement planning and management in all countries

11.3.1 Ratio of land consumption rate to population growth rate

11.3.2 Proportion of cities with a direct participation structure of civil society in urban planning and management that operate regularly and democratically

11.4 Strengthen efforts to protect and safeguard the world's cultural and natural heritage

11.4.1 Total expenditure (public and private) per capita spent on the preservation, protection and conservation of all cultural and natural heritage, by type of heritage (cultural, natural, mixed and World Heritage Centre designation), level of government (national, regional and local/municipal), type of expenditure (operating expenditure/investment) and type of private funding (donations in kind, private non-profit sector and sponsorship)

11.5 By 2030, significantly reduce the number of deaths and the number of people affected and substantially decrease the direct economic losses relative to global gross domestic product caused by disasters, including water-related disasters, with a focus on protecting the poor and people in vulnerable situations

11.5.1 Number of deaths, missing persons and directly affected persons attributed to disasters per 100,000 population

11.5.2 Direct economic loss in relation to global GDP,damage to critical infrastructure and number of disruptions to basic services, attributed to disasters

11.6 By 2030, reduce the adverse per capita environmental impact of cities, including by paying special attention to air quality and municipal and other waste management

11.6.1 Proportion of urban solid waste regularly collected and with adequate final discharge out of total urban solid waste generated, by cities

11.6.2 Annual mean levels of fine particulate matter (e.g. PM2.5 and PM10) in cities (population weighted)

11.7 By 2030, provide universal access to safe,inclusive and accessible, green and public spaces, in particular for women and children, older persons and persons with disabilities

11.7.1 Average share of the built-up area of cities that is open space for public use for all, by sex, age and persons with disabilities

11.7.2 Proportion of persons victim of physical or sexual harassment, by sex, age, disability status and place of occurrence, in the previous 12 months

11.a Support positive economic, social and environmental links between urban, peri-urban and rural areas by strengthening national and regional development planning

11.a.1 Proportion of population living in cities that implement urban and regional development plans integrating population projections and resource needs, by size of city

Report of the Inter-Agency and Expert Group on Sustainable Development Goal Indicators (E/CN.3/2017/2)

16/26

Goals and targets (from the 2030 Agenda) Indicators

11.b By 2020, substantially increase the number of cities and human settlements adopting and implementing integrated policies and plans towards inclusion, resource efficiency, mitigation and adaptation to climate change, resilience to disasters, and develop and implement, in line with the Sendai Framework for Disaster Risk Reduction 2015-2030, holistic disaster risk management at all levels

11.b.1 Number of countries that adopt and implement national disaster risk reduction strategies in line with the Sendai Framework for Disaster Risk Reduction 2015-2030

11.b.2 Proportion of local governments that adopt and implement local disaster risk reduction strategies in line with national disaster risk reduction strategies

11.c Support least developed countries, including through financial and technical assistance, in building sustainable and resilient buildings utilizing local materials

11.c.1 Proportion of financial support to the least developed countries that is allocated to the construction and retrofitting of sustainable, resilient and resource-efficient buildings utilizing local materials

Goal 12. Ensure sustainable consumption and production patterns

12.1 Implement the 10-Year Framework of Programmes on Sustainable Consumption and Production Patterns,all countries taking action, with developed countries taking the lead, taking into account the development and capabilities of developing countries

12.1.1 Number of countries with sustainable consumption and production (SCP) national action plans or SCP mainstreamed as a priority or a target into national policies

12.2 By 2030, achieve the sustainable management and efficient use of natural resources

12.2.1 Material footprint, material footprint per capita, and material footprint per GDP

12.2.2 Domestic material consumption, domestic material consumption per capita, and domestic material consumption per GDP

12.3 By 2030, halve per capita global food waste at the retail and consumer levels and reduce food losses along production and supply chains, including post-harvest losses

12.3.1 Global food loss index

12.4 By 2020, achieve the environmentally sound management of chemicals and all wastes throughout their life cycle, in accordance with agreed international frameworks, and significantly reduce their release to air,water and soil in order to minimize their adverse impacts on human health and the environment

12.4.1 Number of parties to international multilateral environmental agreements on hazardous waste, and other chemicals that meet their commitments and obligations in transmitting information as required by each relevant agreement

12.4.2 Hazardous waste generated per capita and proportion of hazardous waste treated, by type of treatment

12.5 By 2030, substantially reduce waste generation through prevention, reduction, recycling and reuse

12.5.1 National recycling rate, tons of material recycled

12.6 Encourage companies, especially large and transnational companies, to adopt sustainable practices and to integrate sustainability information into their reporting cycle

12.6.1 Number of companies publishing sustainability reports

Report of the Inter-Agency and Expert Group on Sustainable Development Goal Indicators (E/CN.3/2017/2)

17/26

Goals and targets (from the 2030 Agenda) Indicators

12.7 Promote public procurement practices that are sustainable, in accordance with national policies and priorities

12.7.1 Number of countries implementing sustainable public procurement policies and action plans

12.8 By 2030, ensure that people everywhere have the relevant information and awareness for sustainable development and lifestyles in harmony with nature

12.8.1 Extent to which (i) global citizenship education and (ii) education for sustainable development (including climate change education) are mainstreamed in (a) national education policies; (b) curricula; (c) teacher education; and (d) student assessment

12.a Support developing countries to strengthen their scientific and technological capacity to move towards more sustainable patterns of consumption and production

12.a.1 Amount of support to developing countries on research and development for sustainable consumption and production and environmentally sound technologies

12.b Develop and implement tools to monitor sustainable development impacts for sustainable tourism that creates jobs and promotes local culture and products

12.b.1 Number of sustainable tourism strategies or policies and implemented action plans with agreed monitoring and evaluation tools

12.c Rationalize inefficient fossil-fuel subsidies that encourage wasteful consumption by removing market distortions, in accordance with national circumstances, including by restructuring taxation and phasing out those harmful subsidies, where they exist, to reflect their environmental impacts, taking fully into account the specific needs and conditions of developing countries and minimizing the possible adverse impacts on their development in a manner that protects the poor and the affected communities

12.c.1 Amount of fossil-fuel subsidies per unit of GDP (production and consumption) and as a proportion of total national expenditure on fossil fuels

Goal 13. Take urgent action to combat climate change and its impacts*a*

13.1 Strengthen resilience and adaptive capacity to climate-related hazards and natural disasters in all countries

13.1.1 Number of deaths, missing persons and directly affected persons attributed to disasters per 100,000 population

13.1.2 Number of countries that adopt and implement national disaster risk reduction strategies in line with the Sendai Framework for Disaster Risk Reduction 2015-2030

13.1.3 Proportion of local governments that adopt and implement local disaster risk reduction strategies in line with national disaster risk reduction strategies a Acknowledging that the United Nations Framework Convention on Climate Change is the primary international, intergovernmental forum for negotiating the global response to climate change

Report of the Inter-Agency and Expert Group on Sustainable Development Goal Indicators (E/CN.3/2017/2)

18/26

13.2 Integrate climate change measures into national policies, strategies and planning

13.2.1 Number of countries that have communicated the establishment or operationalization of an integrated policy/strategy/plan which increases their ability to adapt to the adverse impacts of climate change, and foster climate resilience and low greenhouse gas emissions development in a manner that does not threaten food production (including a national adaptation plan, nationally determined contribution, national communication, biennial update report or other)

13.3 Improve education, awareness-raising and human and institutional capacity on climate change mitigation,adaptation, impact reduction and early warning

13.3.1 Number of countries that have integrated mitigation, adaptation, impact reduction and early warning into primary, secondary and tertiary curricula

13.3.2 Number of countries that have communicated the strengthening of institutional, systemic and individual capacity-building to implement adaptation,mitigation and technology transfer, and development actions

13.a Implement the commitment undertaken by developed-country parties to the United Nations Framework Convention on Climate Change to a goal of mobilizing jointly $100 billion annually by 2020 from all sources to address the needs of developing countries in the context of meaningful mitigation actions and transparency on implementation and fully operationalize the Green Climate Fund through its capitalization as soon as possible

13.a.1 Mobilized amount of United States dollars per year between 2020 and 2025 accountable towards the $100 billion commitment

13.b Promote mechanisms for raising capacity for effective climate change-related planning and management in least developed countries and small island developing States, including focusing on women,youth and local and marginalized communities

13.b.1 Number of least developed countries and small island developing States that are receiving specialized support, and amount of support, including finance, technology and capacity-building, for mechanisms for raising capacities for effective climate change-related planning and management, including focusing on women, youth and local and marginalized communities

Goal 14. Conserve and sustainably use the oceans, seas and marine resources for sustainable development

14.1 By 2025, prevent and significantly reduce marine pollution of all kinds, in particular from land-based activities, including marine debris and nutrient pollution 14.1.1 Index of coastal eutrophication and floating plastic debris density

14.2 By 2020, sustainably manage and protect marine and coastal ecosystems to avoid significant adverse impacts, including by strengthening their resilience, and take action for their restoration in order to achieve healthy and productive oceans

14.2.1 Proportion of national exclusive economic zones managed using ecosystem-based approaches

Report of the Inter-Agency and Expert Group on Sustainable Development Goal Indicators (E/CN.3/2017/2)

19/26

14.3 Minimize and address the impacts of ocean acidification, including through enhanced scientific cooperation at all levels

14.3.1 Average marine acidity (pH) measured at agreed suite of representative sampling stations

14.4 By 2020, effectively regulate harvesting and end overfishing, illegal, unreported and unregulated fishing and destructive fishing practices and implement science-based management plans, in order to restore fish stocks in the shortest time feasible, at least to levels that can produce maximum sustainable yield as determined by their biological characteristics

14.4.1 Proportion of fish stocks within biologically sustainable levels

14.5 By 2020, conserve at least 10 per cent of coastal and marine areas, consistent with national and international law and based on the best available scientific information

14.5.1 Coverage of protected areas in relation to marine areas

14.6 By 2020, prohibit certain forms of fisheries subsidies which contribute to overcapacity and overfishing, eliminate subsidies that contribute to illegal, unreported and unregulated fishing and refrain from introducing new such subsidies, recognizing that appropriate and effective special and differential treatment for developing and least developed countries should be an integral part of the World Trade Organization fisheries subsidies negotiation

14.6.1 Progress by countries in the degree of implementation of international instruments aiming to combat illegal, unreported and unregulated fishing 14.7 By 2030, increase the economic benefits to small island developing States and least developed countries from the sustainable use of marine resources, including through sustainable management of fisheries, aquaculture and tourism

14.7.1 Sustainable fisheries as a proportion of GDP in small island developing States, least developed countries and all countries

14.a Increase scientific knowledge, develop research capacity and transfer marine technology, taking into account the Intergovernmental Oceanographic Commission Criteria and Guidelines on the Transfer of Marine Technology, in order to improve ocean health and to enhance the contribution of marine biodiversity to the development of developing countries, in particular small island developing States and least developed countries

14.a.1 Proportion of total research budget allocated to research in the field of marine technology

14.b Provide access for small-scale artisanal fishers to marine resources and markets

14.b.1 Progress by countries in the degree of application of a legal/regulatory/policy/institutional framework which recognizes and protects access rights for small-scale fisheries *b* Taking into account ongoing World Trade Organization negotiations, the Doha Development Agenda and the Hong Kong ministerial mandate.

Report of the Inter-Agency and Expert Group on Sustainable Development Goal Indicators (E/CN.3/2017/2)

20/26

14.c Enhance the conservation and sustainable use of oceans and their resources by implementing international law as reflected in the United Nations Convention on the Law of the Sea, which provides the legal framework for the conservation and sustainable use of oceans and their resources, as recalled in paragraph 158 of "The future we want"

14.c.1 Number of countries making progress in ratifying, accepting and implementing through legal, policy and institutional frameworks, ocean-related instruments that implement international law, as reflected in the United Nation Convention on the Law of the Sea, for the conservation and sustainable use of the oceans and their resources Goal 15. Protect, restore and promote sustainable use of terrestrial ecosystems, sustainably manage forests, combat desertification, and halt and reverse land degradation and halt biodiversity loss

15.1 By 2020, ensure the conservation, restoration and sustainable use of terrestrial and inland freshwater ecosystems and their services, in particular forests,wetlands, mountains and drylands, in line with obligations under international agreements

15.1.1 Forest area as a proportion of total land area

15.1.2 Proportion of important sites for terrestrial and freshwater biodiversity that are covered by protected areas, by ecosystem type

15.2 By 2020, promote the implementation of sustainable management of all types of forests, halt deforestation, restore degraded forests and substantially increase afforestation and reforestation globally

15.2.1 Progress towards sustainable forest management

15.3 By 2030, combat desertification, restore degraded land and soil, including land affected by desertification, drought and floods, and strive to achieve a land degradation-neutral world

15.3.1 Proportion of land that is degraded over total land area

15.4 By 2030, ensure the conservation of mountain ecosystems, including their biodiversity, in order to enhance their capacity to provide benefits that are essential for sustainable development

15.4.1 Coverage by protected areas of important sites for mountain biodiversity

15.4.2 Mountain Green Cover Index

15.5 Take urgent and significant action to reduce the degradation of natural habitats, halt the loss of biodiversity and, by 2020, protect and prevent the extinction of threatened species

15.5.1 Red List Index

15.6 Promote fair and equitable sharing of the benefits arising from the utilization of genetic resources and promote appropriate access to such resources, as internationally agreed

15.6.1 Number of countries that have adopted legislative, administrative and policy frameworks to ensure fair and equitable sharing of benefits

15.7 Take urgent action to end poaching and trafficking of protected species of flora and fauna and address both demand and supply of illegal wildlife products

15.7.1 Proportion of traded wildlife that was poached or illicitly trafficked

15.8 By 2020, introduce measures to prevent the introduction and significantly reduce the impact of invasive alien species on land and water ecosystems and control or eradicate the priority species

15.8.1 Proportion of countries adopting relevant national legislation and adequately resourcing the prevention or control of invasive alien species

Report of the Inter-Agency and Expert Group on Sustainable Development Goal Indicators (E/CN.3/2017/2)

21/26

15.9 By 2020, integrate ecosystem and biodiversity values into national and local planning, development processes, poverty reduction strategies and accounts

15.9.1 Progress towards national targets established in accordance with Aichi Biodiversity Target 2 of the Strategic Plan for Biodiversity 2011-2020

15.a Mobilize and significantly increase financial resources from all sources to conserve and sustainably use biodiversity and ecosystems

15.a.1 Official development assistance and public expenditure on conservation and sustainable use of biodiversity and ecosystems

15.b Mobilize significant resources from all sources and at all levels to finance sustainable forest management and provide adequate incentives to developing countries to advance such management, including for conservation and reforestation

15.b.1 Official development assistance and public expenditure on conservation and sustainable use of biodiversity and ecosystems

15.c Enhance global support for efforts to combat poaching and trafficking of protected species, including by increasing the capacity of local communities to pursue sustainable livelihood opportunities

15.c.1 Proportion of traded wildlife that was poached or illicitly trafficked

Goal 16. Promote peaceful and inclusive societies for sustainable development, provide access to justice for all and build effective, accountable and inclusive institutions at all levels

16.1 Significantly reduce all forms of violence and related death rates everywhere

16.1.1 Number of victims of intentional homicide per 100,000 population, by sex and age

16.1.2 Conflict-related deaths per 100,000 population,by sex, age and cause

16.1.3 Proportion of population subjected to physical,psychological or sexual violence in the previous 12 months

16.1.4 Proportion of population that feel safe walking alone around the area they live

16.2 End abuse, exploitation, trafficking and all forms of violence against and torture of children

16.2.1 Proportion of children aged 1-17 years who experienced any physical punishment and/or psychological aggression by caregivers in the past month

16.2.2 Number of victims of human trafficking per 100,000 population, by sex, age and form of exploitation

16.2.3 Proportion of young women and men aged 18-29 years who experienced sexual violence by age 18

Report of the Inter-Agency and Expert Group on Sustainable Development Goal Indicators (E/CN.3/2017/2)

22/26

16.3 Promote the rule of law at the national and international levels and ensure equal access to justice for all

16.3.1 Proportion of victims of violence in the previous 12 months who reported their victimization to competent authorities or other officially recognized conflict resolution mechanisms

16.3.2 Unsentenced detainees as a proportion of overall prison population

16.4 By 2030, significantly reduce illicit financial and arms flows, strengthen the recovery and return of stolen assets and combat all forms of organized crime

16.4.1 Total value of inward and outward illicit financial flows (in current United States dollars)

16.4.2 Proportion of seized, found or surrendered arms whose illicit origin or context has been traced or established by a competent authority in line with international instruments

16.5 Substantially reduce corruption and bribery in all their forms

16.5.1 Proportion of persons who had at least one contact with a public official and who paid a bribe to a public official, or were asked for a bribe by those public officials, during the previous 12 months

16.5.2 Proportion of businesses that had at least one contact with a public official and that paid a bribe to a public official, or were asked for a bribe by those public officials during the previous 12 months

16.6 Develop effective, accountable and transparent institutions at all levels

16.6.1 Primary government expenditures as a proportion of original approved budget, by sector (or by budget codes or similar)

16.6.2 Proportion of population satisfied with their last experience of public services

16.7 Ensure responsive, inclusive, participatory and representative decision-making at all levels

16.7.1 Proportions of positions (by sex, age, persons with disabilities and population groups) in public institutions (national and local legislatures, public service, and judiciary) compared to national distributions

16.7.2 Proportion of population who believe decision making is inclusive and responsive, by sex, age, disability and population group

16.8 Broaden and strengthen the participation of developing countries in the institutions of global governance

16.8.1 Proportion of members and voting rights of developing countries in international organizations

16.9 By 2030, provide legal identity for all, including birth registration

16.9.1 Proportion of children under 5 years of age whose births have been registered with a civil authority, by age

Report of the Inter-Agency and Expert Group on Sustainable Development Goal Indicators (E/CN.3/2017/2)

23/26

16.10 Ensure public access to information and protect fundamental freedoms, in accordance with national legislation and international agreements

16.10.1 Number of verified cases of killing,kidnapping, enforced disappearance, arbitrary detention and torture of journalists, associated media personnel, trade unionists and human rights advocates in the previous 12 months

16.10.2 Number of countries that adopt and implement constitutional, statutory and/or policy guarantees for public access to information

16.a Strengthen relevant national institutions, including through international cooperation, for building capacity at all levels, in particular in developing countries, to prevent violence and combat terrorism and crime

16.a.1 Existence of independent national human rights institutions in compliance with the Paris Principles

16.b Promote and enforce non-discriminatory laws and policies for sustainable development

16.b.1 Proportion of population reporting having personally felt discriminated against or harassed in the previous 12 months on the basis of a ground of discrimination prohibited under international human rights law

Goal 17. Strengthen the means of implementation and revitalize the Global Partnership for Sustainable Development

Finance

17.1 Strengthen domestic resource mobilization,including through international support to developing countries, to improve domestic capacity for tax and other revenue collection

17.1.1 Total government revenue as a proportion of GDP, by source

17.1.2 Proportion of domestic budget funded by domestic taxes

17.2 Developed countries to implement fully their official development assistance commitments, including the commitment by many developed countries to achieve the target of 0.7 per cent of gross national income for official development assistance (ODA/GNI) to developing countries and 0.15 to 0.20 per cent of ODA/GNI to least developed countries; ODA providers are encouraged to consider setting a target to provide at least 0.20 per cent of ODA/ GNI to least developed countries

17.2.1 Net official development assistance, total and to least developed countries, as a proportion of the Organization for Economic Cooperation and Development (OECD) Development Assistance Committee donors' gross national income (GNI)

17.3 Mobilize additional financial resources for developing countries from multiple sources

17.3.1 Foreign direct investments (FDI), official development assistance and South-South Cooperation as a proportion of total domestic budget

17.3.2 Volume of remittances (in United States dollars) as a proportion of total GDP

Report of the Inter-Agency and Expert Group on Sustainable Development Goal Indicators (E/CN.3/2017/2)

24/26

17.4 Assist developing countries in attaining long-term debt sustainability through coordinated policies aimed at fostering debt financing, debt relief and debt restructuring, as appropriate, and address the external debt of highly indebted poor countries to reduce debt distress

17.4.1 Debt service as a proportion of exports of goods and services

17.5 Adopt and implement investment promotion regimes for least developed countries

17.5.1 Number of countries that adopt and implement investment promotion regimes for least developed countries Technology

17.6 Enhance North-South, South-South and triangular regional and international cooperation on and access to science, technology and innovation and enhance knowledge-sharing on mutually agreed terms, including through improved coordination among existing mechanisms, in particular at the United Nations level,and through a global technology facilitation mechanism

17.6.1 Number of science and/or technology cooperation agreements and programmes between countries, by type of cooperation

17.6.2 Fixed Internet broadband subscriptions per 100 inhabitants, by speed

17.7 Promote the development, transfer, dissemination and diffusion of environmentally sound technologies to developing countries on favourable terms, including on concessional and preferential terms, as mutually agreed

17.7.1 Total amount of approved funding for developing countries to promote the development, transfer, dissemination and diffusion of environmentally sound technologies

17.8 Fully operationalize the technology bank and science, technology and innovation capacity-building mechanism for least developed countries by 2017 and enhance the use of enabling technology, in particular information and communications technology

17.8.1 Proportion of individuals using the Internet

Capacity-building

17.9 Enhance international support for implementing effective and targeted capacity-building in developing countries to support national plans to implement all the Sustainable Development Goals, including through North-South, South-South and triangular cooperation

17.9.1 Dollar value of financial and technical assistance (including through North-South, South-South and triangular cooperation) committed to developing countries

Trade

17.10 Promote a universal, rules-based, open,non-discriminatory and equitable multilateral trading system under the World Trade Organization, including through the conclusion of negotiations under its Doha Development Agenda

17.10.1 Worldwide weighted tariff-average

17.11 Significantly increase the exports of developing countries, in particular with a view to doubling the least developed countries' share of global exports by 2020

17.11.1 Developing countries' and least developed countries' share of global exports

Report of the Inter-Agency and Expert Group on Sustainable Development Goal Indicators (E/CN.3/2017/2)

25/26

17.12 Realize timely implementation of duty-free and quota-free market access on a lasting basis for all least developed countries, consistent with World Trade Organization decisions, including by ensuring that preferential rules of origin applicable to imports from least developed countries are transparent and simple,and contribute to facilitating market access

17.12.1 Average tariffs faced by developing countries, least developed countries and small island developing States

Systemic issues

Policy and institutional coherence

17.13 Enhance global macroeconomic stability,including through policy coordination and policy coherence

17.13.1 Macroeconomic Dashboard

17.14 Enhance policy coherence for sustainable development

17.14.1 Number of countries with mechanisms in place to enhance policy coherence of sustainable development

17.15 Respect each country's policy space and leadership to establish and implement policies for poverty eradication and sustainable development

17.15.1 Extent of use of country-owned results frameworks and planning tools by providers of development cooperation

Multi-stakeholder partnerships

17.16 Enhance the Global Partnership for Sustainable Development, complemented by multi-stakeholder partnerships that mobilize and share knowledge, expertise, technology and financial resources, to support the achievement of the Sustainable Development Goals in all countries, in particular developing countries

17.16.1 Number of countries reporting progress in multi-stakeholder development effectiveness monitoring frameworks that support the achievement of the sustainable development goals

17.17 Encourage and promote effective public, public private and civil society partnerships, building on the experience and resourcing strategies of partnerships

17.17.1 Amount of United States dollars committed to public-private and civil society partnerships

Data, monitoring and accountability

17.18 By 2020, enhance capacity-building support to developing countries, including for least developed countries and small island developing States, to increase significantly the availability of high-quality, timely and reliable data disaggregated by income, gender, age, race, ethnicity, migratory status, disability, geographic location and other characteristics relevant in national contexts

17.18.1 Proportion of sustainable development indicators produced at the national level with full disaggregation when relevant to the target, in accordance with the Fundamental Principles of Official Statistics

17.18.2 Number of countries that have national statistical legislation that complies with the Fundamental Principles of Official Statistics

17.18.3 Number of countries with a national statistical plan that is fully funded and under implementation, by source of funding

Report of the Inter-Agency and Expert Group on Sustainable Development Goal Indicators (E/CN.3/2017/2)

26/26

17.19 By 2030, build on existing initiatives to develop measurements of progress on sustainable development that complement gross domestic product, and support statistical capacity-building in developing countries

17.19.1 Dollar value of all resources made available to strengthen statistical capacity in developing countries

17.19.2 Proportion of countries that (a) have conducted at least one population and housing census in the last 10 years; and (b) have achieved 100 per cent birth registration and 80 per cent death registration

Appendix - 4

An Overview of Sustainable Development Goals Report 2017

The *Sustainable Development Goals Report 2017* reviews progress made towards the 17 Goals in the second year of implementation of the 2030 Agenda for Sustainable Development. The report is based on the latest available data. It highlights both gains and challenges as the international community moves towards full realization of the ambitions and principles espoused in the 2030 Agenda. While considerable progress has been made over the past decade across all areas of development, the pace of progress observed in previous years is insufficient to fully meet the Sustainable Development Goals (SDGs) and targets by 2030. Time is therefore of the essence. Moreover, as the following pages show, progress has not always been equitable. Advancements have been uneven across regions, between the sexes, and among people of different ages, wealth and locales, including urban and rural dwellers. Faster and more inclusive progress is needed to accomplish the bold vision articulated in the 2030 Agenda.

Goal 1. End poverty in all its forms everywhere

Giving people in every part of the world the support they need to lift themselves out of poverty in all its manifestations is the very essence of sustainable development. Goal 1 focuses on ending poverty through interrelated strategies, including the promotion of social protection systems, decent employment and building the resilience of the poor.

- An estimated 767 million people lived below the extreme poverty line in 2013,down from 1.7 billion people in 1999. This represents a reduction in the global rate of extreme poverty from 28 per cent in 1999 to 11 per cent in 2013.

- Almost 10 per cent of the employed population worldwide lived with their families on less than 1.90 US dollars per person per day in 2016. Vulnerability was much higher for younger workers: 9 per cent of adult workers and their families lived in extreme poverty compared to 15 per cent of youth workers.
- In 2016, only 22 per cent of the unemployed worldwide received unemployment benefits, 28 per cent of people with severe disabilities collected a disability pension,35 per cent of children were covered by social protection, 41 per cent of women giving birth received maternity benefits, and 68 per cent of people above retirement age collected a pension.
- Economic losses from natural hazards are now reaching an average of 250 billion to 300 billion US dollars a year, with a disproportionate impact on small and vulnerable countries.

Goal 2. End hunger, achieve food security and improved nutrition and promote sustainable agriculture35%

Goal 2 addresses a fundamental human need—access to nutritious, healthy food, and the means by which it can be sustainably secured for everyone. Tackling hunger cannot be addressed by increasing food production alone. Well-functioning markets, increased incomes for smallholder farmers, equal access to technology and land, and additional investments all play a role in creating a vibrant and productive agricultural sector that builds food security.

- The proportion of undernourished people worldwide declined from 15 per cent in 2000-2002 to about 11 per cent in 2014-2016. Globally, about 793 million people were undernourished in 2014-2016, down from 930 million in 2000-2002.
- Southern Asia and sub-Saharan Africa accounted for 63 per cent of undernourished people worldwide in 2014-2016.
- In 2016, an estimated 155 million children under age 5 were stunted (low height for their age), 52 million were suffering from wasting (low weight for their height), and 41 million were overweight. Globally, the stunting rate fell from 33 per cent in 2000 to 23 per cent in 2016.
- The share of aid to agriculture in sector-allocable aid from member countries of the Development Assistance Committee of the Organisation for Economic Co-operation and Development fell from nearly 20 per cent in the mid-1980s to 7 per cent in 2015.

Goal 3. Ensure healthy lives and promote well-being for all at all ages

Goal 3 addresses all major health priorities and calls for improving reproductive, maternal and child health; ending communicable diseases; reducing non-communicable diseases and other health hazards; and ensuring universal access to safe, effective, quality and affordable medicines and vaccines as well as health coverage.

- Between 2000 and 2015, the global maternal mortality ratio declined by 37 per cent,and the under-5 mortality rate fell by 44 per cent. However, 303,000 women died during pregnancy or childbirth and 5.9 million children under age 5 died worldwide in 2015. Most of these deaths were from preventable causes.
- The period between 2000 and 2015 saw a 46 per cent reduction in HIV incidence;a 17 per cent decline in the incidence of tuberculosis; a 41 per cent decrease in the incidence of malaria; and a 21 per cent drop in people requiring mass or individual treatment and care for neglected tropical diseases.
- The risk of dying between the ages of 30 and 70 from one of four main noncommunicable diseases (NCDs)—cardiovascular disease, cancer, diabetes or chronic respiratory disease—fell from 23 per cent to 19 per cent between 2000 and 2015, not rapidly enough to meet the 2030 target.
- Nearly 800,000 suicides occurred worldwide in 2015, with men about twice as likely to die by suicide as women.
- In 2013, around 1.25 million people died from road traffic injuries, an increase of 13 per cent since 2000.
- Globally in 2012, household air pollution from cooking with unclean fuels and inefficient technologies led to an estimated 4.3 million deaths; another 3 million deaths were attributed to ambient air pollution from traffic, industrial sources, waste burning and residential fuel combustion.

Goal 4. Ensure inclusive and equitable quality education and promote lifelong learning opportunities for all

Goal 4 aims to ensure that all people have access to quality education and the opportunity for lifelong learning. The Goal goes beyond school enrolment and looks at proficiency levels, the availability of trained teachers and adequate school facilities, and disparities in education outcomes.

- In 2014, 2 out of 3 children worldwide participated in pre-primary or primary education in the year prior to the official entrance age for primary school, compared to only 4 in 10 children in the poorest countries.
- Despite considerable gains in primary school enrolment between 2000 and 2014,9 per cent of primary-school-aged children worldwide were out of school in 2014,with little progress since 2008.

- Surveys undertaken between 2007 and 2015 in selected countries show that children and adolescents from the richest 20 per cent of households achieved greater proficiency in reading than those from the poorest 20 per cent of households, and urban children scored higher in reading than rural children.
- Data for 2011 indicate that only about one quarter of schools in sub-Saharan Africa had electricity, less than half had access to drinking water, and only 69 per cent had toilets (with many lacking separate sanitation facilities for girls and boys).

Goal 5. Achieve gender equality and empower all women and girls

Gender inequality persists worldwide, depriving women and girls of their basic rights and opportunities. Achieving gender equality and the empowerment of women and girls will require more vigorous efforts, including legal frameworks, to counter deeply rooted gender-based discrimination often resulting from patriarchal attitudes and related social norms.

- One in five girls and women (aged 15 to 49) who have ever been married or in union reported they had been subjected to physical and/or sexual violence by an intimate partner in the previous 12 months, according to surveys undertaken between 2005 and 2016 in 87 countries.
- Around 2000, nearly one in three women between 20 and 24 years of age reported that they were married before age 18; around 2015, the ratio had declined to roughly one in four.
- According to surveys undertaken around 2015 in 30 countries where the practice of female genital mutilation is concentrated, over a third (35 per cent) of girls between the ages of 15 and 19 had been subjected to the procedure.
- On average, women spent almost triple the amount of time on unpaid domestic and care work as men, based on data from 2000 to 2016.
- Women's participation in single or lower houses of national parliaments worldwide reached only 23.4 per cent in 2017. In the majority of the 67 countries with data from 2009 to 2015, fewer than a third of senior- and middle-management positions were held by women.

Goal 6. Ensure availability and sustainable management of water and sanitation for all

Goal 6 aims to tackle challenges related to drinking water, sanitation and hygiene for populations, as well as to water-related ecosystems. Without quality, sustainable water resources and sanitation, progress in many other areas across the SDGs, including health,education and poverty reduction, will also be held back.

- In 2015, 5.2 billion people (71 per cent of the global population) used a "safely managed" drinking water service—an improved source located on premises, available when needed and free from contamination.
- In 2015, 2.9 billion people (39 per cent of the global population) used a "safely managed" sanitation service—a basic facility that safely disposed of human waste.
- Open defecation, practised by 892 million people (12 per cent of the global population) in 2015, continues to pose serious health risks.
- More than 2 billion people globally are living in countries with excess water stress.Northern Africa and Western Asia, as well as Central and Southern Asia, experience water stress levels above 60 per cent, indicating the strong probability of future water scarcity.

Goal 7. Ensure access to affordable, reliable, sustainable and modern energy for all

Universal access to affordable, reliable and sustainable energy services requires expanding access to electricity and clean cooking fuels and technologies, as well as improving energy efficiency and increasing the use of renewable energy. To achieve this Goal, bolder financing and policies will be needed, along with the willingness of countries to embrace new technologies on a much more ambitious scale.

- In 2014, 85.3 per cent of the global population had access to electricity, up from 77.6 per cent in 2000. However, 1.06 billion people still lived without this basic service.
- While 96 per cent of urban residents could access electricity in 2014, the share was only 73 per cent in rural areas.
- Access to clean fuels and technologies for cooking climbed to 57 per cent in 2014, up from 50 per cent in 2000. Still, more than 3 billion people, most of them in Asia and sub-Saharan Africa, lack access to clean cooking fuels and technologies and are exposed to high levels of household air pollution.
- The share of renewable energy in final energy consumption grew modestly from 2010 to 2014—from 17.5 to 18.3 per cent. Water, solar and wind power generation accounted for most of the increase.
- Globally, primary energy intensity improved by 2.1 per cent a year from 2012 to 2014. However, this pace is insufficient to double the global rate of energy efficiency improvements as called for in the target.

Goal 8. Promote sustained, inclusive and sustainable economic growth, full and productive employment and decent work for all

Economic growth is a principal driver of sustainable development. When this growth is sustained and inclusive, more people can escape poverty as opportunities for full and productive employment expand. To allow future generations to benefit from today's economic growth, such growth should be environmentally sound and not the result of unsustainable exploitation of resources.

- The average annual growth rate of real gross domestic product (GDP) per capita expanded from 0.9 per cent over the period 2005-2009 to 1.6 per cent in 2010-2015.Real GDP growth in the least developed countries (LDCs) averaged 4.9 per cent in 2010-2015, short of the target of at least 7 per cent annually.
- Growth in labour productivity—measured by GDP per worker—slowed sharply after the financial crisis of 2008-2009. It grew at an average annual rate of 1.9 per cent between 2009 and 2016, compared to 2.9 per cent between 2000 and 2008.
- The global unemployment rate fell from 6.1 per cent in 2010 to 5.7 per cent in 2016. Despite progress overall, youth (aged 15 to 24 years) were nearly three times more likely than adults to be without a job, with unemployment rates of 12.8 per cent and 4.4 per cent, respectively.
- The number of children aged 5 to 17 engaged in child labour declined from 246 million in 2000 to 168 million in 2012. Still, around 1 in 10 children worldwide were engaged in child labour in 2012; more than half of them (85 million) were exposed to hazardous forms of work.

Goal 9. Build resilient infrastructure, promote inclusive and sustainable industrialization and foster innovation

Infrastructure, industrialization and innovation are three drivers of economic growth. When inclusivity, resilience and sustainability are factored into the implementation of these driving forces, economic growth can support sustainable development.

- In 2015, the economic impact of air transport was 2.7 trillion US dollars (3.5 per cent of global GDP). The least developed countries (LDCs), landlocked developing countries (LLDCs) and small island developing States (SIDS) accounted for limited air travel and freight volumes—each country group comprised only a small fraction (1 to 2.7 per cent) of the global total.
- Between 2005 and 2016, manufacturing value added (MVA) per capita increased by almost 59 per cent in LDCs, yet was still only about 2 per cent of that in Europe and Northern America.

- Between 2000 and 2014, steady reductions were observed in carbon dioxide (CO_2) emissions from manufacturing per unit of MVA in most regions of the world and in all 10 of the largest manufacturing countries.
- Global investment in research and development increased at an average annual rate of 4.5 per cent between 2000 and 2014. It reached 1.8 trillion US dollars (purchasing power parity) in 2014—1.7 per cent of global GDP.
- Coverage by a mobile cellular signal has become almost universal. In 2016, 95 per cent of the world's population was in range of at least a second-generation (2G) signal and 84 per cent received at least a third-generation (3G) signal.

Goal 10. Reduce inequality within and among countries

Goal 10 calls for reducing inequality within and among countries, ensuring safe,orderly and regular migration, and strengthening the voices of developing countries in international economic and financial decision-making.

- In 49 of 83 countries with data for the period 2011-2015, the per capita incomes of the poorest 40 per cent of the population grew more rapidly than the national average,leading to a reduction in income inequality.
- Reforms at the International Monetary Fund have led to increased voting shares for eveloping countries, yet in many international organizations their voting shares remain far below their overall membership levels.
- The international trade community continues to grant more favourable access conditions to LDCs: the proportion of tariff lines for exports from LDCs with zero tariffs increased from 49 per cent in 2005 to 65 per cent in 2015.
- On average, the cost of sending remittances home is above 7 per cent of the amount remitted, significantly higher than the 3 per cent target. New and improved technologies, such as prepaid cards and mobile operators, helped reduce these fees to between 2 per cent and 4 per cent, but are not yet widely available or used in many remittance corridors.

Goal 11. Make cities and human settlements inclusive, safe, resilient and sustainable

The pace of urban growth has been unprecedented. More than half the world's population,or nearly 4 billion people, lived in cities in 2015. However, while cities are incubators of innovation and help foster increased employment and economic growth, rapid urbanization has brought with it enormous challenges, including inadequate housing,increased air pollution, and lack of access to basic services and infrastructure.

- The proportion of the urban population living in slums worldwide fell from 28 per cent in 2000 to 23 per cent in 2014. However, in sub-Saharan Africa, more than half (56 per cent) of urban dwellers lived in slum conditions.
- From 2000 to 2015, in all regions of the world, the expansion of urban land outpaced the growth of urban populations, resulting in urban sprawl.
- According to data from cities in 101 countries from 2009 to 2013, approximately 65 per cent of the population was served by municipal waste collection.
- In 2014, 9 in 10 people living in urban areas breathed air that did not meet the World Health Organization's air quality guidelines value for particulate matter (PM 2.5).
- As of May 2017, 149 countries had fully or partially implemented national-level urban policies, most of which are aligned with priority areas identified in the SDGs.

Goal 12: Ensure sustainable consumption and production patterns

Sustainable consumption and production patterns enable efficient resource use and can reduce the impact of economic activities on the environment. To that end, this Goal focuses on decoupling economic growth from resource use, and ensuring that hazardous chemicals and wastes are managed in a way that minimizes their impact on human lives and the environment.

- Globally, the material footprint of human beings increased from 48.5 billion metric tons in 2000 to 69.3 billion metric tons in 2010. The material footprint per capita increased from 8 metric tons per person to 10 metric tons per person over the same period.
- In 2010, Australia and New Zealand had the highest material footprint per capita (35 metric tons per person), followed by Europe and Northern America (20 metric tons per person); sub-Saharan Africa had the lowest (2.5 metric tons per person).
- Eastern and South-Eastern Asia accounted for 42 per cent of global domestic material consumption (DMC), reflecting rapid industrialization in the region.
- Almost all United Nations Member States are party to at least one global environmental greement on chemicals and hazardous waste. However, between 2010 and 2014, only 51 per cent of Parties to the Stockholm Convention, 57 per cent of Parties to the Basel Convention, and 71 per cent of Parties to the Rotterdam Convention fully met their reporting commitments under these agreements.

Goal 13. Take urgent action to combat climate change and its impactsa

Planetary warming continued in 2016, setting a record of about 1.1 degrees Celsius above the pre-industrial period. The extent of global sea ice fell to 4.14 million square kilometres in 2016, the second lowest on record. Mitigating climate change and its impacts will require building on the momentum achieved by the Paris Agreement on Climate Change. Stronger efforts are also needed to build resilience and limit climate-related hazards and natural disasters.

- The Paris Agreement entered into force on 4 November 2016, marking a shift in focus towards implementation of action for the climate and sustainable development.
- As of 7 June 2017, 148 Parties had ratified the Paris Agreement; of these, 142 Parties (141 countries and the European Commission) had communicated their first nationally determined contributions to the United Nations Framework Convention on Climate Change Secretariat.
- The number of deaths attributed to natural hazards continues to rise, despite progress in implementing disaster risk reduction strategies. From 1990 to 2015, more than 1.6 million people died in internationally reported natural hazards.
- Many countries have begun implementing national and local disaster risk reduction strategies. In 2014-2015, most reporting countries indicated that environmental impact assessments, legislation on protected areas, climate change adaptation projects and programmes, and integrated planning played a major role in reducing underlying risk factors.

Goal 14. Conserve and sustainably use the oceans, seas and marine resources for sustainable development

Oceans cover almost three quarters of the planet, comprising the largest ecosystem on Earth. The increasingly adverse impacts of climate change (including ocean acidification),overfishing and marine pollution are jeopardizing recent gains in protecting portions of the world's oceans.

- In 2017, protected areas cover 13.2 per cent of the marine environment under national jurisdiction, 0.25 per cent of the marine environment beyond national jurisdiction,and 5.3 per cent of the total global ocean area. The average coverage of marine key biodiversity areas (KBAs) by protected areas has risen from 32 per cent in 2000 to 45 per cent in 2017.
- The proportion of marine fish stocks worldwide that have been overfished—that is, are at biologically unsustainable levels—increased from 10 per cent in 1974 to 31 per cent in 2013.

- Oceans absorb up to 30 per cent of the annual emissions of CO2 generated by human activity. However, the absorbed CO2 also leads to an increase in the acidity of seawater,which weakens the shells and skeletons of many marine species, such as corals.As atmospheric CO2 levels rise, estimates indicate that oceans could be nearly 150 per cent more acidic by 2100.
- Of the 63 large marine ecosystems evaluated under the Transboundary Waters Assessment Programme, 16 per cent are in the "high" or "highest" risk categories for coastal eutrophication. By 2050, it is estimated that coastal eutrophication will increase in 21 per cent of these large ecosystems.

Goal 15. Protect, restore and promote sustainable use of terrestrial ecosystems, sustainably manage forests, combat desertification, and halt and reverse land degradation and halt biodiversity loss

Protected and restored ecosystems and the biodiversity they support can help mitigate climate change and provide increased resilience in the face of mounting human pressures and natural disasters. Healthy ecosystems also produce multiple benefits for communities that rely on them. Goal 15 focuses on preserving and sustainably using the Earth's terrestrial species and ecosystems.

- From 2010 to 2015, the annual net loss of forest area globally was less than half that of the 1990s. The proportion of land area covered by forest decreased from 31.6 per cent in 1990 to 30.8 per cent in 2010 and 30.6 per cent in 2015.
- From 2000 to 2017, average worldwide coverage of terrestrial, freshwater and mountain KBAs by protected areas increased from 35 per cent to 47 per cent, from 32 per cent to 43 per cent, and from 39 per cent to 49 per cent, respectively.
- Biodiversity loss, however, continues at an alarming rate. Corals, amphibians and cycads are in serious decline due to distinct and worsening threats. Bleaching, driven by climate change and local impacts, has affected the health of coral reefs worldwide, which could disappear completely by 2050. Amphibians also face a high risk of extinction, with 41 per cent already threatened.
- Illicit poaching and trafficking of wildlife continues to thwart conservation efforts,with nearly 7,000 species of animals and plants reported in illegal trade involving 120 countries. In 2013, elephant ivory, rosewood, rhinoceros horn and reptiles comprised 70 per cent of total wildlife seizures.

Goal 16. Promote peaceful and inclusive societies for sustainable development, provide access to justice for all and build effective, accountable and inclusive institutions at all levels

Peace, justice and effective, accountable and inclusive institutions are at the core of sustainable development. Progress in promoting peaceful and inclusive societies remainsuneven across and within countries. Violent conflicts have increased in recent years, and a number of high-intensity armed conflicts are causing large numbers of civilian casualties and driving millions of people from their homes.

- In 2015, the intentional homicide rate in countries with high income inequality (Gini index >0.45) was nine times that of countries with low income inequality (Gini index <0.35).
- In 76 countries with available data from 2005 to 2016, about 8 in 10 children aged 1 to 14 years were subjected to some form of psychological aggression and/or physical punishment on a regular basis.
- More than 570 different human trafficking flows, which criss-cross the globe, were identified by law enforcement officers between 2012 and 2014. The large majority of identified trafficking victims in 2014 were women and girls (71 per cent), and more than a quarter were children.
- Globally, the proportion of people held in detention without being tried or sentenced for a crime was 31 per cent in 2013-2015.
- According to data from 2005 to 2016, over 18 per cent of firms worldwide reported receiving at least one bribery payment request. The share of firms in low- and lowermiddle- income countries was 25 per cent, versus 4 per cent in high-income countries.
- Data reported for 147 countries from 2010 to 2016 indicate that 71 per cent of children under age 5 worldwide have had their births registered; the birth registration rate in sub-Saharan Africa stands at just 46 per cent.

Goal 17. Strengthen the means of implementation and revitalize the Global Partnership for Sustainable Development

A stronger commitment to partnership and cooperation is needed to achieve the SDGs. Attaining the Goals will require coherent policies, an enabling environment for sustainable development at all levels and by all actors, and a reinvigorated Global Partnership for Sustainable Development. Meeting the means of implementation targets is key to realizing the 2030 Agenda, as is the full implementation of the Addis Ababa Action Agenda. Incremental progress has been made in these areas, but more is needed.

- From 2015 to 2016, official development assistance (ODA) rose by

8.9 per cent in real terms to 142.6 billion US dollars, reaching a new peak. Despite this progress, bilateral aid to LDCs fell by 3.9 per cent in real terms.

- Debt service is trending upwards. From 2000 to 2011, debt service in lower-middle income countries fell from 12.9 per cent to 3.6 per cent, before rising slowly to 6.1 per cent in 2015.
- In 2016, international remittances totalled 575 billion US dollars, 75 per cent of which (429 billion US dollars) flowed to developing countries. However, remittances to developing countries fell in 2016 for a second consecutive year, declining by 2.4 per cent over 2015.
- In 2016, about 80 per cent of the population in developed regions had Internet access, compared to 40 per cent in developing regions and 15 per cent in LDCs.
- In 2014, financial support for statistical capacity in developing countries (338 million US dollars) accounted for only 0.18 per cent of total ODA. From 2007 to 2016,89 per cent of countries or areas around the world conducted at least one population and housing census; 25 countries or areas failed to conduct a census during this period.

Index

O

P

Q

R

V

W